Lecture Notes in Electrical Engineering

Volume 1423

The book series *Lecture Notes in Electrical Engineering* (LNEE) publishes the latest developments in Electrical Engineering—quickly, informally and in high quality. While original research reported in proceedings and monographs has traditionally formed the core of LNEE, we also encourage authors to submit books devoted to supporting student education and professional training in the various fields and applications areas of electrical engineering. The series cover classical and emerging topics concerning:

- Communication Engineering, Information Theory and Networks
- Electronics Engineering and Microelectronics
- Signal, Image and Speech Processing
- Wireless and Mobile Communication
- Circuits and Systems
- Energy Systems, Power Electronics and Electrical Machines
- Electro-optical Engineering
- Instrumentation Engineering
- Avionics Engineering
- Control Systems
- Internet-of-Things and Cybersecurity
- Biomedical Devices, MEMS and NEMS

For general information about this book series, comments or suggestions, please contact leontina.dicecco@springer.com.

To submit a proposal or request further information, please contact the Publishing Editor in your country:

China

Jasmine Dou, Editor (jasmine.dou@springer.com)

India, Japan, Rest of Asia

Swati Meherishi, Editorial Director (Swati.Meherishi@springer.com)

Southeast Asia, Australia, New Zealand

Ramesh Nath Premnath, Editor (ramesh.premnath@springernature.com)

USA, Canada

Michael Luby, Senior Editor (michael.luby@springer.com)

All other Countries

Leontina Di Cecco, Senior Editor (leontina.dicecco@springer.com)

**** This series is indexed by EI Compendex and Scopus databases. ****

Bhavesh N. Gohil · Sankita J. Patel ·
Naveen Kumar Chaudhary · S. S. Iyengar ·
Chirag Modi · Mukti Padhya
Editors

Information Security, Privacy and Digital Forensics

Select Proceedings of the International Conference, ICISPD 2023

Springer

Editors
Bhavesh N. Gohil
Department of Computer Science
and Engineering
Sardar Vallabhbhai National Institute
of Technology
Surat, Gujarat, India

Naveen Kumar Chaudhary
School of Cyber Security and Digital
Forensics
National Forensic Sciences University
Gandhinagar, Gujarat, India

Chirag Modi
Department of Computer Science
and Engineering
National Institute of Technology Goa
Ponda, Goa, India

Sankita J. Patel
Department of Computer Science
and Engineering
Sardar Vallabhbhai National Institute
of Technology
Surat, Gujarat, India

S. S. Iyengar
Florida International University
Miami, FL, USA

Mukti Padhya
National Forensic Sciences University
Gandhinagar, Goa, India

ISSN 1876-1100 ISSN 1876-1119 (electronic)
Lecture Notes in Electrical Engineering
ISBN 978-981-96-9442-6 ISBN 978-981-96-9443-3 (eBook)
https://doi.org/10.1007/978-981-96-9443-3

This Springer imprint is published by the registered company Springer Nature Singapore Pte Ltd.
The registered company address is: 152 Beach Road, #21-01/04 Gateway East, Singapore 189721, Singapore

Contents

About the Editors

Bhavesh N. Gohil received his Ph.D. from the Sardar Vallabhbhai National Institute of Technology (SVNIT), Surat, in 2019. Since 2009, he has been associated with the Department of Computer Science and Engineering at SVNIT, Surat, as Associate Professor. His research interests include performance and security issues in distributed computing like cloud/edge/fog computing, IoTs, etc. Prior to SVNIT, he worked with Amdocs as Subject Matter Expert. He is working as Joint Investigator in a research project funded by the Gujarat Council of Science and Technology, Government of Gujarat, and as Co-PI for the ISEA phase III project.

Sankita J. Patel is associated with the Department of Computer Science and Engineering at Sardar Vallabhbhai National Institute of Technology (SVNIT), Surat, since 2009. Her research interests focus on applied research in information security and privacy application domains like cyber-physical systems, online social networks, data analytics, cloud computing, big data, etc. She has worked as Joint Investigator in research projects funded by the Ministry of Electronics and Information Technology (MeitY), Government of India, and the Gujarat Council of Science and Technology, Government of Gujarat.

Naveen Kumar Chaudhary is Professor of Cyber Security and Dean, at National Forensic Sciences University, Gandhinagar, Gujarat, India, since 2019. He is Courtesy Research Professor at Knight Foundation School of Computing and Information Science, Florida International University, Miami, USA. He holds Bachelor of Technology degree in information technology and telecommunication engineering and Master of Engineering degree in digital communication. He earned his Ph.D. in engineering and advanced certifications in cyber and network security. He has experience of more than 25 years in education, research, and Government. He is Editor-in-Chief of *NFSU Journal of Cyber Security and Digital Forensic*. His research focus is cybersecurity, digital forensics, drone forensics, cyber-physical systems, and cyber-forensic investigations.

S. S. Iyengar is currently Distinguished University Professor, Founding Director of the Discovery Lab, and Director of the US Army funded Center of Excellence in Digital Forensics at Florida International University, Miami. He is also Distinguished Chaired Professor (Hon.) at National Forensics Sciences University, Gandhinagar, India. He is involved with research and education in high-performance intelligent systems, data science and machine learning algorithms, sensor fusion, data mining, and intelligent systems. Since receiving his Ph.D. degree in 1974 from MSU, USA, he has directed over 65 Ph.D. students, 100 Master's students, and many undergraduate students who are now Faculty at major universities worldwide or scientists or engineers at National Labs/Industries around the world. He has published more than 900 research papers. His books are published by MIT Press, John Wiley and Sons, CRC Press, Prentice Hall, Springer Verlag, IEEE Computer Society Press, etc. During the last thirty years more recently in Spring 2021, Dr. Iyengar was awarded a $2.25 M funding for setting up a Digital Forensics Center of Excellence over a period of 5 years (2021–2026).

Chirag Modi is working as Associate Professor in the Department of Computer Science and Engineering at National Institute of Technology Goa (NIT Goa). His research areas include security and privacy, blockchain, and data analytics. He has successfully disseminated his research output in premier international conferences and journals. He holds 5 granted utility patents including 02 Indian patents. He has established a security research lab at NIT Goa, and his group is currently exploring offensive and defensive security solutions such as AI/ML enabled malware mutation, static and runtime time semantics based malware detection, etc.

Mukti Padhya is Assistant Professor at the School of Cyber Security and Digital Forensics at the National Forensic Sciences University (NFSU) in Gandhinagar, India. She has earned her Ph.D. and M.Tech. in Computer Science Engineering from S.V. National Institute of Technology (SVNIT) Surat. Her research interests include information security, cryptography, and cloud security. Throughout her academic career, Dr. Mukti Padhya has been recognized with several awards, such as a Gold Medal from S. V. National Institute of Technology (SVNIT) Surat and the Visvesvaraya Fellowship. She is qualified in the Graduate Aptitude Test in Engineering (GATE) 2012 with an AIR of 753.

MQTT FuzzSecure: Enhancing Robust Security Measures in MQTT Brokers Through Fuzzing

Hemanshu Kailash Bisht, Ramya Shah, Digvijaysinh Rathod, and Sarang Rajvansh

Abstract Among the technologies that have witnessed rampant growth in recent years, a significant one is the IoT (Internet of Things). This transformative paradigm involves the connection of various devices, including smartphones, tablets, and objects equipped with sensors, thereby expanding the scope of IoT to virtually any sensor-enabled entity. The rapid growth of the Internet of Things (IoT) has transformed everyday activities, requiring efficient communication protocols between IoT devices and their servers. In the quest for a communication protocol that effectively addresses the diverse constraints of IoT devices, Message Queuing Telemetry Transport (MQTT) has emerged as a highly popular and widely embraced protocol within this domain. However, our initial investigation revealed a significant number of MQTT brokers hosted on the internet with critical misconfigurations or lacking proper security measures. These challenges include the utilization of outdated versions of MQTT, employment of outdated broker versions, the absence of robust authentication methods, and inadequate access controls once a client establishes a connection with a broker. To address this issue and enhance MQTT broker security, we propose QT-Killer, an automated testing tool specifically designed for MQTT brokers. The tool employs a generation-based fuzzing technique as its fundamental approach to perform fuzzing along with multithreading in order to increase the throughput. Additionally, it incorporates a Graphical User Interface (GUI) for effective interaction between the program and the user. The efficacy of the tool is evaluated by conducting a series of experiments to assess its performance.

Keywords IoT · MQTT · Fuzzing · Brute force

H. K. Bisht (✉) · R. Shah · D. Rathod · S. Rajvansh
School of Cyber Security and Digital Forensics, National Forensic Sciences University, Gandhinagar, Gujarat, India
e-mail: h3manshubisht@gmail.com

B. N. Gohil et al. (eds.), *Information Security, Privacy and Digital Forensics*,
Lecture Notes in Electrical Engineering 1423,
https://doi.org/10.1007/978-981-96-9443-3_1

1 Introduction

The world of the Internet of Things is growing at an exponential pace where the exact definition of IoT is still a topic up for debate and various definitions [1–3] have been devised to define IoT. According to [4], The Internet of Things (IoT) is an emerging concept in the field of wireless telecommunications, characterized by the widespread presence of interconnected objects and devices. These objects, including RFID tags, sensors, actuators, and mobile phones, interact with each other using unique addressing schemes and collaborate to achieve shared objectives. The Internet of Things provides a means through which things i.e. machines can communicate with each other and humans, machines could include programmable devices which have various types of sensors and actuators that help in achieving a physical action based on data. IoT devices are widely employed in the consumer sector and various industries to streamline and automate tasks [5]. IoT devices designed for consumer applications encompass a range of smart technologies, such as sensors, televisions, health trackers, IP cameras, and home automation systems [5].

Although there is no universally adopted IoT architecture, the three-layer architecture [6–8] is widely recognized as a fundamental framework in the field. This architecture was initially introduced during the early stages of IoT research and consists of three layers: the perception layer, the network layer, and the application layer.

The perception layer, also known as the physical layer, encompasses the sensors responsible for sensing and gathering information from the surrounding environment. These sensors capture various physical parameters or identify other intelligent objects within the environment.

The network layer plays a crucial role in establishing connections between smart devices, network infrastructure, and servers. It facilitates the transmission and processing of sensor data, ensuring efficient communication and interoperability among IoT components.

While the three-layer architecture serves as the foundation for the Internet of Things (IoT), it may not suffice for comprehensive research purposes. In order to provide a more comprehensive framework, the five-layer architecture expands upon the three-layer model by incorporating the processing and business layers. The five layers include the perception, transport, processing, application, and business layers (refer to Fig. 1). The perception and application layers retain their roles from the three-layer architecture, focusing on collecting sensor data and delivering application-specific services, respectively. The remaining three layers serve distinct functions within the system.

The transport layer facilitates seamless communication by transferring sensor data between perception and processing layers, utilizing wireless, 3G, LAN, Bluetooth, RFID, and NFC technologies. The processing layer, or middleware, is responsible for storing, analyzing, and processing vast IoT data, leveraging databases, cloud computing, and big data modules. While not extensively discussed here, the business layer, covering applications, business models, and user privacy, plays a crucial role

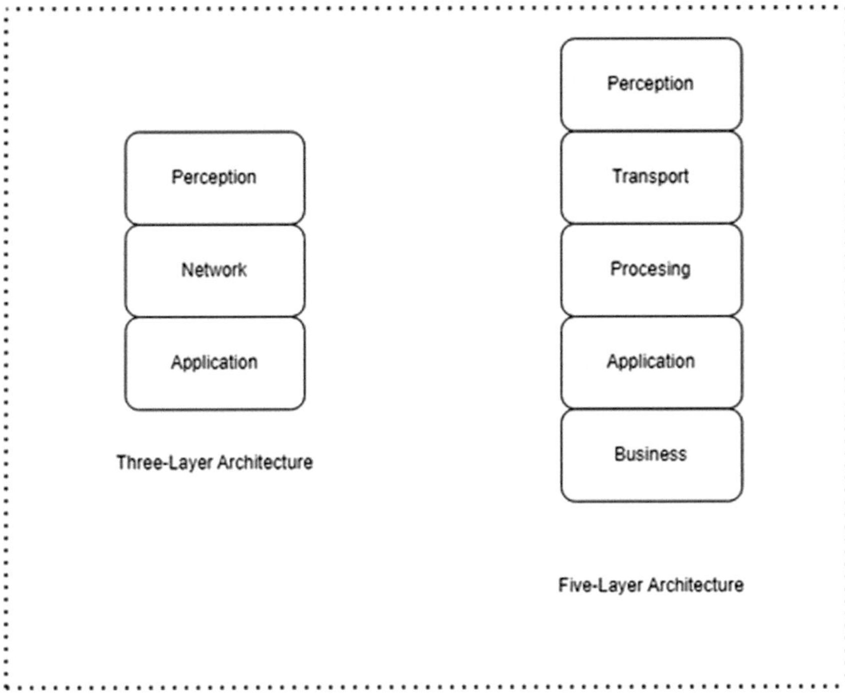

Fig. 1 IoT architecture

in managing the entire IoT system. Despite being beyond this research's scope, its significance in governing IoT functionality is acknowledged. The five-layer architecture, incorporating these layers, provides a comprehensive framework for IoT research, enhancing understanding of layer roles in delivering services and addressing user needs [9].

The IoT concept holds great potential for significantly impacting various aspects of people's daily lives and behaviors. For individual users, the introduction of IoT technology will have notable effects in both professional and domestic settings. Assisted living, e-health, and enhanced learning are just a few examples of the diverse application scenarios where the IoT will play a prominent role in the near future. Likewise, from a business perspective, sectors such as automation, industrial manufacturing, logistics, business/process management, and intelligent transportation of people and goods will experience visible consequences resulting from the adoption of IoT solutions [6]. These devices have significantly enhanced our lives by enabling us to accomplish a wide array of tasks, ranging from everyday routines to more intricate activities like health monitoring.

The IoT's rapid growth has resulted in a diverse array of smart devices connecting to the internet, posing communication challenges due to their heterogeneous and constrained nature, including limited computing power and battery capacity. To address this, alternative communication protocols like CoAP, MQTT, and AQMP have been developed. AQMP enhances messaging interoperability, CoAP uses UDP for secure data transmission, and MQTT relies on a publish-subscribe architecture. The IoT market is expected to grow significantly, with a projected CAGR of 26.1% from $662.21 billion in 2023 to $3352.97 billion in 2030, making it an attractive target for hackers. McKinsey estimates the IoT cloud's potential economic value to be between $5.5 trillion and $12.5 trillion globally. The widespread deployment of interconnected devices intensifies security challenges due to extensive data generation and communication [10–12].

2 Attack Taxonomy on IoT Devices and Protocols

Various attacks are possible in IoT devices and protocols. These attacks include Denial-of-Service (DoS), Man-in-the-Middle (MitM), device spoofing, firmware or software vulnerabilities, data breaches, fuzzing, and physical tampering. Attackers exploit these weaknesses to disrupt device functionality, compromise data integrity and privacy, and gain unauthorized access. Fuzzing is a testing methodology to identify software application vulnerabilities [13]. It involves sending unexpected input data to target systems and subsequently analyzing the outcomes to detect any potential weaknesses.

Fuzzers can be categorized into two main types: mutation-based and generation-based fuzzers [14]. Mutation-based fuzzers generate test cases by applying mutations to existing data samples, expanding the test space. On the other hand, generation-based fuzzers construct test cases from scratch by modeling the target protocol or file format.

The rise in Internet of Things (IoT) devices and the frequency of attacks against them are exhibiting a parallel trajectory. This association draws attention to a worrying pattern where an equal rise matches the growing popularity of IoT devices in security concerns. This finding emphasizes the urgent need for thorough study and protective measures to address IoT devices' growing dangers and weaknesses.

The research paper is structured into distinct sections, each dedicated to various topics about the subject matter. These sections are outlined as follows: Sect. 2, provides an inventory of the diverse IoT protocols, with a particular focus on the structure and specifications of the MQTT protocol (referenced documentation).

Section 3, delves into the existing studies and research conducted on the MQTT protocol, examining the methodologies employed in these investigations.

Section 4 showcases the practical implementation and outcomes of the research, including the steps taken and documented screenshots capturing the resulting outputs.

Finally, Sect. 5 presents the conclusion drawn from the research findings and offers insights into potential avenues for future advancements in the field (Table 1).

Table 1 Lists down a few of the attacks where either IoT systems were directly targeted or used as an accessory to another attack [15–18]

Sr. No.	Attack name	Year	Industry affected
1	Smart device malware	2016	Smart devices
2	Mirai Botnet	2016	Various industries
3	Digital video recorder RCE	2016	Security industry
4	Dyn attack	2016	Various industries
5	Ripple20	2020	Various industries
6	CVE-2021-35,394	2021	Smart IoT devices

3 Preliminary Study

A communication protocol is a predefined set of rules that allows two or more systems or servers to send information [19]. When stringent communication constraints are imposed, like limited bandwidth and low processing capabilities, a distinct need arises for dedicated protocols catering to the required conditions [20]. A few of the most commonly used protocols for IoT are Hypertext Transfer Protocol (HTTP), Extensible Messaging and Presence Protocol (XMPP), Advanced Message Queuing Protocol (AQMP), and MQ Telemetry Protocol (MQTT) [21]. Before opting for any protocol, some factors must be taken into account like energy efficiency (total consumed energy for the given execution time), performance (total transmission time), resource usage (CPU and RAM), and reliability (ability to avoid packet loss) [22] (Fig. 2).

MQTT was developed by Andy Stanford-Clark of IBM and Arlen Nipper of Arcom in 1999 and standardized in 2013 by Organization for the Advancement of Structured Information Standards (OASIS) [24, 25]. The MQTT (Message Queuing Telemetry Transport) protocol due to its capability to safely and consistently link millions of devices to the Internet, MQTT has become the de facto standard for data transmission. MQTT uses limited resources since it is quick and effective, provides

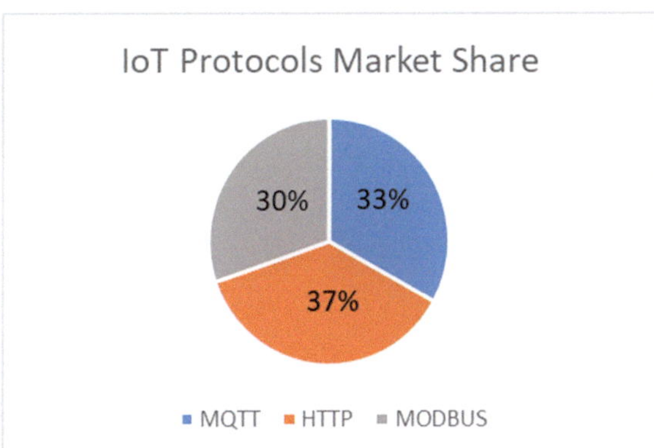

Fig. 2 Depicts the market share of IoT protocols. [23]

bi-directional messaging from the device to the cloud, operates on unstable networks, and offers security [8]. MQTT has a whopping market share of 50.3% [23], this is primarily due to MQTT's low overhead and power consumption [24, 26]. A simple shodan [27] query of "MQTT" gives an overall result of 463,951 hosts (as of June 21, 2023) [27] (Fig. 3).

MQTT follows a publish/subscribe architecture comprising publishers, subscribers, and a broker. The publishers and subscribers exchange messages through brokers with the help of control packets [5]. Publishers are unaware of the number of subscribers that exist. The subscriber first needs to subscribe to a particular topic or use a wildcard (#) to subscribe to all the topics for receiving notifications from the broker when new data is published (Fig. 4).

In addition, one of the advantages of MQTT has a predefined size of header i.e. 2 Bytes, resulting in low packet overhead. Being built upon TCP protocol for reliable message delivery [5].

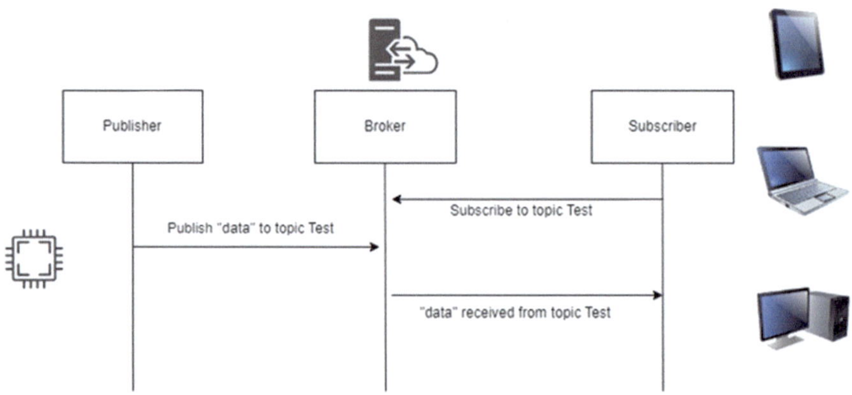

Fig. 3 Explains the communication model of the MQTT protocol [28]

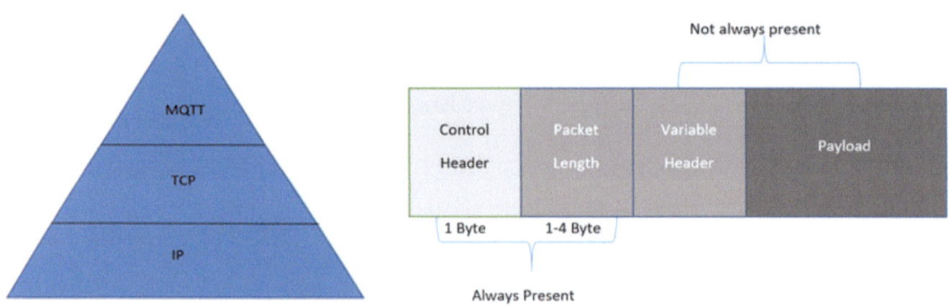

Fig. 4 MQTT header

4 Literature Work

In [29], the research paper adopts a mutation-based approach for fuzzing and introduces a novel technique based on templates. The template-based approach involves a three-step process: Firstly, a template acts as a sniffer between the broker and the client, filtering packets based on specified parameters. Secondly, the user generates legitimate traffic with the broker. Lastly, the processed package results in the automatic creation of a .json template. To facilitate the automatic generation of test cases, an external application called Radamsa is employed. However, one limitation of mutation-based fuzzing is its potential for limited coverage of various functionalities.

In [30], the research paper presents a comprehensive framework for identifying potential vulnerabilities in MQTT brokers and proposes solutions to address these vulnerabilities. It encompasses various attack vectors such as Data Parsing, Authentication brute-forcing, Data Tampering, and Denial of Service. One notable feature of this framework is its ability to generate a detailed report as part of its output. The testing was conducted using version 1.4.8 of the MQTT Mosquitto broker, although it is worth noting that version 2.0.15 is the latest release as of 2022–08–16. The partial success of the DoS attack was observed, as it did not fully disconnect the clients. Similarly, during the Data Tampering testing, the framework was unable to expose broker exceptions or errors.

In [31], the paper puts forward a Fuzzer for the MQTT protocol using Scapy (Scapy documentation) to forge packets. It generates a payload from a randomly selected number of randomly selected characters and that is sent to the brokers. The payload's effectiveness is judged based on the error it produces in the log file. If the word "error" is detected in the logs, the score is incremented by 1000. Furthermore, the paper outlines an advanced packet generation method that could be used to enhance the fuzzer's capabilities. The tool could be further expanded and improved by working on the packet generation technique.

5 Architecture

To implement the tool, a specific testbed architecture was established to facilitate the desired results. The VirtualBox [32] platform was utilized for setting up the clients and the target server, which in this case is an MQTT Broker. VirtualBox is a versatile virtualization software that enables the creation of dynamic architectures tailored to specific requirements [32] (Fig. 5).

The laboratory setup comprises three machines, including one host machine (HM) and two virtual machines (VMs), all connected within the same network. One of the VMs is running Kali Linux, serving as the attacker machine where the attack script is deployed. The other VM is running Ubuntu and functions as the Mosquitto broker, specifically version 2.0.10 [28]. The tool will be executed on the attacker machine, where the user will initiate the selected modules along with their specified

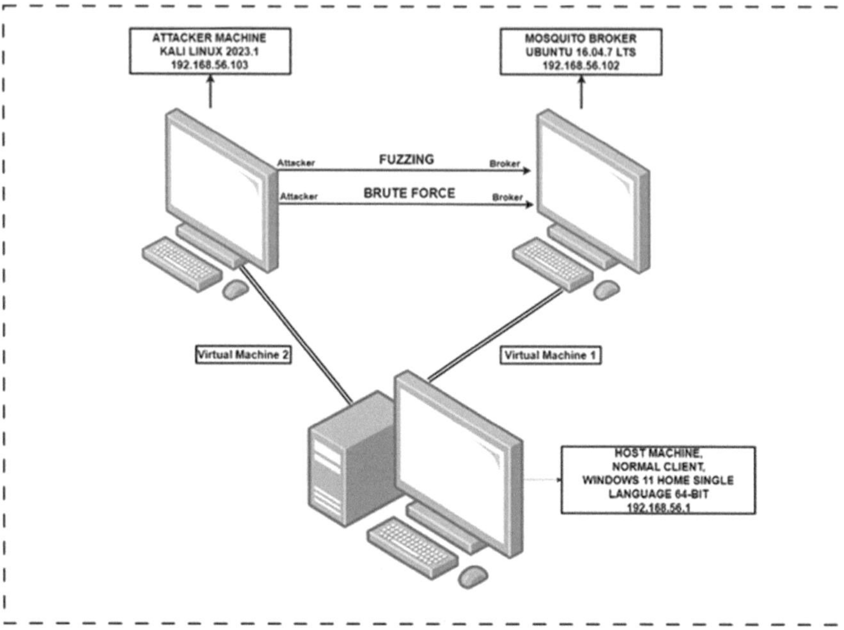

Fig. 5 Overview of the lab setup

configurations. This setup enables the user to control and customize the execution of the tool according to their requirements and preferences.

6 Research Methodology

This section introduces our GUI-based tool that offers a unique approach to evaluate and strengthen the security of MQTT protocol brokers. In the implementation described in [28], an instance of the tool is utilized to create a malicious MQTT server. The test suite encompasses a comprehensive set of test cases designed which can be specifically used to find security flaws and robustness problems in test MQTT clients. In contrast, our tool offers the capability to evaluate both the security and performance aspects of the MQTT broker through the utilization of various modules. The test cases sent to the broker are specifically designed using a generation-based fuzzing technique (Fig. 6).

The packets used in our research are crafted using the Python programming language [28] and leveraging the built-in "Random" function [29]. We have developed multiple custom functions that generate input data, which is subsequently inserted into specific fields within the packets intended for transmission to the MQTT broker (Fig. 7).

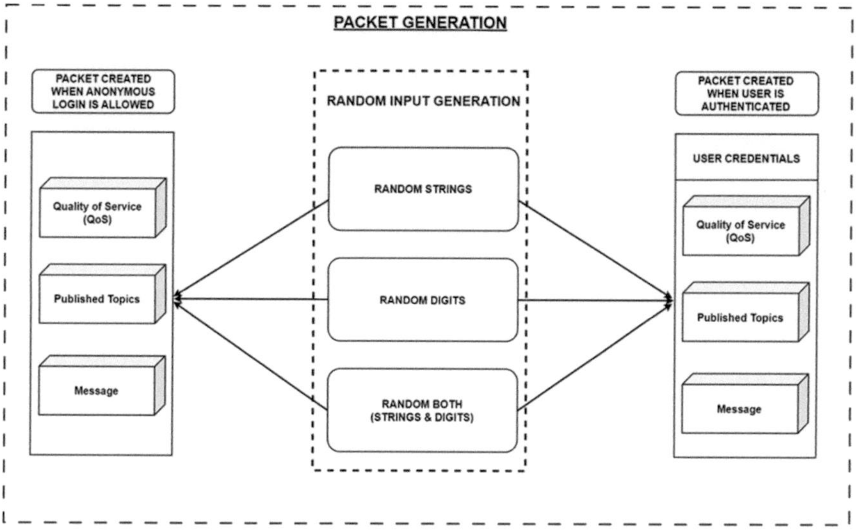

Fig. 6 Packet generation model

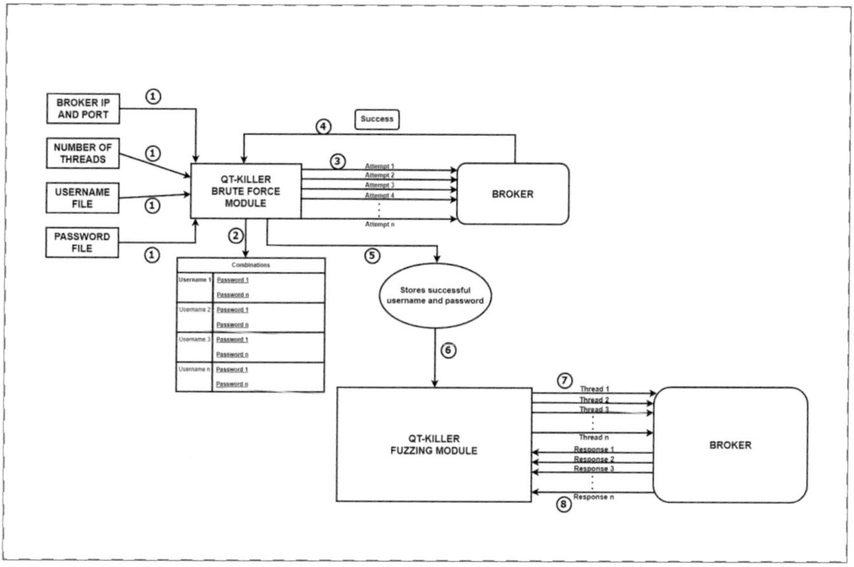

Fig. 7 Technical architecture

Scenario 1: When Anonymous login is not enabled:

In the first step, the user is prompted to provide initial details about the MQTT broker, including the broker's IP address, port number, number of threads, execution mode, and optional username and password files.

Moving to step 2, the tool iterates through the username and password files, generating combinations of each username with every password listed.

Step 3 involves the tool attempting to establish a connection with the broker using the generated combinations as credentials.

Upon successful connection in step 4, the tool saves the credentials that were used to establish the connection.

Similarly, in step 5, the saved credentials are used to reconnect to the broker, ensuring the validity of the credentials.

The Fuzzer module is activated in step 6, where multiple packets are simultaneously sent to the broker using a multi-threading technique. The number of threads created is determined by the user's input in step 1.

Step 7 signifies that the tool captures the responses received from the broker during the testing process.

Lastly, in step 8, the captured responses can be further analyzed to gain insights into the behaviour and performance of the MQTT broker.

Scenario 2: When Anonymous login is enabled:

Step 1: Directly the Fuzzer module is activated, in which multiple packets are simultaneously sent to the broker using a multi-threading technique. The number of threads to be created is dependent on the user's input.

In this approach, since no credentials are required, the tool proceeds directly to packet generation and execution of the Fuzzer module. It skips the steps related to establishing a connection using username and password combinations. Instead, the tool focuses on generating packets and initiating the Fuzzer module for testing the MQTT broker's security and performance.

Pseudocode:

Algorithm 1: Flow of the tool pseudocode.

Input: broker_ip, broker_port, no_threads, mode, username and password files.

(1) if the user selects mode = Fuzzer then

    (a) Fuzzer function is called.

(2) if the user selects mode = Bruteforce and Fuzzer then

    (b) Fuzzer and Bruteforce function is called.

Algorithm 2: Packet generator pseudocode for a CONNECT packet.

(1) packet_generation function:
(2) variable quality = random_digits(0,1,2);
(3) variable publish_topic = random_string and random_digits of length 100;
(4) variable test_message = random_string of length 10;

(5) A packet is created with the above-mentioned variations.

Algorithm 3: Fuzzer module pseudocode.

(1) if user selects mode = Fuzzer Input: IP and Port
    (a) packet_genertion function is called.
(2) Send multiple packets simultaneously using multi-threading.

Algorithm 4: Brute force module pseudocode.

(1) Input: Username and Password Files.
(2) Every username will be paired with each and every password from the file.
    (a) Packet of CONNECT type is sent.
(3) It will check if the result is Successful
    (a) Store those pair of credentials.

Output:

The user interface is presented to the user upon launching the tool, where the user is required to provide several inputs in order to generate results. Upon selecting the Brute force and Fuzzer mode and providing the file containing the Usernames and Passwords, the user is required to initiate the execution by clicking the Start Execution button (Figs. 8, 9 and 10).

During the execution, the brute force function systematically examines every conceivable combination of usernames and passwords (Fig. 11).

Upon invoking the Fuzzer function, numerous packets are concurrently transmitted to the broker using a multi-threading technique. To monitor the incoming packets, MQTT-Explorer-0.4.0-beta1 was employed.

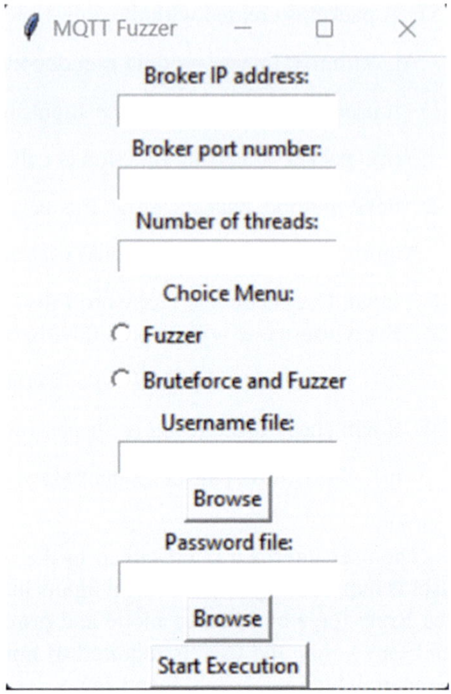

Fig. 8 User interface

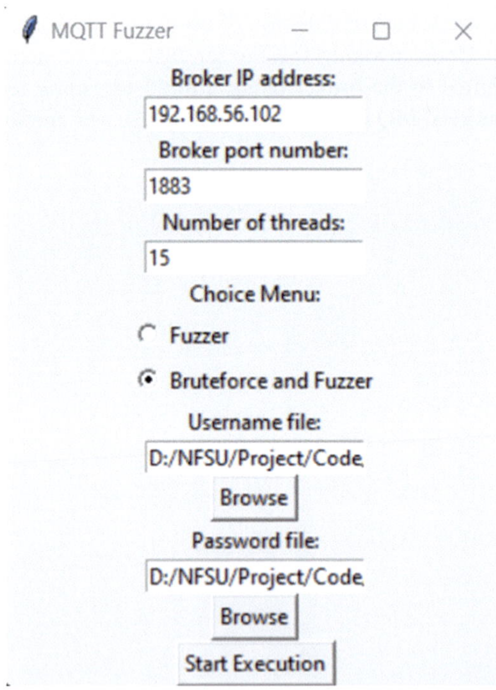

Fig. 9 Scenario 1

Fig. 10 Brute force function

Fig. 11 Fuzzer Function

7 Conclusion and Future Work

This research paper introduces QT-Killer, a unique tool designed to identify potential vulnerabilities in MQTT brokers. The tool automates the process of initiating a predefined set of attack vectors, enabling efficient detection of security weaknesses. To the best of our knowledge, this tool is the first of its kind to leverage the multi-threading technique for implementing a fuzzing attack on MQTT brokers.

In terms of future work, we plan to expand the tool's functionality by incorporating additional modules that cover a broader range of attack vectors. These modules will include assessments for Information Disclosure and evaluation of the status of past Common Vulnerabilities and Exposures (CVE).

References

1. Li S, Xu LD, Zhao S (2014) The internet of things: a survey. Springer Link 243–259
2. Perera C, Zaslavsky A, Christen P, Georgakopoulos D (2014) Context aware computing for the internet of things: a survey. IEEE 16(1):414–454
3. Minerva R, Biru A, Rotondi D (2015) Towards a definition of the Internet of Things (IoT). IEEE 1

4. Akyildiz IF (2002) Wireless sensor networks: a survey. Comput Netw 38(4):393–422
5. Firdous SN, Baig Z, Valli C, Ibrahim A (2017) Modelling and evaluation of malicious attacks. IEEE 748–755
6. Atzori L, Iera A, Morabito G (2010) The internet of things: a survey. Comput Netw 54(15):2787–2805
7. The Constrained Application Protocol (CoAP) 2014. [Online]. Available: https://www.rfc-editor.org/rfc/rfc7252
8. MQTT [Online]. Available: https://mqtt.org/
9. Sethi P, Sarangi SR (2017) Internet of things: architectures, protocols, and applications. J Electr Comput Eng
10. Internet of Things (IoT) Market Size, Share & COVID-19 Impact Analysis by Component (Platform, Solution & Services), By End-use Industry, and Regional Forecast, 2023–2030. Fortune Business Insights, 2023
11. McKinsey & Company (2021) IoT value set to accelerate through 2030: where and how to capture it. McKinsey
12. Roman R, Zhou J, Lopez J (2013) On the features and challenges of security and privacy in distributed internet of things. Comput Netw 57(10):2266–2279
13. Yang H, Zhang Y, Hu YP, Liu QX (2013) IKE vulnerability discovery based on fuzzing. Secur Commun Netw 889–901
14. Sutton M, Greene A, Amini P (2007) Fuzzing: brute force vulnerabilty discovery
15. Shapiro SJ (2023) The strange story of the teens behind the mirai botnet. IEEE [Online]. Available: https://spectrum.ieee.org/mirai-botnet
16. Woolf N (2016) DDoS attack that disrupted internet was largest of its kind in history, experts say. The Guardian, Oct 26 [Online]. Available: https://www.theguardian.com/technology/2016/oct/26/ddos-attack-dyn-mirai-botnet.
17. "Ripple20 Network Vulnerabilities," NHS 75 Digital, 18 06 2020 [Online]. Available: https://digital.nhs.uk/cyber-alerts/2020/cc-3504
18. "CVE-2021-35394," NVD, 16 08 2021. [Online]. Available: https://nvd.nist.gov/vuln/detail/CVE-2021-35394
19. Communication protocol, Wikipedia [Online]. Available: https://en.wikipedia.org/wiki/Communication_protocol
20. Joseph Jose Anthraper JK Security, Privacy and Forensic Concern of MQTT Protocol," 19 03 2019. [Online]. Available: https://papers.ssrn.com/sol3/papers.cfm?abstract_id=3355193
21. Niruntasukrat A, Issariyapat C, Pongpaibool P, Meesublak K, Aiumsupucgul P, Panya A (2016) Authorization mechanism for MQTT-based Internet of Things. IEEE 290–295
22. Mun DH, Le Dinh M, Kwon YW (2016) An assessment of internet of things protocols for resource-constrained applications. IEEE 555–560
23. Skerrett I "[Survey Results] MQTT Widely Used in IIoT," IIOT World, 03 02 2022 [Online]. Available: https://www.iiot-world.com/industrial-iot/connected-industry/survey-results-mqtt-widely-used-in-iiot#:~:text=MQTT%20Widely%20Used%20Today%20in%20IIoT&text='%2C%20the%20most%20popular%20was%20//,and%20then%20Modbus%20(45.9%25)
24. Al-Fuqaha A, Guizani M, Mohammadi M, Aledhari M, Ayyash M (2015) Internet of things: a survey on enabling technologies. IEEE 17:2347–2376
25. "MQTT Version 3.1.1," OASIS, 10 12 2015. [Online]. Available: http://docs.oasis-open.org/mqtt/mqtt/v3.1.1/mqtt-v3.1.1.html
26. Waher P (2015) Learning internet of things. Packt Publishing
27. Shodan Report, [Online]. Available: https://www.shodan.io/search/report?query=mqtt
28. MQTT Version 5.0, OASIS, 2019. [Online]. Available: https://docs.oasis-open.org/mqtt/mqtt/v5.0/mqtt-v5.0.html
29. Hernández Ramos S, Villalba MT, Lacuesta R (2018) MQTT security: a novel fuzzing approach. Wirel Commun Mob Comput
30. Palmieri A, Prem P, Ranise S, Morelli U, Ahmad T (2019) MQTTSA: a tool for automatically assisting the secure deployments of MQTT brokers. IEEE 47–53

31. Casteur G, Aubaret A, Blondeau B, Clouet V, Quemat A, Pical V, Zitouni R (2020) Fuzzing attacks for vulnerability discovery within MQTT protocol. IEEE 420–425
32. Virtual Box, [Online]. Available: https://www.virtualbox.org/

An Efficient Approach for Reliable Verification of Immunization Data Using Blockchain Technology

V. J. Charles, Sharon Justine, and V. Panchami

Abstract There is a huge importance of a reliable and secure database system for storing sensitive data related to vaccination records. Traditional methods of centralized storage have several drawbacks such as mutable data, lack of transparency, and a single point of failure. To address these limitations, this research proposes a novel Blockchain based architecture that provides a decentralized, tamper proof, and easy to manage database for vaccination records. The proposed system consists of a smart contract that acts as the backend logic and a web application for data creation and retrieval. To ensure the authenticity of vaccination records, the proposed scheme employs a unique universal identification system created using cryptographic algorithms. Leveraging the advantages of Blockchain architecture, this proposed system offers a solution that addresses the limitations of centralized data storage and provides a secure and transparent platform for managing vaccination records. The system uses Polygon Blockchain as its base architecture and also provides a justification as to why this Blockchain is used by providing a detailed cost and time analysis of different chains.

Keywords Blockchain · Smart contract · SHA-256

1 Introduction

With the advent of COVID-19, there has been an increase in the number of loopholes found in traditional medical data management [1]. A lot of pressure has been put on the current database systems, and it has led to more and more faults being exposed.

V. J. Charles · S. Justine (✉) · V. Panchami
IIIT Kottayam, Kottayam, Kerala, India
e-mail: sharonjustine.22phd1100@iiitkottayam.ac.in

V. J. Charles
e-mail: charles2019@iiitkottayam.ac.in

V. Panchami
e-mail: panchamam036@iiitkottayam.ac.in

B. N. Gohil et al. (eds.), *Information Security, Privacy and Digital Forensics*,
Lecture Notes in Electrical Engineering 1423,
https://doi.org/10.1007/978-981-96-9443-3_2

There have been many reports of providers facing logistical challenges such as lack of vaccination records [2]. Poor access to children's immunization record is one of the major barriers to vaccination. Numerous cases of fake and unauthenticated vaccination records leading to increased spread of pandemic indicates that a change in the method of medical data is of utmost importance. Corruption in the times of a pandemic also has not contributed positively for a hassle-free record management system.

In our proposed system for reliable verification of immunization data, introduced a decentralized application. In the existing works [3, 4] etc. they haven't mentioned any decentralized application for their system. In Alrebdi et al. [5] even they proposing a searchable and verifiable medical record system there is no way to check the authenticity of the records. In the existing systems many systems are handling the medical records using Blockchain network, even then there is no decentralized application for the same and also there is no methods are there in those systems to ensure the authenticity and integrity of the medical data which is achieved in our proposed system.

Ethereum-based blockchain is considered for medical applications, including vaccine record management, for several reasons:

- Security and Immutability: Ethereum's blockchain offers a high level of security and immutability. Once data is recorded on the Ethereum blockchain, it is difficult to alter or tamper with, providing a secure and reliable record-keeping system.
- Smart Contracts: Ethereum supports smart contracts, which are self-executing contracts with the terms of the agreement directly written into code. This feature can automate processes in healthcare, such as ensuring that vaccine records are updated when a dose is administered.
- Decentralization: Ethereum operates on a decentralized network of nodes, making it resistant to censorship and single points of failure. This can be crucial in healthcare applications where data integrity and accessibility are paramount.
- Interoperability: Ethereum's open-source nature allows for interoperability with other systems and applications. This can facilitate the integration of healthcare data with other platforms and services.
- Polygon is chosen to mitigate cost concerns of the transactions. An average transaction costs about Dollar 0.015 which is affordable

The privacy of the users can be achieved by the use of Blockchain technology. The users are anonymous in the case of Blockchain paradigm. The users identity or any information that can deduce the user identity is not revealed in Blockchain. Each user is identified using a hexadecimal address. For the entire Blockchain network the user appears with the address and other users or anyone else may not able to identify the user. In our proposed system we added gas relayer for ensuring privacy and correctness of the data communicated between Blockchain network. The relayer is used to communicate between different Blockchain networks and it ensures that the data communicated correctly.

1.1 Centralized Systems

Observing deeply in our current database management systems, we can somewhat infer where the root of the problem lies. Traditional systems uses a centralized structure which makes it almost impossible to entrust it with sensitive information [6]. A single entity handling the entirety of a structure poses a ton of problems. It forms a single critical point of failure. A malfunction in a part would mean the whole system shutting down. This also means it provides a single point for any cyber attack. Sensitive information being vulnerable to cyber attacks should be discarded completely. Such databases are not transparent and need a level of authentication to access data, making it tough for nation wide projects. In terms of authentication, administrators need to make sure that the data is accurate which leads to more man power being needed. A project which will have a huge impact and will be used by a number of people should avoid all limitations at any cost. These problems are therefore solved by the advent of decentralized systems.

1.2 Blockchain Technology

Blockchain is a cryptographically secure open, immutable, distributed ledger. A Blockchain consists of large number of blocks. Whenever a transaction is initiated, after the validation of the transaction and the block will be mined by the miners and it will be added to the Blockchain as a block.

Blockchain can be majorly of three different types being:

- Public Blockchain: The consensus mechanism in public Blockchain is performed by the miners. And the consensus mechanism is permission less. This Blockchain concept is nearly impossible to tamper. It follows a purely decentralized approach.
- Private Blockchain: The consensus mechanism is performed by a single organization and the consensus mechanism is permissioned. This Blockchain concept could be tampered. And this follows a centralized approach.
- Consortium Blockchain: The consensus is performed by a set of nodes and the consensus mechanism is permissioned. Consortium Blockchain could be tampered. These type of Blockchain has a semi-decentralized nature.

2 Related Works

This section coves all the current work that has been done related to our problem statement. This is done to get meaningful information regarding the problems faced, the ideas used and improvements that can be made. Eventually, helping to create an even better understanding of the problem and possible solutions for it.

Wan and Huang [7] proposed Adoption and Optimization of Blockchain Technology in the Regulation of Class II Vaccines. They studied the vulnerabilities in the second class medicine supervision and also they discussed the impact of Blockchain technology in second class medicine supervision and they proposed a modular and sustainable supply chain integration optimization design for the second-class vaccine safety supervision. The system uses Blockchain for supply chain management. The entire system need to rely on different technologies namely RFID, Artificial Intelligence, Image Processing, etc. The complexity of processing the system will be high.

Sajedi et al. [8] proposed Global data sharing of SARS-CoV-2 based on Blockchain. This paper proposes the concept of data sharing world wide in a decentralized manner. For the pandemic medical data by using the Blockchain technology can be shared to any lab or hospital or to any one who want to access the data. Hence makes the data accessible to the authorised persons who want to access the data. Secure data storage can be guaranteed using Blockchain.

Paik et al. [3] proposed a summary of data management in Blockchain based systems is described, more specifically, usage of Blockchain based system for storage of data at a large scale. It also describes the factors that contribute to the safety and security of a Blockchain based system. The paper discusses on chain data storage using different types of Blockchain such as public, private, consortium etc. The key takeaways form this paper are combination of on chain and off chain data in a large software system with a Blockchain. The data storage in Blockchain while compared with other centralized database is discussed in this paper in detail. The Blockchain data store is clearly explained as four layers namely logical data store, physical data store, data access, and data processing layer. The smart contract technology for managing the data is not discussed in this paper.

Rotbi et al. [4] proposed Blockchain based system which is used for the complete vaccination process. The architecture of the system has five actors : Manufacturer, Distributor, Patient, Doctor and medical center. In this paper leveraging IoT for contract tracing and tracking. However, the authenticity and ethical behavior of the patients still posed a problem, indicating stricter authentication measures needed to be adopted. There is a need for participants in the supply chain to set up the environment and their commercial agreements. The covid-19 vaccination reports are stored in the immutable Blockchain. It can be shared among all the participants in a transparent way. Any participant in this scenario can verify the data stored in the Blockchain. All the information related to vaccines are also stored in Blockchain. Hence the correctness of the information can be verified. The major issue faced by the system is

Antal et al. [9] specifies Blockchain structure for vaccine supply management. A decentralized smart contracts based solution for monitoring the proper vaccine transportation conditions in a cold chain and real-time awareness of all peers. Pseudocode of the data structure that specifies all the relevant data that is needed. The medical center, the doctors, vaccine producers, vaccine storage, the beneficiaries constitute the Blockchain network. All the vaccination activities will be recorded in the immutable Blockchain network. Hence anyone can validate the transactions. Limitations of the system is latency is high for the system.

Buterin and Vitalik [10] proposed discusses the architecture on which our proposed solution can be made, ethereum. It shows in detail the technology and structure behind a Blockchain network: The intent of Ethereum is to create an alternative protocol for constructing dapps, with a different set of tradeoffs that will be very beneficial for a number of decentralized applications, with a focus on circumstances where continuous improvement time, security for small and rarely used applications, and the ability of different applications to interact very efficiently are important. The paper describes a protocol for building and connecting ethereum-compatible Blockchain networks. Polygon works basically like ethereum, but has some notable differences which make it more suitable for our use cases. The consensus algorithm used in Polygon, Proof-of-Stake, is more environment friendly, considering it does not require much computational power.

Alrebdi et al. [5] discusses in detail about a searchable and verifiable medical record system. This paper uses Interplanetary File Storage (IPFS) for the decentralized storage of files. Uses encryption algorithms to encrypt the sensitive files and then store the hash of it. The system uses cloud database for the storage of encrypted files. Along with Blockchain, cloud database is also used for storage of the encrypted data which will increase the latency of the system. And cloud is a centralized database which is a single point of failure.

Nabil and Salekin [11] proposed a Blockchain based COVID vaccination registration and monitoring. In this paper they proposed a system which is based on Blockchain that can integrate testing and vaccination mechanisms. And also they implemented a QR (quick response) code-based "Digital Vaccine Passport" (DVP) mechanism which will reduce the corruption in COVID testing and vaccination. They also proposed a Vaccination prioritization, i.e., vaccination is given to the areas and peoples based on some priority criteria.

Binbin et al. [12] proposed a Blockchain based system for safe vaccine supply and supervision. Ethereum based smart contracts are designed in this paper for consumers, vaccine institutions and government for storing the vaccination data. They resolved the vaccine accountability problem by using the vaccine Blockchain system. Along with Blockchain technology, machine learning and deep learning technologies are used for intelligent vaccine recommendation. By querying the Blockchain the expired vaccination details and vaccine information can be gathered.

In the literature we have discussed so far, most of the system used the Blockchain for storage of the vaccination data. When compared with our system the latency of execution of the other systems [5, 9, 12], the proposed system have low latency of execution. In most of the papers the platform used for smart contract is Ethereum ide whereas in the proposed system and [10] uses the polygon matic network for the execution of smart contract. The scalability of the proposed system when compared with the existing papers is high. The gas consumption of the proposed system is low when other existing works is considered.

3 System Model

The system has been designed keeping in mind it will serve 3 kinds of users, which are:

- Vaccination authorities: This is the actor which will be able to create/update the data entries, this is done so that any individual can easily be registered as soon as he/she gets vaccinated.
- Medical center: For any verification of the vaccination records that has to be made for a patient, the medical center just has to enter the unique identification number of the patient that was created during vaccination.
- Patient: The beneficiary will be able to read his/her own data, and can be notified of next vaccination time etc.

This is the interaction between the various modules and actors of the system, the medical center actor will be able to read any value using the given ID (Figs. 1, 2 and 3; Table 1).

The unique ID plays an important role in the authenticity and security of the whole system. Thus it is important for a safe and secure generation of the IDs. We use some of the well known cryptographic hash functions for creating this. The unique ID will be a combination of a private and a public ID. The private ID will act as a password and the public ID will be derived from the private ID using cryptography algorithms that have been tested to be secure and will have a huge range to avoid collisions. A hash function can be defined mathematically as a mapping that takes an input and returns a fixed-size unique string of characters, which is typically a hexadecimal

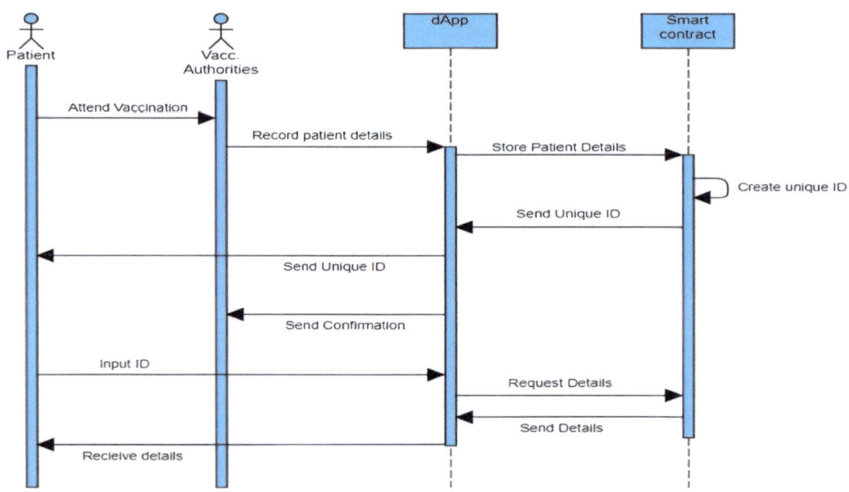

Fig. 1 Proposed system sequence diagram

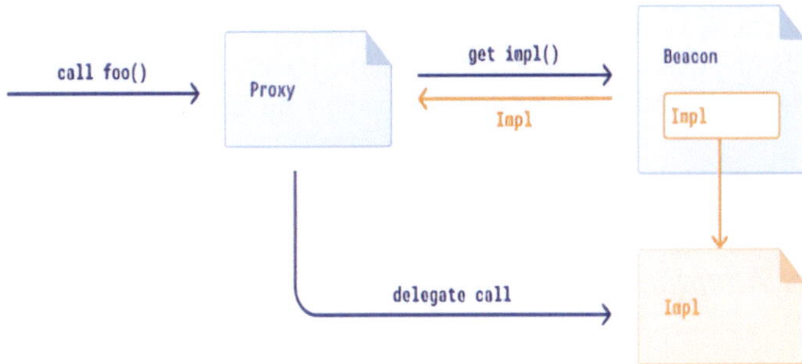

Fig. 2 Proxy transaction flow

```
User ---- tx ---> Proxy ----------> Implementation_v0
                    |
                     ------------> Implementation_v1
                    |
                     ------------> Implementation_v2
```

Fig. 3 Concept of proxies

Table 1 Privileges of the user

	Create	Read	Update	Delete
Vaccination authorities	Yes	Yes	Yes	No
Medical center	No	Yes	No	No
Patient	No	Yes	No	No

number. For each input to the hash function there will be a unique, collision free output.

Let H be a hash function and x be the input to the hash function then H(x) = h, where h is the output hash value. The cryptographic algorithm that is used in the proposed system is SHA-256. SHA-256 is a part of the SHA-2 family of algorithms, where SHA stands for Secure Hash Algorithm. Some of the important characteristics that have been kept in mind while choosing an algorithm is:

- Since vaccination has to be done in a huge number, therefore a hashing function of a wide range and lesser collision probability was required.
- The hashing should be irreversible. This contributes to the safety of the system. A reversible algorithm will be harmful to the privacy of individuals since any person can get the details of any other person

For any individual to prove that the record is genuine and authenticated, they just need to hash the private ID and obtain the public ID. For the sake of uniqueness, the unix timestamp of time of vaccination and aadhar number was taken as the private ID.

3.1 User Adoption

Due to only the recent advent of Blockchain technology, users may find the whole process of creating wallet, signing transactions and querying the Blockchain to be confusing. For making all of this easier, we are going to be using gasless transactions and social login:

- Gasless transactions: Gasless transactions refer to a mechanism in Ethereum that enables users to interact with smart contracts without having to pay for gas. In the traditional Ethereum network, gas is the amount of ether required to execute a transaction on the network. This means that every time a user wants to update a smart contract or initiate a transaction, they need to pay for gas in the form of ether. However, with gasless transactions, users can interact with smart contracts without needing to own ether.
- Social Login: For many users, creating a wallet, managing their public and private keys might seem a bit of a hassle. To tackle this, the system will have an option for social login using email accounts. Biconomy's social login feature ensures that through their social accounts, a wallet is created.
- Sending notifications: Sending Notifs comprises of smart contracts (and later p2p nodes) that acts like a middleware through which all notifs/communication from a service to their subscribers needs to flow.

3.2 Proxies

Basically what happens in a normal transaction in any Blockchain is that a user (also called the signer) will execute a transaction and a smart contract deployed on the Blockchain will carry the logic/code out and change/read state as needed. The blocker that we hit is that this smart contract is immutable, so suppose we find a bug in this smart contract there is nothing that we can do to change or update it. To solve this pain point, we use proxies. Proxies are basically surface contracts. The whole concept of proxies includes 2 contracts - Proxy contract and implementation contract.

This proxy contract will be linked to implementation contract through the means of impl. contract's address. And this address can be changed by executing a func in proxy contract. Implementation contract contains the main logic that the intended contract should carry out, so when a user initiates a transaction, it is done on the proxy contract, this proxy contract will redirect us to the implementation contract (which holds the logic) and then transaction will be completed.

4 Methodology

The proposed system is built upon the Polygon Blockchain which uses the Blockchain architecture. This is advantageous in 2 ways :

- Less gas fees: making it cost effective
- Less computational power: making it more efficient and environment friendly.

The tech stack of creating the system would look like:

- Polygon Blockchain
- Solidity smart contracts
- React frontend
- Ethers and web3 helper libraries

Polygon is built upon ethereum, therefore the underlying fundamentals remain the same. The smart contracts govern the backend of our system and it is written in solidity language. Remix is a tool which was used to test out the smart contracts for detecting any faults or security holes. Hardhat is a development environment that was used for local deployment and testing.

The tech stack mentioned here refers to the technologies that would be used to develop a system that operates on the Polygon Blockchain network. The Polygon network is a Layer 2 scaling solution for Ethereum, which provides faster transaction speeds and lower gas fees compared to the Ethereum mainnet. Solidity is a programming language used to write smart contracts that execute on the Ethereum Blockchain and other compatible networks. Solidity is used to write smart contracts that would be executed on the Polygon network.

Figure 4 shows the workflow of our proposed decentralized application. The user access the site through the web application. The web application checks the user role, the user need to register in this phase if the user is using the application for the first time, else the user want to log in to the web application. If the user is patient, then the user can access the vaccination record and if any editing want to perform then that changes can be made, then that change is stored. The user is vaccination official, then then they can add the data of the vaccinated individuals, and that change can be stored. So as a patient as well as a vaccination official one can enter the decentralized web application and add the data and store the records. Gas relayer is a third-party service that helps users execute transactions on the Blockchain without having to pay gas fees. Relayer act as a middle layer that you send a message or make a transaction without having to pay for it yourself.

Algorithm for Vaccination and Registration smart contract is specified below:

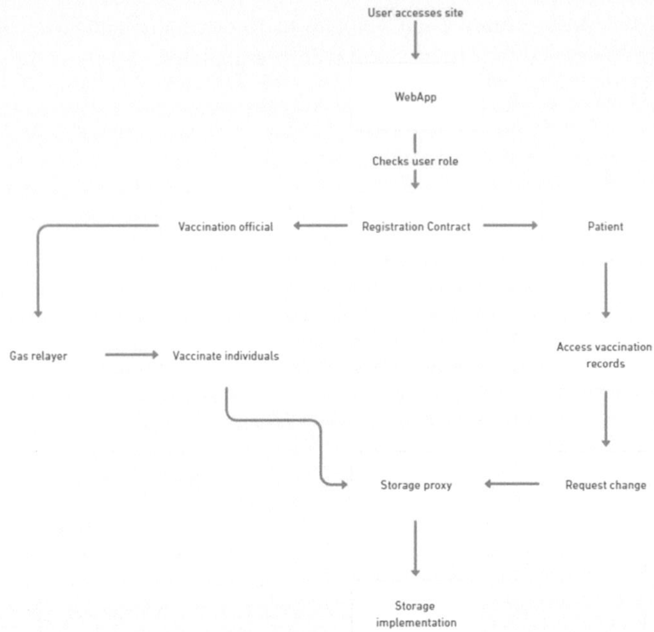

Fig. 4 Workflow of proposed decentralized application

Algorithm 1 Storage contract

---

procedure VACCINATE($aadhar, place, name, doseNumber$)
  Check if correct role
  if $registered == True$ **then**
    Set timestamp as last recorded entry
    Set place of vaccination
    Set dose number of vaccination
    Set name of vaccination
    if $registered == firsttime$ **then**
      Concatenate aadhar, block.timestamp, address
      Generate sha256 hash of concatenated value
      Return ID
    else
      Revert

---

5 Implementation

The implementation of vaccination system using Blockchain with a decentralized application was successful.The deployment details can be found in figures given below. Block explorer transaction details are also attached as figures. An image of the decentralized application is shown below. A block explorer is a tool used to

Algorithm 2 Registration contract

procedure REGISTER($aadhar, role$)
    Check if already registered
    if $registered == True$ **then**
        Revert
    else
        Assign role based on id and owner of address =0

browse and view the contents of a Blockchain network. It allows users to view the transactions that have taken place on the network, along with details such as the amount of cryptocurrency transferred, the time of the transaction, and the addresses of the sender and receiver.

Block explorers are typically web-based applications that connect to the Blockchain network and display information in an easy-to-understand format. They allow users to search for specific transactions by entering the transaction hash, wallet address, or other identifying information. In addition to displaying transaction data, block explorers can also show information about the current state of the Blockchain network, including the total number of blocks, the difficulty level of mining new blocks, and the current block reward.

Figure 5 is the smart contract deployment on polygon test network. The transaction hash, transaction status, the block number of the newly created block, the sender and receiver address, timestamp and the transaction fee in matic, these much information of the transaction are available from the diagram.

Figure 6 shows the gas consumption after the successful transaction. From the figure we can find the total amount of gas consumed in the transaction and also the nonce value of the transaction. The gas consumption is represented in terms of Matic coins.

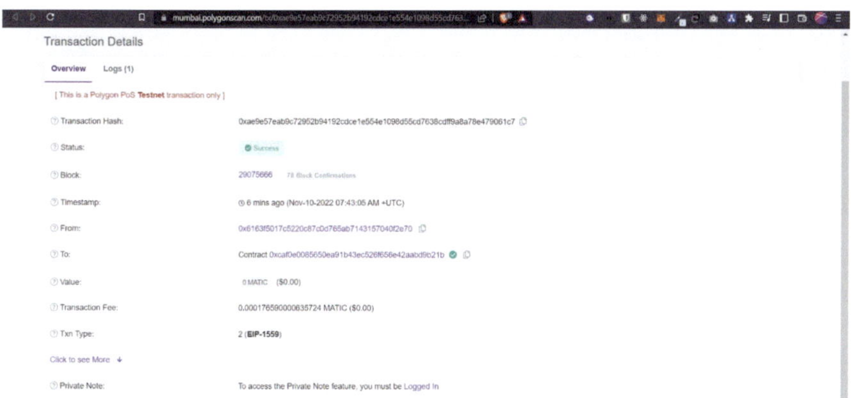

Fig. 5 Contract deployment

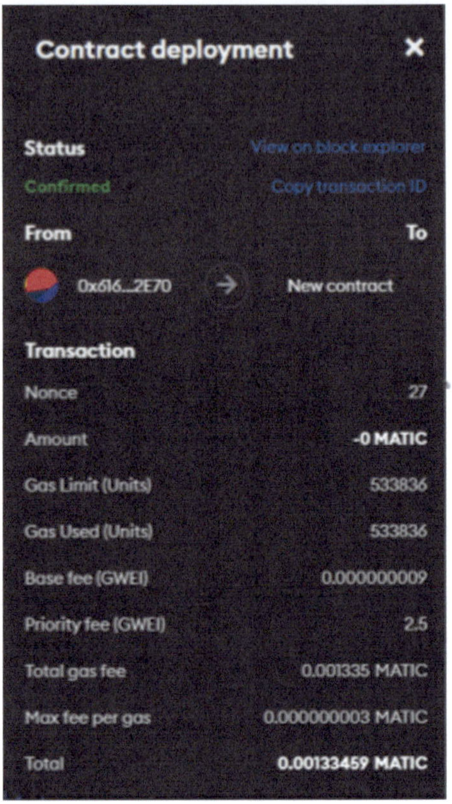

Fig. 6 Gas consumption in contract deployment

6 Performance Analysis

Testnets are experimental Blockchain networks created to test new features, upgrades, and fixes before deploying them to the mainnet. They provide a safe environment for developers to test and refine their ideas without risking real assets or disrupting the main network. However, as with any Blockchain network, testnets can experience bottlenecks, congestion, and other performance issues that affect their speed and reliability.

The Mumbai testnet is the test network of the Polygon network, which replicates the features of the Polygon mainnet. The Mumbai testnet enables developers to deploy, test, and execute their decentralized Applications in the Blockchain environment. Since Mumbai testnet is a replica of the Polygon mainnet, this allows developers to clearly visualize how their decentralized Application work during excecution. Furthermore, because Polygon is Ethereum Virtual Machine (EVM) compatible, the testnet provides an easy way for developers who wish to migrate their dApps from the Ethereum main chain to connect to Polygon to test them before deploying onto the mainnet.

Sepolia is a test network build on Proof of Work consensus algorithm, but now switched to Proof of Stake consensus algorithm. Sepolia is maintained by client developers which ensures the safety and accuracy. An amount of gas is required to pay for on-chain transactions. Sepolia is almost replica of Ethereum which Web3 developers can run test on Web3.

Goerli is a cross-client testing network for Ethereum. In which the ledger is separate from the main Ethereum ledger, so transactions do not cross over between the two. Goerli uses Proof of Authority instead of the mainnet consensus algorithm Proof of Stake. Developers build their dApps on the Goerli testnet because Goerli supports a wider variety of node softwares like Geth, Parity, Nethermind, Hyperledger etc. The most common time analysis metrics for Blockchain networks are transaction confirmation time, block propagation time, and block validation time. Transaction confirmation time is the time it takes for a transaction to be included in a block and added to the Blockchain. This metric depends on several factors, including the size of the transaction, the current network load, and the transaction fee.

Lower confirmation times are desirable for applications that require fast and responsive transactions, such as micropayments, gaming, and trading. Different testnets may have different performance characteristics and time analysis results, depending on their design, consensus mechanism, and network parameters. Therefore, it is important to conduct time analysis on multiple testnets under various conditions to obtain a comprehensive understanding of their performance and scalability.

Cost analysis for test chains Mumbai, Sepolia and Goerli based on contract deployment and contract method call is performed and cost in dollars for various chains is plotted. The test chain Mumbai has low contract deployment and contract method call cost. Sepolia and Goerli have almost same cost in dollars for contract deployment and contract method call.

Time analysis .i.e., time for contract deployment in Metamask and time for state change in Metamask is performed for the test chains like Mumbai, Sepolia and Goerli is performed. The time taken by metamask in seconds is low for Mumbai test network. The time taken for Sepolia and Goerli is almost same. But the time taken by Sepolia is a bit lower than time taken by Goerli (Figs. 7 and 8).

7 Conclusion and Future Work

The decentralized application and the smart contracts required to integrate it were deployed for public use successfully. In our proposed system a decentralized web application for the verification of the immunization data is introduced. The proposed system was actualized on the polygon Blockchain architecture. The report was also successful in analysing and comparing different testnet network for a proper deployment decision. The various metrics used for comparing were cost and time and a clear better testnet was decided in Polygon Mumbai testnet. The current deployment system needs a secure private mechanism to hide all private data, for this there will

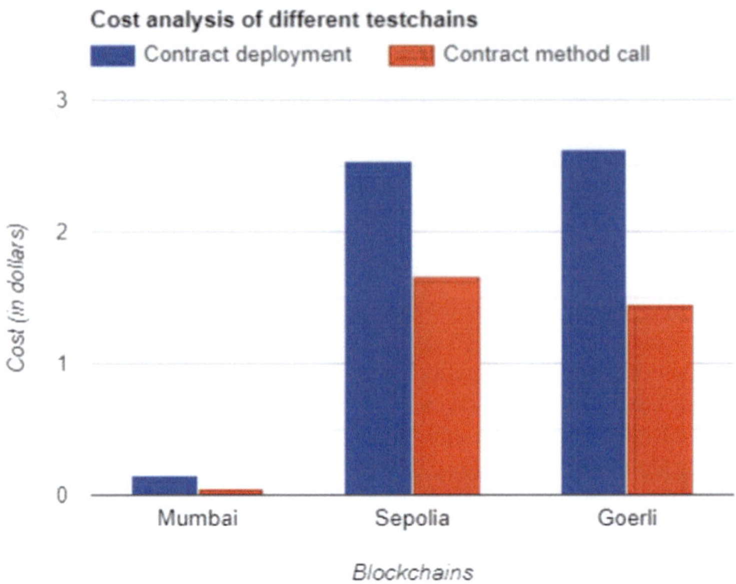

Fig. 7 Cost analysis of test chains

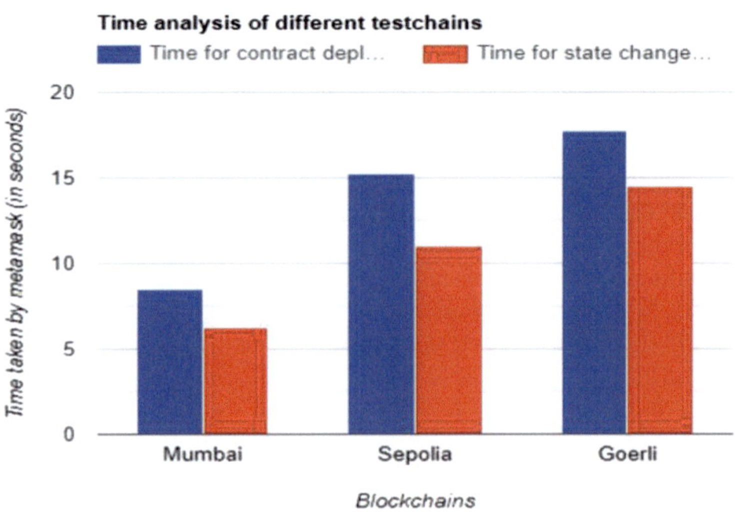

Fig. 8 Time analysis of test chains

be a need to introduce zero knowledge concept. Future scope will include adding Zero Knowledge SNARKS to secure and privatise all kinds of data.

Incorporating privacy metrics is the next step, this is in order to improve the security of the platform since the data that is being stored is highly sensitive. Implementing privacy metrics also helps to improve the security of the platform as a whole. By evaluating and monitoring privacy, it becomes easier to detect and prevent potential breaches. Additionally, using privacy metrics can help to identify areas of weakness in the platform's security architecture, allowing for more targeted improvements to be made.

References

1. Awotunde JB et al (2021) Big data and data analytics for an enhanced COVID-19 epidemic management. Artif Intell COVID-19. Springer International Publishing, Cham, pp 11–29
2. Arji G et al (2023) Identifying resilience strategies for disruption management in the healthcare supply chain during COVID-19 by digital innovations: a systematic literature review. Inf Med Unlocked, pp 101199
3. Paik H-Y et al (2019) Analysis of data management in Blockchain-based systems: from architecture to governance. IEEE Access 7:186091–186107
4. Rotbi MF, Motahhir S, El Ghzizal A (2021) Blockchain technology for a safe and transparent covid-19 vaccination. ArXiv preprint arXiv:2104.05428
5. Alrebdi N et al (2022) SVBE: searchable and verifiable Blockchain-based electronic medical records system. Sci Rep 12(1):266
6. Scobie HM et al (2020) Improving the quality and use of immunization and surveillance data: summary report of the working group of the strategic advisory group of experts on immunization. Vaccine 38(46):7183–7197
7. Wan Y, Huang H (2023) Adoption and optimization of blockchain technology in the regulation of class II vaccines. IEEE Access 11:84607–84619. https://doi.org/10.1109/ACCESS.2023.3301772
8. Sajedi H, Mohammadipanah F (2023) Global data sharing of SARS-CoV-2 based on blockchain. Int J Inf Technol 1–9
9. Antal C et al (2021) Blockchain platform for COVID-19 vaccine supply management. IEEE Open J Comput Soc 2:164–178
10. Marbouh D et al (2020) Blockchain for COVID-19: review, opportunities, and a trusted tracking system. Arab J Sci Eng 45:9895–9911
11. Nabil SS et al (2022) Blockchain-based covid vaccination registration and monitoring. Blockchain: Res Appl 3(4):100092
12. Yong B et al (2020) An intelligent blockchain-based system for safe vaccine supply and supervision. Int J Inf Manage 52:102024
13. Anderson EL (2014) Recommended solutions to the barriers to immunization in children and adults. Missouri Med 111(4):344
14. Mahmud H, Joan L, Qiang X (2018) A blockchain-based service provider validation and verification framework for health-care virtual organization. UHD J Sci Technol 2(2):24–31
15. Hirano T et al (2020) Data validation and verification using Blockchain in a clinical trial for breast cancer: regulatory sandbox. J Med Internet Res 22(6):e18938
16. Sheikh S, Azmathullah RM, Rizwan F (2018) Proof-of-work vs proof-of-stake: a comparative analysis and an approach to Blockchain consensus mechanism. Int J Res Appl Sci Eng Technol 6(12):786–791
17. Buterin V (2013) Ethereum: a next-generation generalized smart contract and decentralized application platform. Curated Cryptoasset Publications, Blockchain Papers, pp 475–483
18. Zheng Z et al (2017) An overview of Blockchain technology: architecture, consensus, and future trends. In: 2017 IEEE international congress on big data (BigData congress). IEEE 2017

Cryptanalysis of User Authentication Scheme for Public Cloud Server

Samidha Saxena, Payal Chaudhari, and Nishant Doshi

Abstract Public cloud servers have become a energy efficient fundamental component of modern computing, providing flexible and scalable resources to a wide range of users. However, ensuring the security of data stored in the public cloud is still a serious concern. Authentication protocols are essential for ensuring secure access to cloud resources. The Authentication and Key Agreement (AKA) system is frequently used for this purpose. In this study, we conducted a comprehensive cryptanalysis of the authentication scheme for public cloud server which was recently proposed by Khan et al. in 2023. Through meticulous examination, we discovered flaws in the areas of perfect forward secrecy, susceptibility to Denial of Service (DoS) attacks, lack of timestamp usage, and susceptibility to replay attacks.

Keywords Energy · Privacy preserving · Public cloud server · Authentication protocol

1 Introduction

With the increasing popularity of cloud computing more and more users are want use Public Cloud Servers for their data processing, there is no doubt cloud computing market is rapidly growing, it is anticipated that revenue in the public cloud industry will reach US$525.60bn in 2023, and it will increase by $881.90 till 2027 [1]. However, this also raises concerns around the security and privacy of user data.

S. Saxena
L.D. College of Engineering, Gujarat, India

P. Chaudhari (✉) · N. Doshi
School of Technology, Pandit Deendayal Energy University, Gujarat, India
e-mail: payal.chaudhari@sot.pdpu.ac.in

N. Doshi
e-mail: nisahnt.doshi@sot.pdpu.ac.in

B. N. Gohil et al. (eds.), *Information Security, Privacy and Digital Forensics*,
Lecture Notes in Electrical Engineering 1423,
https://doi.org/10.1007/978-981-96-9443-3_3

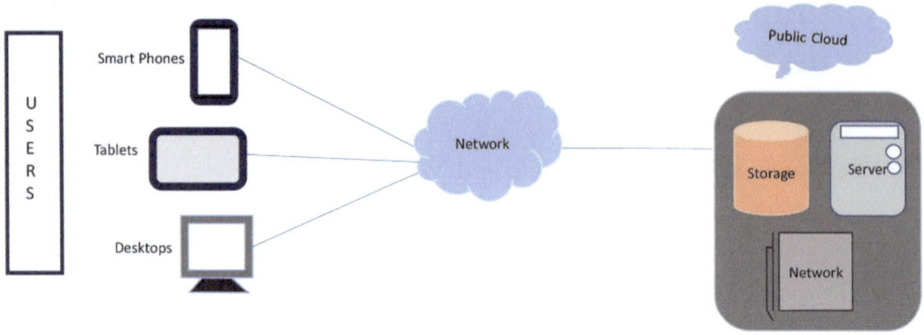

Fig. 1 Public cloud server scenario

Because huge number of user's use cloud network for banking and storing sensitive information and cloud server used by industrialist and government also. All the operation done over an insecure medium. So, one of the main challenges is an Authentication, because for intruder's it is very easy and effortless to steal data and/or inject malicious data or virus in user's wireless devices such as laptop and smartphones etc. These attacks may result in very serious events like service interruptions, data breaches, data loss, and illegal access to critical information. Therefore, authentication is very important for cloud server's and wireless devices as mentioned in Fig. 1.

First authentication scheme was proposed in 1981 by the Lamport [2] After that many authentication schemes were proposed by many researchers. Author of [3] and [4]also proposed authentication scheme but unfortunately their suggested protocol is prone to impersonation and offline password guessing attacks. In another scheme which is proposed by author of [5], provided the designing principle, these principles aim to ensure robust security. Multiple techniques have been presented by different researchers to improve security features while lowering computational costs. Author of [6] proposed anonymous authentication protocol scheme for Radio Frequency Identification using PUF. Similarly, author of [7] proposed Biometric based authentication scheme for multi-server environment. And SIP proposed by [8], author of [9] proposed A Dynamic ID based remote user authentication scheme for IIoT. and author of [10].

Asymmetric cryptography is quite common in the field of cryptography, Examples of asymmetric cryptographic techniques include ECC, Bilinear Pairing, Chaotic maps and RSA. That are frequently utilized in the development of AKA schemes for secure communication. The first AKA scheme using chaotic maps for e-commerce was proposed in 2005 by the author of [11]. But later according to author of [12], it was found to be vulnerable to counterfeiting attacks. But later in 2007 the author of [13] used chaotic maps to improve the scheme used in [11]. Since then, using chaotic maps many more approaches were proposed for various application [14–18], these proposed solutions, introduced two-factor authentication using a smartcard or biometric in addition to a password. However, some researchers [17, 19] have proposed two factor authentication AKA scheme to protect your confidentiality and safety. Furthermore, three factor AKA scheme is more reliable and secure than one and two factor scheme According to [3, 4, 19] some researchers three factor AKA schemes are unable to achieve other security objectives.

The authentication schemes proposed by authors of [3, 20] does not adhere to the three factor authentication scenario. And [16] scheme does not support user untracebility. Furthermore, the schemes [20, 21] are vulnerable to session key security and password guessing attacks. The author's [19] proposed scheme is susceptible to counterfeiting assaults.

1.1 Our Contribution

In this study, we present the cryptanalysis of the suggested system by Naveed Khan, we identified and evaluated the security vulnerabilities present in the proposed schemes.

- Key Escrow
- SSTIA
- Replay Attack
- DoS
- Perfect forward secrecy

By emphasising these flaws, our goal is to contribute to the understanding of the constraints and potential risks associated with the proposed authentication schemes. This study provides a useful foundation for further development of stronger authentication systems for public cloud services.

1.2 Paper Organization

The research is introduced in Sect. 1 of the paper. Section 2 gives a summary of the relevant work done in this area, highlighting the existing literature and advancements. In Sect. 3, the scheme proposed by Khan et al. is discussed. Section 4 presents the cryptanalysis of Khan et al.'s scheme, where a comprehensive analysis is conducted to identify potential weaknesses and security vulnerabilities. In Sect. 5, we have given the conclusion. Lastly, An extensive list of referenced sources is provided in the References section.

2 Related Work

Although mobile cloud computing has many advantages, it also carries some concerns, one of which is the outsourcing of data storage. Unauthorised physical access is more likely when data in the cloud is spread across several different places. Encryption is frequently used as the primary method to safeguard data from unauthorised access in order to reduce this risk. Both criminal users and cloud service providers are prevented from accessing the data without valid authorization by encrypting the data before transferring it to the cloud. To preserve data security even if an adversary steals the secret key, it is crucial to constantly improve encryption methods.

Users need authentication and key agreement techniques in order to connect to remote servers via insecure networks. In 1981, author of [2] suggested the first authentication and key agreement technique, in which server authenticates the user using a username and password. However, because this system keeps a password table, it is open to being intercepted by outsiders, who can then use the passwords to execute replay attacks and gain access to the server. The author [22] suggested a two-factor authentication system in 1991 to overcome this problem. To increase security and defend against replay attacks, this technique combines the usage of a login, password, and use smart card as a second factor.

A two-factor AKA technique based on chaos theory was suggested by author of [23] in 2013. However, another author found that the [23] scheme's session key security and anonymity were lacking in [24]. The technique described in [24] was also subject to a cryptanalysis by the author of [17], which revealed that it was unprotected against insider assaults and susceptible to Denial-of-Service (DoS) attacks.

The author of [17] presented a new two-factor AKA approach to overcome the flaws of the suggested protocol by [24]. However, the technique described in [17] is not effective at fending off key compromise, information leakage attacks, and impersonation, and it is also unable to give local password updates and detect erroneous passwords, according to the author of [25].

These results underline how crucial it is to carefully assess authentication and key agreement techniques in order to guarantee their security and efficacy in thwarting various forms of attacks. The process of creating reliable systems that can withstand potential flaws and respond to changing security threats is ongoing.

Due to their effectiveness in stopping smart card loss attacks, key agreement systems and three-factor authentication are currently gaining popularity. These protocols typically use three factors: biometric identity, a smart card, and a username/password combination. However, commercial services operate in multiserver contexts, whereas conventional authentication and key agreement techniques are primarily created for single-server setups [26]. As a result, these conventional techniques do not offer users with anonymity and untraceability in multiserver environments.

A three-factor system with biometric authentication as the third component was suggested in [24]. The system described in [24] does not, ensure user anonymity, in the author's opinion [27], and thus is susceptible to impersonation assaults. Other three-factor multiserver systems, however, have been put out in [28, 29]. However, the author of [30] points out that the [28] approach is judged defenceless against user impersonation assaults.

These results highlight the necessity for strong and secure key agreement and three-factor authentication protocols that are specially designed for multiserver systems. These protocols must also address weaknesses like user impersonation and guarantee user anonymity. The security and performance of these protocols in practical settings must be improved through ongoing research and development.

In the literature, various schemes have been proposed to address the security issues of existing authentication and key agreement protocols. However, many of these schemes also have their own security drawbacks, leading to subsequent improvements and alternative solutions.

For instance, the system [31] security enhancements were suggested in [32]. The scheme in [32]still has security issues, though, like privileged insider attacks and lost smart cards. The plan given in [33, 34] provides a remedy for these flaws and addresses the vulnerabilities mentioned in [32].

The author of [35] were find out the security flaws of [36, 37] and also suggested improvements for [38], Similar to this, [39, 40] also has drawbacks.

In addition, the author of [41] observed that the protocol described in [42] is expensive to compute and communicate with, and is also susceptible to a number of assaults, as a solution, the author of [41] proposed an alternative protocol.

An authentication and key agreement (AKA) technique with three factors was put up in 2014 by author of [43], this method is vulnerable to attacks that steal smart cards, and guessing of offline passwords, and probable biometric sample leaks, according to [18]. Similarly, schemes proposed in [3, 4, 21, 44] are also susceptible to security threats such as password guessing attempts.

Furthermore, the scheme [45] lacked traceability and mutual authentication. To address these limitations, Elliptic Curve Cryptography based three-factor authentication scheme was suggested by authors [46, 47] to attain perfect forward secrecy. Nevertheless, these protocols still fell short in providing perfect forward secrecy, user anonymity, and resistance against replay attacks.

The technique proposed in [48] provides security features but comes with higher computing expenses. However, the author of [49] suggested a lightweight authentication scheme, but it has a high key generation time.

The author of [50] suggested a scheme specifically designed for cloud-assisted autonomous vehicles, the scheme proposed in [50] was found to have several loopholes and security weaknesses.

These results emphasise the significance of carefully analysing authentication and key agreement procedures, taking into account their functionality, security attributes, and potential weaknesses. To create strong schemes that can withstand diverse assaults and offer safe authentication and key agreement in various application contexts, ongoing research and improvement is required.

3 Scheme by Khan et al. [51]

We have provided the khan et al. [51]approach in this section. This plan has 3 steps, which is given below.

User's Registration Phase

It will be between User and Public cloud registration centre (PCRC).

USER

- User choose identity ID_{mu}
- Password PW_{mu} and imprints biometric $bio(B_{mu})$
- Choose a random number r_2 and calculate
- $S_1 = h((h(ID_{mu} \| PW_{mu}) \| r_2 \| bio(B_{mu}))$
- $S_2 = h(PW_{mu} \| r_2)$
- $S_3 = S_1 \oplus r_2 ID_{mu}, S_{2,} S_3$
- $ID_{mu,} S_{2,} S_3 \rightarrow$ (PCRC)

PCRC

- Calcute : $PK_{mu} = r_1.P$
- $SK_{mu} = r_1.\, P \oplus h\ (ID_{mu} \oplus\ PK_{mu})$
- $N = S_3 \oplus SK_{mu}$
- $M = h(ID_{mu} \oplus r_1) \oplus h(ID_{mu} \| S_2 \| SK_{mu}$
- $O = h(ID_{mu} \| S_3 \| Pk_{mu})$
- $SC\{PK_{mu,} \| N, M, O\} \rightarrow$ (User)

USER

- Calcute : $SC\{Pk_{mu,} N, M, O\}$
- $C = r_2 \oplus bio(B_{mu})$
- $N\prime = N \oplus r_2$
- Store $= \{O, M, N\prime, PK_{mu}\}$ in smart card

Public Cloud Server (PCS)'s Registration Phase-

It will be between Public Cloud Server and Public cloud registration centre (PCRC).

PCS

- SelectID_{PCS} and 160 – bits big integer q
- $PID_{PCS} = ID_{PCS} \| q$
- $PID_{PCS} \rightarrow$ (PCRC)

PCRC

- Choose random number r_1
- $PK_{PCS} = r_1.q$
- $Sk_{PCS} = (r_1.P) \oplus h(PID_{PCS} \| Pk_{PCS})$
- $PK_{PCS}, SK_{PCS}, r_1 \rightarrow PCS$

PCS

- Store $\{SK_{PCS}, r_1\}$ and publish PK_{PCS}

Login and Authentication Phase-

It will be between User and Public cloud server (PCS).

USER

- Input ID_{mu}, PW_{mu}, and $bio(B_{mu})$
- Calculate :
- $e = C \oplus bio(B_{mu})$
- $O\prime = h(ID_{mu} \| S_3 \| SK_{mu})$
- Check $O\prime = O$ proceed further
- $J = (r_2 \| P)$
- $MSG_1\{J\} \rightarrow PCS$

PCS

- Compute : $Pk_{mu} = (r_1 \| P)$
- $Q = r_1 \oplus SK_{PCS} \| h(r_1 \| P \oplus r_2 \| P)$
- $MSG_2\{r_1, P, Q\} \rightarrow User$

USER

- Compute : $Q\prime ? = r_1 \oplus Pk_{PCS} \oplus h(r_1 \| P) \oplus (r_2 \| P)$
- $S_1 = h(h(ID_{mu} \| PW_{mu}) \| r_2 \; bio\ (B_{mu})$
- $D = (r_1 \oplus Pk_{mu}) \oplus (PID_{PCS} \oplus (r_1 \| P) \oplus (r_2 \| P))$
- $M = h(ID_{mu} \oplus r_1) \oplus h(ID_{mu} \| S_2 \| SK_{mu})$
- $PK_u = (r_1 \| P)$
- $SK_{mu} = h(r_1 \| P \oplus (r_2.P) \| h\ )(ID_{mu} \| SK_{mu}) \| r_1 \| h\,(ID_{mu} \| PID_{PCS})$
- $Y = h((SK_{mu} \| r_1) \oplus (r_1 \| P) \oplus (r_2 \| P) \| ID_{mu})$
- $W = h((r_1 \| P) \oplus (r_2 \| P))$
- $MSG_3\{W, Y, D\} \rightarrow PCS$

PCS

- Compute : $W\prime = h((r_1 \| P) \oplus (r_2 \| P))$
- $D\prime = (r_1 \oplus PK_{mu}) \oplus (PID_{PCS} \oplus (r_1 \| P) \oplus (r_2 \| P))$
- Check $W\prime = W$, and $D\prime = D$, proceed further
- $SK_{PCS} = h(r_1 \| P) \oplus (r_2 \| P) \| \; h\,(ID_{mu} \| PK_{mu}) \| r_1 \| h\,(ID_{mu} \| PID_{PCS})$
- Compare : $Y ? = h(SK_{mu} \| r_1) \oplus (r_1 \| P) \oplus (r_2 \| P) \| ID_{mu})$

USER

- *Session key* $= Sk_{mu} = SK_{PCS}$

4 Analysis

We consider the following Threat model with following adversaries and possible attacks:

Adversary—Through an insecure channel, this adversary can intercept, modify, block, add, or remove messages sent between mobile users and public cloud servers. They are unable to retrieve the cloud server's secret key, but they can divulge every parameter that has been put on the smart card as shown in Fig. 2.

Adversary's Identity: An algorithm or group of statements or programmes with defined capabilities and objectives might serve as the adversary.

Objectives: The adversary's main goal is to undermine the security of the system by obtaining sensitive credentials and getting unauthorised access.

- **Interaction with Mobile Cloud Architecture:** By impersonating a malicious user on a cloud server, the adversary communicates with the mobile cloud architecture and performs the following activities:
- **Data Extraction:** The adversary can leverage stored data that has been extracted from the memory of cloud server to validate confidential information.
- **Manipulation of Public Network Channel:** The attacker has the power to change, delete, update, corrupt, or inject fake information into the public network channel.
- **Manipulation of Private Channel:** The valuable information transmitted between individuals over a secret route may be replayed, altered, or erased by the adversary.

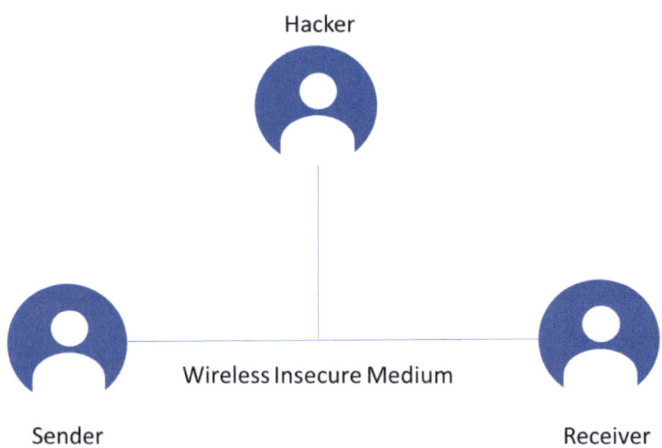

Fig. 2 Adversary scenario

Table 1 Required computational power

Operation	USER	PCS
Bitwise XOR (⊕)	13	5
Concatenation (‖)	22	5
Hash (h)	9	2
Biometric (bio)	11	–

- **Acquisition of Internal Sensitive Credentials:** Using reverse engineering methods or crucial tags, the adversary can change the memory of a hacked or lost mobile device in order to gain access to internal sensitive credentials.
- **Key Escrow:** Khan et al. scheme is vulnerable to key escrow attack, PCRC has the capability to obtain the ID of a mobile user, this exposure of user information could facilitate a key escrow attack.
- **Session Specific Temporary Information Attack (SSTIA):** An attacker may be able to gain the Public Cloud Server's (PCS) secret key if they are able to compromise the random numbers r1 and r2, the attacker can take unauthorised control of the PCS and its associated functionality if they have access to the secret key.

  By using r1 and r2 attacker will calculate the session key, which is equal to

$$h(r_1 \| P) \oplus (r_2 \| P) \| h(ID_{mu} \| PK_{mu}) \| r_1 \| h(ID_{mu} \| PID_{PCS}$$

- **Replay Attack:** A replay attack, in which an attacker sends the same message repeatedly to take advantage of the system, The Khan et al. scheme is susceptible to replay attack, detecting and mitigating this attack would require a substantial amount of computational power. In this attacker will resend $MSG_1\{J\}$ and $MSG_3\{W, Y, D\}$ (Table 1)

- **DoS:** The lack of timestamp usage for the messages makes the Khan et al. techniques susceptible to a Denial of Service (DoS) attack. which can be considered a broader version of a Replay attack.
- **Perfect forward secrecy:** Khan et al. schemes have been found to be vulnerable to a perfect forward secrecy attack, in which the compromise of the long-term key also compromises the session key.

In this scenario attacker will get ID_{mu}, PW_{mu}, B_{mu} and then it will launch the attack to get the session key

$$h(r_1 \| P) \oplus (r_2 \| P) \| h(ID_{mu} \| PK_{mu}) \| r_1 \| h(ID_{mu} \| PID_{PCS})$$

from this parameter attacker will get the session key.

5 Conclusion

Security is must for public cloud servers, and current authentication schemes are not secure enough. We conducted a cryptanalysis of Naveed Khan's scheme, which revealed vulnerabilities to various attacks. We hope that in the future, a robust and secure authentication scheme will be designed for public cloud servers.

References

1. Public Cloud—| Statista Market Forecast. https://www.statista.com/outlook/tmo/public-cloud/worldwide. Accessed 22 May 2023
2. Jones AK, Lamport L (1981) Password authentication with insecure communication
3. Wazid M, Das AK, Kumar N, Rodrigues JJPC (2017) Secure three-factor user authentication scheme for renewable-energy-based smart grid environment. IEEE Trans Industr Inform 13(6):3144–3153. https://doi.org/10.1109/TII.2017.2732999
4. Islam SH, Vijayakumar P, Bhuiyan MZA, Amin R, Rajeev V, Balusamy B (2018) A provably secure three-factor session initiation protocol for multimedia big data communications. IEEE Internet Things J 5(5):3408–3418. https://doi.org/10.1109/JIOT.2017.2739921
5. Ma CG, Wang D, Zhao SD (2014) Security flaws in two improved remote user authentication schemes using smart cards. Int J Commun Syst 27(10):2215–2227. https://doi.org/10.1002/dac.2468
6. Gope P, Lee J, Quek TQS (2018) Lightweight and practical anonymous authentication protocol for RFID systems using physically unclonable functions. IEEE Trans Inf Forensics Secur 13(11):2831–2843. https://doi.org/10.1109/TIFS.2018.2832849
7. Chatterjee S, Roy S, Das AK, Chattopadhyay S, Kumar N, Vasilakos AV (2018) Secure biometric-based authentication scheme using Chebyshev chaotic map for multi-server environment. IEEE Trans Dependable Secure Comput 15(5):824–839. https://doi.org/10.1109/TDSC.2016.2616876
8. Arkko J, Torvinen V, Camarillo G, Niemi A Google Scholar https://scholar.google.com/scholar?hl=en&as_sdt=0%2C5&q=J.+Arkko%2C+V.+Torvinen%2C+G.+Camarillo%2C+A.+Niemi%2C+and+T.+Haukka%2C+%E2%80%9CSecurity+Mechanism+Agreement+for+SIP+Sessions%2C%E2%80%9D+IETF+Internet+Draft+%28Draft-ietf-sipsecagree-04.+txt%29%2C+2002.&btnG= . Accessed 22 May 2023
9. Das ML, Saxena A, Gulati VP (2004) A dynamic ID-based remote user authentication scheme. IEEE Trans Consum Electron 50(2):629–631. https://doi.org/10.1109/TCE.2004.1309441
10. Yang Z, He J, Tian Y, Zhou J (2020) Faster Authenticated key agreement with perfect forward secrecy for industrial internet-of-things. IEEE Trans Industr Inform 16(10):6584–6596. https://doi.org/10.1109/TII.2019.2963328
11. Xiao D, Liao X, Wong KW (2005) An efficient entire chaos-based scheme for deniable authentication. Chaos Solitons Fractals 23(4):1327–1331. https://doi.org/10.1016/J.CHAOS.2004.06.069
12. Alvarez G (2005) Security problems with a chaos-based deniable authentication scheme. Chaos Solitons Fractals 26(1):7–11. https://doi.org/10.1016/J.CHAOS.2004.12.023
13. Xiao D, Liao X, Deng S (2007) A novel key agreement protocol based on chaotic maps. Inf Sci (N Y) 177(4):1136–1142. https://doi.org/10.1016/J.INS.2006.07.026
14. Li X, Wu F, Khan MK, Xu L, Shen J, Jo M (2018) A secure chaotic map-based remote authentication scheme for telecare medicine information systems. Futur Gener Comput Syst 84:149–159. https://doi.org/10.1016/J.FUTURE.2017.08.029

15. Han L, Xie Q, Liu W, Wang S (2017) A new efficient chaotic maps based three factor user authentication and key agreement scheme. Wirel Pers Commun 95(3):3391–3406. https://doi.org/10.1007/S11277-017-4003-Z/METRICS
16. Liu Y, Xue K (2016) An improved secure and efficient password and chaos-based two-party key agreement protocol. Nonlinear Dyn 84(2):549–557. https://doi.org/10.1007/S11071-015-2506-2/METRICS
17. Lee TF, Hsiao CH, Hwang SH, Lin TH (2017) Enhanced smartcard-based password-authenticated key agreement using extended chaotic maps. PLoS One 12(7). https://doi.org/10.1371/journal.pone.0181744
18. Jiang Q, Wei F, Fu S, Ma J, Li G, Alelaiwi A (2016) Robust extended chaotic maps-based three-factor authentication scheme preserving biometric template privacy. Nonlinear Dyn 83(4):2085–2101. https://doi.org/10.1007/S11071-015-2467-5/METRICS
19. Zhu H, Hao X (2015) A provable authenticated key agreement protocol with privacy protection using smart card based on chaotic maps. Nonlinear Dyn 81(1–2):311–321. https://doi.org/10.1007/S11071-015-1993-5/METRICS
20. Tsai JL, Lo NW, Wu TC (2013) Novel anonymous authentication scheme using smart cards. IEEE Trans Industr Inform 9(4):2004–2013. https://doi.org/10.1109/TII.2012.2230639
21. Roy S, Chatterjee S, Das AK, Chattopadhyay S, Kumari S, Jo M (2018) Chaotic map-based anonymous user authentication scheme with user biometrics and fuzzy extractor for crowd-sourcing internet of things. IEEE Internet Things J 5(4):2884–2895. https://doi.org/10.1109/JIOT.2017.2714179
22. Hwang T, Chen Y, Laih CS (1991) Non-interactive password authentications without password tables, pp 429–431. https://doi.org/10.1109/TENCON.1990.152647
23. Guo C, Chang C-C (2013) Chaotic maps-based password-authenticated key agreement using smart cards. Commun Nonlinear Sci Numer Simul 18(6):1433–1440. https://doi.org/10.1016/j.cnsns.2012.09.032
24. Lin HY (2015) Improved chaotic maps-based password-authenticated key agreement using smart cards. Commun Nonlinear Sci Numer Simul 20(2):482–488. https://doi.org/10.1016/J.CNSNS.2014.05.027
25. Qiu S, Wang D, Xu G, Kumari S (2022) Practical and provably secure three-factor authentication protocol based on extended chaotic-maps for mobile lightweight devices. IEEE Trans Dependable Secure Comput 19(2):1338–1351. https://doi.org/10.1109/TDSC.2020.3022797
26. Jan SU, Abbasi IA, Algarni F (2021) A key agreement scheme for IoD deployment civilian drone. IEEE Access 9:149311–149321. https://doi.org/10.1109/ACCESS.2021.3124510
27. Lin H, Wen F, Du C (2015) An improved anonymous multi-server authenticated key agreement scheme using smart cards and biometrics. Wirel Pers Commun 84(4):2351–2362. https://doi.org/10.1007/s11277-015-2708-4
28. He D, Wang D (2015) Robust biometrics-based authentication scheme for multiserver environment. IEEE Syst J 9(3):816–823. https://doi.org/10.1109/JSYST.2014.2301517
29. Jiang P, Wen Q, Li W, Jin Z, Zhang H (2015) An anonymous and efficient remote biometrics user authentication scheme in a multi server environment. Front Comput Sci 9(1):142–156. https://doi.org/10.1007/s11704-014-3125-7
30. Odelu V, Das AK, Goswami A (2015) A secure biometrics-based multi-server authentication protocol using smart cards. IEEE Trans Inf Forensics Secur 10(9):1953–1966. https://doi.org/10.1109/TIFS.2015.2439964
31. Hsieh W-B, Leu J-S (2014) An anonymous mobile user authentication protocol using self-certified public keys based on multi-server architectures. J Supercomput 70(1):133–148. https://doi.org/10.1007/s11227-014-1135-8
32. Amin R, Biswas GP (2015) Design and analysis of bilinear pairing based mutual authentication and key agreement protocol usable in multi-server environment. Wirel Pers Commun 84(1):439–462. https://doi.org/10.1007/s11277-015-2616-7
33. Chandrakar P, Om H (2017) Cryptanalysis and improvement of a biometric-based remote user authentication protocol usable in a multiserver environment. Trans Emerg Telecommun Technol 28(12):e3200. https://doi.org/10.1002/ETT.3200

34. Chandrakar P, Om H (2017) A secure and robust anonymous three-factor remote user authentication scheme for multi-server environment using ECC. Comput Commun 110:26–34. https://doi.org/10.1016/j.comcom.2017.05.009
35. Park YH, Park YH (2016) Three-factor user authentication and key agreement using elliptic curve cryptosystem in wireless sensor networks. Sensors 16(12):2123. https://doi.org/10.3390/S16122123
36. Chang IP, Lee TF, Lin TH, Liu CM (2015) Enhanced two-factor authentication and key agreement using dynamic identities in wireless sensor networks. Sensors 15(12):29841–29854. https://doi.org/10.3390/S151229767
37. Choi Y, Lee Y, Won D (2016) Security improvement on biometric based authentication scheme for wireless sensor networks using fuzzy extraction. Int J Distrib Sens Netw 2016. https://doi.org/10.1155/2016/8572410
38. Yoon EJ, Kim C (2013) Advanced biometric-based user authentication scheme for wireless sensor networks. Sens Lett 11(9):1836–1843. https://doi.org/10.1166/SL.2013.3014
39. Reddy AG, Yoon E-J, Das AK, Odelu V, Yoo K-Y (2017) Design of mutually authenticated key agreement protocol resistant to impersonation attacks for multi-server environment. IEEE Access 5:3622–3639. https://doi.org/10.1109/ACCESS.2017.2666258
40. Irshad A, Sher M, Chaudhary SA, Naqvi H, Farash MS (2016) An efficient and anonymous multi-server authenticated key agreement based on chaotic map without engaging Registration Centre. J Supercomput 72(4):1623–1644. https://doi.org/10.1007/s11227-016-1688-9
41. Jan SU, Qayum F (2018) A robust authentication scheme for client-server architecture with provable security analysis. Netw Commun Technol 3(1):6. https://doi.org/10.5539/nct.v3n1p6
42. Hassan A, Eltayieb N, Elhabob R, Li F (2018) An efficient certificateless user authentication and key exchange protocol for client-server environment. J Ambient Intell Humaniz Comput 9(6):1713–1727. https://doi.org/10.1007/s12652-017-0622-1
43. Islam SKH (2014) Provably secure dynamic identity-based three-factor password authentication scheme using extended chaotic maps. Nonlinear Dyn 78(3):2261–2276. https://doi.org/10.1007/s11071-014-1584-x
44. Guo X, Zhang J (2010) Secure group key agreement protocol based on chaotic Hash. Inf Sci (N Y) 180(20):4069–4074. https://doi.org/10.1016/j.ins.2010.06.013
45. Chaudhry SA, Kim IL, Rho S, Farash MS, Shon T (2019) An improved anonymous authentication scheme for distributed mobile cloud computing services. Cluster Comput 22(1):1595–1609. https://doi.org/10.1007/s10586-017-1088-9
46. Hathaliya JJ, Tanwar S, Evans R (2020) Securing electronic healthcare records: a mobile-based biometric authentication approach. J Inf Secur Appl 53:102528. https://doi.org/10.1016/j.jisa.2020.102528
47. Li X, Peng J, Obaidat MS, Wu F, Khan MK, Chen C (2020) A secure three-factor user authentication protocol with forward secrecy for wireless medical sensor network systems. IEEE Syst J 14(1):39–50. https://doi.org/10.1109/JSYST.2019.2899580
48. Nikooghadam M, Amintoosi H (2023) Secure communication in CloudIoT through design of a lightweight authentication and session key agreement scheme. Int J Commun Syst 36(1):e4332. https://doi.org/10.1002/DAC.4332
49. El Zouka HA, Hosni MM (2021) Secure IoT communications for smart healthcare monitoring system. Internet of Things 13:100036. https://doi.org/10.1016/j.iot.2019.01.003
50. Jiang Q, Zhang N, Ni J, Ma J, Ma X, Choo K-KR (2020) Unified biometric privacy preserving three-factor authentication and key agreement for cloud-assisted autonomous vehicles. IEEE Trans Veh Technol 69(9):9390–9401. https://doi.org/10.1109/TVT.2020.2971254
51. Khan N, Zhang J, Jan SU (2022) A robust and privacy-preserving anonymous user authentication scheme for public cloud server. Secur Commun Netw. https://doi.org/10.1155/2022/1943426

Hybrid Cryptography for Securing IoT: Elliptic Curve and Isogeny-Based

Kalyan Banerjee, Jasleen Kaur, Nilesh Tiwari, and Nikhil Nair

Abstract With the proliferation of the Internet of Things (IoT) and the ever-increasing number of devices interconnected through it, security has become a paramount concern. In this paper, we introduce an innovative strategy to bolster IoT security through the fusion of Elliptic Curve Cryptography (ECC) and Isogeny-Based Cryptography. Our approach is underpinned by a bespoke algorithm crafted with IoT security in mind. This approach leverages the strengths of both ECC and Isogeny-Based cryptography to not only enhance the efficiency of encryption and decryption but also to fortify the security of IoT systems, as illustrated in the accompanying IoT diagrams—a vital component of this paper. We offer a fundamental implementation centered on the core principles of our security analysis. This approach acts as a foundational framework, laying the groundwork for a more comprehensive examination in future research. Furthermore, our work extends beyond the immediate present, providing a forward-looking perspective on the evolving landscape of IoT security.

Keywords Internet of Things (IoT) · Elliptic Curve Cryptography (ECC) · Isogeny-based cryptography · Hybrid Encryption Decryption · Key Derivation Function (KDF) · And Security analysis

1 Introduction

The Internet of Things [1] has revolutionized the way we interact with technology, enabling a vast network of interconnected devices to communicate and share data. However, this increased connectivity also poses significant security risks, as sensitive information is transmitted between devices over potentially insecure networks. To address these concerns, researchers have proposed various encryption schemes to secure IoT communication. One promising approach to securing IoT communication is hybrid encryption and decryption using Elliptic Curve Cryptography

K. Banerjee · J. Kaur (✉) · N. Tiwari · N. Nair
Vellore Institue of Technology, Chennai, India
e-mail: jasleen.kaur2021@vitstudent.ac.in

B. N. Gohil et al. (eds.), *Information Security, Privacy and Digital Forensics*,
Lecture Notes in Electrical Engineering 1423,
https://doi.org/10.1007/978-981-96-9443-3_4

[2] and Isogeny-based cryptography [3]. ECC is a widely used public-key cryptosystem that offers high levels of security with small key sizes, making it suitable for resource-constrained systems like IoT devices. Isogeny-based cryptography, on the other hand, is a relatively new approach that relies on the mathematical properties of elliptic curves to provide secure encryption. In this research article, we present a comprehensive security analysis of a hybrid encryption and decryption scheme [4] that combines Elliptic Curve Cryptography and Isogeny-Based cryptography for use in IoT applications. Our primary objective is to evaluate the effectiveness of the scheme against several common attacks, including brute force, man-in-the-middle, and side-channel attacks. Additionally, we analyze the computational efficiency of the scheme, considering the limited resources available on IoT devices. To achieve our objectives, we first provide an overview of ECC and Isogeny-Based cryptography, highlighting their respective strengths and weaknesses. We then describe the hybrid encryption and decryption scheme and its implementation details. Subsequently, we present our security analysis results and discuss the performance and limitations of the scheme. Our study is particularly relevant given the increasing reliance on IoT devices in various critical applications such as healthcare, transportation, and industrial control systems. The security of such systems cannot be compromised; therefore, it is imperative to identify robust and efficient encryption schemes that can withstand sophisticated attacks. By evaluating the ECC-Isogeny hybrid scheme, we aim to contribute to the ongoing efforts to secure IoT communication and facilitate the widespread adoption of IoT technology. The rest of the article is organized as follows: Sect. 2 provides an overview of the ECC and Isogeny-Based cryptography, and their respective strengths and weaknesses. Section 3 describes the hybrid encryption and decryption scheme and its implementation details. Section 4 presents our security analysis results, and IoT implementation with the hardware and software considerations for the implementation followed by a discussion of the performance evaluation and security aspects as well as performance-enhancing techniques and future considerations of the scheme in Sect. 5. In Sect. 6 we will discuss the potential for advancements and future directions of our research field which is ECC and Isogeny-Based Cryptography. Finally, we conclude the article in Sect. 7 followed by the References required for the respective paper.

2 Overview of Elliptic Curve Cryptography and Isogeny-Based Cryptography and Its Implementation

2.1 Description of Elliptic Curve Cryptography (ECC)

Elliptic Curve Cryptography is a cryptographic scheme that harnesses the mathematical properties of elliptic curves over finite fields. ECC offers improved security, efficiency, and key size compared to traditional cryptographic systems like RSA [5].

The mathematical foundation of ECC lies in elliptic curves, which are defined by equations of the form $y^2 = x^3 + ax + b$, where the coefficients a and b determine the curve's shape. These curves, along with a distinguished point at infinity, form an additive group with specific properties. This group structure enables cryptographic operations such as point addition and scalar multiplication. In ECC, participants generate a public–private key pair. The private key is a randomly chosen integer, while the public key is derived by multiplying the base point (generator) on the curve with the private key. The key exchange involves sharing public keys, and the shared secret is computed by multiplying the recipient's private key with the received public key. ECC supports digital signatures and encryption. Digital signatures involve using the private key to generate a signature for a message, which can be verified using the corresponding public key. Encryption typically employs the Diffie-Hellman key exchange protocol [6], where the shared secret is used to derive a symmetric encryption key. The security of ECC relies on the difficulty of solving the elliptic curve discrete logarithm problem (ECDLP) [7]. Known algorithms for solving ECDLP have exponential time complexity, making ECC resistant to brute-force attacks. Moreover, ECC offers equivalent security to RSA but with significantly smaller key sizes, resulting in faster computations and reduced bandwidth requirements.

2.2 *Description of Isogeny-Based Cryptography*

Isogeny-Based cryptography is a relatively recent branch of public-key cryptography that utilizes the mathematical properties of isogenies, which are mappings between elliptic curves. Isogenies possess unique properties that make them suitable for cryptographic purposes. The foundation of Isogeny-Based cryptography lies in the computational hardness of the isogeny problem, which involves finding an isogeny between two given curves. This problem is considered computationally challenging, forming the basis for building cryptographic schemes. The primary application of isogeny-based cryptography is in key exchange protocols. These protocols enable the establishment of a shared secret between two parties over an insecure channel by leveraging isogeny computations. Prominent examples include the Couveignes-Rostovtsev-Stolbunov (CRS) key exchange protocol [8]. One notable advantage of isogeny-based cryptography is its resistance against attacks by quantum computers. Unlike many traditional cryptographic schemes such as RSA and ECC, which can be broken by quantum algorithms, isogeny-based schemes like Commutative Supersingular Isogeny Diffie-Hellman (CSIDH) are considered secure against quantum attacks.

Implementation and Performance Considerations The implementation of elliptic curve cryptography and isogeny-based cryptography necessitates careful attention to security and performance considerations. Several crucial factors to consider include:

Curves and Parameter Selection:

The selection of appropriate elliptic curves and isogeny parameters is vital to ensure security. Recommended curves and parameters provided by reputable standards bodies and research organizations help strike a balance between security and efficiency.

Utilization of Cryptographic Libraries and Tools:

Employing established cryptographic libraries and tools that provide well-tested and efficient implementations of elliptic curves and isogeny-based cryptography is essential. These libraries often incorporate optimized routines and safeguards against side-channel attacks.

Hardware and Software Implementations:

Cryptographic algorithms can be implemented either in software or specialized hardware. Hardware implementations, such as Application-Specific Integrated Circuits (ASICs) or Field-Programmable Gate Arrays (FPGAs) [9], can offer significant performance enhancements.

Guarding Against Side-Channel Attacks:

Side-channel attacks [10] exploit information leaked during cryptographic operations, such as power consumption or timing variations. Employing countermeasures such as constant-time implementations and secure hardware designs is crucial to mitigate these attacks.

Standardization and Interoperability:

Adhering to standardized cryptographic protocols and formats is necessary to ensure interoperability and ease of integration. Organizations such as the National Institute of Standards and Technology (NIST) play a significant role in defining and promoting secure implementations.

In this research article, we have implemented a hybrid encryption and decryption algorithm that combines both ECC and Isogeny-Based Cryptography. The algorithm's implementation details will be discussed in Sect. 3, providing the hybrid encryption and decryption algorithm amalgamation of ECC and Isogeny-Based Cryptography respectively.

3 Hybrid Encryption and Decryption Algorithm Amalgamation of Elliptic Curve Cryptography and Isogeny-Based Cryptography

3.1 Contribution of Ramanujan Graphs in Hybrid Encryption and Decryption

Ramanujan graphs [11], named after the renowned Indian mathematician Srinivasa Ramanujan, have made significant strides in advancing hybrid encryption and decryption in cryptography. These graphs possess distinctive spectral properties that play a pivotal role in enhancing the security and efficiency of cryptographic protocols.

Ramanujan graphs serve as a crucial foundation for establishing secure key exchange protocols in the realm of hybrid encryption and decryption. Their spectral properties enable the construction of efficient and resilient communication channels by leveraging the computational complexity associated with these graphs.

Within the context of hybrid encryption and decryption, Ramanujan graphs provide a valuable framework for facilitating secure and reliable key exchanges between entities. The construction of these graphs relies on arduous mathematical problems, such as the Ramanujan conjecture or the existence of Ramanujan primes.

The unique spectral properties of Ramanujan graphs ensure a substantial spectral gap, characterized by a notable difference between the largest and second-largest eigenvalues. This property guarantees the expansion of the graph, preventing small subsets from becoming isolated, which is pivotal for establishing secure key exchanges.

By harnessing the power of Ramanujan graphs, hybrid encryption, and decryption protocols can achieve robust cryptographic properties. The connectivity and pseudo-randomness exhibited by these graphs enable efficient and secure key exchanges, ensuring that only authorized entities can establish a shared secret key. This shared secret key is then utilized for symmetric encryption and decryption, providing confidentiality and integrity for transmitted data.

Moreover, Ramanujan graphs offer resilience against various attacks, including brute-force attacks and cryptographic attacks targeting graph properties. The pseudo-random nature of these graphs presents challenges for attackers attempting to exploit underlying patterns or vulnerabilities.

The contribution of Ramanujan graphs to hybrid encryption and decryption is invaluable. Their distinctive spectral properties and the computational complexity associated with them provide a robust foundation for secure key exchange protocols. Leveraging Ramanujan graphs facilitates the construction of efficient and reliable communication channels, enhancing the overall security and efficiency of hybrid encryption and decryption algorithms.

3.2 Exploring Alternative Approaches for Hybrid Encryption and Decryption

In addition to the integration of ECC and Isogeny-Based Cryptography, researchers have investigated various alternative techniques to enhance hybrid encryption and decryption. These approaches introduce novel methodologies that strengthen security and optimize performance, adding versatility and adaptability to hybrid cryptographic systems.

Homomorphic Encryption: Homomorphic encryption enables computations to be performed directly on encrypted data, preserving the privacy of sensitive information. It allows for operations on ciphertexts, producing results that are consistent with performing the same operations on plain-texts. This technique facilitates secure and privacy-preserving computations, making it suitable for scenarios where data confidentiality is paramount.

Lattice-Based Cryptography: Lattice-based cryptography leverages the hardness of lattice problems to provide robust security guarantees. By exploiting the complexity of solving certain mathematical problems associated with lattices, such as the Shortest Vector Problem (SVP) or the Learning With Errors (LWE) problem [12], lattice-based schemes offer resistance against various attacks, including those from quantum computers.

Multivariate Cryptography: Multivariate cryptography relies on the computational complexity of solving systems of multivariate polynomial equations. This approach provides resistance against attacks based on linear algebra or factorization methods. Multivariate schemes are known for their efficiency and can be suitable for resource-constrained environments where computational power is limited.

Code-Based Cryptography: Code-based cryptography utilizes error correcting codes to enhance the security of cryptographic systems. It relies on the computational difficulty of decoding random linear codes, making it resilient against attacks based on mathematical algorithms. Code-based schemes have gained attention for their resistance to quantum attacks and have been extensively studied for their reliability and performance.

Post-Quantum Cryptography: Post-quantum cryptography encompasses a wide range of cryptographic techniques specifically designed to withstand attacks from quantum computers. These techniques include lattice-based, code-based, multivariate, and other quantum-resistant schemes. Post-quantum cryptography aims to ensure the long-term security of cryptographic systems in an era where quantum computers can potentially break classical cryptographic algorithms.

These alternative approaches offer diverse security properties and performance characteristics. The selection of an appropriate technique depends on specific requirements, threat models, and computational environments. By exploring and combining these techniques, researchers can further advance the security and efficiency of hybrid cryptographic systems for various applications.

It is essential to note that while ECC and Isogeny-Based Cryptography, as discussed earlier, provide strong foundations, exploring alternative approaches fosters innovation and enables the development of tailored cryptographic solutions to address specific needs and emerging threats.

3.3 *Algorithms of Elliptic Curve Cryptography (ECC) and Isogeny-Based Cryptography*

Algorithm 1 Elliptical point generation

```
INPUT : a,b,p
OUTPUT: Points on the elliptical curve
if ((4a^3 + 27b^2) mod p) = 0 then                ▷ discriminant is zero
    return Invalid Point
end if
result1 ← empty list of length p
result2 ← empty list of length p
for x in range(0, p) do
    result2[x] ← x^2 mod p
end for
XY ← empty list
for i in range(0, p) do
    for j in range(0, p) do
        if result1[i] = result2[j] then
            XY.append((i, j))
        end if
    end for
end for
```

The algorithm takes three input parameters: *a*, *b*, and *p*, which represent the parameters of the elliptical curve. The output of the algorithm is a list of points on the elliptical curve.'The algorithm begins by checking if the discriminant of the elliptical curve is zero. If it is zero, the algorithm returns an "Invalid Points" indicating that the given curve is not valid. Next, two empty lists, *result1*, and *result2*, are initialized. These lists will be used to store intermediate results during the computation. The algorithm then iterates over all possible x-values from 0 to $p - 1$ and computes the value of x^2 mod p. The results are stored in the result2 list. An empty list, XY, is initialized to store the final points on the elliptical curve. The algorithm then iterates over all possible x-values and y-values from 0 to $p - 1$. For each combination of x and y, it checks if the x-value matches the computed y-value. If they match, the point (i, j) is added to the XY list. At the end of the algorithm, the list XY contains all the points on the elliptical curve defined by the parameters *a*, *b*, and *p*.

Algorithm 2 Isogeny Parameter Generation

```
function ISOGENY_PARAMETER_GENERATION
    // Select appropriate Isogeny-Based cryptographic parameters
    isogeny_params = SELECT_ISOGENY_PARAMETERS
    return isogeny_params
end function
```

Description of Isogeny Parameter Generation: The algorithm Isogeny Parameter Generation is responsible for generating suitable isogeny-based cryptographic parameters. Let's elaborate on its steps: The algorithm begins by adding a comment indicating the intention to select appropriate isogeny-based cryptographic parameters. This step implies that specific parameters need to be chosen for the cryptographic scheme that relies on isogeny-based operations. These parameters typically include values such as security levels, curve coefficients, or other relevant settings. The Select Isogeny Parameters function is called to handle the selection process. This function is responsible for determining the specific parameters required for isogeny-based cryptography. It is expected to perform various calculations and evaluations to choose the appropriate parameter values. The implementation of this function will depend on the specific cryptographic scheme being used. The isogeny params variable is assigned the result of the Select Isogeny Parameters function call. This variable holds the chosen isogeny-based cryptographic parameters, which could be a collection of values or a data structure.

Algorithm 3 Isogeny Key Agreement

```
function ISOGENY_KEY_AGREEMENT(isogeny_params, public_key)
    // Perform key agreement using isogeny-based protocol (e.g., CSIDH)
    shared_secret = ISOGENY_KEY_AGREEMENT_PROTOCOL(isogeny params, pub-
lic_key)
    return shared_secret
end function
```

Explanation of Isogeny key Agreement

1. The algorithm begins with a comment indicating the intention to perform key agreement using an isogenybased protocol, such as Commutative Super-singular Isogeny DiffieHellman (CSIDH). Isogeny-Based protocols rely on the mathematics of elliptic curves and isogenies to establish a shared secret between two parties.
2. The function Isogeny Key Agreement [13] is called with two input parameters: isogeny params (isogeny-based cryptographic parameters) and public key (the public key of the other party involved in the key agreement).
3. The output of the algorithm is the shared secret, which represents the agreed-upon secret key between the parties.
4. Inside the function, the Isogeny Key Agreement Protocol function is called, passing the isogeny params and public key as inputs. This function performs the actual key agreement process using the specified isogenybased protocol. The

implementation of this function will depend on the specific isogenybased protocol being used, such as CSIDH.
5. The shared secret variable is assigned the result of the Isogeny Key Agreement Protocol function call. This shared secret represents the agreed-upon secret key between the parties.
6. Finally, the shared secret is returned as the output of the Isogeny-Key-Agreement function. This shared secret can be used for further cryptographic operations or as a basis for establishing secure communication between the parties.

The Isogeny Key Agreement algorithm is responsible for performing the key agreement process using an Isogeny-Based protocol. It takes the Isogeny-Based cryptographic parameters and the public key of the other party as inputs, and it returns the agreed-upon shared secret key. This shared secret can then be used for secure communication or other cryptographic operations.

Algorithm 4 Key Derivation Function (KDF)

```
function KDF(shared_secret, purpose)
    // Use Key Derivation Function (KDF) to derive encryption or decryption key
    key = KDF_FUNCTION(shared_secret, purpose)
    return key
end function
```

Explanation of Key Derivation Function (KDF): This algorithm is responsible for deriving an encryption or decryption key using a Key Derivation Function [14]. Let's break down the steps: The algorithm defines the function KDF, which takes two input parameters: shared secret, which represents the shared secret value obtained from a key agreement protocol, and purpose, which specifies the purpose for which the derived key will be used (e.g., encryption or decryption). Inside the function, there is a comment indicating the intention to use a KDF to derive the encryption or decryption key. This comment serves as a reminder of the purpose of this step in the algorithm. The KDF Function is called to perform the actual key derivation process. This function takes the shared secret and purpose as input parameters and returns the derived key. The implementation of the KDF Function will depend on the specific KDF algorithm being used (e.g., HKDF, PBKDF2). The derived key is assigned to the variable key. Finally, the algorithm returns the key, which represents the derived encryption or decryption key. This allows the calling code or subsequent steps in the cryptographic process to utilize the derived key for encrypting or decrypting data. In summary, the "Key Derivation Function" algorithm focuses on deriving an encryption or decryption key using a Key Derivation Function. It takes a shared secret and a purpose as input, calls the KDF Function to perform the key derivation, and returns the derived key. The algorithm is designed to be easy to understand and can be used in various cryptographic protocols and applications where key derivation is needed.

Algorithm 5 Symmetric Encryption

```
function SYMMETRIC_ENCRYPTION(plaintext, encryption_key)
    // Use symmetric encryption algorithm (e.g., AES) to encrypt plaintext
    ciphertext = SYMMETRIC_ENCRYPTION_ALGORITHM(plaintext, encryption_key)
    return ciphertext
end function
```

Explanation of Symmetric Encryption: This algorithm is used to encrypt a piece of plaintext using a symmetric encryption algorithm like AES. Let's break down the steps: The algorithm defines the function Symmetric Encryption [15], which takes two input parameters: plaintext, which is the message or data to be encrypted, and encryption key, which is a secret key used for encryption.

Inside the function, there is a comment indicating the intention to use a symmetric encryption algorithm (e.g., AES) to encrypt the plaintext. This comment explains the purpose of this step in simple terms.

The Symmetric Encryption Algorithm is called to perform the actual encryption process. This algorithm takes the plaintext and encryption key as input parameters and returns the ciphertext, which is the encrypted version of the plaintext. The specific implementation of the Symmetric Encryption Algorithm will depend on the chosen symmetric encryption algorithm (e.g., AES).

The ciphertext is assigned to the variable ciphertext, which holds the encrypted version of the plaintext. Finally, the algorithm returns the ciphertext. This allows the calling code or subsequent steps in the process to use or transmit the encrypted data. In simpler terms, the "Symmetric Encryption" algorithm takes a message (plaintext) and a secret key (encryption key), and uses a special encryption algorithm (like AES) to scramble the message in a way that can only be unscrambled using the same secret key. The resulting encrypted message (ciphertext) is then returned. This algorithm is commonly used to protect sensitive information during transmission or storage, ensuring that only authorized parties with the correct key can read the encrypted data.

Algorithm 6 Symmetric Decryption

```
function SYMMETRIC_DECRYPTION(ciphertext, decryption_key)
    // Use symmetric encryption algorithm (e.g., AES) to decrypt ciphertext
    plaintext = SYMMETRIC_DECRYPTION_ALGORITHM(ciphertext, decryption_key)
    return plaintext
end function
```

Explanation of Symmetric Decryption: This algorithm is used to decrypt a piece of ciphertext (encrypted message) using a symmetric decryption algorithm, such as AES. Let's break down the steps: The algorithm defines the function Symmetric Decryption [16], which takes two input parameters: cipher-text, which is the encrypted message, and decryption key, which is the secret key used for decryption. Inside the function, there is a comment indicating the intention to use a symmetric

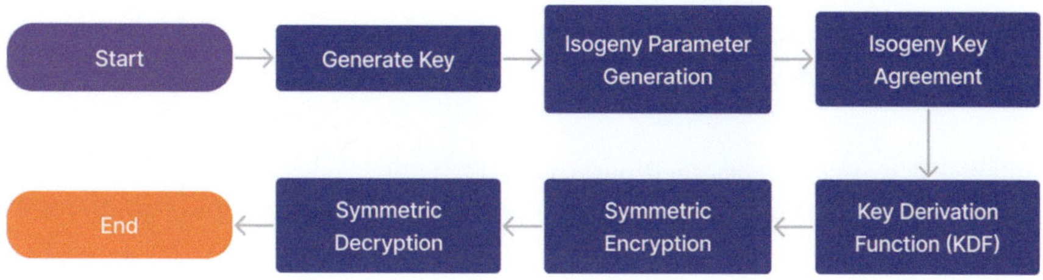

Fig. 1 Control flow diagram

encryption algorithm (e.g., AES) to decrypt the ciphertext. This comment explains the purpose of this step in simple terms.

The Symmetric Decryption Algorithm is called to perform the actual decryption process. This algorithm takes the ciphertext and decryption key as input parameters and returns the plaintext, which is the decrypted version of the ciphertext. The specific implementation of the Symmetric Decryption Algorithm will depend on the chosen symmetric encryption algorithm (e.g., AES). The plaintext is assigned to the variable plaintext, which holds the decrypted version of the ciphertext. Finally, the algorithm returns the plaintext. This allows the calling code or subsequent steps in the process to use the decrypted data.

In simpler terms, the"Symmetric Decryption" algorithm takes an encrypted message (ciphertext) and a secret key (decryption key), and uses a special decryption algorithm (like AES) to reverse the encryption process and obtain the original message (plaintext). This allows the recipient with the correct decryption key to retrieve and read the original content (Fig. 1).

4 Security Analysis and IoT Implementation

4.1 IoT Implementation with ECC and Isogeny-Based Cryptography

This section focuses on the integration of IoT technology within the scope of our research on hybrid encryption and decryption using ECC and Isogeny. IoT devices play a pivotal role in establishing secure and interconnected systems for various applications such as smart homes, industrial automation, and healthcare.

Our approach involves leveraging the capabilities of IoT devices to create a network of interconnected endpoints, enabling secure communication and cryptographic operations using our hybrid scheme. These devices, equipped with sensors, actuators, and communication capabilities, seamlessly integrate encryption and decryption functionalities into IoT environments.

4.2 *Hardware and Software Considerations for Implementation*

Implementing our hybrid encryption and decryption scheme in an IoT context requires careful attention to hardware and software aspects. The following elements should be taken into account:

Hardware Considerations: The selection of hardware components is critical for IoT applications. It involves choosing microcontrollers or system-on-chip (SoC) devices [17] that offer the necessary computational power, memory resources, and connectivity options. Additionally, incorporating hardware security modules (HSMs), secure elements, or trusted platform modules (TPMs) [18] can significantly enhance the overall security of the IoT system (Fig. 2).

Software Considerations: The choice of software is crucial for the successful implementation of our hybrid scheme. Opting for lightweight and real-time operating systems, such as FreeRTOS, ensures efficient resource management and facilitates the execution of cryptographic operations. Leveraging cryptographic libraries like mbedtls [19], which provide optimized implementations of ECC and other cryptographic algorithms, is essential for the hybrid encryption and decryption process (Fig. 3).

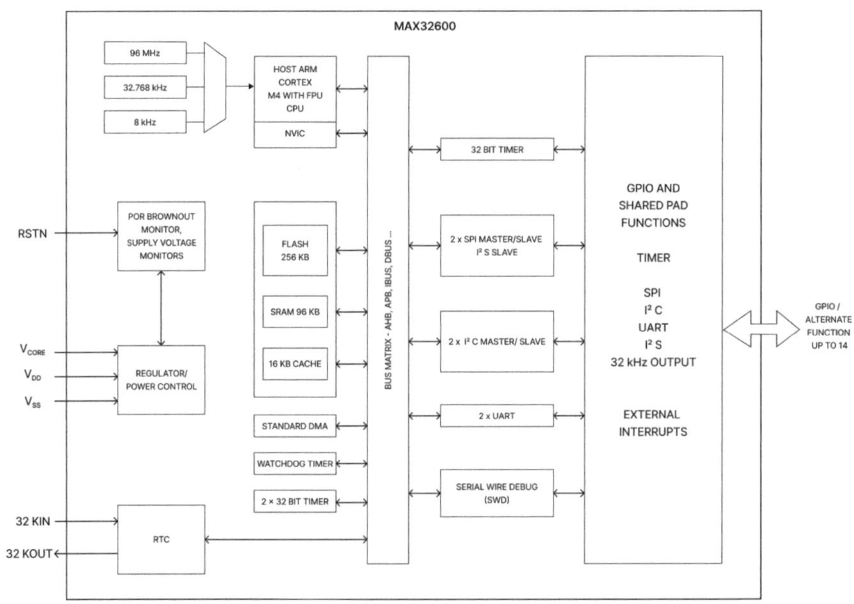

Fig. 2 Architecture of 32-bit microcontroller with an ARM Cortex-M4 core

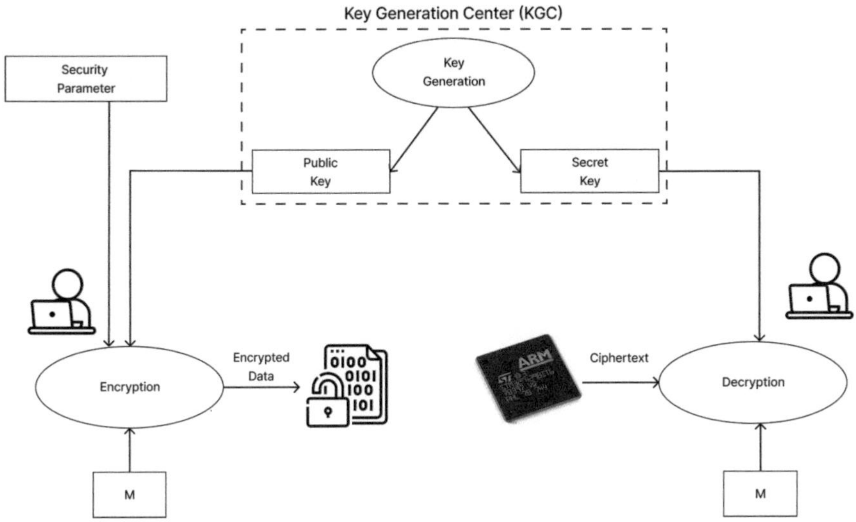

Fig. 3 Functionality of how the IoT is implemented using Hybrid encryption and decryption

4.3 Future Perspectives in the IoT Domain

Examining the security aspects of hybrid encryption and decryption in IoT applications requires considering future developments within the IoT domain. The continuous evolution of IoT presents several opportunities to enhance the security and functionality of IoT systems.

One area of focus is the advancement of dedicated hardware security mechanisms tailored specifically for IoT devices. Manufacturers are actively integrating robust security features into IoT chips, including secure boot mechanisms, hardware-based key storage, and secure communication interfaces. These advancements significantly contribute to the overall security posture of IoT implementations, enhancing their resilience against potential attacks.

Furthermore, the integration of blockchain technology with IoT holds promise for improving the security and privacy of IoT data transactions. Blockchain provides a decentralized and tamper-resistant framework for ensuring data integrity, authentication, and accountability in IoT environments.

Additionally, advancements in machine learning and artificial intelligence (AI) can enhance anomaly detection and threat mitigation in IoT systems. AI algorithms can analyze large volumes of data generated by IoT devices, identify- ing patterns, detecting anomalies, and enabling proactive responses to security incidents.

Moving forward, ongoing research and collaboration between academia, industry, and regulatory bodies will drive innovation and standardization in IoT security. Staying informed about emerging security protocols, best practices, and regulations is crucial to ensure the robustness and resilience of IoT implementations.

By addressing these future perspectives, we can pave the way for secure and trustworthy IoT systems that effectively utilize the hybrid encryption and decryption scheme based on ECC and Isogeny. Such advancements enable a wide range of applications in areas such as smart cities, healthcare, and industrial automation.

The next section presents a comprehensive security analysis of our hybrid encryption and decryption scheme, evaluating its strengths, vulnerabilities, and potential mitigations within the context of IoT applications.

5 Performance Evaluation and Security Aspects of the ECC and Isogeny-Based Cryptography

This section provides a thorough assessment of the performance and security aspects of the ECC and Isogeny-based encryption and decryption scheme specifically designed for IoT applications. Through a comprehensive analysis, we evaluate the scheme's performance, strengths, and vulnerabilities, and propose potential mitigations, focusing on the unique aspects of ECC and Isogeny within the IoT domain.

5.1 Performance Evaluation

The performance evaluation of the ECC and Isogeny-based encryption and decryption scheme in an IoT context revolves around key performance metrics that are crucial for efficient and effective operation. We consider the following aspects: **Computational Efficiency:** We measure the computational complexity of key generation, encryption, and decryption operations, taking into account the computational capabilities of IoT devices. This evaluation helps us understand the scheme's efficiency and its ability to meet the real-time requirements of IoT.

applications.

Memory Utilization: We assess the memory footprint of the scheme to ensure optimal usage of limited resources in IoT devices. By analyzing the memory requirements, we can determine the scheme's scalability and its ability to handle resource-constrained IoT environments.

Energy Consumption: We analyze the energy consumption of the ECC and Isogeny-based scheme to ensure it is suitable for battery-powered IoT devices. By minimizing energy consumption during cryptographic operations, we enhance the overall sustainability and longevity of IoT systems.

5.2 Security Analysis

Security is a critical aspect when implementing ECC and Isogeny-based encryption and decryption in IoT applications. Our security analysis encompasses the following key elements:

Key Generation Strength: We evaluate the strength of the generated ECC and Isogeny-based encryption keys, ensuring they possess the necessary entropy and resistance against attacks. This assessment ensures the scheme's ability to provide secure communication and data protection in IoT environments.

Vulnerability Assessment: We conduct a comprehensive analysis of the scheme's resistance against various cryptographic attacks, such as brute-force attacks, side-channel attacks, and fault attacks. By identifying potential vulnerabilities, we can recommend countermeasures to strengthen the scheme's security posture.

IoT-specific Risks: We consider the unique risks associated with ECC and Isogeny-based cryptography in the IoT domain, including device compromise, network attacks, and key management challenges. By addressing these risks, we enhance the overall security of the scheme within the specific IoT context.

Counter Measures and Enhancements: Based on our findings, we propose suitable countermeasures and security enhancements to mitigate the identified vulnerabilities. These measures may include the adoption of secure key management protocols, improved authentication mechanisms, and the integration of hardware security modules to enhance the scheme's resilience against potential attacks.

5.3 Performance-Enhancing Techniques and Future Considerations

This subsection explores performance-enhancing techniques and future considerations to further optimize the performance and security of the ECC and Isogeny-based encryption and decryption scheme in IoT applications. Key areas of focus include:

Algorithmic Optimization: We investigate algorithmic improvements and optimizations specific to ECC and Isogeny-based cryptography to enhance the scheme's computational efficiency without compromising security. By leveraging advanced mathematical techniques and algorithmic refinements, we can improve the scheme's performance in IoT environments.

Hardware Acceleration: We explore the integration of hardware acceleration mechanisms, such as dedicated cryptographic co-processors or FPGA (Field-Programmable Gate Array) [18] implementations, to enhance the computational speed and efficiency of the scheme. These hardware-level optimizations can significantly improve the performance of ECC and Isogeny-based operations in IoT devices.

Post-Quantum Considerations: Given the emerging threat of quantum computers, we discuss future considerations for post-quantum secure ECC and Isogeny-based schemes in the IoT domain. Exploring alternative cryptographic algorithms and techniques resistant to quantum attacks [20] will ensure the long-term security of IoT systems.

By presenting a comprehensive performance evaluation and security analysis focused on the ECC and Isogeny aspects within the IoT domain, we gain valuable insights into the scheme's performance, strengths, vulnerabilities, and potential improvements. These findings lay the foundation for further research and development efforts aimed at enhancing the security, efficiency, and resilience of ECC and Isogeny-based encryption and decryption in IoT applications (Table 1).

6 Potential for Advancements and Future Directions

Our algorithm for hybrid encryption and decryption, which combines ECC and Isogeny-Based Cryptography, opens up promising possibilities for further advancements in the field. By exploring potential improvements and future research directions, we can enhance the security and efficiency of cryptographic systems. One area that deserves attention is optimizing the performance of our algorithm. Striking the right balance between security and efficiency is a continual challenge. To address this, researchers can investigate techniques to streamline computational operations, reduce overhead, and improve processing speed while maintaining robust security measures. This may involve refining the implementation of cryptographic primitives, leveraging specialized hardware acceleration, or exploring parallel computing approaches.

Additionally, conducting thorough analysis and evaluation to assess the algorithm's resilience against advanced attacks is crucial. Rigorous security assessments, including crypto-analysis and formal verification, can provide insights into its strengths and weaknesses. Exploring potential side-channel threats and implementing effective countermeasures will also contribute to the algorithm's overall robustness in real-world scenarios.

To facilitate practical adoption, implementing the algorithm in a widely used programming language such as Python would be valuable. Creating an opensource Python codebase that implements the algorithm will promote accessibility and encourage collaboration among researchers, developers, and practitioners. This will enable further experimentation, refinement, and integration of the algorithm into various projects and systems.

Table 1 Comparison of ECC and isogeny-based cryptography for IoT security

Aspect	Elliptic curve cryptography (ECC)	Isogeny-based cryptography
Security level	Offers strong security with smaller keys and efficient operations	Provides post-quantum security, resistant to quantum attacks
Key size	Uses shorter key sizes (e.g., 256 bits) for equivalent security	Requires longer key sizes (e.g., 768 bits) due to isogeny-based nature
Computational efficiency	ECC is computationally efficient, making it suitable for resource-constrained IoT devices	Isogeny-based cryptography demands more computational resources, which may not be ideal for low-power devices
Quantum resistance	Vulnerable to quantum attacks, requiring migration to post-quantum algorithms	Offers resistance against quantum attacks, providing long-term security
Algorithm maturity	Well-established and widely adopted invarious security protocols	Relatively newer and less standardized
Standardization and ecosystem support	Supported by industry standards and extensive libraries	Lacks the same level of standardization and ecosystem support
Performance in IoT environments	Efficient for constrained devices with limited processing power and memory	Potentially less efficient due to longer key sizes and more complex operations
Key exchange methods	Supports widely used key exchange methods like ECDH	Utilizes different key exchange techniques specific to isogeny-based cryptography
Post-quantum transition	Requires transitioning to post-quantum cryptography in the future	Already considered a post-quantum alternative
Research and development	Constantly evolving and benefiting from ongoing research	Continues to be an active area of research and development
Patent and licensing issues	Some ECC algorithms may have patent or licensing concerns	Patent issues are less common in the field of isogeny-based cryptography
Implementation and optimization	Well-optimized for a variety of platforms	Optimization may be more challenging due to its relative newness

Looking ahead, future research can explore the algorithm's applicability in specific domains or use cases. Evaluating its performance in resource-constrained environments, such as IoT devices or embedded systems, will be particularly relevant. Additionally, investigating its compatibility with existing cryptographic standards and protocols will ensure seamless integration into diverse systems and networks.

Furthermore, ongoing advancements in post-quantum cryptography, especially in the field of Isogeny-Based Cryptography, will shape the future of hybrid encryption and decryption. Research efforts should focus on exploring novel techniques, expanding the range of supported operations, and addressing emerging security concerns. This will ensure the algorithm remains resilient and effective against evolving cryptographic threats.

Our algorithm represents an important step forward in hybrid encryption and decryption. By identifying areas for improvement and outlining future research directions, we aim to contribute to the continual development of secure and efficient cryptographic solutions. Through collaboration, experimentation, and innovation, we can advance the state of the art in hybrid encryption and decryption, strengthening the security of communication systems in today's digital landscape.

7 Conclusion

In conclusion, this research paper has made substantial strides in enhancing the security of IoT applications through the implementation of a novel approach, combining ECC and Isogeny-based Cryptography in a Hybrid Encryption and Decryption scheme. The comprehensive analysis conducted throughout this study has revealed the effectiveness and resilience of our proposed scheme in establishing secure communication channels and safeguarding sensitive data within the IoT ecosystem. By leveraging the unique strengths of ECC and Isogeny-based Cryptography, we have created a robust solution that ensures both the integrity and confidentiality of IoT systems. The examination of hardware and software considerations has emphasized the importance of strategic choices in implementing our scheme. Careful selection of appropriate hardware components, coupled with the utilization of suitable operating systems, has provided a solid foundation for executing cryptographic operations on resource-constrained IoT devices. The integration of optimized cryptographic libraries has further fortified the security of our scheme, enabling seamless integration of essential cryptographic algorithms. Looking ahead, the future of IoT holds tremendous potential for advancements in security. The integration of dedicated hardware security mechanisms and the exploration of emerging technologies, such as blockchain, offer promising avenues to revolutionize the security and privacy of IoT data transactions. Additionally, the utilization of advanced techniques like machine learning and artificial intelligence can greatly enhance anomaly detection and threat mitigation capabilities, bolstering the overall resilience of IoT systems. To facilitate practical implementation and foster collaboration, we are committed to providing an open-source Python codebase for our proposed scheme. This will empower researchers and practitioners to validate, experiment, and build upon our approach, facilitating further innovation and advancements in IoT security. This research represents a significant contribution toward establishing a more secure and trustworthy IoT ecosystem. By harnessing the power of ECC and Isogeny-based Cryptography, we empower IoT applications to thrive in an interconnected world. As we continue to push the boundaries of knowledge and innovation, we pave the way for a future where IoT systems seamlessly integrate with robust security measures, unlocking their full potential to transform industries and enrich our daily lives.

References

1. Gubbi J, Buyya R, Marusic S, Palaniswami M (2013) Internet of Things (IoT): a vision, architectural elements, and future directions. Futur Gener Comput Syst 29(7):1645–1660
2. Bos JW, Halderman JA, Heninger N, Moore J, Naehrig M, Wustrow E (2014) Elliptic curve cryptography in practice. In: Financial cryptography and data security: 18th international conference, FC 2014, Christ Church, Barbados. Revised Selected Papers 18. Springer, pp 157–175
3. Koziel B, Azarderakhsh R, Kermani MM (2018) A high-performance and scalable hardware architecture for isogeny-based cryptography. IEEE Trans Comput 67(11):1594–1609
4. Kurosawa K, Desmedt Y (2004) A new paradigm of hybrid encryption scheme. In: Crypto, vol 3152, pp 426–442
5. Dixit P, Gupta AK, Trivedi MC, Yadav VK (2018) Traditional and hybrid encryption techniques: a survey. In: Networking communication and data knowledge engineering: volume 2. Springer, pp 239–248
6. Li N (2010) Research on Diffie-Hellman key exchange protocol. In: 2010 2nd International conference on computer engineering and technology. IEEE, vol 4, pp V4–634
7. Menezes A (2001) Evaluation of security level of cryptography: the Elliptic Curve Discrete Logarithm Problem (ECDLP). University of Waterloo, vol 14
8. De Feo L, Kieffer J, Smith B (2018) Towards practical key exchange from ordinary isogeny graphs. In: Advances in cryptology–ASIACRYPT 2018: 24th International conference on the theory and application of cryptology and information security, Brisbane, QLD, Australia, Proceedings, Part III 24. Springer, pp 365–394
9. Selmane N, Bhasin S, Guilley S, Danger J-L (2011) Security evaluation of application-specific integrated circuits and field programmable gate arrays against setup time violation attacks. IET Inf Secur 5(4):181–190
10. Lawson N (2009) Side-channel attacks on cryptographic software. IEEE Secur Priv 7(6):65–68
11. Costache A, Feigon B, Lauter K, Massierer M, Puska's A (2019) Ramanujan graphs in cryptography. In Research directions in number theory: women in numbers IV. Springer, pp 1–40
12. Lyubashevsky V, Peikert C, Regev O (2013) On ideal lattices and learning with errors over rings. J ACM (JACM) 60(6):1–35
13. Azarderakhsh R, Jalali, A, Jao D, Soukharev V (2019) Practical supersingular isogeny group key agreement. Cryptology ePrint Archive
14. Krawczyk H, Eronen P (2010) HMAC-based extract-and-expand key derivation function (HKDF)
15. Kamara S, Papamanthou C, Roeder T (2012) Dynamic searchable symmetric encryption. In: Proceedings of the 2012 ACM conference on computer and communications security, pp 965–976
16. Wu C, Li Z (2021) Local thinning of 3D stereo images based on symmetric decryption algorithm. Microprocess Microsyst 82:103803
17. Kumar S, Sahoo S, Mahapatra A, Swain AK, Mahapatra KK (2017) Security enhancements to system on chip devices for IoT perception layer. In 2017 IEEE International symposium on nanoelectronic and information systems (iNIS). IEEE, pp 151–156
18. Murtaza MH, Tahir H, Tahir S, Alizai ZA, Riaz Q, Hussain M (2022) A portable hardware security module and cryptographic key generator. J Inf Secur Appl 70:103332
19. Nemec M, Klinec D, Svenda P, Sekan P, Matyas V (2017) Measuring popularity of cryptographic libraries in internet-wide scans. In: Proceedings of the 33rd annual computer security applications conference, pp 162–175
20. Yan SY (2013) Quantum attacks on public-key cryptosystems, vol 207. Springer

A Classification Approach for Hyperspectral Images Through Multi-feature Extraction

Prabhu Ram Kancharla, Radhesyam Vaddi, and Bhargav Teki

Abstract An innovative method for extracting useful spectral-spatial characteristics from hyper-spectral imaging for remote sensing is presented in this research. The procedure comprises merging three feature sub-cubes produced by separate feature extraction methods into a single feature sub-cube. The resulting multi-feature extraction sub-cube is then enhanced using an intrinsic structure-preserving recursive filter to improve its spatial features. Then, the produced sub-cube is trained for classification using a SVM that has an RBF kernel. The Indian Pines and Salinas datasets are used to evaluate the performance of the proposed architecture. The results show that the overall accuracy achieved with this model is 96.28% for Indian Pines and 94.23% for Salinas, surpassing the performance of existing methods. This framework highlights its adaptability and relevance across a range of domains, including geological surveying and environmental monitoring.

Keywords Probabilistic principal component analysis · Hyperspectral ımage classification · Principal component analysis · Factor analysis · Structure preserving recursive filter · And Support vector machine

---

P. R. Kancharla (✉) · R. Vaddi · B. Teki
Department of IT, VR Siddhartha Engineering College, JNTU-Kakinada, Vijayawada, India
e-mail: prabhuramkancharla1@gmail.com

R. Vaddi
e-mail: syam.radhe@gmail.com

B. Teki
e-mail: bhargavteki9376@gmail.com

B. N. Gohil et al. (eds.), *Information Security, Privacy and Digital Forensics*,
Lecture Notes in Electrical Engineering 1423,
https://doi.org/10.1007/978-981-96-9443-3_5

1 Introduction

Numerous scholars are now working on the examination of hyperspectral image classification, also known as HSI classification. This classification method is a reliable one that differentiates between different land cover categories within a three-dimensional dataset. The hyperspectral cube, often referred to as the H-cube, is obtained using hyperspectral sensors and features three dimensions: variable, which represents the number of rows; variable, which represents the number of columns; and variable, which represents the count of adjacent spectral bands with distinct wavelengths. Hyperspectral sensors capture Earth's surface information in a continuous manner, generating images with rich three-dimensional data [1]. Within these images, the initial two dimensions depict spatial data, while the third dimension captures spectral information. Each material's reflectance is depicted as a spectral response, as illustrated in Fig. 1 for the materials present in the Indian Pines dataset.

Although these images contain a wealth of information, they also display notable high correlation and redundancy, further exacerbated by the limited quantity of training samples. This issue has drawn considerable attention within the research community [2]. Hence, there is a crucial requirement for dimensionality reduction in these images. A new paradigm for spectral-spatial feature dimensionality reduction is presented in this research.

Many different industries make use of hyperspectral pictures, spanning from agriculture to defense applications. Figure 1 delineates the key areas of application for hyperspectral image classification. Hyperspectral image (HSI) classification finds applications in various domains, including mineral mapping, change detection, rock identification, land use and land cover analysis, fruit defect detection, defense applications, disease prediction, and agriculture. It enables precise identification and classification of materials and features, making it a versatile tool in remote sensing and scientific research.

2 Literature Review

Hughes' phenomenon [2] is being studied by researchers right now. This is an interesting finding that shows that adding more training samples for classifiers causes the number of spectral bands to grow exponentially. This is attributed to the significant amount of three-dimensional data [1, 3]. Nevertheless, it's crucial to understand that this high-dimensional data frequently produces inconsistent classification accuracy. [4]. As a result, there is a pressing need to develop mechanisms that can address these challenges without compromising classification accuracy.

Scholars in the field of literature have used machine learning methods to tackle the problems caused by hyperspectral data, making good use of both spectral and geographical data. A variety of statistical and non-statistical approaches have been proposed to address the Hughes phenomenon and enhance accuracy. Additionally,

Fig. 1 Applications of hyperspectral imaging

Kakhani and Mokhtarzade [5] introduced a neural-based classification approach that incorporates general PCA for feature reduction. A more modern method that combines spatial and spectral elements was also introduced. This method involves projecting hyperspectral data while keeping the highest level of noise for feature extraction. This method uses contextual and local covariance matrices to train a support vector classifier, showing that it is better than other methods for extracting features.

In another vein, [6] introduced a technique for extracting inherent properties from individual pixels. In the realm of remote sensing, [7] delves into the extraction of spatial structures using attribute profiles, followed by the training of a random forest classifier for hyperspectral image identification. It's worth noting that many researchers initially adopt linear PCA to identify uncorrelated spectral bands, as evident in studies like [8, 9]. Moreover, various feature extraction methods, such as

Table 1 Description of the dataset

S. No.	Item	Indian pines	Salinas
1	Size	145 × 145x224	512 × 217 x 204
2	No. of bands	224	224
3	Spatial resolution	145 × 145	512 × 217
4	Area of Acquisition	North-western Indiana	Salinas Valley, California
5	Sensor	AVIRIS	AVIRIS
6	No of classes	16	16

those found in [8, 10, 11], have been employed to obtain features that hold relevance for classifiers.

In the medical dataset context, Luukka [6] proposed a methodology where a nonlinear technique is initially applied. Subsequently, a similarity classifier is used that employs principal component analysis (PCA) to capture spatial data. These spatial features, often representing neurons, are then relayed to the classifier for the extraction of spectral features. Nonetheless, as mentioned in [7], although a membership-based kernel PCA enables robust classification, it does have its constraints, primarily due to its extensive reliance on iterations.

Additionally, as detailed in [12], a clustering technique is presented for extracting spatial information, and on top of that, methods for SVMs and extreme learning are used. Furthermore, the literature has delved into a dimensionality reduction strategy grounded in factor analysis, as documented in [13]. This approach works well for hyperspectral images (HSIs) by separating useful spectral bands, making them SVM-compatible. Notably, ranking-based feature extraction and band fusion [14] are also used in this area for HSI categorization. These approaches collectively contribute to the ongoing efforts aimed at solving the challenges posed by hyperspectral data while preserving classification accuracy.

3 Description of Dataset

The proposed framework is examined using two hyperspectral data sets. The detailed description can be found in Table 1. The visual representation, demonstrated by ground truths, is depicted in Figs. 2 and 3.

4 Proposed Methodology

The schematic diagram in Fig. 4 illustrates the proposed framework, comprising key stages that include sub-cube generation, dimensionality reduction, spectral feature extraction, spatial feature extraction, and the classification process.

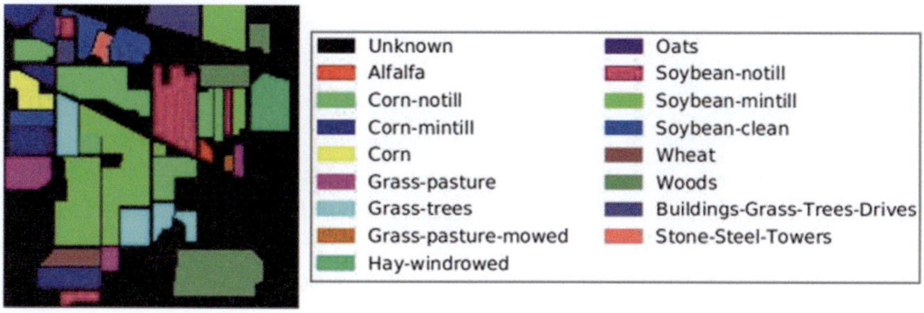

Fig. 2 Indian Pines dataset

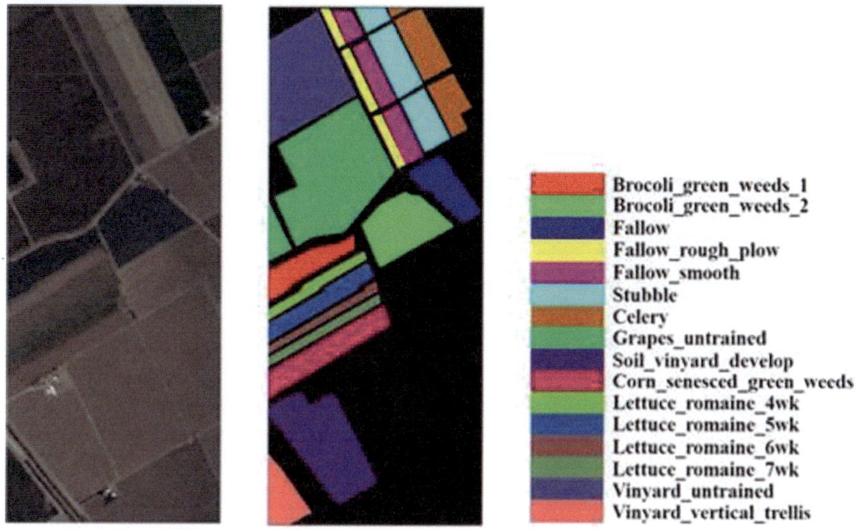

Fig. 3 Salinas dataset

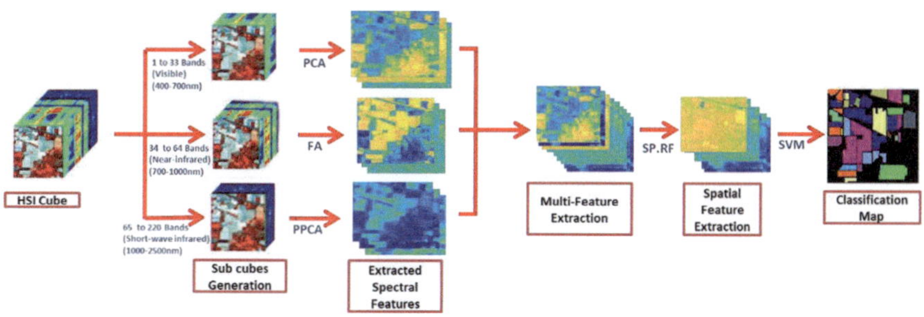

Fig. 4 Suggested hyperspectral image (HSI) classification approach

4.1 Input

This paper utilizes a hyperspectral cube obtained through the AVIRIS sensor. The sensor records information across 220 spectral bands, which are segmented into three separate images. The initial sub-cube encompasses bands 1 to 33, representing the visible spectrum (400–700 nm). The second sub-cube includes bands 34 to 64, which cover the near-infrared (NIR) range (700–1000 nm). Lastly, the third sub-cube comprises bands 65 to 220, covering the short-wave infrared (SWIR) spectrum (1000–2500 nm). Subsequently, these spectral images are extracted from the input cube.

4.2 Spectral Feature Extraction:

The three partitioned pictures are subjected to three separate feature extraction methods in this article. Here are several methods:

1. Principal Component Analysis
2. Factor Analysis
3. Probabilistic Principal Component Analysis

The first image utilizes the principal component analysis algorithm; the second image employs the factor analysis algorithm; and for the third image, the spectral feature extraction is carried out using the probabilistic principal component analysis algorithm. Subsequently, the outputs from these three images are amalgamated into a single cube.

4.3 Spatial Feature Extraction

This technique uses a structure-preserving recursive filter approach (SPRF) to take the sub-cube that is made by spectral feature extraction, which is explained in (B). It is then put through something called spatial feature extraction [9]. This approach captures the inherent features of the image. The features extracted are then trained using a support vector machine (SVM), specifically employing a radial basis function kernel [10]. This kernel is particularly well-suited for multi-class classification [15].

Presented in Algorithm 1 is the complete algorithm that will be used for the framework that has been suggested. Using this approach, a comprehensive explanation is provided on how the methodology combines a variety of feature extraction methods in order to attain the highest possible level of accuracy and performance.

Algorithm 1: HSI Multi-Feature Classification

1. Input: An image H ∈ R^{mxnxr} with m × n pixels by r bands
2. Output: Image Y
3. Feature extraction. Obtain the first 3 components of the multi-feature cube as given int the subsection
   a. Bands 1–33: PCA → 3PCA's
   b. Bands 34–64: FA → 3 Factor scores
   c. Bands 65–220: PPCA → 3 PCA's
4. Merge the extracted PCA and factor scores
5. Apply structure-preserving Recursive Filter
6. SVM classifier on the extracted

5 Result Analysis

5.1 Comparision of the Outcomes Across Various Feature Reduction Techniques

In this part, we have carried out a comparative examination of the findings of the HSI classification using a number of different feature reduction strategies. These techniques include factor analysis [16], probabilistic principal component analysis [17], principal component analysis (PCA) [15, 18], and an approach that involves the extraction of multiple features. This investigation was carried out on two different datasets, namely the Salinas and the Indian Pines datasets. The outcomes for each dataset are presented in (Table 2 and Fig. 5) and (Table 3 and Fig. 6) for reference.

5.2 Analysis of Results

We do a dual analysis in this part. The Kappa, average accuracy (AA), and overall accuracy (OA) are the first metrics we compare. Secondly, we evaluate the outcomes while adjusting the quantity of training samples. This comprehensive analysis is conducted on two datasets, namely Indian Pines and the Salinas. The results are visually presented in (Figs. 7 and 8) and (Figs. 9 and 10), respectively. These comparisons underscore the superior performance of the Proposed method when contrasted with the other feature reduction techniques.

This data highlights significant variations in the performance of four classification methods across three distinct classes (AA, OA, & Kappa). Notably, the Proposed method consistently outperforms the others, achieving the highest classification accuracy in all three classes, suggesting its promise for effective classification. PCA and

Table 2 Class wise analysis for Indian pines dataset

Classes	PCA	FA	PPCA	Proposed
C1	92.00	70.97	19.66	85.19
C2	84.46	83.72	76.58	93.06
C3	74.69	85.95	83.23	94.01
C4	86.67	84.28	78.19	90.87
C5	87.94	84.17	88.21	99.54
C6	93.15	89.68	68.35	94.62
C7	56.52	45.16	72.22	82.35
C8	67.20	87.84	79.56	100
C9	73.25	18.87	29.41	100
C10	82.17	80.46	65.97	95.67
C11	89.12	82.84	83.75	96.33
C12	65.77	70.34	60.46	98.04
C13	78.35	73.75	85.99	100
C14	65.20	89.84	59.92	100
C15	73.09	75.11	66.38	97.28
C16	88.55	88.51	54.81	98.46
OA	65.23	66.35	72.34	94.23
AA	66.12	58.64	71.23	94.65
Kappa	68.04	67.90	75.80	95.74

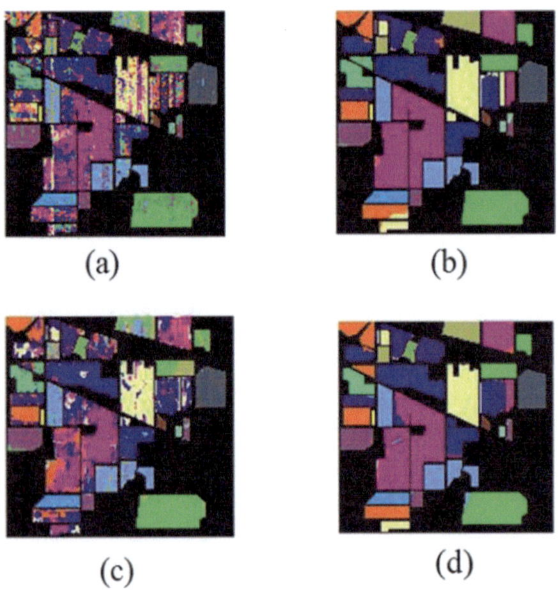

Fig. 5 Indian Pines **a** PCA. **b** FA. **c** PPCA. **d** Proposed

Table 3 Class wise analysis for Salinas dataset

Classes	PCA	FA	PPCA	Proposed
C1	84.17	72.35	75.49	88.82
C2	79.88	54.24	61.56	92.35
C3	72.93	67.06	54.72	93.46
C4	60.58	78.45	57.67	89.97
C5	79.23	69.14	69.63	99.74
C6	64.69	66.55	77.34	95.28
C7	41.45	53.17	59.82	78.23
C8	87.55	57.63	69.93	100
C9	76.54	21.38	37.05	100
C10	77.13	75.26	49.61	92.47
C11	77.11	41.88	61.37	94.62
C12	82.86	75.91	79.39	96.83
C13	79.76	79.02	58.14	100
C14	54.34	48.99	69.96	100
C15	87.67	54.15	73.58	97.01
C16	78.43	58.74	75.91	98.52
OA	66.12	71.23	73.82	95.39
AA	63.92	56.94	69.63	93.72
Kappa	65.64	62.93	71.83	95.74

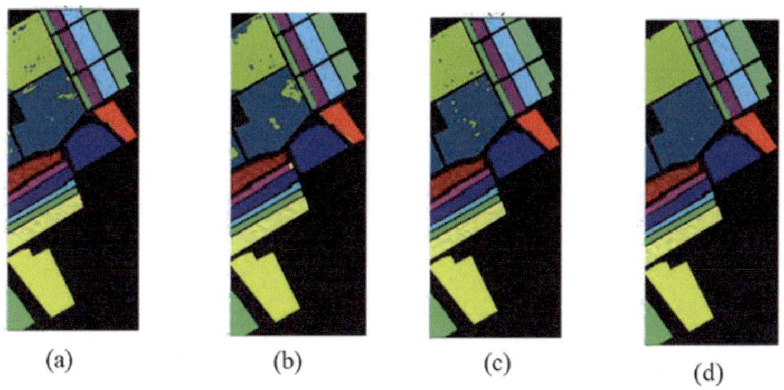

Fig. 6 Salinas **a** PCA. **b** FA. **c** PPCA. **d** Proposed

PPCA exhibit similar performance levels, indicating comparability in their classification capabilities. In contrast, Factor Analysis (FA) consistently yields the lowest accuracy, implying its limited suitability for this specific classification problem.

Increasing the percentage of training data consistently improves classification accuracy for three classes (OA, AA, and Kappa). Notably, even with just 4% training

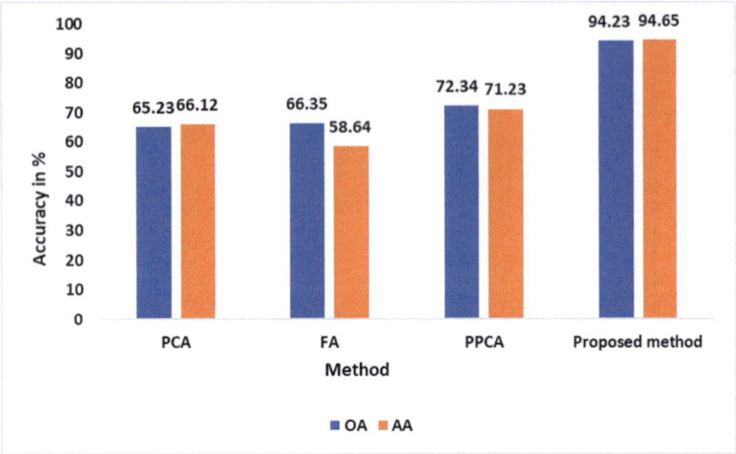

Fig. 7 Examination of various methods in the Indian Pines dataset

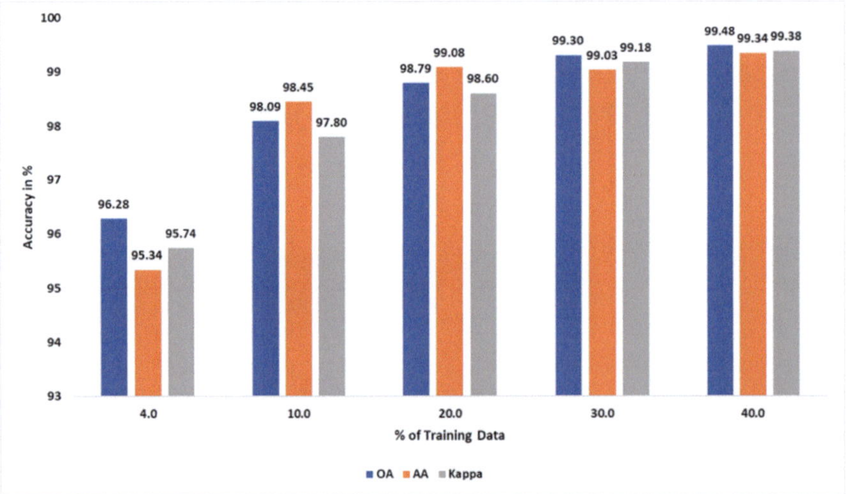

Fig. 8 Assessing the performance of the proposed method on the Indian pines dataset

data, accuracy is high (95.34 to 96.28%). As training data increases to 10, 20, 30, and 40%, accuracy consistently rises, peaking at 99.03 to 99.48% with 40% training data. This highlights the significance of a larger training dataset in enhancing classification accuracy, demonstrating a clear positive correlation between training data proportion and classification performance.

In the Salinas dataset, four classification methods (PCA, FA, PPCA, and the Proposed Method) were evaluated for accuracy in classifying two classes, OA and AA. The Proposed Method consistently outperforms the other three methods,

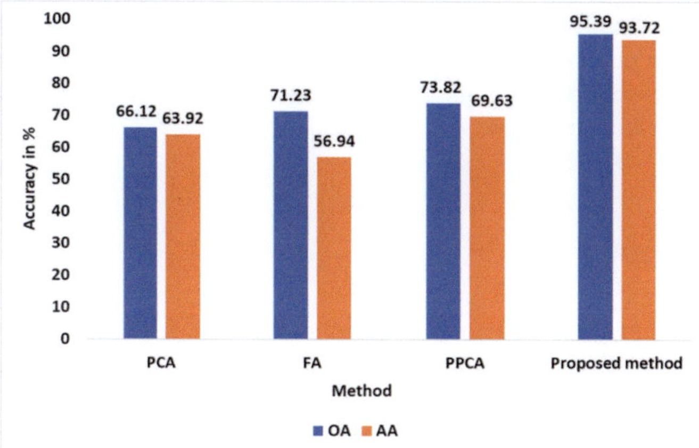

Fig. 9 Examination of various methods in the Salinas dataset

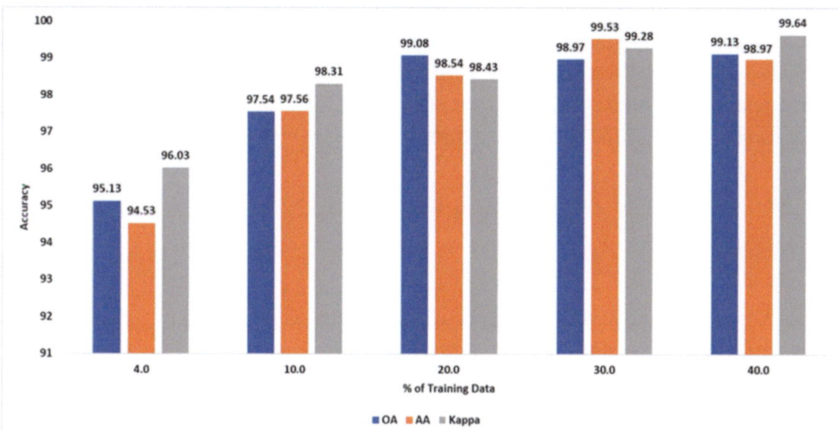

Fig. 10 Assessing the performance of the proposed method on the Salinas dataset

achieving the highest accuracy percentages of 94.23% for class OA and 94.65% for class AA. PCA and PPCA show intermediate performance, while FA consistently delivers the lowest accuracy percentages, suggesting it may not be well-suited for this dataset. This highlights the potential of the Proposed Method as an effective choice for classification in the Salinas dataset.

Increasing the training data percentage consistently enhances classification accuracy across OA, AA, and Kappa metrics. At 4% training data, accuracy ranges from 94.53 to 95.13%, significantly improving at 10, 20, 30, and 40%. The highest accuracy, notably 99.64% for Kappa, 99.53% for AA, and 99.13% for OA, is achieved with 30 and 40% training data, emphasizing the value of a larger dataset. This underscores a strong positive correlation between training data proportion and classification performance, highlighting the importance of ample training data for high accuracy, especially in OA and AA metrics.

6 Conclusion

The purpose of this study is to provide an efficient, multi-feature extraction method for spectral characteristics. Following the division of the original data cube into three sub-cubes, various implementations of principal component analysis and factor analysis are applied to each of the sub-cubes. A new sub-cube is then generated, which incorporates the components and scores that were taken from the original cube. After that, a structure-preserving recursive filter (SPRF) is used in order to carry out a spatial feature extraction method on this single sub-cube. Non-linear support vector machine training is used to further refine the characteristics that have been collected. The suggested framework was able to attain a performance indicator known as overall accuracy (OA) of 96.28% when applied to the Indian Pines dataset. The suggested methodology achieves an OA of 94.23% when used with the Salinas dataset, comparable to the previous example.

References

1. Ding Y, Pan S, Chong Y (2019) Robust spatial-spectral block-diagonal structure representation with fuzzy class probability for hyperspectral image classification. IEEE Trans Geosci Remote Sens 58:1747–1762
2. Vaddi R, Prabukumar M (2017) Comparative study of feature extraction techniques for hyperspectral remote sensing image classification: a survey. In 2017 International conference on ıntelligent computing and control systems (ICICCS), pp 543–548
3. Dalla Mura M (2010) Morphological attribute profiles for the analysis of very high-resolution images. IEEE Trans Geosci Remote Sens 48:3747–3762
4. Boggavarapu L, Prabukumar M (2017) Survey on classification methods for hyperspectral remote sensing imagery. In: 2017 International conference on ıntelligent computing and control systems (ICICCS), pp 538–542
5. Li W et al (2012) Locality-preserving dimensionality reduction and classification for hyperspectral image analysis. IEEE Trans Geosci Remote Sens 50:1185–1198
6. Luukka P (2011) A new nonlinear fuzzy robust PCA algorithm and similarity classifier in the classification of medical data sets. Int J Fuzzy Syst 13:153–162
7. Heo G, Gader P, Frigui H (2009) Robust kernel PCA using fuzzy membership. In: 2009 International joint conference on neural networks, pp 1213–1220
8. Phaneendra Kumar BLN, Manoharan P (2021) Whale optimization-based band selection technique for hyperspectral image classification. Int J Remote Sens 42:5109–5147. https://doi.org/10.1080/01431161.2021.1906979
9. Manoharan P, Phaneendra Kumar BLN (2021) Improved whale optimization based band selection for hyperspectral remote sensing image classification. Infrared Phys Technol 119:103948. https://doi.org/10.1016/j.infrared.2021.103948

10. Gastal ES, Oliveira MM (2011) Domain transform for edge-aware image and video processing. In: ACM SIGGRAPH 2011 papers, pp 1–12
11. Patro RN, Subudhi S, Biswal PK (2019) Spectral clustering and spatial Frobenius norm-based Jaya optimisation for BS of hyperspectral images. IET Image Proc 13(2):307–315. https://doi.org/10.1049/iet-ipr.2018.5109
12. Sigirci IO, Bilgin G (2017) Hyperspectral image classification using fuzzy C-means based composite kernel approach. In: 2017 25th Signal processing and communications applications conference (SIU), pp 1–4
13. Boggavarapu LNP, Prabukumar M (2020) Classification of hyperspectral remote sensing imagery using intrinsic parameter estimation. In: Abraham A et al (eds) Intelligent systems design and applications, pp 852–862. Springer International Publishing, Switzerland
14. Prasad S, Bruce L (2008) Limitations of principal components analysis for hyperspectral target recognition. IEEE Geosci Remote Sens Lett 5:625–629
15. van der Maaten LJP, Postma EO, van den Herik HJ (2009) Dimensionality reduction: a comparative review. Tilburg University Technical Report, TiCC-TR 2009–005
16. Zhang T, Zhang P, Zhong W, Yang Z, Yang F (2020) JL-GFDN: a novel gabor filter-based deep network using joint spectral-spatial local binary pattern for hyperspectral image classification. Remote Sensing 12:1–14. https://doi.org/10.3390/rs12122016
17. Vaddi R, Prabukumar M (2020) CNN based hyperspectral image classification using unsupervised band selection and structure-preserving spatial features. Infrared Phys Technol 110:103457. https://doi.org/10.1016/j.infrared.2020.103457
18. Zhan K, Wang H, Huang H, Xie Y (2016) Large margin distribution machine for hyperspectral image classification. J Electron Imaging 25(6):063024. https://doi.org/10.1117/1.JEI.25.6.063024

CSBC: Cloud-Based Secret Image Sharing Using Bit-Flip and Counting Scheme

Bhawana Parihar, Maroti Deshmukh, and Arjun Singh Rawat

Abstract This paper introduces an innovative approach to securely and efficiently share a single secret image in a system with limited resources. Although traditional secret sharing techniques are efficient, they often require significant processing and storage resources, making them impractical in environments with limitations. While there are existing counting based secret sharing techniques applicable to systems with limited resources, that handle numerical data, text, watermarking, and steganography, schemes designed specifically for multimedia images exhibit some noticeable gaps. By employing bit-flip and parallel bit-counting techniques, our proposed model offers a counting-based single-image sharing solution to bridge this gap. The core components of our scheme encompass share generation of share and recovering of the secret. In share generation, we utilize a bit-flip operation to create the shares, and for enhanced confidentiality, a reverse bit operation is applied before distribution on a cloud network. In the case of secret reconstruction which follows the perfect secret sharing scheme, parallel bit operations are employed. By integrating all the shares and using parallel bit-counting techniques at the bit level, the secret image is successfully recovered. The experimental results showcase the average level of randomness in the shares generated by our method. Metrics like PSNR, RMSE, and correlation are used to assess the effectiveness of the suggested scheme, yielding compelling results. This approach has a significant drawback in that if the quantity of shares drops below the required threshold 'n', reconstruction of the secret image becomes impossible.

Keywords Counting bits scheme for secret sharing · Parallel bits counting · Bit flip · Limited resources · Cloud network

---

B. Parihar · M. Deshmukh (✉)
National Institute of Technology Srinagar, Srinagar, Uttarakhand, India
e-mail: marotideshmukh@nituk.ac.in

B. Parihar
e-mail: bhawana.phd2020@nituk.ac.in

A. S. Rawat
National Institute of Technology Delhi, Delhi, India

B. N. Gohil et al. (eds.), *Information Security, Privacy and Digital Forensics*,
Lecture Notes in Electrical Engineering 1423,
https://doi.org/10.1007/978-981-96-9443-3_6

1 Introduction

The Internet of Things (IoT) has introduced a new era of data abundance, seamlessly becoming an integral part of our daily existence. Managing this data deluge often involves its storage on cloud computing platforms. Cloud computing essentially delivers a range of computing services, including networking, processing, and storage, via the internet. Cloud service providers offer immediate access to a diverse array of resources, reducing the need for extensive on-site infrastructure and empowering businesses to efficiently manage and analyze their data. While cloud computing offers significant benefits such as scalability and cost-effectiveness, it also raises privacy concerns in the realm of technology. To address these privacy concerns, encryption emerges as a pivotal strategy. Since user data is encrypted, anyone lacking the key cannot decrypt it. However, there are a number of difficulties with encryption, especially when it comes to key management. Safeguarding decryption keys is a major issue. If the cloud service provider possesses these keys, or if they fall into the wrong hands, the provider could potentially decrypt the data at will. Conversely, users who store the keys themselves risk losing them, which could prevent access to their encrypted data. Furthermore, data that cloud service providers maintain but are unable to access without the necessary key. Cryptographic methods like 'Secret Sharing' are employed to mitigate these challenges. The original secret can only be recovered if a legitimate access structure is established, which frequently calls for a threshold scheme a minimum number of shares after this method splits secret data into multiple shares. Cloud computing offers scalable and user-friendly storage options, while secret-sharing techniques give a cryptographic method to transfer and secure sensitive content, such as encryption keys and private information. When combined, these technologies solve a number of security and privacy issues pertaining to cloud data storage. Using a split-and-combine technique, the cloud-based Secret Image Sharing Scheme divides the secret image into several shares to prevent any one sharing from disclosing sensitive information. The share generation process uses a number of methods, including as modulo, Boolean, and polynomial operations, to preserve anonymity. This approach spreads confidence among several cloud servers as opposed to depending just on one. In order to recreate the secret data, a predetermined number of shares kept on these cloud servers are merged using the combine technique or secret reconstruction process. Integrating secret-sharing systems into cloud computing environments offers significant security and privacy benefits. This integration enhances the protection of sensitive data, improves access management, and mitigates various security concerns. The combination of cloud computing and secret-sharing techniques enhances the security and privacy of data processing and storage on the cloud, reducing vulnerability to data loss, unauthorized access, and breaches. The benefits of cloud services are also utilized in this connection. There are strong arguments for researchers to switch from conventional secret-sharing techniques to counting-based approaches. Counting-based techniques increase resource efficiency in resource-constrained contexts by lowering computing demands and resource requirements. They are ideal for resource-constrained applications and reduce storage overhead. Additionally, counting-based techniques are more flexible and can handle non-numeric data formats, such as multimedia. Their potential to increase security by introducing a high degree of unpredictability further emphasizes their popularity. Additionally, they are useful in real-world situations like cloud networks for secret image sharing. Adoption of counting-based secret-sharing systems, which provide better performance, scalability, and lower complexity, has the potential to progress data sharing and cryptography.

However, the fact that counting-based secret-sharing systems are only applicable to text, steganography, watermarking, and numerical data is a significant disadvantage. Therefore, a solution is required to address this gap, particularly for multimedia images. In line with our findings, we propose a counting-based scheme for secret image in resource-constrained environments while enhancing both security and efficiency.

The organization of the remaining sections in this paper is as follows: the literature survey is introduced in Sect. 2, the suggested scheme is elaborated in Sect. 3, the experimental results of the proposed scheme are shown in Sect. 4, and the conclusion and future work are provided in Sect. 5.

2 Literature Survey

The need for secure communication and data protection has led to the rise in popularity of counting-based secret sharing (CBSS) systems in recent years. This article examines the various CBSS strategies covered in the 2.1 through 2.4 subsections.

2.1 Distributed Key Security

Adnan et al. [1], Ghamdi et al. [2], and Qurashi et al. [3] have all conducted research on the application of CBSS in Distributed Key Security. They introduce new methods such as simultaneous counting of ones and statistical randomness testing. The security levels of CBSS are reliant on data and have high computational costs, but it also offers simplicity, utility, and improved security.

2.2 Text Steganography

Aziz et al. [4], Gutub et al. [5], and Gutub et al. [6] have improved Arabic text steganography, demonstrating the use of CBSS in text steganography. Improved security, practical capability, and share retention are among the benefits; steganographic changes provide difficulties.

2.3 Image-Based Steganography

CBSS techniques in Image-Based Steganography offer improved security, efficiency, and lossless reconstruction; these have been studied by Gutub et al. [7], Gutub et al. [8], and Alkhodaidi et al. [9]. Among the challenges are the optimization of share size, memorizing key, and the potential instability of the scheme.

2.4 Multi-user Authentication and Beyond

Gutub et al. [10] employ a 64-bit key to increase security when using CBSS to multi-user authentication. Gutub et al. [11] increase participant capacity by extending counting-based sharing for multi-user systems. Alkhodaidi et al. [12] offer a sophisticated method that enhances security and scalability while permitting limitless share key generation, but with drawbacks.

3 Proposed Methodology

Protecting sensitive data from potential threats is crucial, and secret-sharing strategies play a vital role in achieving this. However, in scenarios with limited resources, such as constraints on computation cost and storage space, or within resource-constrained environments, the demand for lightweight schemes that deliver both advanced security and improved performance becomes evident. Although counting based method have advanced, they have primarily been proposed for numerical data and did not address the unique challenges posed by multimedia images. Therefore, this work employs operations such as bit flips and bit counting to propose a novel method for creating a secret-sharing scheme for a single image. These operations are strategically distributed across multiple cloud servers to enhance trust and security. Figure 1 shows the flowchart of a cloud-based, counting-based method for sharing a single secret.

This scheme comprises two primary phases: the generation and distribution of shares across multiple cloud servers, and the secret recovery process. The share generation applies the bit flip method and distributes the shares in different cloud servers, strengthening trust and security. In the secret reconstruction phase, the scheme utilizes parallel bit counting across all distributed shares. This approach follows the perfect secret image-sharing mechanism, requiring the incorporation of all distributed shares in the parallel bit-counting process to successfully recover the original secret.

Figure 2 illustrates the process of share generation using the bit flip method for different test cases applicable to sharing a secret image. In test case 1 and test case 2, the target key values are 254 and 255, respectively, and these values are repeated for the required number of shares. In the given illustration, the number of shares to

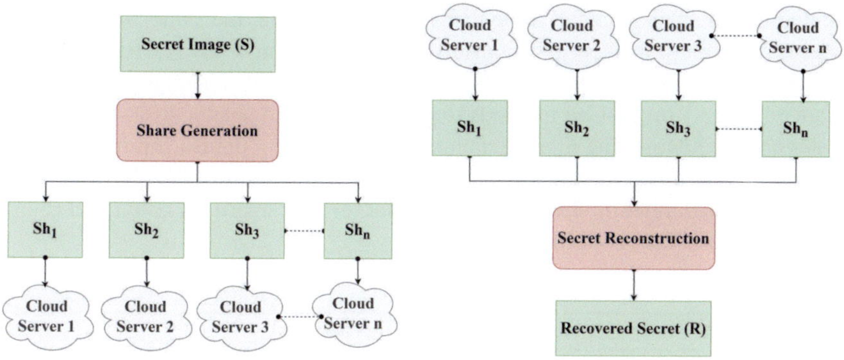

(a) Process of Generation of Shares (b) Process of Reconstruction of Secret

Fig. 1 Flow diagram

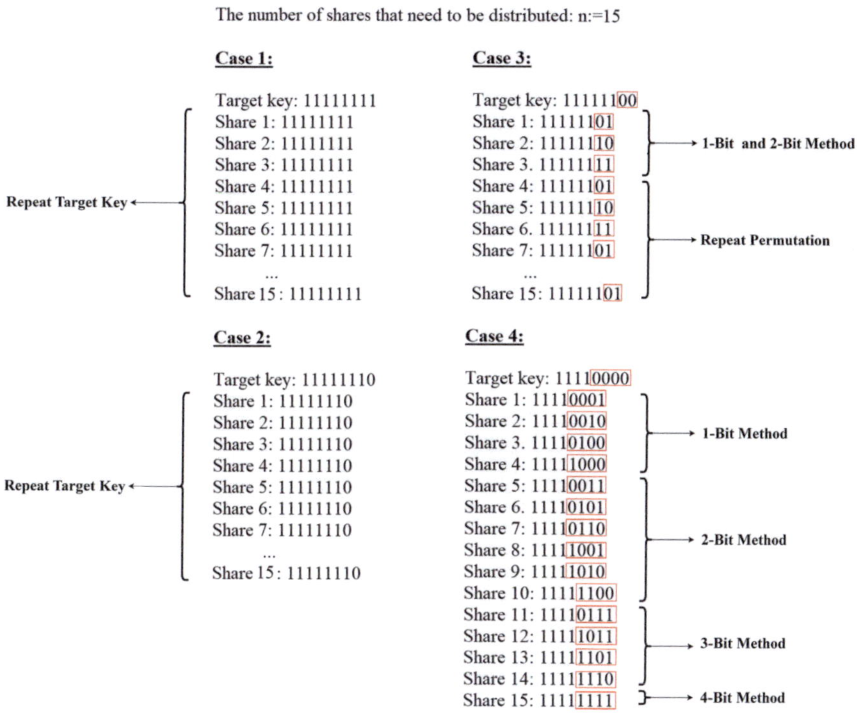

Fig. 2 Proposed share generation process

be distributed is denoted as $n := 15$. As a result, all shares will have the same value as the target key. In test case 3, the target key value is 252, which has only three different possible permutations, namely 253, 254, and 255, all of which are less than the number of shares needed to be distributed. Therefore, the same permutation is repeated until there are $n := 15$ shares. In test case 4, the target key value is 240, which has 15 possible permutations other than the target key itself. These permutations are arranged using 1-bit to 4-bit methods to generate $n := 15$ shares.

Algorithm 1 shows the Share generation process using the Bit flip method. This algorithm is designed to generate shares from a given Target Key. The number of shares to be generated is denoted by n. he Target Key's zero bit count determines which share generation mechanism is used.

Algorithm 1: Share Generation using Bit Flip Method

Data: Target Key, Number of Distributed Shares (n)
Result: Shares
if *Number of Zero Bits in Target Key* $\leq$ *1* **then**
    /** If the number of zero bits in the Target Key is less than or equal to 1, we simply repeat the Target Key until we have generated n shares. **/
    Repeat the Target Key until we have n shares;
else if $2^{Number\ of\ Zero\ Bits\ in\ Target\ Key} - 1 < n$ **then**
    /** If the number of zero bits is more than 1 and $2^{NumberofZeroBits} - 1$ is less than n, we use all possible permutations of the Target Key (excluding target key) until we have n shares. **/
    To create n shares, use every permutation of the target key (apart from the target key).;
else
    /** If the number of zero bits is more than 1 and $2^{NumberofZeroBits} - 1$ is greater than or equal to n, we employ all possible permutations of the Target Key using 1-bit to 8-bit methods to generate 'n' shares. **/
    Use all possible permutations of the Target Key, utilizing 1-bit to 8-bit methods, to generate n shares;

The process of secret reconstruction utilizing the parallel bit-counting approach, in which the shares' bits are focused in parallel, is shown in Fig. 3. With n denoting the number of distributed shares, a bit value of 1 is produced if the count is exactly equal to n; if it is less than n, a bit value of 0 is produced.

4 Experiment Analysis

The experiment findings intended to assess the effectiveness of the proposed method are presented in this section. We used the Pycharm IDE, which is compatible with Python 3.8, and an Intel Pentium 4417U CPU with 4 GB of RAM for the study. In order to carry out the experiment, we used a limited subset of images for explanatory purposes and a diversified set of datasets focusing more than ten thousand images to evaluate the model. We use both qualitative and quantitative evaluations in our analysis. We used a 256 × 256 Zelda's image as a secret in our experimental setup for both grayscale and color images.

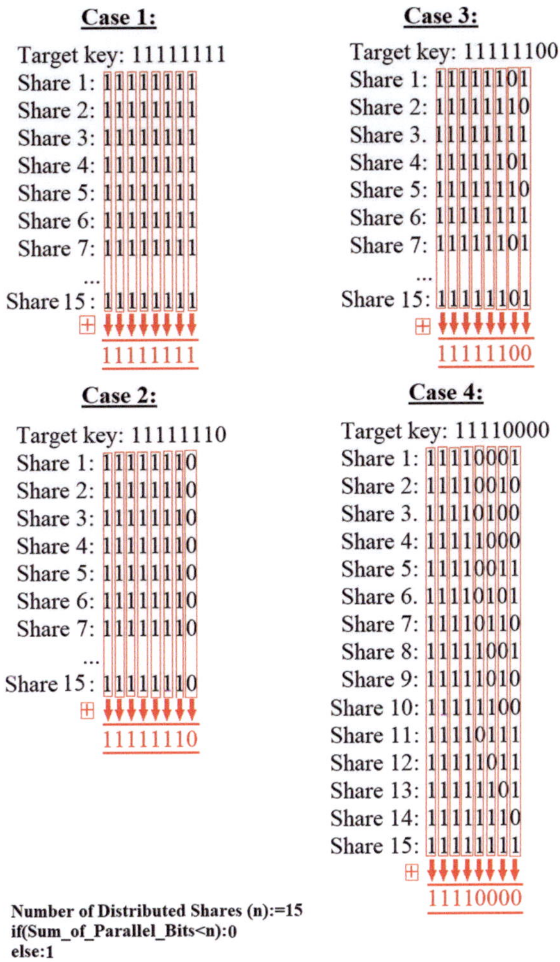

Fig. 3 Proposed secret reconstruction process

The results of the proposed model, which utilizes a counting-based approach for a single secret image-sharing scheme, are visually represented in Fig. 4. The original secret, sized at 256 × 256, is displayed in Fig. 4a. The shares, distributed via the cloud and generated using the bit-flip method, are shown in Fig. 4b–e. Finally, Fig. 4f unveils the recovered image, produced by applying the parallel bit counting operation to all the distributed shares.

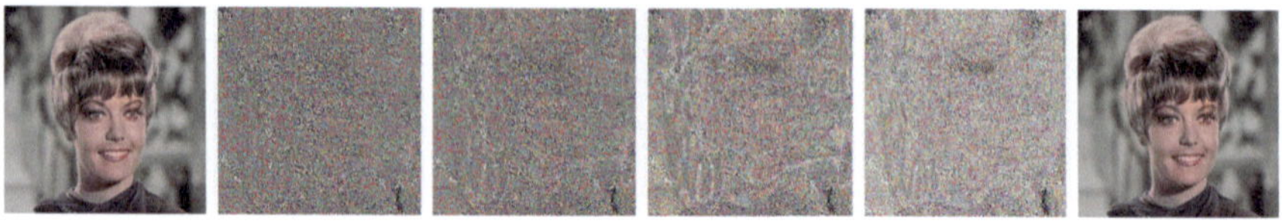

(a) S (b) Sh_1 (c) Sh_2 (d) Sh_3 (e) Sh_4 (f) R

Fig. 4 Proposed CSBC scheme : **a** original secret, **b–e** shared images, **f** secret recovery

4.1 Statistical Analysis

In the context of secret-sharing schemes using bit flip and parallel bits counting, the division of a secret into multiple shares is a key component, and these shares are subsequently distributed among multiple cloud servers. The evaluation of the secret image's efficiency and confidentiality, along with that of its associated shares and retrieved secrets, relies on statistical measurements. The effectiveness and security of counting-based secret-sharing techniques are evaluated using a number of statistical measures, including correlation, Root Mean Square Error (RMSE), and Peak Signal-to-Noise Ratio (PSNR).

1. **Correlation**: Telationship between two images, uses the correlation coefficient. Values close to 0 on a scale of –1 to 1 indicate no connection, values close to –1 show a negative correlation, and values close to 1 show a positive correlation. The correlation coefficient evaluation between images is determined using Eq. 1.

$$C_{X,Y} = \frac{\frac{1}{L}\sum_{i=1}^{L}(X_i - \bar{X})(Y_i - \bar{Y})}{\sqrt{\frac{1}{L}\sum_{i=1}^{L}(X_i - \bar{X})^2} \cdot \sqrt{\frac{1}{L}\sum_{i=1}^{L}(Y_i - \bar{Y})^2}} \tag{1}$$

   where the averages of X and Y are denoted as $\bar{X}$ and $\bar{Y}$ respectively.
2. **RMSE**: The Root Mean Square Error (RMSE) is a metric used to quantify how different two images are from one another. We compute the amount of error between these images using the Eq. 2.

$$RMSE = \sqrt{\frac{1}{s}\sum_{i=1}^{t}(X_i - Y_i)^2} \tag{2}$$

   The pixel value of images X and Y at location i is represented by X_i and Y_i, whereas s indicates the total pixels.
3. **PSNR**: The quality of an imagae is commonly conducted through the calculation of Peak Signal-to-Noise Ratio (PSNR). PSNR can be determined using Eq. 3:

$$PSNR = 20\log_{10}\left(\frac{255}{MSE}\right) \tag{3}$$

Table 1 Statistical analysis between secrets and shares

	Correl.	RMSE	PSNR
S, Sh_1	0.064	64.48	11.94
S, Sh_2	0.100	64.95	11.87
S, Sh_3	0.176	72.38	10.93
S, Sh_4	0.170	83.72	9.67

Table 2 Statistical analysis between shares

	Correl.	RMSE	PSNR
$Sh_{1,2}$	0.990	8.12	29.93
$Sh_{1,3}$	0.858	33.50	17.62
$Sh_{1,4}$	0.807	50.59	14.04
$Sh_{2,3}$	0.889	27.91	19.21
$Sh_{2,4}$	0.812	46.09	14.85
$Sh_{3,4}$	0.731	38.92	16.32

The term Mean Squared Error, or MSE, appears in this equation.

Several datasets and a 256×256 secret imags were used in the experimental analysis. Table 1 presents a statistical comparison using correlation, RMSE (Root Mean Square Error), and PSNR (Peak Signal-to-Noise Ratio) metrics between the secret and shares. The correlation value between the secret image and its shares is found to be very near to zero, indicating a significant difference. The larger RMSE value indicates a significant degree of inaccuracy between the shared image and the secret image, suggesting a higher level of randomization or dissimilarity between the two. The PSNR value reflects the difference between the secret image and its shares when it falls below 27 dB.

Table 2 presents a statistical analysis of the shares using correlation, RMSE (Root Mean Square Error), and PSNR (Peak Signal-to-Noise Ratio) metrics. The observed correlation value is approximately 0, indicating no relation between the shares. The high RMSE figure indicates a high degree of randomization and a certain amount of inaccuracy among the shares. The PSNR value, which is less than 27 dB, suggests that the shares are quite distinct. Overall, these statistical results support the notion that the proposed method generates moderately randomized shares, although the correlation values do not meet the required improvement criteria.

4.2 Parameter Comparison

A parameter comparison between the proposed scheme and various current schemes is shown in Table 3.

Table 3 Parameters comparison

Parameters	[13]	[14]	[15]	[16]	[17]	Proposed
Sharing type	Perfect-(n, n)	Perfect-(n, n)	Perfect-(n, n)	Perfect-(n, n)	Perfect-(n, n)	Perfect-(n, n)
Reveal information	No	No	No	No	Partial	Partial
Randomness of shares	High	–	–	High	Average	Average
Sharing capacity	$1/n$	$1/n$	$1/n$	n/t	$1/n$	$1/n$
Approach	CRT,XOR	DWT,AM	BO	CRT	CBSS	CSBC

1. **Sharing Type**: The counting single secret sharing system of (n, n) is used in the suggested scheme, where the shares needed for secret reconstruction are indicated by the following n and the shares to be distributed by the first n. The (n, n) variation of the single secret sharing scheme is likewise supported by the current schemes [13–17].
2. **Reveal Information**: The proposed scheme discloses partial information about the secret. Similarly, existing schemes [13–17] do not reveal any form of secret information. The proposed scheme is suitable for applications where minor degradation in security is acceptable if it enhances resource efficiency. Examples of such applications include encrypted backup systems and multi-party computation.
3. **Randomness of Shares**: Compared to existing schemes, the proposed scheme demonstrates average randomness when evaluated using statistical measures.
4. **Approach**: The suggested method uses a bit-flip and counting approach to share secret images in a lightweight cloud-based manner.
5. **Sharing Capacity**: The ratio of shared data (images) to secret data (images) determines sharing capacity. The proposed scheme is $\frac{1}{n}$. Current schemes [13–15, 17] support a $\frac{1}{n}$ sharing capacity, while scheme [16] supports a $\frac{n}{t}$ sharing capacity.

5 Conclusion and Future Work

This work introduces an innovative approach for securely sharing individual images within resource-constrained environments. The method generates shares using a counting-based bit-flip mechanism and then distributes them over a cloud network, then reconstruction process ensures lossless recovery through the utilization of the parallel bits counting technique. The technique yields moderately randomized shares and demonstrates impressive performance in various metrics, including correlation, RMSE, and PSNR, highlighting its potential. However, it is vital to acknowledge the scheme's limitations, especially its susceptibility to recovery when only a limited number of shares are available. To address this vulnerability and enhance the scheme's practicality in real-world scenarios with resource constraints, future research endeavors could focus on strengthening its security measures and overcoming the limitation.

References

1. Gutub A, Al-Juaid N, Khan E (2019) Counting-based secret sharing technique for multimedia applications. Multimed Tools Appl 78:5591–5619
2. Al-Ghamdi M, Al-Ghamdi M, Gutub A (2019) Security enhancement of shares generation process for multimedia counting-based secret-sharing technique. Multimed Tools Appl 78:16283–16310
3. Al-Qurashi A, Gutub A (2018) Reliable secret key generation for counting-based secret sharing. J Comput Sci Comput Math 8(4):87–101
4. Gutub A, Aydh Alaseri K (2021) Refining Arabic text stego-techniques for shares memorization of counting-based secret sharing. J King Saud Univ-Comput Inf Sci 33(9):1108–1120
5. Gutub A, Alaseri K (2020) Hiding shares of counting-based secret sharing via Arabic text steganography for personal usage. Arab J Sci Eng 45(4):2433–2458
6. Gutub A (2022) Regulating watermarking semi-authentication of multimedia audio via counting-based secret sharing. Pamukkale Üniversitesi Mühendislik Bilimleri Dergisi 28(2):324–332
7. Gutub A, Al-Ghamdi M (2019) Image based steganography to facilitate improving counting-based secret sharing. 3D Research 10:1–36
8. Gutub A, Al-Ghamdi M (2020) Hiding shares by multimedia image steganography for optimized counting-based secret sharing. Multimed Tools Appl 79(11–12):7951–7985
9. AlKhodaidi T, Gutub A (2021) Refining image steganography distribution for higher security multimedia counting-based secret-sharing. Multimed Tools Appl 80:1143–1173
10. Gutub A, Al-Qurashi A (2020) Secure shares generation via M-blocks partitioning for counting-based secret sharing. J Eng Res 8(3)
11. Gutub A, AlKhodaidi T (2020) Smart expansion of target key for more handlers to access multimedia counting-based secret sharing. Multimed Tools Appl 79:17373–17401
12. Alkhodaidi TM, Gutub AA (2022) Scalable shares generation to increase participants of counting-based secret sharing technique. Int J Inf Comput Secur 17(1–2):119–146
13. Pande D et al (2023) Single secret sharing scheme using Chinese remainder theorem, modified Shamir's scheme and XOR operation. Wirel Pers Commun 130(2):957–985
14. Rawat AS, Deshmukh M, Singh M (2023) QR shares based secret sharing scheme using DWT, random permutation and arithmetic modulo operation for QR secret. In: 10th International conference on signal processing and integrated networks (SPIN), pp 772–777. IEEE
15. Rawat AS, Deshmukh M, Singh M (2023) Natural share-based lightweight (n, n) single secret image sharing scheme using LSB stuffing for medical images. J Supercomput 79:1–30
16. Rawat AS, Deshmukh M, Singh M (2023) A novel multi secret image sharing scheme for different dimension secrets. Multimed Tools Appl 82:1–37
17. Parihar B, Deshmukh M, Rawat AS (2023) Efficient single secret image sharing in resource-constrained environment using counting-based secret sharing over cloud. Procedia Comput Sci 230:158–167

Android Malware Detection Based on Permissions and API Calls Using Ensemble Based Model

Monika, Yogesh K. Sharma, Deepak S. Tomar, and R. K. Pateriya

Abstract The Android operating system has revolutionized the mobile industry and society with its versatility and customization options. However, the increasing popularity of the Android system has caused a rise in the number of malware attacks, making it challenging to combat these threats. This study proposes a malware detection framework for Android systems that combines permissions and API calls as features. An autoencoder is used to reduce the feature set's dimensionality, and an ensemble model is employed for classification. The results show that the ensemble models outperform individual classifiers, achieving an accuracy of 98.99%. The study concludes that combining multiple classifiers and feature sets can lead to more accurate and reliable malware detection, providing a foundation for future research in the field of Android malware detection.

Keywords Android malware analysis · Static analysis · API-Calls · Permission

1 Introduction

Android is an open-source, free operating system, due to this fact its architecture may be thoroughly understood. As a result, a large number of manufacturers, including Google Pixel, Motorola, Samsung, and Sony, are using this OS to create mobile devices (smartphones, smartwatches, and smart glasses). Notably, the usage of OS has caused a sharp rise in the proportion of Android users. With a 71.52% market share in August 2022 [1], Android has risen to become the most popular mobile operating system at the moment. Due to its popularity, Android has been more frequently attacked by attackers than any other mobile operating system [2]. As a result, Android malware analysis has emerged as one of the most intriguing study topics.

Monika (✉) · Y. K. Sharma · D. S. Tomar · R. K. Pateriya
Department of Computer Science and Engineering, Maulana Azad National Institute of Technology, Bhopal, Madhya Pradesh, India
e-mail: monikarawat8991@gmail.com

B. N. Gohil et al. (eds.), *Information Security, Privacy and Digital Forensics*, Lecture Notes in Electrical Engineering 1423,
https://doi.org/10.1007/978-981-96-9443-3_7

Security experts often use malware analysis to detect malware in Android applications, which can be done through dynamic or static analysis or both in some cases. Applications are categorized as malicious or benign based on features, which pertain to the characteristics of the application. These features are typically used as inputs by machine learning classifiers for making decisions. In order to improve accuracy, i.e., create a more accurate predictive model with fewer data, minimize the complexity of the detection model, and limit the amount of noisy and irrelevant data, it is best to have a minimum number of useful features. This can help to create a more accurate predictive model.

By introducing a novel model that makes use of machine learning techniques and a fusion of various feature sets derived from unprocessed applications, the proposed work aims to improve the field of Android malware detection. This method is intended to identify and classify applications that could be malicious by behavior. The remainder of this paper is structured as follows: An overview of earlier studies in the subject of malware detection is given in Sect. 2. Section 3 delves into the proposed methodology. Section 4 talks about the analysis and results. Section 5 serves as the conclusion of the paper, accompanied by a discussion of potential future directions for this study.

2 Literature Review

With the growing popularity of Android, the number of malicious applications targeting it has increased. One common technique used by malware developers is to exploit the permission-based system in Android to gain unauthorized access to sensitive information. Over the past few years, numerous methods have been put forth for the identification of Android malware, with a focus on utilizing permissions as feature indicators.

There are two primary techniques employed in Android malware detection: static analysis and dynamic analysis. Static analysis entails the examination of an application's code without its execution, making it capable of uncovering hidden malware within the code [3]. Dynamic analysis involves executing the application and monitoring its behavior to detect malware that is activated at runtime [4]. A combination of both methods is often used in practice to provide more comprehensive coverage in detecting malware called as hybrid analysis.

2.1 *Static Analysis*

Rathore et al. [5] employed opcodes and their frequency of occurrence as characteristics to identify Android malware, making use of the Malicia Project dataset. Random Forest achieved the best level of accuracy at 99.74% when various machine learning methods (NB, KNN, and SVM) were used. Nonetheless, the dataset employed in this research was discontinued in 2016, and newer malware samples might have different characteristics, limiting the applicability of the study to current Android malware detection.

Idrees et al. [6] developed a machine learning-based Android app classifier called PIndroid, which utilizes both permissions and intent APIs for training. The classifier's overall accuracy in categorizing Android apps was 97.9% after it was trained on a dataset of more than 20,000 Android apps. The study highlights the importance of analyzing manifest file components such as permissions and intents for detecting mobile malware and suggests the need to find the best combination of permissions and intents for better accuracy in malware detection.

2.2 Dynamic Analysis

Dynamic features in Android malware detection often incorporate system calls due to their ability to furnish valuable insights into an application's behavior. Burguera et al. introduced CrowDroid, a malware detection framework that uses dynamic analysis to extract system calls and then clusters applications as benign or malware using K-means clustering. CrowDroid achieved high detection rates and a false positive rate of zero for a self-written malware dataset of 10 applications. However, the small size of the datasets used in the study could restrict how widely results can be used.

The stateless input generating tools Dynodroid [7] and Monkey [8] are used to simulate interactions. For the same function, DroidBot [9] is a stateful tool. A technique that identifies fraudulent Android apps using stateful input creation and deep learning was proposed by Alzaylaee et al. [10] in 2020. Theoretically, dynamic analysis is less resourceefficient but more reliable. However, due to the limitations on simulation duration and trigger methods, dynamic analysis cannot account for all program actions.

2.3 Permission-Based Android Malware Detection

Wang et al. [11] proposed a methodology for identifying Android malware that ranked permissions based on the risks involved, using T-test and Information Gain techniques to select the top 20 permissions with the highest ranks for analysis. They applied the Support Vector Machine algorithm and outperformed other machine learning algorithms in detecting Android malware. However, the ability to recognize covert programs that download malware while running is constrained by static approaches like this one.

In order to maximize the efficacy of their malware detection strategy, Sun et al. [12] used permission pruning techniques to narrow the available permissions count from 135 to 22. To evaluate the effectiveness of the selected permissions, they used a variety of classification algorithms, with FT achieving the greatest detection rate of

93.62%. The dataset used for this study, however, only includes applications that were published between 2012 and 2015, and has since been discontinued, limiting its applicability to current Android malware threats. Nonetheless, the study provides valuable insights into the potential of permission pruning methods for effective Android malware detection.

A system for Android malware detection that relies on permissions and makes use of numerous linear regression algorithms was introduced by Sahin et al. [13]. Permissions are extracted through static analysis, and machine learning techniques are used to analyze the security of applications. Two classifiers that used multiple linear regression techniques are compared to basic machine learning techniques, and the classification performance is improved using the bagging method. The outcomes indicate that classifiers built upon linear regression models exhibit strong performance, eliminating the necessity for exceedingly intricate classification algorithms.

3 Proposed Work

The proposed research aims to develop a method for identifying whether Android applications are benign or malicious using static features such as API calls and permissions. The method involves extracting features from the Smali files and AndroidManifest.xml, reducing the number of features using an autoencoder, classifying the applications using ensemble learning techniques, and evaluating the model's performance. This research aims to provide a more accurate and efficient way of detecting malicious Android applications.

The proposed workflow for creating the initial feature set is illustrated in Fig. 1. The main objectives are:

- To create an android malware feature set using API calls and permissions extracted from component files of android apk i.e., Smali files and AndroidManifest.xml respectively.
- To perform feature reduction using Autoencoders.
- To classify the android application as malicious or benign using ensemble learning techniques such as, bagging and boosting ensemble technique.
- To assess the classification outcomes and gauge the model's accuracy and efficacy.

3.1 Dataset

The dataset used in this study includes APKs obtained from two different sources: the Drebin dataset [14] and the AndroZoo dataset. The Drebin dataset is widely known and highly recommended for use in studies pertaining to Android malware analysis [15]. It consists of 5560 samples of malware across 179 distinct malware families, as well as 123,453 benign samples collected during the years 2010 and 2012. Conversely, the AndroZoo dataset [16] serves as an expanding archive of Android

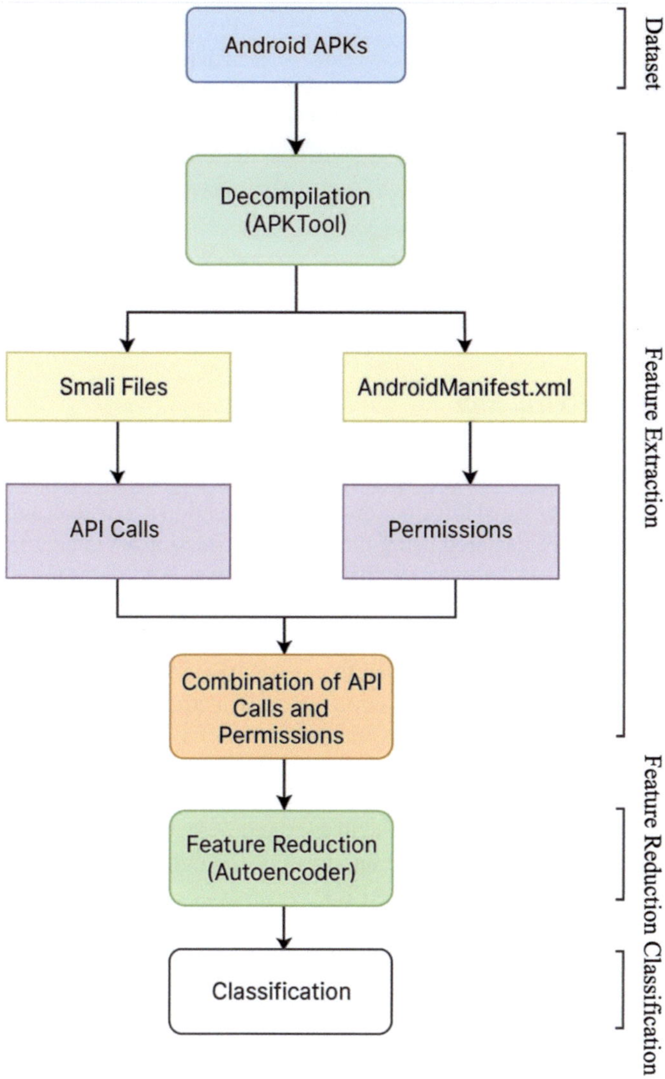

Fig. 1 Proposed workflow diagram

apps taken from diverse origins, including the Microsoft Google Play store. Two sets of Android applications were selected from these datasets: one comprising 250 applications and the other comprising 500 applications.

```
<uses-permission android:name="com.google.android.permission.PROVIDE_BACKGROUND"/>
<uses-permission android:name="android.permission.VIBRATE"/>
<uses-permission android:name="android.permission.WAKE_LOCK"/>
```

Fig. 2 Android permissions in AndroidManifest.xml

```
invoke-virtual {v0, v2}, Landroid/os/Parcel;->writeInterfaceToken(Ljava/lang/String;

invoke-virtual {v0, p1}, Landroid/os/Parcel;->writeInt(I)V

invoke-virtual {v0, p2}, Landroid/os/Parcel;->writeTypedList(Ljava/util/List;)V
```

Fig. 3 API calls in Smali files

3.2 Feature Extraction

APK files were decompiled using APKTool to extract the AndroidManifest.xml and Smali Files, which provided information on the application's metadata and low-level code. Permissions are declared using the < uses-permission > element in AndroidManifest.xml files. In order to extract these permissions, AndroidManifest.xml files were scanned to extract permissions following the keyword "android.permission" as shown in Fig. 2.

Similarly, Smali files were scanned to extract API calls following the keyword "invoke". The term "invoke" is often associated with method invocation, which refers to calling a method or function in the Smali code (which is a low-level representation of Android application code), this is shown in Fig. 3.

The extraction process was implemented using Python, resulting in the extraction of 124,083 API Call features from Smali files and 130 permissions from AndroidManifest.xml files. Combining these features into a single feature set allowed for a more comprehensive analysis of the APKs.

3.3 Feature Reduction

However, to manage the large number of features extracted, an autoencoder [17] is employed to convert the initial set of features into a more efficient and refined set of features for training and testing. The autoencoder [18] is a kind of neural network that can learn the most important features of a dataset and transforming them into a lower-dimensional space, while still retaining most of the original information (Fig. 4).

An autoencoder consists of an encoder and a decoder. The encoder takes in input data, such as a picture, and compresses it into a bottleneck or code layer, which is a representation in reduced dimensions. The key components of the input are captured by this layer. The bottleneck layer typically contains fewer neurons than the input layer, its goal is to reduce the error between the input and the decoder's output while

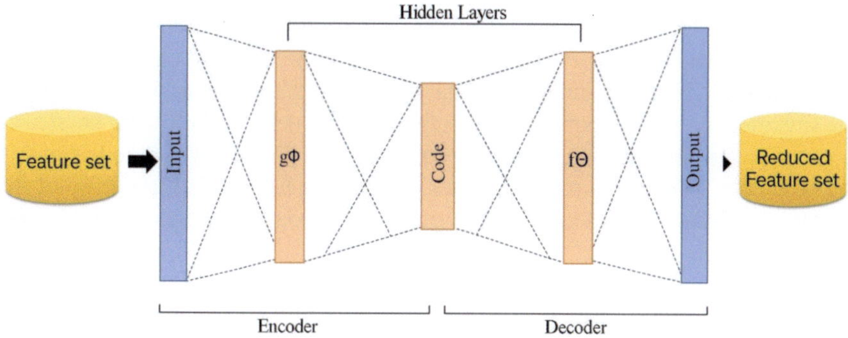

Fig. 4 Architecture of autoencoder

reconstruction, this forces the autoencoder to learn a more efficient and compact representation of the data, which can be used for various tasks such as classification or data visualization [19].

The calculation of the reconstruction error is performed using the following equation:

$$L(\theta, \emptyset) = \frac{1}{n}\sum_{i=1}^{n}(x_i - f_\theta(g_\emptyset(x_i)))^2$$

where Ø and θ are the parameters that define the encoder and the decoder respectively, $g_\emptyset$ and f_θ represent the encoder and decoder respectively. They are the weights and bias of the neural network. x_i is the original image whereas f_θ $(g_\emptyset(x_i))$ is the reconstructed image.

As a result, the bottleneck layer can serve as a set of features for the training and testing of machine learning models. The decoder then takes this code and reconstructs the original input data as closely as possible.

Using autoencoder the feature set is reduced from 124,213 features to just 300 features. This reduction in the number of features made it easier to process the data and improved the performance of the machine learning models. Following the reduction of the feature set to 300 features through an autoencoder, this condensed feature set is subsequently divided into separate training and testing datasets. The training dataset is employed for machine learning model training purposes, while the testing dataset is utilized to assess the models' performance.

3.4 Classification

Two ensemble learning models, Bagging [20] and AdaBoost [21], were used for classification in this study. In the boosting ensemble method, multiple weak models are trained sequentially, where each subsequent model focuses on correcting the errors made by the previous model [22]. During training, the boosting algorithm assigns higher weights to the misclassified data points in each iteration, which increases the importance of these points in the subsequent models. The ultimate prediction is generated by amalgamating the projections of all individual weak models within the ensemble. This technique contributes to enhancing the overall accuracy of the model, particularly in scenarios involving imbalanced data or an abundance of noisy features.

Bagging, short for Bootstrap Aggregating, represents an ensemble learning approach employed to enhance the precision and reliability of machine learning models. Within a bagging ensemble model, numerous models undergo training on distinct subsets of the training data, with these subsets being sampled with replacement from the original dataset [22].

Each model within the ensemble is autonomously trained, employing a subset of the data that is taken at random, and the ultimate prediction is generated by taking an average of the output produced by all the models within the ensemble.

The bagging method contributes to mitigating overfitting and enhancing the model's stability by diminishing the influence of noisy or irrelevant features present in the dataset. The random sampling of the training data also helps to increase the diversity among the models in the ensemble, which can boost the model's general performance. These models were implemented using three different base classifiers, including decision tree, decision stump, and naive Bayes.

The decision tree is a popular classifier that works by modeling decisions and possible outcomes in the form of a tree like model [23]. Decision stumps are simple decision trees with only one split, which are often used as weak classifiers in ensemble learning [24]. The Naive Bayes classifier, which is based on the Bayes theorem, makes solid assumptions about the independence of the features [25]. By combining these base classifiers using the bagging and AdaBoost algorithms, the ensemble models succeeded in enhancing the accuracy of the classification task while diminishing overfitting.

4 Results

Initially, the experiment is conducted using a feature set that exclusively consisted of permissions. This is a feature set containing 130 permissions as features for 250 applications. The results as shown in Table 1, suggest that the ensemble model performed better than the individual base classifiers for all three machine learning models.

For the Decision Tree and Decision Stump classifier, the accuracy of the ensemble model increased to 88.33%, compared to the individual base classifiers which both had an accuracy score of 83.8%. This indicates that the ensemble model is able to produce a more accurate classification. Similarly, for the Naïve Bayes classifier, the accuracy of the ensemble model increased to 86.33%, compared to the accuracy of

Table 1 Machine Learning model performance for individual feature set and combination of features

Features	Sample	Base classifier	Model type	Accuracy (%)
Permission	250	Decision	Individual Classifier	83.8
		Tree	Bagging	88.33
		Decision	Individual Classifier	83.8
		Stump	AdaBoost	88.33
		Naïve	Individual Classifier	76.52
		Bayes	AdaBoost	86.33
API calls	250	Decision	Individual Classifier	88.67
		Tree	Bagging	91.56
		Decision	Individual Classifier	85.49
		Stump	AdaBoost	89.43
		Naïve	Individual Classifier	82.84
		Bayes	AdaBoost	88.26
Combination of permission and API Call	250	Decision	Individual Classifier	92.03
		Tree	Bagging	97.82
		Decision	Individual Classifier	90.55
		Stump	AdaBoost	98.29
		Naïve	Individual Classifier	82.56
		Bayes	AdaBoost	95.89
Permission	500	Decision	Individual Classifier	85.8
		Tree	Bagging	89.54
		Decision	Individual Classifier	84.18
		Stump	AdaBoost	86.69
		Naïve	Individual Classifier	80.22
		Bayes	AdaBoost	84.33
API calls	500	Decision	Individual Classifier	89.27
		Tree	Bagging	93.64
		Decision	Individual Classifier	86.99
		Stump	AdaBoost	91.36
		Naïve	Individual Classifier	80.84
		Bayes	AdaBoost	89.12
Combination of permission and API call	500	Decision	Individual Classifier	93.73
		Tree	Bagging	98.25
		Decision	Individual Classifier	92.15
		Stump	AdaBoost	98.99
		Naïve	Individual Classifier	85.61
		Bayes	AdaBoost	97.29

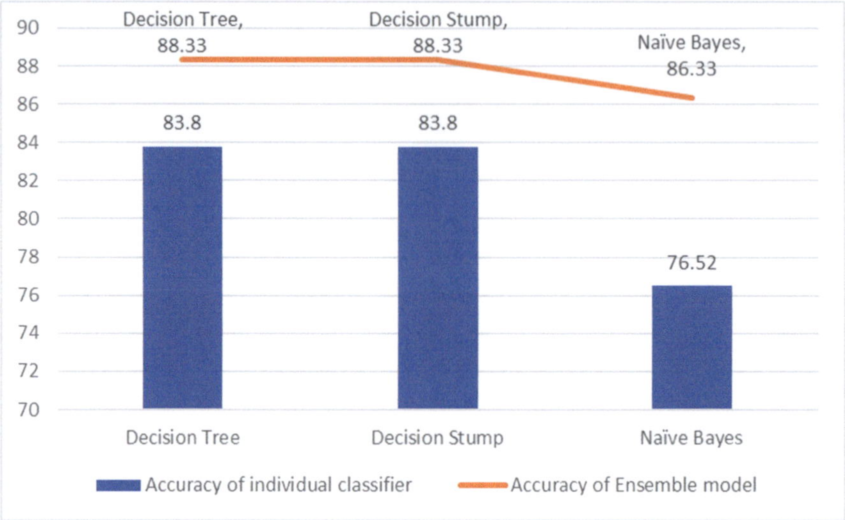

Fig. 5 Graph showing accuracy of individual classifiers and ensemble models using only permission-based feature set (250 applications)

the individual classifier which is 76.52%. This suggests that the ensemble model has the capacity to enhance the classification performance of the weaker base classifier as shown in Fig. 5.

The experiment is also conducted using features consisting of only API calls. As shown in Table 1, the results indicate that utilizing ensemble models can be a promising strategy for enhancing the accuracy of classification models, particularly when employing a variety of base classifiers with diverse strengths and limitations.

After the initial experiment using a feature set that included only a single feature, the experiment is repeated using a combined feature set that included both permissions and API calls as shown in Table 1. This allowed for a more comprehensive analysis of the classification performance by incorporating additional features that could provide more information about the behavior of the apps. By expanding the feature set, the classification model is able to capture more nuanced patterns and potentially improve the accuracy of the model.

The results as shown in the Table 1, suggest that for all three machine learning models, the accuracy of the ensemble model is higher than that of the individual base classifiers, indicating that ensemble models can effectively improve the classification performance.

For the Decision Tree classifier, the accuracy of the ensemble model increased to 97.82%, compared to the accuracy of the individual classifier which is 92.03%. Similarly, for the Decision Stump classifier, the accuracy of the ensemble model

Table 2 Comparison of proposed work with previous works

Study	Features	Classifier	Accuracy (%)
Wang et al. [11]	Permissions	SVM, Decision Tree and Random Forest,	94.62
SigPID [12]	Permissions	Rotation Forest, Random Forest, FT, PART, SVM	93.62
LinRegDroid [13]	Permissions	KNN, Naive Bayes, Decision Trees, SMV	96.69
Proposed work	Permissions only	Decision Tree, Decision Stump, KNN, Naive Bayes, Decision Trees	89.54
Proposed work	Permissions and API Calls	Decision Tree, Decision Stump, KNN, Naive Bayes, Decision Trees	98.99

increased to 98.29%, compared to the accuracy of the individual classifier which is 90.55%. This suggests that the ensemble models were able to combine the strengths of both classifiers to produce a more accurate classification. For the Naïve Bayes classifier, the accuracy of the ensemble model increased to 95.89%, compared to the accuracy of the individual classifier which is 82.56%. This indicates that the ensemble model has the capacity to enhance the classification performance of the weaker base classifier.

When the experiment is replicated with a set of a total of 500 applications, similar results are obtained. The ensemble models outperformed the individual classifiers, with AdaBoost achieving the highest accuracy rate of 98.99% as shown in Table 1. Decision stump is used as the base classifier, while the feature set included a combination of permissions and API calls.

Table 2 compares the results of proposed work with the results of existing studies.

As shown in Table 2, studies [11–13] employ permissions as features, achieving a maximum accuracy of 96.69%. When solely relying on permissions as features, the performance of proposed model is comparatively lower. However, when utilizing a feature set that combines both permissions and API calls, the performance increases by approximately 2%, reaching 98.99%, surpassing [13]. This emphasizes that using permissions alone is not sufficient to classify an android application into malware and good ware the proposed model's (Fig. 6).

The results suggest that ensemble models can be an effective approach for improving the accuracy of classification models, especially when using multiple base classifiers with different strengths and weaknesses. Additionally, the experiment demonstrated that expanding the feature set to include both permissions and API calls can significantly improve the classification performance, as seen by the high accuracy scores for all three machine learning models.

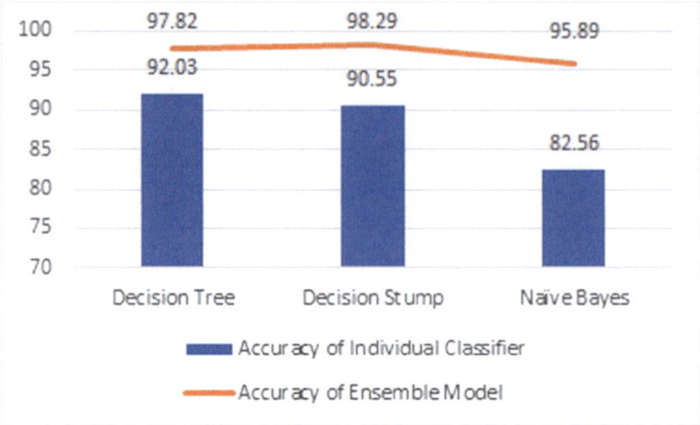

Fig. 6 Graph showing accuracy of individual classifiers and ensemble models using combination of permissions and API Call-based feature set (250 applications)

5 Conclusion

A study is conducted to identify malicious application built for Android systems using a combination of permissions and API calls as features. An autoencoder is used to reduce the feature set, and an ensemble model is used to combine the predictions of base classifiers for improved accuracy. The findings demonstrated that ensemble models can effectively enhance the accuracy of classifying security threats in mobile apps. The inclusion of API calls as features significantly improved the classification accuracy, and the ensemble model achieved high levels of accuracy.

The study's findings illustrate the efficacy of employing a combination of Android system features such as permissions requested by the Android application and API calls generated, for Android malware detection. The inclusion of API calls as features significantly improved the classification accuracy for all three machine learning models, suggesting that the additional information provided by API calls can better distinguish between malicious and benign apps. The ensemble model achieved high levels of accuracy, with an overall accuracy of 98.99% for the Decision Stump base classifier. These findings provide valuable insights into the development of more effective approaches for detecting Android malware and can inform future research in this area. The experiments demonstrate the effectiveness of ensemble models and the significance of feature selection for machine learning in improving the accuracy of classification models for mobile app security threats. These findings can help guide future research in developing more effective approaches for identifying and mitigating mobile app security threats.

References

1. StatCounter (2022) Mobile Operating System Market Share Worldwide. https://gs.statcounter.com/os-market-share/mobile/worldwide. Last Accessed: 2022/09/03
2. More than 99 percent of all malware designed for mobile devices targets Android devices, explained Olaf Pursche, Head of Communications at AV-TEST, in the F-Secure State of Cyber Security 2017. https://blog.f-secure.com/another-reason-99-percent-of-mobile-malware-targets-androids/. Last Accessed: 2022/08/31
3. Pan Y, Xiuting G, Chunrong F, Yong F (2020) A systematic literature review of android malware detection using static analysis. IEEE Access 8:116363–116379
4. Amin MR, Zaman M, Hossain MS, Atiquzzaman M (2016) Behavioral malware detection approaches for Android. In: 2016 IEEE International conference on communications (ICC). IEEE, pp 1–6
5. Rathore H, Swati A, Sanjay KS, Mohit S (2018) Malware detection using machine learning and deep learning. In: Big data analytics: 6th international conference, BDA 2018, Warangal, India, 2018, Proceedings 6. Springer International Publishing, pp 402–411
6. Idrees F, Muttukrishnan R, Mauro C, Thomas MC, Yogachandran R (2017) PIndroid: a novel Android malware detection system using ensemble learning methods. Comput Secur 68:36–46
7. Machiry A, Rohan T, Mayur N (2013) Dynodroid: an input generation system for android apps. In: Proceedings of the 2013 9th Joint meeting on foundations of software engineering, pp 224–234
8. Xu J, Yingjiu L, Robert D, Ke X (2020) Sdac: a slow-aging solution for android malware detection using semantic distance based api clustering. In: IEEE transactions on dependable and secure computing
9. Li Y, Ziyue Y, Yao G, Xiangqun C (2017) Droidbot: a lightweight ui-guided test input generator for android. In: 2017 IEEE/ACM 39th International conference on software engineering companion (ICSE-C). IEEE, pp 23–26
10. Alzaylaee MK, Yerima SK, Sakir S (2020) DL-Droid: deep learning based android malware detection using real devices. Comput Secur 89:101663
11. Wang W, Wang X, Feng D, Liu J, Han Z, Zang X (2014) Exploring permission-induced risk in android applications for malicious application detection. In: IEEE transactions on information forensics and security, vol 9, pp 1869–1882
12. Sun L, Li Z, Yan Q, Witawas S, Yu P (2016) SigPID: significant permission identification for android malware detection. In: 11th International conference on malicious and unwanted software (MALWARE). IEEE, pp 1–8
13. Sahin DQ, Sedat A, Erdal K (2022) LinRegDroid: detection of android malware using multiple linear regression models-based classifiers. IEEE Access 10:14246–14259
14. Arp D, Spreitzenbarth M, Hubner M, Gascon H, Rieck K, Siemens CERT (2014) Drebin: effective and explainable detection of android malware in your pocket. Ndss 23
15. Monika M, Yogesh KS, Deepak ST, Pateriya RK (2023) Analysing mobile forensic datasets: a systematic review on availability, efficacy, and limitations. In: ITM Web of conferences, vol 54. EDP Sciences, p 03002
16. Allix K, Bissyande´ TF, Klein J, Traon YL (2016) Androzoo: collecting millions of android apps for the research community. In: IEEE/ACM 13th Working conference on mining software repositories (MSR), vol 468
17. Srivastava A, Ankita A, Mohd AN, Abdullah N, Aradhana T (2022) MalTDec3: malicious traffic detection in a network using 3 layer inspection. In: 2022 Fifth international conference on computational intelligence and communication technologies (CCICT), pp 568–575. IEEE
18. Gao N, Ling G, Yi-yue H, Hai W (2017) A lightweight intrusion detection model based on autoencoder network with feature reduction. In: ACTA electonica sinica 45(3):730
19. Zavrak S, Murat I (2020) Anomaly-based intrusion detection from network flow features using variational autoencoder. IEEE Access 8:108346–108358

20. Sifat S, Sakir MH, Sadia Afrin T, Bejoy M, Riftana M, Hossain MS (2023) Android ransomware attacks detection with optimized ensemble learning. In: Advances in cybersecurity, cybercrimes, and smart emerging technologies, pp 41–53. Springer International Publishing, Cham
21. Bhagwat S, Govind PG (2022) Android malware detection using hybrid meta-heuristic feature selection and ensemble learning techniques. In: Advances in computing and data sciences: 6th international conference, ICACDS 2022, Kurnool, India. Revised Selected Papers, Part I. Springer International Publishing, Cham, pp 145–156
22. Ganaie MA, Hu M, Malik AK, Tanveer M, Suganthan PN (2022) Ensemble deep learning: a review. Eng Appl Artif Intell 115:105151
23. Bansal M, Apoorva G, Apoorva C (2022) A comparative analysis of K-Nearest Neighbour, genetic, support vector machine, decision tree, and long short-term memory algorithms in machine learning. Decis Anal J 100071
24. Chen Y, Yuanqing Z, Yulei T A comparative study of the cost–benefit strategy with the learning ensembles of decision stumps in polymetallic prospectivity modelling. In: Earth science informatics, pp 1–16
25. Wickramasinghe I, Harsha K (2021) Naive Bayes: applications, variations and vulnerabilities: a review of literature with code snippets for implementation. In: Soft computing, vol 25, no. 3, pp 2277–2293

Fighting Cybercrime at Domain Names Level: A Comparative Analysis of Tools and Techniques for Identifying Malicious Domain Names

Harish Chowdhary and Naveen Kumar Chaudhary

Abstract This study makes a pivotal contribution to cybersecurity research by conducting a comprehensive analysis of global tools and techniques for detecting malicious domain names. Setting itself apart from existing literature, it thoroughly evaluates the strengths and weaknesses of these tools, offering a global viewpoint and underscoring the specific cybersecurity needs of India. At the core of this research is an in-depth examination of the Domain Name System (DNS), a fundamental component of various Internet services, which is frequently exploited in cyber-attacks. We delve into the sophisticated tactics of malicious actors who use domain names for disseminating malware, orchestrating C&C communications, and hosting phishing sites, thereby highlighting the critical role of DNS in these threats. A significant facet of our study is the comparative analysis of widely-used Malicious Domain Detection (MDD) techniques, such as DNS analysis and DNS traffic measurement. This analysis provides an insightful perspective on their benefits and limitations, showcasing the depth of our methodological comparative analysis. Distinctly, this paper proposes an innovative system dedicated to monitoring and detecting malicious '.in' domains. This system is not just a response to the gap in India's cybersecurity defenses but also a strategic approach to combating domain name abuse in the country's ccTLD. It offers a scalable and robust model, potentially adaptable for other regions with similar challenges. This approach is crucial for bolstering cybersecurity in India to provide a template for global cybersecurity enhancements.

Keywords Malicious domain names · DNS measurements · .IN domains · Cyber-security · ccTLD of India · Malicious domain detection · Domain name abuse

---

H. Chowdhary (✉)
School of Doctoral Studies and Research, National Forensic Sciences University, Gandhinagar, Gujarat, India
e-mail: intern3tgovernance@gmail.com

N. K. Chaudhary
School of Cyber Security and Digital Forensics, National Forensic Sciences University, Gandhinagar, Gujarat, India
e-mail: naveen.chaudhary@nfsu.ac.in

B. N. Gohil et al. (eds.), *Information Security, Privacy and Digital Forensics*, Lecture Notes in Electrical Engineering 1423,
https://doi.org/10.1007/978-981-96-9443-3_8

1 Introduction

The exponential growth of the Internet has precipitated a parallel increase in cyber-attacks, employing benign services and protocols to advance malicious objectives. These attacks often exploit domain names, URLs, and IP addresses, necessitating their accurate identification to mitigate cyber threats.Central to this dynamic is the Domain Name System (DNS), introduced in 1983 (IETF RFCs 882), which plays a crucial role in mapping domain names to IP addresses and supporting Internet services [1]. The analysis of DNS data for malicious domain detection, due to its relative smallness in overall network traffic, emerges as an effective solution [2, 3].

Malicious actors exploit domain names to facilitate numerous cybercrime activities, such as spam, phishing, malware distribution, and botnet command and control [4, 5]. The complex issue of designing a reliable and flexible server infrastructure and command and control mechanism is a significant challenge faced by these attackers. One common method they employ is the use of botnets—executable applications found on hacked hosts, which receive their instructions from a Command and Control (C&C) server controlled by the malicious actors, known as a bot-master. Botnets attempt to increase the number of impacted hosts, often leading to large-scale cyber security threats such as Distributed Denial of Service (DDoS) attacks, widespread spam campaigns, and identity theft [6].

In response to this ongoing issue, numerous tools and techniques have been developed to detect malicious domains. These methods employ different identifiers such as DNS analysis, DNS traffic measurement, each with their unique advantages and disadvantages. This paper aims to undertake a comprehensive comparative analysis of these significant tools and techniques used worldwide, comparing their strengths and weaknesses. A particular focus will be on the use of a security measure involving the C&C server that the botnets attempt to contact. Attackers often employ DNS agility or fluxing methods, rapidly changing their domain names or IP addresses to evade detection and inclusion on organizational blacklists [1, 7, 8].

Given the absence of a specific Internet and DNS measurement system for India's ".in" domains, this research also emphasizes the need for such a mechanism. Despite more than 3.0 million active.in domains, no dedicated system currently exists for detecting malicious.in domains, representing a significant vulnerability in India's sovereign digital space [9, 10]. In light of these factors, the objective of this study is to conduct an exhaustive comparative analysis of existing tools and techniques for detecting malicious domains, compare them, and propose a dedicated system "intelli" for monitoring and detecting malicious '.in' domains. This system would amalgamate the benefits of existing tools while also addressing their shortcomings, providing a more comprehensive and targeted approach to countering cyber threats in India's digital landscape.

1.1 The Importance of Detection of Malicious Domain Names to Understand and Prevent Cybercrime

The detection of malicious domain names is a critical aspect of cybersecurity, given the increasing number of internet users and the subsequent rise in domain registrations, a significant portion of which are malicious [11]. The challenge has been further complicated by the introduction of Internationalized Domain Names in Applications (IDNA), allowing non-English Unicode domain names, making recognition and validation more complex [12]. To address this, research efforts have focused on employing machine learning algorithms like AdaBoost and Random Forest to analyze domain characteristics and identify potential threats, utilizing WHOIS records and DNS-based features for early threat detection. Furthermore, the early identification and blocking of malicious domains at the registration stage by domain registries and registrars can significantly mitigate cyber threats, emphasizing the importance of proactive methods [11]. Research has shown that cybercriminals often use strategies like mass registration and reusing domains for malicious purposes. These findings underscore the effectiveness of using machine learning techniques, dynamic graph models, and spatial–temporal analyses to accurately detect such domains while minimizing false positives. Proposed methods like Premadoma, DomainProfiler, and DyDom show promise in thwarting malicious registrations. Hence, the detection of malicious domain names is crucial for safeguarding the internet and ensuring its integrity and safety. Continuous research in this domain is imperative to refine detection methods and develop robust countermeasures against cybercrime, as evidenced by the insights provided by various studies.

1.2 Important Steps for Detection of Malicious Domain Names

Collection of DNS Information: The process involves acquiring data from different segments of the DNS framework, each offering varying depths of information. Data sourcing ranges from the recursive DNS servers of businesses or ISPs to more sophisticated authority servers. This data might appear as detailed query/response logs or in condensed summaries. The source and depth of this data play a pivotal role in identifying patterns linked to harmful domains, significantly influencing the conceptualization and formulation of detection algorithms [13].

Improving DNS Data Analysis: To comprehensively understand malicious activities, integrating DNS data with varied network and application insights is crucial. This typically involves adding details like domain registration information, autonomous system numbers, and geographical locations associated with the IP addresses hosting these domains [14].

Formulating Detection Algorithms: These algorithms target potential malicious domains by leveraging DNS data, supplementary insights, and sometimes, knowledge of known benign and malevolent domains. Various machine learning approaches, including supervised, semi-supervised, and unsupervised models, are modified to suit this context, based on different assumptions about the behavior of harmful domains [15]. Establishing a Ground Truth: Developing and accessing these algorithms requires a baseline set of domains, categorized as harmful or safe. For supervised and semi-supervised models, this ground truth is crucial to train the algorithm and tweak vital parameters for maximum efficacy. The collection, purification, and implementation of this dataset significantly affect the evaluation of the algorithms [16].

2 Background and Literature Review

The Internet relies heavily on the Domain Name System (DNS) and domain names. DNS serves as the digital directory of the internet, translating human-friendly domain names into numerical Internet Protocol (IP) addresses that computers use to identify each other on the network. Domain names serve as the identifier for internet resources, such as web sites and email servers.

DNS and domain names play an integral role in cyber-attacks. DNS, being a critical internet infrastructure, often becomes a focal point for cybercriminals. A common form of DNS-based attack is DNS spoofing or cache poisoning, where hackers manipulate a DNS server's cache, causing it to provide an incorrect IP address and redirect users to malicious sites [17].

Similarly, domain names are exploited in phishing attacks. Malicious actors can create deceptive domain names, designed to mimic genuine ones, leading users to fraudulent sites [18]. Further, attackers use domain generation algorithms (DGAs) to produce numerous pseudo-random domain names, making it challenging for defenders to block malicious sites [19].

Recognizing these security vulnerabilities, standards like DNS Security Extensions (DNSSEC) have been developed. DNSSEC adds a layer of security to the DNS lookup process by enabling DNS responses to be digitally signed. By verifying these signatures, it ensures that the users are directed to the correct IP address, thus mitigating the risk of DNS spoofing [20]. However, despite its advantages, DNSSEC adoption has been slow due to various reasons such as complexity of implementation, lack of perceived necessity, and potential performance issues [21].

In the wake of increasing cyber-attacks, it is imperative that the adoption of security measures like DNSSEC is prioritized. Efforts need to be made to address the barriers preventing their implementation, and greater awareness needs to be fostered regarding the importance of these security standards. It's essential for the safety of the digital space that mechanisms that fortify the security of domain names and DNS are developed and effectively implemented.

3 Methodology

In this section, we detail the methodology adopted for our study on malicious domain registration detection and prevention. This approach encompasses a comprehensive literature review, a nuanced comparison of machine learning models, in-depth data analysis, and the development of the "Intelli" system.

3.1 Literature Review

- **Selection and Analysis of Papers**: Commencing with an extensive search across academic databases, we identified 110 papers using targeted keywords. The rigorous selection process, which involved screening based on abstracts followed by full-paper review, refined this pool to 72 papers. Our criteria focused on relevance, citation count, recency, and empirical robustness.
- **Review Process**: This stage laid the groundwork for the study, ensuring a robust foundation of current knowledge and methodologies in the field and presented in presented in Table 1.

3.2 Comparative Analysis of Machine Learning Techniques

- **Development of Comparison Table**: Transitioning from the broad literature review, we focused on a detailed comparative analysis. A comprehensive Table 3 was constructed to analyze machine learning models like Random Forest, AdaBoost, XGBoost, and GPT-based models, considering factors such as architecture, efficiency, and specific performance metrics.
- **Criteria for Comparison**: This analytical step was crucial in identifying the most effective models for detecting malicious domains, paving the way for the development of our unique system, "Intelli".

3.3 Aggregated Analysis: "Insights from Malicious Domain Detection Studies"

- **Compilation of Cybersecurity Metrics**: Building upon the comparative analysis, we synthesized cybersecurity metrics from the literature. This encompassed Web and Domain Security, Redirection Campaigns, and Phishing Detection, among others and presented in Table 4.
- **Analytical Approach**: The insights gained here were instrumental in both understanding the landscape of malicious domain detection and in shaping the direction of our subsequent data analysis.

Table 1 Comparative study of malicious domain name detection systems

References	Research aim and objective of the study	Technique/method used	Statistics/key data/ findings
[24]	This study extensively scrutinizes 14 months of registration data to identify large-scale malicious campaigns present in the. eu TLD	Analysis of registration data	80.04% malicious domains belonged to 20 larger campaigns. Processes were only partially automated
[25]	This paper discusses Premadoma, a solution for DNS registries to predict malicious intent well before a domain name becomes operational	Premadoma—predictive system	Decrease in malicious registrations in.eu ccTLD registry. Three evasion patterns identified
[26]	This study proposes a system for discovering malicious domain names that will likely be abused in future, by exploiting temporal variation patterns (TVPs) of domain names	Exploiting temporal variation patterns (TVPs)	Predicted malicious domain names 220 days ahead with a true positive rate of 0.985
[27]	Study examines the registration process of domains used by spammers. It finds that spammers use bulk registration and often re-use domains previously registered by others	Analysing registration processes of spammers	Spammers use bulk registration and reuse domains
[28]	This study aims to investigates cybercrime in new gTLDs	Comparative study of new gTLD and legacy gTLD	New gTLDs diverted abuse from legacy ones. Increased tendency to register than hack domain names
[29]	This paper discusses the problem of residual domain trust and how it can be exploited by adversaries. It proposes a technical remedy (Alembic) and discusses several policy remedies	Observational study and algorithm	27,758 domains from blacklists and 238,279 domains resolved by malware were maliciously re-registered. Proposed "Alembic" for passive DNS observations
[30]	This paper discusses a method for mining DNS data to find malicious domain registrations	Random Forest classifier based on second order Markov models	Effective in identifying malicious domains with a minimal false positive rate

(continued)

Table 1 (continued)

References	Research aim and objective of the study	Technique/method used	Statistics/key data/ findings
[31]	This paper aims provide an operational solution for DNS registries to prevent malicious domain registrations	Premadoma—predictive system	Detected and prevented malicious registrations. Contributed to the takedown of 58,966 registrations in 2018
[32]	This study explores the Tunnelling Behaviours in Malicious Domains with Self-Organizing Maps	Unsupervised learning using Self-organizing Maps (SOMs)	F1 measure reached 99% across varied testing conditions
[33]	This paper objective is to discuss typo squatting, a practice where typo squatters register misspelled variants of existing domain names to profit from users' typing mistakes. It describes how typo squatting is a widespread issue which plays an important role in exposing users to malice	Large-scale measurement study	Identified millions of overlooked typo squatting domains
[34]	This study Discover Malicious Domains through Alias-Canonical Graph	Calculating probabilities of domains being malicious using DNS CNAME records	Accuracy over 97.25% with a false positive rate of less than 0.027%
[35]	Objective of this study is to discovering Malicious Domains through Passive DNS Data Graph Analysis	Global associations among domains	High true positive rates with low false positive rates
[36]	Detection of Newly Registered Malicious Domains through Passive DNS	Machine learning using LightGBM	Average AUC of 0.9763 and F1-score of 0.905
[37]	This work proposes COMAR, an approach to differentiate between compromised and maliciously registered domains	An approach to differentiate between compromised and maliciously registered domains, complementary to previously proposed domain reputation systems	COMAR can achieve high accuracy (97% accuracy with a 2.5% false-positive rate) without using any privileged or non-publicly available data

(continued)

Table 1 (continued)

References	Research aim and objective of the study	Technique/method used	Statistics/key data/ findings
[38]	Objective of this study is to proposes a system, DyDom, to detect malicious domains by employing spatial–temporal analysis on domains Behaviours and their temporal variations	Dynamic graphs and spatial–temporal analysis	Effective malicious domain detection with real-world data
[39]	This paper presents an approach for detecting Domain Generation Algorithm (DGA) using frequency analysis of the character distribution and the weighted scores of the domain names	Frequency analysis of character distribution and weighted scores	Less than 45 weighted score resulted in only 15% of domains identified as non-human generated
[40]	Aim of the study to use Linkage analysis and open-source threat intelligence to visualize the relationship of malicious domain names while verifying their categories	Graph-based model using linkage analysis and open-source threat intelligence	Effective in revealing group patterns of malicious domain names
[41]	This paper presents a study that evaluates how well participants distinguish malicious from benign domains before and after they learned and applied domain squatting techniques themselves	Multiphase survey to gauge user perceptions of malicious domains	Users struggled to identify legitimate domains, especially with domain squatting characteristics
[42]	A malicious domain names detection algorithm based on N-gram is proposed	N-Gram method on top 100,000 domain names	Accuracy: 94.04%, False Negative: 7.42%, False Positive: 6.14%
[43]	This paper discusses a novel algorithm to detect malicious domains and relate them to a specific malware campaign	Identification of Malicious Domain Campaigns (IMDoC) algorithm	Detected malicious domains and associated them with specific malware campaigns
[44]	This paper explores the use of machine learning algorithms to classify websites as malicious or not	Machine learning algorithms combined with dynamic and static analysis	Potential utility of machine learning in identifying web-based security threats

(continued)

Table 1 (continued)

References	Research aim and objective of the study	Technique/method used	Statistics/key data/findings
[45]	This paper presents "Ringer", a scalable method to detect malicious domains by dynamic Graph Convolutional Network (GCN)	Ringer method using dynamic Graph Convolutional Network (GCN)	High performance with an average accuracy of 96.8%
[46]	A unified analysis system combining current defence solutions to build actionable threat intelligence from malicious domain names	Implemented a unified analysis system	Actionable Threat Intelligence
[47]	This paper proposes MalHunter, a technique to determine a domain's reputation via only a single DNS query	MalHunter technique using a deep neural network to determine a domain's reputation through a single DNS query	Reduced detection time to approximately ten microseconds with high accuracy
[48]	Aim of this paper is to propose a novel method to detect malicious BDNs	Detection method for malicious Blockchain Domain Names (BDNs) using Heterogeneous Information Network (HIN) and graph convolutional network algorithm	Detected malicious BDNs with an F1 score of 0.9901
[49]	Objective of this study is Lexical analysis of domain names can contribute to increasing the precision and decreasing the number of false positives when combined with other basic domain features	Lexical analysis of domain names combined with other basic domain features	Increased precision and reduced false positives in malicious domain identification, but methodology was not detailed
[50]	This paper discusses a system for detecting malicious domains and IP addresses using graph inference	Graph inference method	High detection rates and reasonably low false positive rates
[51]	nDEWS system is proposed which is Hadoop-based automatic early warning system of malicious domains for domain name registry operators	Hadoop-based early warning system	Demonstrated system's ability to detect various forms of domain abuse
[52]	Lexical analysis is effective and efficient for proactive detection of malicious URLs	Lexical analysis of URLs	Efficacy proven over an evaluation of 110,000 URLs

(continued)

Table 1 (continued)

References	Research aim and objective of the study	Technique/method used	Statistics/key data/ findings
[53]	Objective to showcase Unsupervised clustering based on passive DNS records and other inherent network information can identify malicious domains	Unsupervised clustering based on passive DNS records	This method achieve up to 2.1 $\times$ expansion from a seed of known campaign domains with less than 4% false positives
[54]	This paper discusses the ecosystem of malicious URL redirection. It describes a honeypot-based monitoring system that was used to collect data on malicious redirect URLs	Longitudinal analysis of malicious URL redirection	Over 100,000 malicious redirect URLs collected
[55]	This paper reviews existing methods for detecting malicious domains	Retrospective analysis	Data sources for malicious domain detection can be divided into two types: DNS data and DGA data and Detection methods can be divided into four types: signature-based, machine learning-based, graph-based, and hybrid-based
[56]	This paper surveys existing approaches to malicious domain detection through DNS data analysis	Review of malicious domain detection using DNS data	Systematic categorization of existing methods
[57]	The first multiclass approach to indicate the threat present in the malicious domain is proposed	Multiclass classification of malicious domains using passive DNS with XGBoost	Link between TLDs and maliciousness of a domain
[58]	This study proposes a malicious domain detection approach based on domain relationship features, PDNS features, and domain character features	Detecting malicious domains using domain relationship and graph models	Effective combination of relationship features to surpass two existing methods
[59]	Aim of the study to show Malicious domains are rarely deployed independently	Identifying and characterizing COVID-19 themed malicious domain campaigns	Emphasized correlations between malicious domains related to public events

(continued)

Table 1 (continued)

References	Research aim and objective of the study	Technique/method used	Statistics/key data/ findings
[60]	Objective is to propose a proactive algorithm to uncover redirection networks in real-time given a small set of seed domains	Real-time discovery of URL redirection networks	Detected 3 major redirection campaigns from 2,300 popular fake news sites. Majority of domains were re-registered
[61]	Aim of the study to show Blacklisting domains should not be one-way function and need to be regularly re-evaluated	Analysis of blacklisted domains	Emphasizes the vulnerability of users to malicious domains due to outdated software
[62]	This paper proposes a method for proactively detecting malicious domain names by exploring abnormal WHOIS records	Feature-Based Rules	The proposed method can be adopted as the first layer of defence to identify malicious domains on the domain registration stage
[63]	This paper proposes MalShoot, a graph embedding technique for detecting malicious domains using passive DNS database	MalShoot	High true positive rate of 96.08% and a low false positive rate of 0.1%
[64]	The proposed model, using domain name features, Whois features, and N-gram features, effectively detects Domain Generation Algorithms (DGA) and reduces detection time	Model development and comparison	Key results include construction of a feature set with domain name features, Whois features, and N-gram features, the development of a deep learning model based on BiLSTM
[65]	This paper proposes a new method, Domain Observer, for detecting malicious domains. It is based on dynamic time warping and passive traffic measurements	DomainObserver	Based on dynamic time warping and passive traffic measurements
[66]	Aim of this study to showcase the majority of malicious websites are hosted under apex domains that attackers do not own	Analysis of VirusTotal URL scans	65.6% attackers compromised benign websites, 81.7% of malicious websites were under domains not owned by attackers

(continued)

Table 1 (continued)

References	Research aim and objective of the study	Technique/method used	Statistics/key data/ findings
[67]	Félegyházi, Kreibich, Paxson	Proactive domain blacklisting	93% of inferred domains appeared suspect, 73% ended up on blacklists, median lead time of about two days
[68]	This paper presents a case study in one top-level domain (TLD) operator (.nl) with diverse longitudinal datasets	Longitudinal case study on.nl TLD	Revealed eight business models for DNS abusers. Focused on.nl TLD operator
[69]	The binary particle swarm optimization (BPSO)-based feature selection method is shown to be an effective way to improve the performance of classifiers	Machine learning classifiers (both single and ensemble) with BPSO based feature selection	Enhanced accuracy in detecting malicious domains from benign ones using machine learning classifiers
[70]	The study propose method for detecting phishing sites involves utilizing ChatGPT to generate prompts based on data collected from websites using a web crawler	ChatGPT for phishing site detection with web crawler for website data collection	Precision rate of 98.3% and recall rate of 98.4%. Improvement noted in GPT-4 over GPT-3.5 in minimizing false negatives
[71]	This paper describes the composition of dictionary-based AGDs using meaningful word segmentation, introduces the standard deviation	Feature fusion of meaningful word segmentation & N-Gram sequences for detecting AGDs	Accuracy of 97.24% on the full dataset. Improved accuracy and F1 values for both dictionary-based and character-based AGDs
[72]	This paper discusses the use of machine learning to classify malicious domains. It describes how to extract features from DNS traffic and use them to train a classification mode	ML techniques focusing on lexical-based, DNS statistical-based, and third party-based features from DNS traffic	Best F1-Score using k-NN: 94.8% for balanced and 99.4% for imbalanced data ratios

3.4 Data Analysis

- **Analysis Techniques**: Utilizing statistical methods and data visualization tools and Generative Pre-Trained Modals (GPTs) we thoroughly analyzed the findings from our literature review. This included advanced correlational studies and trend analyses (Fig. 1).
- **Creation of Comparative Figure**: The insights were crystallized in a figure that highlighted the relationship between cybersecurity metrics and their false positive rates, providing a clear visual representation of our findings in Fig. 2.

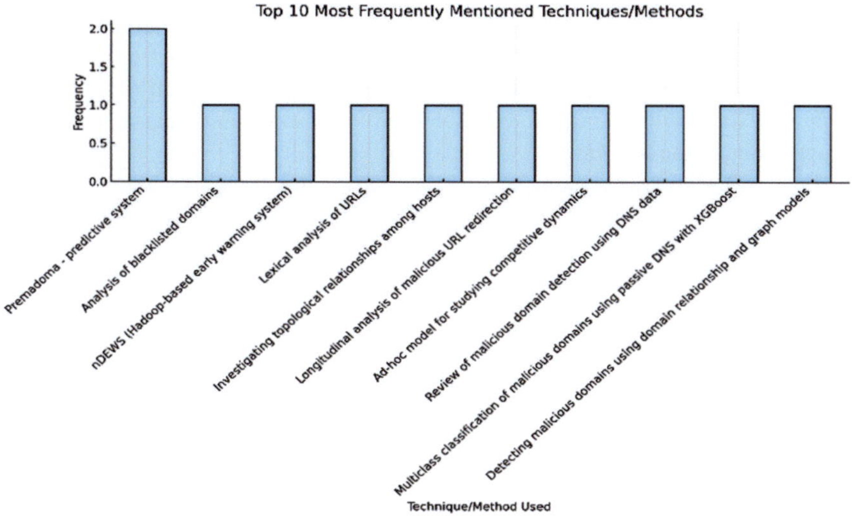

Fig. 1 Top 10 most frequently mentioned techniques/methods in malicious domain detection research

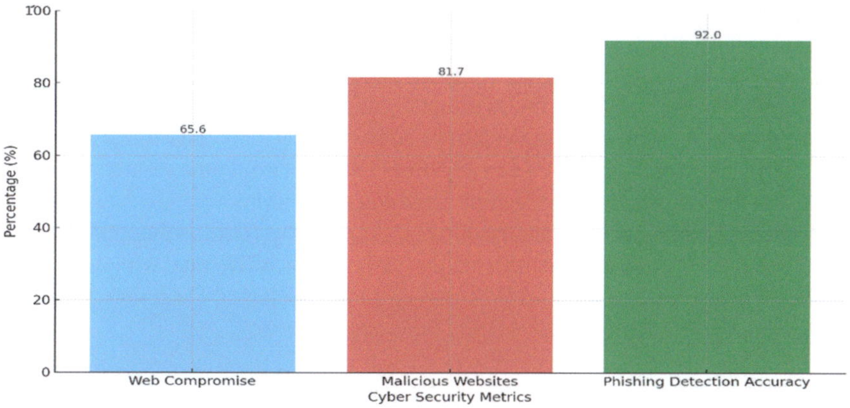

Fig. 2 Malicious domain detection rates based on various techniques

3.5 *Development of "Intelli"*

- **Data Set Generation**: We created a unique data set for "Intelli", initially capturing active domain names from the internet using tools like Scrapy and Beautiful Soup, followed by meticulous cleaning to extract domain names. This dataset was enriched with domain names from diverse sources, ensuring its comprehensiveness.

- **Passive Data Gathering**: In addition to active data collection, we utilized passive sources such as the Tranco list, government domain names from sites like data.gov.in, and various GitHub repositories. This combination of active and passive data gathering methods ensured a robust and varied dataset, forming a solid foundation for "Intelli".
- **System Design and Rationale**: With this rich dataset, "Intelli" was meticulously developed to fill gaps in existing domain security solutions. Its focus on both active and passive data sources is a testament to our commitment to creating a holistic and effective solution.

3.6 Limitations

In recognizing the limitations of our study, we offer a balanced perspective of our methodology, acknowledging areas for future improvement and research.

A key focus of this evaluation is testing the resilience of these methods against adversaries who may change their tactics to avoid detection [22, 23].

4 Results and Discussion

The studies have revealed key findings that highlight numerous successful outcomes related to specific techniques for detecting and preventing malicious domain registrations. Table 2 presents several commonly observed successful outcomes and Table 3, represents the Comparison of Machine Learning Algorithms.

Figure 3 is derived from a synthesis of research papers, contrasting the accuracy rate of various cybersecurity metrics against their false positive rate, with data points for Web Compromise, Malicious Websites Accuracy, Phishing Detection Accuracy, GPT-4 Detection Accuracy, and AI/ML Detection Accuracy.

5 Proposed Recommendations for a Dedicated Detection System for Malicious ".in" Domains Considering India's Vast and Diverse Digital Space

- Localized Machine Learning Models: Adapt machine learning algorithms specifically for ".in" domains, training them on datasets that include a variety of Indian-specific domain patterns, and behaviors.
- Multilingual Domain Analysis: Incorporate capabilities to analyze and detect anomalies in domains registered in different Indian scripts. This is crucial given India's linguistic diversity and the presence of 22 Internationalized Domain Names Country Code Top Level Domains (IDNccTLDs).

Table 2 Summary of techniques and key studies in malicious domain registration

Technique used	Key studies	Key findings
Predictive systems	"Premadoma", "DomainProfiler"	Effective in decreasing malicious registrations and predicting malicious domains with high true positive rates
Comparative analysis	"Cybercrime After the Sunrise"	Highlights abuse shift from legacy to new gTLDs, providing insights into changing domain abuse trends
Machine learning and statistical analysis	"Mining DNS for malicious domain registrations", "Detection of Newly Registered Malicious Domains through Passive DNS"	Demonstrates high accuracy and minimal false positives in identifying malicious domains using ML and statistical methods
Behavioral analysis	"Understanding the domain registration behavior of spammers", "Exploring Tunnelling Behaviors in Malicious Domains with Self-Organizing Maps"	Analyzes spammers' registration processes, using unsupervised learning to understand and prevent malicious behaviors
Graph-based models and DNS data analysis	"Discovering Malicious Domains through Alias-Canonical Graph", "Graph-based model using linkage analysis and open-source threat intelligence"	Emphasizes the effectiveness of graph-based models and DNS data analysis in identifying patterns and associations in malicious domains

- Region-Specific Feature Analysis: Focus on analyzing regional internet behavior patterns and cultural nuances within the ".in" domain space. This involves understanding local cyber threat landscapes and customizing detection mechanisms.
- Enhanced DNS Analysis with Local Focus: Employ DNS analysis techniques specifically targeting ".in" domains, identifying unique patterns and potential malicious activities inherent to the Indian digital environment.
- Integration with National Cybersecurity Frameworks: Align the detection system with India's national cybersecurity strategies and regulations, ensuring compliance and enhancing collaborative efforts with government cybersecurity agencies.
- Utilization of Indigenous Technologies and Expertise: Leverage locally developed technologies and methodologies, tapping into India's rich pool of IT and cybersecurity talent.
- Dynamic System Adaptation: Design the system for regular updates and adaptability based on AI/ML, reflecting the evolving nature of cyber threats in the Indian context and to provide the access to Law Enforcement agencies malicious domain data to support Indian criminal justice system.

Table 3 Comparison of machine learning algorithms: random forest, AdaBoost, XGBoost, and GPT-based models

Model/ algorithm	Architecture	Strengths	Weaknesses	Performance metrics
Random forest	Ensemble of decision trees	Robust to overfitting, Handles both categorical and numerical data well	Can be computationally intensive, not as interpretable as simpler models	Accuracy: high, precision: moderate-high, Recall: moderate-high, F1 score: high
AdaBoost	Ensemble of weak learners (often decision trees)	Improves classification accuracy, less prone to overfitting	Sensitive to noisy data and outliers, Performance depends on the choice of weak learner	Accuracy: high, precision: high, recall: moderate-High, F1 score: high
XGBoost	Optimized gradient boosting algorithm	Handles missing data, Efficient and scalable, Outperforms other algorithms frequently	Requires careful tuning, can overfit if not tuned properly	Accuracy: very high, precision: High, recall: high, F1 Score: Very High
GPT-based models	Transformer-based neural networks	Excellent at understanding context and semantics, can be fine-tuned for specific tasks	Requires large datasets for training, computationally intensive	Accuracy: high, precision: high, Recall: high, F1 score: high

- Collaboration with Local Stakeholders and Communities: Engage closely with ISPs, domain registrars, local tech communities, and cybersecurity experts within India to foster a collaborative approach to monitoring and managing ".in" domains.
- Public Awareness Programs: Implement educational initiatives focused on safe cyber practices, particularly emphasizing the safe use and registration of ".in" domains, in multiple Indian languages to cater to a diverse population.
- Comprehensive Multilingual Support: Ensure that the system is equipped to handle queries and reports in multiple Indian languages, reflecting the linguistic diversity of the country. These recommendations aim to create a detection system that is not only technically robust but also deeply integrated with the unique digital and legal landscape of India, enhancing the security and integrity of the ".in" domain space.

Table 4 Insights from malicious domain detection studies: an aggregated analysis based on derived cybersecurity metrics

Cybersecurity metric	Key findings and observations
Web and domain security	65.6% of benign websites experienced successful cyber infiltration; 81.7% of malicious websites operated under domains not initially registered to the attackers; A total of 58,966 proactive malicious domain registrations were neutralized in 2018; 93% of inferred domains exhibited suspect traits, with 73% blacklisted within a median of two days
Redirection campaigns and ownership	Three significant redirection campaigns were linked to around 2300 high-traffic faux news websites, with a trend towards domain re-registration; A focus on the ownership analysis revealed that a large portion of malicious websites were regulated under domains not owned by the cyber attackers
Phishing detection	Phishing site detection achieved over 92% accuracy, with a false positive rate below 8%; Of the detected phishing sites, 73% were compromised and 27% were intrinsically malicious
Advanced detection technologies	The 'Alembic' methodology is proposed to enhance passive DNS observation techniques; Machine learning and AI, including GPT-4, showed high accuracy rates (GPT-4: 98.3% precision, 98.4% recall) in threat detection, marking an improvement over previous models; Advanced Grammatical Domain (AGD) detection techniques reached a 97.24% accuracy rate
Domain classification and campaigns	Enhanced precision in malicious domain detection with reduced false positives; 80.04% of malicious domains were attributed to 20 major semi-automated campaigns; Challenges were noted in discerning legitimate domains, particularly those with squatting characteristics
gTLD and TLD analysis	A shift in abuse patterns from legacy domains to new generic Top-Level Domains (gTLDs) was observed, highlighting a preference for domain registration over traditional hacking; The study emphasized the potential for pre-registration detection, with a bias towards specific TLDs

6 Proposed Model

This modal is proposed in Figure 4 is to calculates the probability of a domain being harmful. It uses specific characteristics of the domain, like its age or how often it changes, and combines them with certain fixed values (coefficients) to estimate this likelihood, which ranges from 0 (not harmful) to 1 (very harmful). Further, it utilizes the existing customized Large Language Models (LLMs) with the highly refined specialized data for ".in" domain names.

$$P(M) = 1/1 + \mathrm{e} - (b0 + b1F1 + \mathrm{b}2F2 + \cdots + bnFn) \tag{1}$$

where:

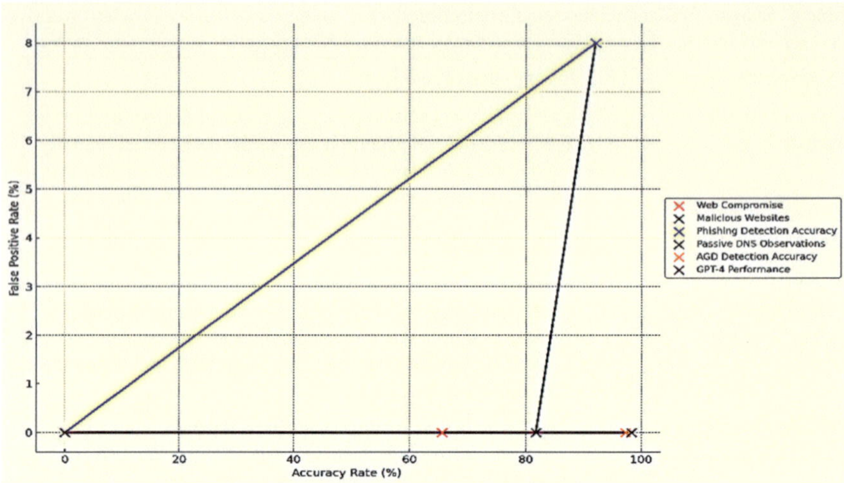

Fig. 3 Accuracy versus false positive rate of techniques to find malicious domains

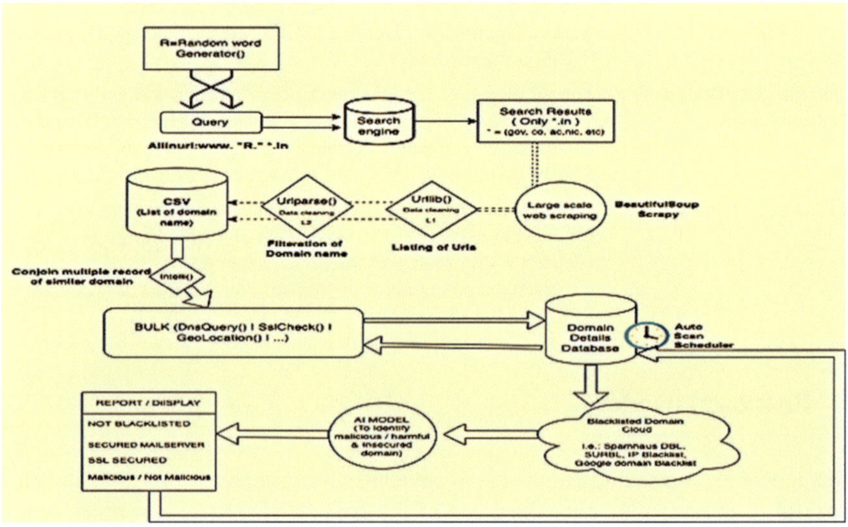

Fig. 4 Intelli—the proposed model

- *P(M)* is the probability that a domain is malicious.
- *e* is the base of natural logarithms.
- *b*0 is the intercept, and *b*1, *b*2,…,*bn* are the coefficients of the features *F*1, *F*2,…,*F*n.
- *F*1, *F*2,…,*F*n are the features or parameters based on the dataset. These could be attributes like domain age, frequency of updates, associated IP addresses, etc.

6.1 Features Important to Find the Malicious Domain Names

- **Domain Age**: Older domains may have a lower likelihood of being malicious.
- **Frequency of Updates**: Domains that update very frequently might be more suspicious.
- **Associated Protocols**: Security protocols deployed.
- **Associated Networks**: Domains associated with known malicious networks could have a higher likelihood of being malicious.
- **Redirection Count**: Domains that redirect users multiple times might be more suspicious.
- **Registration Behavior**: Domains registered in bulk or using certain patterns might indicate algorithmically generated domains.

7 Conclusion

The study offers an in-depth analysis of the domain registration landscape, highlighting the significant vulnerability of benign websites to cyber-attacks, with a notable 65.6% infiltration rate by cybercriminals. It also identifies three major redirection campaigns originating from counterfeit news platforms, illustrating the sophisticated and evolving nature of cyber threats. This dynamic environment requires constantly evolving detection and mitigation strategies. The effectiveness of advanced tools like GPT-4 and novel methodologies such as "Alembic" in countering these cyber threats is emphasized. This progress is crucial in domain name security within cybersecurity, although it also underscores the challenge of staying ahead of cybercriminals, who are always refining their tactics. The study stresses the need for ongoing research and innovation, particularly in creating custom solutions for domains like India's ".in," given its diverse digital environment and the presence of numerous Internationalized Domain Names (IDNs). While significant progress has been made in identifying and mitigating domain registration risks, the study concludes that the continually evolving nature of cyber threats necessitates persistent vigilance and innovative approaches. Insights into cybercriminal tactics, along with the development of sophisticated detection tools, are critical for future cybersecurity strategies. Collaboration, both nationally and internationally, and the integration of advanced technology with local expertise, are imperative for a safer digital future.

Future research directions include refining methodologies like "Alembic," reducing false positives in threat detection, shifting towards proactive cybersecurity strategies, further exploring the potential of machine learning and AI, especially Large Language Models like GPT-4, addressing the challenges of domain squatting, investigating new threat vectors in emerging generic Top-Level Domains (gTLDs), and encouraging collaborative, interdisciplinary research. These steps are crucial for staying ahead of cyber threats and ensuring robust security in the digital domain registration landscape.

References

1. Zhauniarovich Y et al (2018) A survey on malicious domains detection through DNS data analysis. ACM Comput Surveys (CSUR) 51(4):1–36
2. Torabi S et al (2018) Detecting internet abuse by analyzing passive DNS traffic: a survey of implemented systems. IEEE Commun Surveys Tutor 20(4):3389–3415
3. Lyu M, Gharakheili HH, Sivaraman V (2022) A survey on dns encryption: Current development, malware misuse, and inference techniques. ACM Comput Surveys 55(8):1–28.
4. Liu Y et al (2019) A comparative study of blockchain-based dns design. In: Proceedings of the 2019 2nd international conference on blockchain technology and applications
5. Li Z et al (2021), B-DNS: a secure and efficient DNS based on the blockchain technology. IEEE Trans Netw Sci Eng 8(2):1674–1686. https://doi.org/10.1109/TNSE.2021.3068788
6. Bilge L et al (2011) Exposure: Finding malicious domains using passive DNS analysis. In: Ndss
7. Ghafir I, Prenosil V (2015) DNS traffic analysis for malicious domains detection. In: 2015 2nd international conference on signal processing and integrated networks (SPIN), IEEE
8. Antonakakis M et al (2011) Detecting malware domains at the upper dns hierarchy. in USENIX security symposium
9. Hoang XD, Nguyen QC (2018) Botnet detection based on machine learning techniques using DNS query data. Future Internet 10(5):43
10. Nabeel M et al (2020) Following passive dns traces to detect stealthy malicious domains via graph inference. ACM Trans Privacy and Security (TOPS) 23(4):1–36
11. Zhang J, Sun H, Wang J (2022) Malicious domain name detection model based on CNN-LSTM. https://doi.org/10.1117/12.2659649
12. Alexopoulos A (2021) Entropy-based evaluation of DNS activity for threat hunting, https://doi.org/10.47260/jamb/1112
13. Mukhopadhyay A et al (2018) Aquatic salinization and mangrove species in a changing climate: impact in the Indian sundarbans. https://doi.org/10.1596/1813-9450-8532
14. Altavilla C, Ragusa G (2013) Anchoring the yield curve using survey expectations. https://doi.org/10.1920/wp.cem.2013.5213
15. McIntyre MSF et al (2011) Consequences of double negative regulatory T cell and antigen presenting cell interaction on immune response suppression. Int Immunopharmacol. https://doi.org/10.1016/j.intimp.2010.11.015
16. Xiao H et al (2017) Detecting malicious behavior in computer networks via cost-sensitive and connectivity constrained classification. https://doi.org/10.1137/1.9781611974973.14
17. Grießhammer HW. (2013) Dissecting deuteron Compton scattering I: the observables with polarised initial states. Eur Phys J A 49(1–31)
18. Nikiforakis N et al Uncovering the use of homophones in domain squatting
19. Yadav S et al (2010) Detecting algorithmically generated malicious domain names. In: Proceedings of the 10th ACM SIGCOMM conference on Internet measurement
20. Eastlake 3rd D (1999) Domain name system security extensions
21. Hoffman P (2023) RFC 9364: DNS Security Extensions (DNSSEC). RFC Editor
22. Choo E et al (2022) A large scale study and classification of VirusTotal reports on phishing and malware URLs. https://doi.org/10.48550/arxiv.2205.13155
23. Sperotto A et al (2009) Hidden Markov model modeling of SSH brute-force attacks. https://doi.org/10.1007/978-3-642-04989-7_13
24. Vissers T et al (2017) Exploring the ecosystem of malicious domain registrations in the. eu tld. in Research in Attacks, Intrusions, and Defenses: 20th International Symposium, RAID 2017, Atlanta, GA, USA, September 18–20, 2017, Proceedings. Springer
25. Desmet L et al (2021), Premadoma: An operational solution to prevent malicious domain name registrations in the. eu tld. Digital Threats: Research and Practice. 2(1):1–24
26. Chiba D et al (2016) DomainProfiler: Discovering domain names abused in future. In: 2016 46th annual IEEE/IFIP international conference on dependable systems and networks (DSN). IEEE

27. Hao S et al (2013) Understanding the domain registration behavior of spammers. in Proceedings of the 2013 conference on Internet measurement conference
28. Korczynski M et al (2018) Cybercrime after the sunrise. In: Proceedings of the 2018 on Asia conference on computer and communications security. ACM
29. Lever C et al (2016) Domain-z: 28 registrations later measuring the exploitation of residual trust in domains. In: 2016 IEEE symposium on security and privacy (SP). IEEE
30. He Y et al (2010) Mining dns for malicious domain registrations. In: 6th international conference on collaborative computing: networking, applications and Worksharing (CollaborateCom 2010). IEEE
31. Spooren J et al (2019) Premadoma: an operational solution for DNS registries to prevent malicious domain registrations. In: Proceedings of the 35th Annual Computer Security Applications Conference
32. Campbell AJ, Zincir-Heywood N (2020) Exploring tunneling behaviours in malicious domains with self-organizing maps. In: 2020 IEEE symposium series on computational intelligence (SSCI). IEEE
33. Szurdi J (2020) Measuring and analyzing typosquatting toward fighting abusive domain registrations
34. Peng C et al (2017) Discovering malicious domains through alias-canonical graph. In: 2017 IEEE Trustcom/BigDataSE/ICESS. IEEE
35. Khalil I, Yu T, Guan B (2016) Discovering malicious domains through passive DNS data graph analysis. In: Proceedings of the 11th ACM on Asia conference on computer and communications security
36. Silveira MR et al (2021) Detection of newly registered malicious domains through passive DNS. In: 2021 IEEE international conference on big data (Big Data). IEEE
37. Maroofi S et al (2020) COMAR: classification of compromised versus maliciously registered domains. IEEE
38. Li Y et al (2021) DyDom: detecting malicious domains with spatial-temporal analysis on dynamic graphs. In: 2021 IEEE 23rd international conference on High performance computing and communications; 7th International Conference on Data Science & Systems; 19th international conference on Smart City; 7th International Conference on Dependability in Sensor, Cloud & Big Data Systems & Application (HPCC/DSS/SmartCity/DependSys). IEEE
39. Agyepong E, Buchanan W, Jones K (2018) Detection of algorithmically generated malicious domain using frequency analysis. Int J Comput Sci Inf Technol 10:91–111
40. Huang S-Y et al (2018) Comprehensible categorization and visualization of orchestrated malicious domain names using linkage analysis. In: 2018 16th annual conference on privacy, Security and Trust (PST), IEEE
41. Quinkert F et al (2020) Be the phisher–understanding users' perception of malicious domains. In: Proceedings of the 15th ACM Asia conference on computer and communications security
42. Zhao H et al (2019) Malicious domain names detection algorithm based on N-gram. J Comput Netw Commun
43. Lazar, D., et al.(s), IMDoC: identification of malicious domain campaigns via DNS and communicating files. IEEE Access, 2021. 9(45242–45258.
44. Urcuqui C et al (2017) Machine learning classifiers to detect malicious websites. SSN, 1950(14–17)
45. Liu Z et al (2020) Ringer: systematic mining of malicious domains by dynamic graph convolutional network. In: Computational science–ICCS 2020: 20th International Conference, Amsterdam, The Netherlands, June 3–5, 2020, Proceedings, Part III 20. 2020. Springer
46. Chiba D et al (2017) DomainChroma: providing optimal countermeasures against malicious domain names. IEEE
47. Peng C et al (2018) Malhunter: performing a timely detection on malicious domains via a single DNS query. In: Information and communications security: 20th international conference, ICICS 2018, Lille, France, October 29–31, 2018, Proceedings. 2018. Springer
48. Han J et al (2022) Malicious Blockchain domain detection based on heterogeneous information network. In: GLOBECOM 2022–2022 IEEE global communications conference. IEEE

49. Kidmose E, Stevanovic M, Pedersen JM (2018) Detection of malicious domains through lexical analysis. In: 2018 international conference on cyber security and protection of digital services (Cyber Security). IEEE
50. Najafi P et al (2018) Guilt-by-association: detecting malicious entities via graph mining. In: Security and privacy in communication networks: 13th international conference, secure Comm 2017, Niagara Falls, ON, Canada, October 22–25, 2017, Proceedings 13. Springer
51. Moura GC et al (2016) ndews: A new domains early warning system for tlds. In: NOMS 2016–2016 IEEE/IFIP network operations and management symposium. IEEE
52. Mamun MSI et al (2013) Detecting malicious urls using lexical analysis. In: Network and system security: 10th international conference, NSS 2016, Taipei, Taiwan, September 28–30, 2016, Proceedings 10. Springer
53. Weber M, Wang J, Zhou Y (2018) Unsupervised clustering for identification of malicious domain campaigns. ACM
54. Akiyama M et al Analyzing the ecosystem of malicious URL redirection through longitudinal observation from honeypots. Comput Secur 69:155–173
55. Li K, Yu X, Wang J (2021) A review: how to detect malicious domains, in advances in artificial intelligence and security. Springer International Publishing, pp 152–162
56. Zhauniarovich Y et al (2018) A survey on malicious domains detection through DNS data analysis. ACM Comput Surveys (CSUR) 51:1–36
57. Silva LMD et al (2020) Multiclass classification of malicious domains using passive DNS with XGBoost: (Work in Progress). In: IEEE 19th international symposium on network computing and applications (NCA), pp 1–3
58. He W et al (2019) Malicious domain detection via domain relationship and graph models. In: 2019 IEEE 38th international performance computing and communications conference (IPCCC), pp 1–8
59. Xia P et al (2021) Identifying and characterizing COVID-19 themed malicious domain campaigns. In: Proceedings of the eleventh ACM conference on data and application security and privacy
60. Chen Z, Freire J (2021) Discovering and measuring malicious URL redirection campaigns from fake news domains. In: 2021 IEEE security and privacy workshops (SPW), pp 1–6
61. Jensen Ø, Shalaginov A, Dyrkolbotn GO (2020) Study of blacklisted malicious domains from a microsoft windows end-user perspective: is it safe behind the wall?
62. Cheng Y et al (2021) Detecting malicious domain names with abnormal WHOIS records using feature-based rules. Comput J 65(9):2262–2275. https://doi.org/10.1093/comjnl/bxab062
63. Peng C et al (2018) *MalShoot: shooting malicious domains through graph embedding on passive DNS data.* In: International conference on collaborative computing
64. Sun X, Liu Z (2023) Domain generation algorithms detection with feature extraction and Domain Center construction. PLOS ONE 18
65. Tan G et al (2018) *DomainObserver:* a lightweight solution for detecting malicious domains based on dynamic time warping. In: International conference on conceptual structures
66. Silva RD et al (2021) Compromised or attacker-owned: a large scale classification and study of hosting domains of malicious URLs. In: USENIX Security Symposium
67. Félegyházi M, Kreibich C, Paxson V (2010) On the potential of proactive domain blacklisting. in USENIX workshop on large-scale exploits and emergent threats
68. Moura GCM et al (2017) Domain names abuse and TLDs: from monetization towards mitigation. In: 2017 IFIP/IEEE symposium on integrated network and service management (IM), pp 1077–1082
69. Hu Z et al (2016) Identifying malicious web domains using machine learning techniques with online credibility and performance data. In: 2016 IEEE congress on evolutionary computation (CEC), pp 5186–5194
70. Koide T et al (2023) Detecting phishing sites using ChatGPT. ArXiv, 2023. abs/2306.05816
71. Chen S et al (2023) Detection of algorithmically generated malicious domain names with feature fusion of meaningful word segmentation and N-Gram sequences. Appl Sci

72. Mahdavifar S et al (2021) Classifying malicious domains using DNS traffic analysis. In: 2021 IEEE international conference on dependable, autonomic and secure computing, international conference on pervasive intelligence and computing, international conference on cloud and big data computing, international conference on cyber science and technology congress (DASC/PiCom/CBDCom/CyberSciTech), pp 60–67

Utilizing Convolutional Neural Networks for Android Malware Detection via Permission and Opcode Sequences

Pragat Gadilohar, Deepak Singh Tomar, Vasudev Dehalwar, and Yogesh Kumar Sharma

Abstract Our contemporary digital existence is intricately intertwined with the realm of Android-based smart devices, delivering unparalleled convenience across personal, professional, and social dimensions. However, this profound connectivity exposes us to an escalating barrage of malicious attacks, with Android smartphones emerging as prominent targets. To cultivate a secure, intelligent, and lasting digital environment, we must advance the field of Android malware detection while mitigating the need for frequent retraining. Presently, existing solutions for malware detection on Android devices grapple with persistent challenges, chief among them being the high incidence of false positives and the limited capacity to identify emerging threats. In response, this paper introduces an innovative approach that achieves an outstanding 98% accuracy in malware detection through the power of deep learning techniques. This study is grounded in a dataset comprising 1000 APK files, evenly distributed between benign and malicious samples (500 each), and leverages advanced deep learning methodologies and feature extraction strategies. The overarching objective is to fortify Android-based smart devices against the ever-evolving landscape of cyber threats. In summary, the research charts a course towards elevated security, heightened resilience, and the enduring relevance of Android-based smart devices in the fabric of daily lives, all made possible through the capabilities of deep learning. Furthermore, detailed classification results for varying dataset sizes, including 200, 500, and 1000 APK files, showcase the scalability and robustness of the approach in effectively detecting malware.

Keywords Android malware · Dalvik opcode · CNN · Malware detection

P. Gadilohar (✉) · D. S. Tomar · V. Dehalwar · Y. K. Sharma
Maulana Azad National Institute of Technology (MANIT), Bhopal, M.P., India
e-mail: pragatgadilohar16@gmail.com

D. S. Tomar
e-mail: deepaktomar@manit.ac.in

V. Dehalwar
e-mail: vasudevd@manit.ac.in

B. N. Gohil et al. (eds.), *Information Security, Privacy and Digital Forensics*,
Lecture Notes in Electrical Engineering 1423,
https://doi.org/10.1007/978-981-96-9443-3_9

1 Introduction

Technological progress has led to a connected world facilitated by rapid and energy-efficient tools such as laptops, and smartphones. This evolution has given rise to a secure environment termed ubiquitous computing [1], aiming to prevent and mitigate various cyber-attacks, both known and unknown [2]. Android-powered smart devices have seen significant popularity, commanding a 72.44% share of the worldwide mobile operating system market in 2021 [3]. The attraction of Android devices can be attributed to their intuitive and user-friendly characteristics [4]. These characteristics render Android devices versatile for practical applications, encompassing data sharing, banking, entertainment, and social connectivity [5]. Furthermore, the open-source framework of Android permits customization and adjustment to suit specific device needs. Nevertheless, the extensive dependence on these intelligent devices in various aspects of daily life has emphasized the pressing necessity to tackle cybersecurity issues.

To accommodate the unique needs of users, the Android operating system runs application packages. These packages are concise components containing code for business logic, essential libraries, and manifest files [6]. A Manifest file provides a list of permissions and intents that an application requests during installation or when it's being used. Cybercriminals are exploiting these intents and permissions skillfully to infiltrate and inject malware, imitating regular programs and making detection and classification challenging [7]. Subsequently, these malicious programs engage in various detrimental activities to compromise device security. Furthermore, due to the constantly evolving nature of malware, the security of the Android operating system can be compromised, even though attempts have been made to assign different privilege levels to authenticate and grant requested permissions [8]. Nonetheless, an uneven distribution of data across different categories of malware attacks can impede the overall capability of these trained models to make precise generalizations [9].

This research significantly contributes to the field of cybersecurity by focusing on Android applications and malware detection. The primary contributions can be summarized as follows:

Effective Utilization of Convolutional Neural Networks (CNNs): This study maximizes the potential of Convolutional Neural Networks (CNNs), a robust deep learning architecture, for classifying a dataset of 1000 APK files into benign and malware categories. By leveraging CNNs, the research achieves an exceptional 98% accuracy in distinguishing between benign and malicious applications.

Customized Feature Extraction Techniques for CNNs: The research integrates feature extraction techniques specifically designed for CNNs, enhancing the model's performance. These techniques help identify and prioritize the most pertinent features, streamlining the model training process and improving its interpretability, thus contributing to the high accuracy achieved.

Thoughtful Dataset Balance for Unbiased Assessment: Careful attention is given to the dataset's balance, ensuring an equal representation of 500 benign and 500 malware samples. This equilibrium is vital to ensure the model's performance assessment remains unbiased and reflects real-world utility accurately. It mitigates any potential bias that imbalanced data could introduce, particularly in cybersecurity applications.

Promising Practical Applications: The outstanding 98% accuracy rate achieved by the CNN-based model holds promise for various practical applications, particularly in the domain of mobile app security assessments, malware detection, and risk mitigation. The high accuracy instills confidence in deploying this model in real-world scenarios, where precise classification of APK files is critical.

This paper follows a structured progression organized into four main sections. Section 2, "Related Works," succinctly summarizes existing research on Android malware detection, providing a foundational understanding essential for comprehending proposed methodology. Moving forward, Sect. 3, "A Comprehensive Methodology," elaborates on innovative approach for detecting Android malware categories, outlining the techniques and methodologies employed. In Sect. 4, "Results and Discussion," we discuss the experimental setup, present obtained results, and conduct a detailed analysis to evaluate the effectiveness of our proposed methodology in Android malware detection. Finally, Sect. 5, "Conclusion," encapsulates the research, emphasizing its key contributions and presenting potential directions for future research in the domain of Android malware detection.

2 Related Works

In this section, a summary of prior research related to the recognition and detection of malicious applications is presented.

2.1 Malware Detection

Binary files can be analyzed to determine if they are malicious using information from their file format. For example, the Windows PE format or Linux ELF format can provide valuable data. By examining certain features of the file, such as the opcode sequence, it is possible to understand its behavior without actually executing it [10].

The study [11] involved the extraction of opcode sequences from benign and malicious files, followed by a comprehensive statistical analysis. The experimental findings revealed notable disparities in opcode frequencies and distribution across various malware types. Remarkably, the analysis demonstrated that opcodes can serve as reliable indicators for malware detection.

In another study [11], the process of feature selection was conducted using permissions and API calls, with the utilization of a genetic algorithm. Diverse machine learning algorithms like decision trees, random forests, and naive Bayes were utilized, yielding an accuracy of approximately 97% with a dataset consisting of 6000 Android samples.

Utilizing static analysis and the DBN algorithm, DroidDeep [12] achieved an overall accuracy ranging from 92% to 97.5% for various acceptable ratios of benign to malware samples.

In a related study [13], static analysis was utilized to extract permissions, API calls, and code, which were then input into various machine learning algorithms, including SVM, Random Forest, and Logistic Regression. The highest level of accuracy achieved was approximately 97.5% when using datasets such as AMD, Drebin, and UpDroid.

Articles [14–17] followed a similar approach, incorporating both permissions and API calls were integrated into various machine learning algorithms, including random forest, SVM, and logistic regression. Through the utilization of different datasets, these studies produced varying accuracy rates, spanning from 87 to 98%.

This paper [18] proposed a distinctive learning-based framework aiming to minimize reliance on prior knowledge and pre-training models without labels. The results highlighted the effectiveness of this approach, achieving an accuracy exceeding 96% in identifying malware from publicly available records.

2.2 *Features of Android Malware Detection*

Permissions in Android applications: In the realm of Android, every application functions within a confined-access sandbox. Should an application necessitate access to resources or data beyond its designated sandbox, it is obligated to make precise permission requests. This system plays a pivotal role in identifying potential malware since the requested permissions are clearly defined in the AndroidManifest.xml file. The Android permission framework can be divided into two main categories: official permissions and customized permissions.

Official permissions, totaling 166 in number [19], are preestablished permissions in Android, such as "android.permission.INTERNET", permitting applications to initiate network connections. All developers possess the ability to request these official permissions. Conversely, custom permissions are crafted by developers and facilitate resource and functionality sharing among applications. For example, developers can create custom permissions to restrict specific users from accessing particular activities within an app. Once defined, these custom permissions become employable within component definitions.

The permissions specified in an Android application's manifest file offer insights into the app's behavior. Researchers have utilized these permissions as features in conjunction with machine-learning algorithms for Android malware detection. For instance, Sanz et al. [20] utilized this approach, while Wang et al. [21] thoroughly analyzed individual and collaborative permission risks using machine learning techniques. Talha et al. [22] introduced APK Auditor, a permission-centric Android malware detection system, achieving an impressive accuracy of 88% and specificity of 92.5%.

Dalvik opcode features: In the initial stages of Android's development, applications ran within a virtual machine called Dalvik. During runtime, Dalvik would dynamically interpret portions of Dalvik bytecode into machine code. It's important to note that starting with Android 5.0, the Dalvik virtual machine was replaced by Android Runtime. However, the compilation process for the fundamental opcodes remained compatible. These opcodes hold significant value, as they can, to a certain extent, mirror an application's behavioral patterns by interpreting the underlying machine code. Hence, they are commonly utilized as features in static analysis.

3 A Comprehensive Methodology

In this manuscript, an approach grounded in static analysis is introduced. Here, significant and observed features are extracted from Android applications.

3.1 Gathering Android Applications

The applications utilized in this study were sourced from an open-access dataset. To ensure the integrity of malicious and legitimate samples, the collected samples were meticulously examined using antivirus engines. Further elaboration on this process will be provided in the experiment section.

3.2 Feature Extraction and Preprocessing

Permissions in Android applications: The key objective behind the inclusion of permissions in the Android system is to ensure the protection of Android users' privacy [23]. Android applications must request permission before they can access sensitive user data, like contacts and text messages, or specific system features such as the camera and internet connectivity. These permissions can be granted automatically by the system or by user-initiated approval prompts. Android categorizes permissions into four protection levels, which determine whether runtime permission requests are necessary.

- *Normal Permission*: This classification pertains to instances where an application necessitates access to data or resources beyond its designated sandbox. Typically, such scenarios pose minimal risks to user privacy or the functionality of other applications.

- *Dangerous Permission*: Unlike normal permissions, dangerous permissions involve permissions that, when obtained, expose the user's private data to potential misuse or tampering by the application.
- *Exclusive Permissions*: Limited to apps with identical digital signatures, this category ensures only apps with matching signatures can access specific data, despite attempts by others to mimic these permissions in AndroidManifest.xml.
- *SignatureOrSystem Permission*: This classification of permission is akin to signature permissions but adds a layer. It necessitates not only the same digital signature but also similarities with system-level applications. SignatureOrSystem permissions are commonly reserved for pre-installed applications developed by leading mobile phone manufacturers.

Creating Feature Vectors: APKs are broken down using an APK tool [24] that reverses the APK structure to understand its components. Creating a dictionary to represent opcodes using characters, simplifying their notation. Extracting opcode sequences in a simplified form from .smali files using the previously created dictionary. It allows for the exploration of the Android file organization by decompiling and extracting static features. This enables the extraction of permissions and opcode sequences from each application by analyzing both the AndroidManifest.xml file and classes.dex file.

In this research, the goal was to address the complexity of feature vectors and maximize the utility of derived features. Emphasis lay on extracting the 166 official permissions while excluding custom permissions. Additionally, for the Dalvik opcode sequences obtained, a mapping table was utilized to capture simplified opcode sequences separated by branch instructions. The combination of these features forms the initial feature set.

To construct feature vectors, numerical representations were assigned to this feature set in the following manner. Consider an Android application 'a,' and a feature set derived from all applications encompassing 'n' features, denoted as 'S.' The feature vector for application 'a' is denoted by Eq. (1).

$$V_a = \{v_1, v_2, v_3, \ldots v_n\}$$

$$v_i = \{1, v_i \in a\, and\, v_i \in S, 1 \le i \le n; 0,\ otherwise \tag{1}$$

Hence, the feature vector can be denoted as $V_a = \{0, 1, 0, 0, 1, 1, 0, \ldots 1\}$ where '1' signifies the inclusion of the feature in the application and '0' indicates its absence. Regarding sample labels, 'M' denotes malware, and 'B' signifies benign instances (Fig. 1).

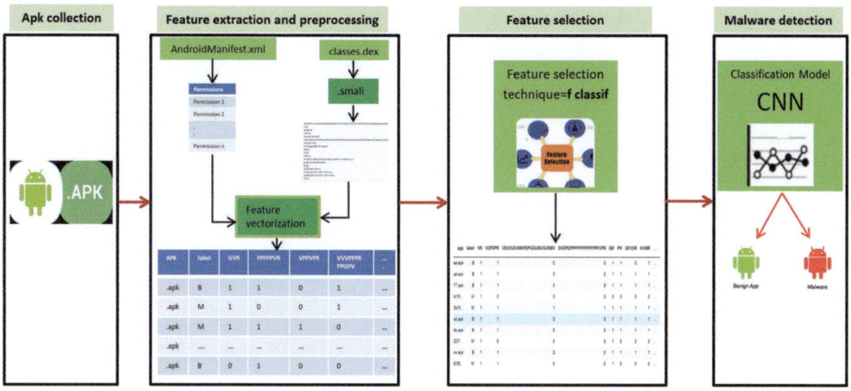

Fig. 1 Proposed model

3.3 Feature Selection Method—f_classif

The f_classif function is a part of the scikit-learn library and is used to compute the F-score for feature selection. The F-score is a statistical measure that quantifies the differences in means between classes while considering the variances within classes. It's a useful metric for identifying features that are relevant for classification tasks, as it helps discriminate between classes based on their distributions.

Variance between classes explained by feature:

$$BCV_j = \sum_{i=1}^{k} N_i\left(\mu_{ij} - \mu\right)^2 \tag{2}$$

where

k number of classes.
N_i number of samples in class *i*.
μ_{ij} mean of feature *j* in class *i*.
μ overall mean of feature *j* across all classes.

Variance within classes:

$$WCV_j = \sum_{i=1}^{k} (N_i - 1)\sigma_{ij}^2 \tag{3}$$

where

σ_{ij}^2 variance of feature *j* within class *i*.

The formula for the F-score of a feature is calculated using the following equation:

$$F(j) = \frac{Variance\ between\ classes\ explained\ by\ feature}{Variance\ within\ classes} = \frac{BCV_j}{WCV_j} \quad (4)$$

where

BCV_j between-class variance explained by the feature j.
WCV_j is the within-class variance of feature j.

SelectPercentile and k_best: SelectPercentile is a class provided by scikit-learn that allows to perform feature selection by selecting a certain percentage of top-scoring features based on a scoring function (like F-score in this case).

k_best is an instance of the SelectPercentile class that is created. By passing score_func = f_classif and percentile = 20 to it, use the F-score as the scoring function and select the top 20% of features based on their F-scores.

3.4 Classification Using Convolutional Neural Networks

In this section, a comprehensive approach is presented to classify files into two categories: malware and benign, utilizing a Convolutional Neural Network (CNN). The aim is to achieve the highest accuracy in the critical task of identifying potentially harmful files.

Dataset: Before diving into the architecture and training, it is crucial to provide insights into the dataset used for the classification task. The dataset consists of a collection of files, each represented as a feature vector of dimensionality (Number of Samples, Number of Features). In this case, the feature vector has approx. 100,000 dimensions, encompassing various file attributes and characteristics.

CNN Architecture: # Define the CNN architecture for malware versus benign classification (Fig. 2).

Activation Function: Softmax (to obtain probability scores).

Model Training:—For training CNN model, Employing the following settings:

Loss Function: Binary Cross-Entropy—An ideal choice for binary classification tasks.

Optimizer: Adam—Adaptive learning rate optimization methods.

Regularization:—To prevent overfitting, incorporated regularization techniques:

Dropout: Applied after dense layers.

Batch Normalization: Normalizes activations between layers, aiding in faster convergence and stable training.

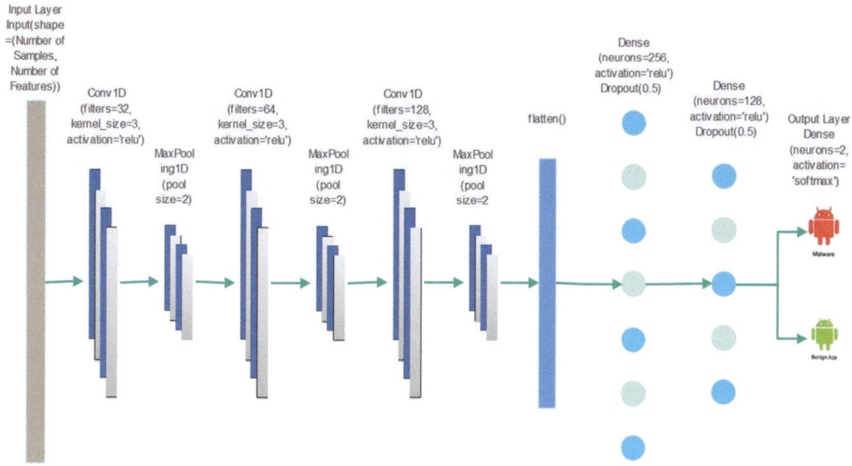

Fig. 2 Architecture of CNN

Model Evaluation: To ensure the robustness and generalization of the model, k-fold cross-validation is employed. This method assesses the performance across multiple splits of the dataset, providing a more comprehensive evaluation.

Hyperparameter Tuning: The architecture's hyperparameters, such as learning rate, batch size, number of filters, and layer depths, are subjected to experimentation and tuning to achieve the optimal configuration.

4 Results and Discussion

Within this section, the attributes of the dataset are discussed, followed by the presentation of the acquired results. Lastly, the tools employed for data preprocessing and model training are detailed.

4.1 Dataset

Data collected from AndroZoo [25], downloading 1000 APK files randomly—500 of them are malware and 500 are benign.

4.2 Model Evaluation

Within this section, the model's performance is assessed using two different versions of the dataset. One version comprises two distinct target classes, namely malware and benign, specifically designed for malware detection.

The malware detection model demonstrated exceptional performance across varying dataset sizes of APK files, as depicted in Table 1. Notably, the selected features, representing the top 20% based on their F-scores, are shown in Table 1, in accordance with the feature selection method.

These results underscore the robustness of malware detection model in effectively discerning between benign and malicious applications. The balance between precision and recall, as indicated by the F1-Score, showcases model's proficiency in accurately identifying malicious files while minimizing false positives. Such advancements significantly fortify the security of Android-based smart devices, contributing to a safer digital environment amidst the evolving landscape of cyber threats. Furthermore, detailed Confusion Matrix (see Fig. 3) and nearly perfect ROC curve (approx. 1) provide comprehensive insights into the model's performance and discriminative power, further affirming the effectiveness of this approach (Table 2).

Table 1 Evaluation metrics results

No. of Apk	No. of selected features	Precision	Recall	F1-score	Accuracy
200	57,982	0.9514	0.98	0.9654	0.9648
500	87,738	0.95	1	0.9743	0.975
1000	107,257	0.9898	0.97	0.9798	0.98

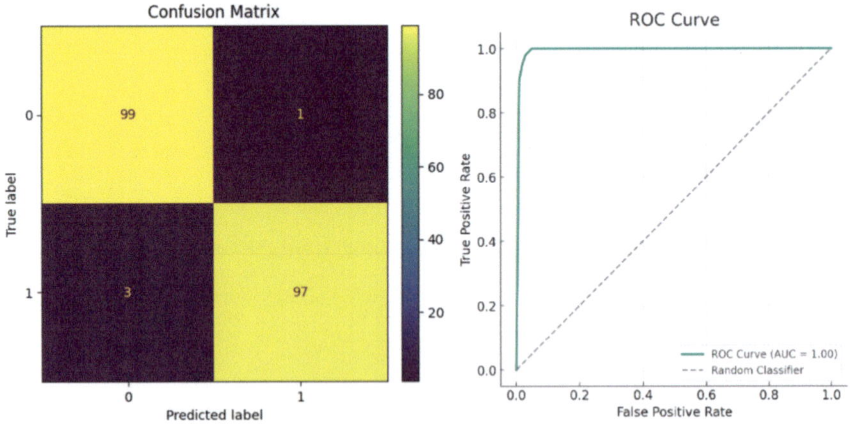

Fig. 3 Confusion matrix and ROC Curve for 1000 APK dataset

Table 2 Comparison with related work

Techniques	Accuracy %	Precision	Recall	F1-score	Data set
Genetic algorithm [11]	97	0.9689	0.965	0.9669	6000 Samples
DroidDeep [12]	92–97.5	–	–	–	3986 Benign and 3986 malware
Framework DL [18]	96	0.926	0.9416	0.9419	CICInvesAndMal2019
RF [14]	95.64	0.97	0.956	0.963	1500 Benign and 1500 malware
SVM [13]	88.87	0.8952	0.8194	0.8556	CICInvesAndMal2019
DL [17]	95.94	0.9932	0.9258	0.9583	CICInvesAndMal2019
Proposed classification model	98	0.9898	0.97	0.9798	500 Benign and 500 malware

5 Conclusion

In conclusion, study vividly demonstrates the efficacy of our chosen CNN-based approach in achieving an impressive accuracy rate when classifying datasets of varying sizes comprising APK files. The dataset was meticulously balanced, including both benign and malware samples, ensuring an unbiased evaluation of model's performance.

For 200 APKs, a remarkable accuracy of 96.48% was achieved, with a precision of 95.14%, recall of 98%, and an F1-score of 96.54%. With a dataset of 500 APKs, the model achieved an accuracy of 97.5%, underlining its consistent performance, with a precision of 95%, perfect recall, and an F1-score of 97.43%. Scaling up to 1000 APKs, the model demonstrated exceptional precision at 98.98%, a recall of 97%, and an impressive F1-score of 97.98%, resulting in an overall accuracy of 98%.

These results underscore the potency of deep learning techniques, particularly CNNs, in discerning between benign and malicious applications with exceptional precision. Additionally, integration of feature extraction techniques tailored for CNNs played a pivotal role in enhancing the model's performance. These techniques efficiently identified and prioritized the most pertinent features, streamlining model training and enhancing interpretability.

Our achievement not only highlights the remarkable capabilities of CNNs as potent tools for classification tasks but also positions them as indispensable assets for data scientists and practitioners across diverse domains. The outstanding accuracy rates achieved across varying dataset sizes hold significant promise for practical applications, instilling confidence in deploying this model in real-world scenarios such as mobile app security assessments, malware detection, and risk mitigation, where precise classification of APK files is of paramount importance. These results emphasize the critical role of judicious feature extraction in developing robust classification models for high-stakes applications in today's dynamic digital landscape.

In the future, our research aims to advance corporate mobile security by tailoring the malware detection model to suit diverse enterprise environments, accommodating varied device usage patterns, and ensuring seamless integration with existing corporate security frameworks. Future educational initiatives will focus on creating interactive tools that leverage the model to educate individuals about mobile application security, reinforcing cyber security practices. Develop a real-time detection system that can analyze and classify applications as they are installed or executed on a device. This would require optimizing the model for efficiency without compromising accuracy. The uses of this trained model exhibits versatile applications, with its integration into mobile security apps promising real-time protection for users against potential threats. Collaboration with app stores ensures a heightened layer of security screening, safeguarding users by preemptively identifying malicious applications before they reach the market.

References

1. Malibari AA et al (2022) A novel metaheuristics with deep learning enabled intrusion detection system for secured smart environment. Sustain Energy Technol Assess 52:102312
2. Kumar P, Gupta GP, Tripathi R (2021) An ensemble learning and fog-cloud architecture-driven cyber-attack detection framework for IoMT networks. Comput Commun 166:110–124
3. Stats, StatCounter Global (2021) Mobile operating system market share worldwide, 2020. Recuperado de: https://gs.statcounter.com/os-market-share/mobile/worldwide
4. Imtiaz SI et al (2021) DeepAMD: detection and identification of Android malware using high-efficient deep artificial neural network. Future Gen Comput Syst 115:844–856
5. Sihag V, Vardhan M, Singh P (2021) A survey of android application and malware hardening. Comput Sci Rev 39:100365
6. Sharma K, Gupta BB (2019) Towards privacy risk analysis in android applications using machine learning approaches. Int J E-Serv Mobile Appl 11(2):1–21
7. Wang C et al (2019) Research on data mining of permissions mode for Android malware detection. Cluster Comput 22:13337–13350
8. Cam NT, Pham V-H, Nguyen T (2019) Detecting sensitive data leakage via inter-applications on Android using a hybrid analysis technique. Clust Comput 22(Suppl 1):1055–1064
9. Shafiq M et al (2020) IoT malicious traffic identification using wrapper-based feature selection mechanisms. Comput Secur 94:101863
10. Bilar D (2007) Opcodes as predictor for malware. Int J Electron Secur Digit Forens 1(2):156–168
11. Lee J et al (2021) Android malware detection using machine learning with feature selection based on the genetic algorithm. Mathematics 9(21):2813
12. Su X et al (2016) A deep learning approach to android malware feature learning and detection. In: 2016 IEEE Trustcom/BigDataSE/ISPA. IEEE
13. Roy A et al (2020) Android malware detection based on vulnerable feature aggregation. Proc Comput Sci 173:345–353
14. Egitmen A et al (2020) Research article combat mobile evasive malware via skip-gram-based malware detection
15. Yerima SY. Sezer S, Muttik I (2014) Android malware detection using parallel machine learning classifiers. In: 2014 Eighth international conference on next generation mobile apps, services and technologies. IEEE
16. Gupta D, Rani R (2020) Improving malware detection using big data and ensemble learning. Comput Electr Eng 86:106729

17. Liu S et al (2019) DeepBalance: deep-learning and fuzzy oversampling for vulnerability detection. IEEE Trans Fuzzy Syst 28(7):1329–1343
18. Musikawan P et al (2022) An enhanced deep learning neural network for the detection and identification of android malware. IEEE Internet Things J
19. Android Permission. https://developer.android.com/reference/android/Manifest.permission
20. Sanz B et al (2013) MAMA: manifest analysis for malware detection in android. Cybern Syst 44(6–7):469–488
21. Wang W et al (2014) Exploring permission-induced risk in android applications for malicious application detection. IEEE Trans Inf Forens Secur 9(11):1869–1882
22. Talha KA, Alper DI, Aydin C (2015) APK auditor: permission-based Android malware detection system. Dig Investig 13:1–14
23. Permissions Overview. https://developer.android.google.cn/guide/topics/permissions/overview. Accessed 27 Oct 2020
24. Apktool. https://apktool.org/
25. AndroZoo. https://androzoo.uni.lu/

Attacking Authentication Mechanisms: From Offense to Defense

Jayant Kumawat, Lavesh Verma, and Mohit Maurya

Abstract Almost every web application on the internet requires an authentication mechanism to let their customers log in. Once a user is authenticated, he or she can perform any action with a particular role assigned (Access controls). These actions can vary from posting a comment on social media to handling an entire corporate enterprise and thereby results in the demand of a robust authentication mechanism with solid access control systems. The mechanism cannot be same for different businesses, the type of authentication is directly linked to the business logic. However, when developers design custom authentication systems, incorporating features like rate limiting, password resets, new user registration, and logins, the promise of ironclad security is not always fulfilled. This paper emphasizes on attacking single factor authentication systems (form based) which are designed on the idea of 'flaws in design of authentication mechanisms' to resist attacks against them. No system is secure if the most common software development practices are not followed, no matter how cutting-edge a website's tech stack may be, adherence to fundamental software development best practices is paramount for security. A compelling case study demonstrates how the implementation of a rate-limiting mechanism, designed with both user experience and security in mind, can inadvertently lead to full account takeovers through phishing attacks. As we dissect various attack vectors, from creating custom captchas to exploiting flawed authentication functions, this paper sheds light on the critical importance of robust authentication systems in an ever-evolving digital landscape.

Keywords Authentication · Rate limit · Client side attacks · XSSI attacks

J. Kumawat (✉)
Sardar Vallabhbhai National Institute of Technology, Surat, Gujarat, India
e-mail: u20ce004@ced.svnit.ac.in

L. Verma
Indian Institute of Information Technology, Lucknow, Lucknow, Uttar Pradesh, India

M. Maurya
ITS Engineering College, Greater Noida, India

B. N. Gohil et al. (eds.), *Information Security, Privacy and Digital Forensics*,
Lecture Notes in Electrical Engineering 1423,
https://doi.org/10.1007/978-981-96-9443-3_10

1 Introduction

Authentication is defined as the act of proving an assertion. In this paper's context, which revolves around application security, authentication could be defined as the process of determining if an entity (a user or an automated application) is who it claims to be. The most widespread authentication method used in web applications is login forms, where a user enters their username and password to prove their identity.

1.1 Background

The background highlights the historical context of authentication methods, narrowing its focus to the challenges posed by form-based authentication. Emphasizing the prevalence and vulnerabilities of this method, the research aims to analyze and propose mitigation strategies within the specific context of form-based authentication systems.

1.2 Scope and Objectives

This research focuses on form-based authentication, aiming to identify and analyze vulnerabilities such as username enumeration and design flaws. Objectives include evaluating attack strategies, proposing effective mitigation measures, and assessing the impact on user experience, ultimately contributing to the enhanced security of form-based authentication systems.

2 Literature Review

The literature reveals the widespread reliance on authentication mechanisms in web applications and the critical role they play in enabling user actions through access controls. Despite the diverse demands of different businesses, custom authentication systems often fall short of delivering promised security features. This paper focuses on the vulnerabilities inherent in single-factor authentication systems, emphasizing the importance of adhering to fundamental software development best practices for robust security. A compelling case study demonstrates how seemingly secure mechanisms, like rate limiting, can inadvertently lead to account takeovers, underscoring the necessity of resilient authentication systems in the evolving digital landscape.

3 Authentication: An Overview

3.1 *Definition and Importance*

Authentication is of paramount importance if the user is to be provided a "service", which simply means performing some action with an identity. Organizations want to streamline the user experience, allowing users to access multiple applications and websites by logging in only once.

3.2 *Taxonomy of Authentication Methods*

Multi-factor Authentication

Multi-Factor Authentication, commonly known as MFA (or 2FA when there are just two factors involved), can result in a much more robust authentication process. Think about a corporate badge or a train ticket. Passing through a turnstile often requires you to swipe a badge that grants you access. In this case, you need no PIN, no identification string, or anything else but a card. This is an edge case because company badges, or train multi-cards, are often used to match a specific user by sending an ID. By swiping, both authorization and a form of authentication are performed.

Form-Based Authentication

The most common authentication method for web applications is Form-Based Authentication (FBA). The application presents an HTML form where the user inputs their username and password, and then access is granted after comparing the received data against a backend. After a successful login attempt, the application server creates a session tied to a unique key (usually stored in a cookie). This unique key is passed between the client and the web application on every subsequent communication for the session to be maintained.

HTTP-Based Authentication

Many applications offer HTTP-based login functionality. In these cases, the application server can specify different authentication schemes such as Basic, Digest, and NTLM.

Source IP Address Verification

While uncommon, it is also possible that authentication is performed by checking the source IP address. A request from localhost or the IP address of a well-known/trusted server could be considered legitimate and allowed because developers assumed that nobody but the intended entity would use this IP address.

Using Third Parties to Authenticate Users

Authentication and authorization frameworks such as OAuth and SAML can help organizations build secure and standard authentication and authorization flows.

4 Attacks Against Single Factor Authentication Mechanisms (Form Based)

Overview of Attacks Against Authentication

Authentication attacks can take place against a total of three domains. These three domains are divided into the following categories:

- The HAS domain
- The IS domain
- The KNOWS domain

Attacking the KNOWS Domain

The 'knows' domain is the one we will dig into in this paper. It is the simplest one to understand, but we should thoroughly dive into every aspect because it is also the most widespread. This domain refers to things a user knows, like a username or a password. This paper focuses on attacks against FBA only. Keep in mind that the same approach could be adapted to HTTP authentication implementations.

4.1 Developers Creating Their Own Captcha

"CAPTCHA, a widely used security measure named after the Completely Automated Public Turing test to tell Computers and Humans Apart" sentence, can have many different forms. It could require, for example, typing a word presented on an image, hearing a short audio sample and entering what you heard into a form, matching an image to a given pattern, or performing basic math operations. Even though CAPTCHA has been successfully bypassed in the past, it is still quite effective against automated attacks. It is also possible for developers to use a custom or weak implementation of CAPTCHA, where for example, the name of the image is made up of the chars contained within the image (see Listing 1). Having weak protections is often worse than having no protection since it provides a false sense of security. The image below shows a weak implementation where the PHP code places the image's content into the id field. This type of weak implementation is rare but not unlikely.

Offense—As an attacker, we can just read the page's source code to find the CAPTCHA code's value and bypass the protection. We should always read the source.

Defense/ Mitigation—As developers, we should not develop our own CAPTCHA but rely on a well-tested one and require it after very few failed logins.

4.2 Custom Security Mechanism Utilizing X-Forwarded-Header to Install Rate Limit in Place

When an attacker can tamper with data taken into consideration to increase security, they can bypass all or some protections. For example, changing the User-Agent header is easy. Some web applications or web application firewalls leverage headers like X-Forwarded-For to guess the actual source IP address (see Listing 2). This is done because many internet providers, mobile carriers, or big corporations usually "hide" users behind NAT. Blocking an IP address without the help of a header like X-Forwarded-For may result in blocking all users behind the specific NAT.

Offense—Unfortunately, this security measure could be bypassed by crafting an X-Forwarded-For header, (see Listing 3). The vulnerable PHP code will think the request originates from the 1.2.3.4 IP address. Some web applications may grant users access based on their source IP address. The behavior we just discussed could be abused to bypass this type of protection.

Defense/Mitigation—From a developer's perspective, all security measures should be considered with both user experience and business security in mind.

4.3 Login Page Too Friendly/verbose Allowing Username Enumeration and Brute Forcing Passwords.

Username enumeration is frequently overlooked, probably because it is assumed that a username is not private information. When you write a message to another user, we commonly presume we know their username, email address, etc. The same username is oftentimes reused to access other services such as FTP, RDP and SSH, among others. Having a list of common users gives an attacker some advantages. In addition to achieving good User Experience (UX), coming across random or non-easily-predictable usernames is uncommon. A user will more easily remember their email address or nickname than a computer-generated and (pseudo)random username.

Offense—Having a list of valid usernames, an attacker can narrow the scope of a brute force attack or carry out targeted attacks (leveraging OSINT) against support employees or users themselves. Also, a common password could be easily sprayed against valid accounts, often leading to a successful account compromise.

Protection against username enumeration attacks can have an impact on user experience. A web application revealing that a username exists or not may help a legitimate user identify that they failed to type their username correctly, but the same applies to an attacker trying to determine valid usernames. Even well-known and mature web frameworks, like WordPress [5], suffer from user enumeration because the development team chose to have a smoother UX by lowering the framework's security level a bit. When a failed login occurs, and the application replies with "Unknown username" or a similar message, an attacker can perform a brute force attack against the login functionality in search of a, "The password you entered for the username X is incorrect" or a similar message. We notice that the application replies with an Unknown username message, and we guess that it uses a different message when the username is valid. We can carry out the brute force attack using wfuzz (see Listing 4) and a reverse string match against the response text.

Defense/Mitigation

- Implement account lockout policies, introducing delays and CAPTCHA challenges to thwart brute force attacks.
- Remove specific feedback on invalid usernames to prevent enumeration, and encourage strong password practices.
- Utilize multi-factor authentication, regularly update software, and monitor for suspicious login activity to enhance overall security.

4.4 Failing to Prioritize Security While Trying to Enhance the User Experience (Username Existence Inference)

Sometimes a web applications may not explicitly state that it does not know a specific username but allows an attacker to infer this piece of information. Some web applications prefill the username input value if the username is valid and known but leave the input value empty or with a default value when the username is unknown. This is quite common on mobile versions of websites and was also the case on the vulnerable WordPress login page we saw earlier.

Defense/Mitigation—While developing, always try to give the same experience for both failed and granted login: even a slight difference is more than enough to infer a piece of information.

4.5 Some Authentication Functions May Contain Flaws by Design

Some authentication functions may contain flaws by design. One example is an authentication function where the username and password are checked sequentially. Let us analyze the below routine, see Listing 5.

The code snippet first connects to the database and then executes a query to retrieve an entire row where the username matches the requested one. If there are no results, the function ends with a generic message. When $result is true (the user exists and is active), the provided password is hashed and compared. If the hashing algorithm used is strong enough, timing differences between the two branches will be noticeable (see Listing 7). By calculating $cpass using a generic hash_password() function, the response time will be higher than the other case.

Offense—Python script to perform username enumeration (see Listing 6).

Defense/Mitigation—This small error could be avoided by checking user and password in the same step, having a similar time for both valid and invalid usernames.

Consider another authentication mechanism used for authenticating digital images, particularly in scenarios where the images may undergo compression. The system is designed to handle JPEG compression, but it may not be effective at detecting malicious manipulations like cutting and pasting. On the receiver's side, the feature vector is extracted from the received image, and it is compared against the extracted watermark. This comparison helps verify whether the image is both intact and genuine.

While it is robust against compression, the system is sensitive to malicious attacks such as cutting and pasting. In other words, it may not be able to detect tampering when portions of the image are manipulated or replaced [3].

4.6 Sub-addressing

One interesting feature of email addresses that many people do not know or do not have ready in mind while testing is sub-addressing. This extension, defined at RFC5233, says that any + tag in the left part of an email address should be ignored by the Mail Transport Agent (MTA) and used as a tag for sieve filters. This means that writing to an email address like *student+nfsu@nfsu.com* will deliver the email to *student@nfsu.com* and, if filters are supported and properly configured, will be placed in folder *nfsu*. Very few web applications respect this RFC, which leads to the possibility of registering almost infinite users by using a tag and only one actual email address.

Defense/Mitigation—Mitigate the misuse of sub-addressing by validating input, stripping sub-addresses on the mail server, and educating users on responsible use. Implement monitoring, user registration policies, and application logic updates to enhance security.

4.7 Password Policy Disclosure

The chances of executing a successful brute force attack increase after a proper policy evaluation. Knowing what the minimum password requirements are, allows an attacker to start testing only compliant passwords. A web app that implements a strong password policy could make a brute force attack almost impossible. As a developer, always choose long passphrases over short but complex passwords. On virtually any application that allows self-registration, it is possible to infer the password policy by registering a new user. Trying to use the username as a password, or a very weak password like 123,456, often results in an error that will reveal the policy (or some parts of it) in a human-readable format.

Families are:

- lowercase characters, like abcd…
- uppercase characters, like ABCD…Z
- digit, numbers from 0 to 9
- special characters, like,./.?! or any other printable one (space is a character)

It is possible that an application replies with a Password does not meet complexity requirements message at first and reveals the exact policy conditions after a certain number of failed registrations. This is why it is recommended to test three or four times before giving up. The same attack could be carried on a password reset page. When a user can resets his password, the reset form may leak the password policy (or parts of it). During a real engagement, the inference process could be a guessing game. Since this is a critical step, we are providing you with another basic example. Having a web application that lets us register a new account, we try to use 123,456 as a password to identify the policy. The web application replies with a Password does not match minimum requirements message. A policy is obviously in place, but it is not disclosed. We then start guessing the requirements by registering an account and entering a keyboard walk sequence for the password like Qwertyiop123!@#, which is actually predictable but long and complex enough to match standard policies. Suppose that the web application accepts such passwords as valid. Now let's decrease complexity by removing special characters, then numbers, then uppercase characters, and decreasing the length by one character at a time. Specifically, we try to register a new user using Qwertyiop123, then Qwertyiop!@#, then qwertyiop123, and so forth until we have a matrix with the minimum requirements.

Within a few tries, we should be able to infer the policy even if the message is generic.

Offense—Let us now suppose that this web application requires a string between 8 and 12 characters, with at least one uppercase and lowercase character (see Listing 8).

Defense/Mitigation—Mitigate password guessing attacks by enforcing strong password policies with complexity requirements and implementing account lockout mechanisms or rate limiting to detect brute-force attempts.

4.8 Weak Token Generation

Some applications create a token using known or predictable values, such as local time or the username that requested the action and then hash or encode the value. This is a poor security practice because a token doesn't need to contain any information from the actual user to be validated and should be a pure-random value. In the case of reversible encoding, it could be enough to decode the token to understand how it is built and forge a valid one. We should try to brute force any weak hash using known combinations like time + username or time + email when a reset token is requested for a given user. Take for example this PHP code (see Listing 9). It is the logical equivalent of the vulnerability reported as CVE-2016–0783 on Apache OpenMeeting [4]

Offense—Predicting the reset token of an admin user by retrieving the server timestamp (see Listing 10) [4]

Defense/Mitigation—Mitigate weak token generation by ensuring tokens are purely random and not derived from predictable values like local time or usernames. Use strong, irreversible hashing methods for token creation to prevent decoding attempts and brute force attacks.

5 Case Study: Authentication Function Containing Flaws by Design: JavaScript File Leaking Tokens to Complete the Authentication Request Replay Which Results into Retrieving Victim's Credentials in Plaintext

5.1 Overview of Authentication Mechanism Used by PayPal

PayPal encapsulates a huge corporate enterprise network and hence already possesses defense mechanisms against authentication attacks. This mechanism is protected against all the attack vectors we have discussed but still a weak implementation of a robust rate limiting mechanism provides an entry point for an attacker to craft a phishing exploit and steal any legit user's password in plaintext. Thinking about UI/UX, an application should at least require a user to solve a CAPTCHA after a few failed attempts. Some developers often skip this protection altogether, and others prefer to present a CAPTCHA after some failed logins to retain a good user experience. PayPal implemented the captcha using the same concept. This implementation serves the purpose of installing a rate-limiting mechanism, which fortifies their defense against brute force attacks. However, it's worth noting that despite these commendable security measures, some fundamental software development best practices were overlooked during the implementation of this rate-limiting mechanism.

Rate Limiting Mechanism

Scenario 1. In the event of an attacker attempting to brute force the login form, the web application responds by prompting the user with a manually designed security challenge. Only after successfully completing this challenge can the user make another login attempt.

Scenario 2. Even if the attacker, after multiple failed login attempts, manages to enter the correct credentials on a final attempt (assuming they have successfully cracked the password), the web application will still require the completion of the security challenge before proceeding with the authentication flow.

This practice is one of the most commonly employed methods for implementing a rate limit, and it simultaneously enhances the user experience. However, its effectiveness in bolstering security remains unverified until it undergoes rigorous testing.

5.2 Session Identifier and CSRF Token Leakage in a JavaScript File

Upon conducting some enumeration, the attacker has uncovered the presence of a JavaScript file within the web application. This JavaScript file contains both a Session Identifier and a CSRF token (see Listing 12), with the notable characteristic that each user, whether authenticated or unauthenticated, possesses a unique CSRF token [2]. This information could be exploited by the attacker to potentially mount targeted attacks or perform malicious activities.

5.3 Possible Attack Vectors

CSRF Attack. Cross-Site Request Forgery (CSRF or XSRF) is an attack that forces an end-user to execute inadvertent actions on a web application in which they are currently authenticated. This attack is usually mounted with the help of attacker-crafted web pages that the victim must visit or interact with, leveraging the lack of anti-CSRF security mechanisms.

Session Hijacking. In session hijacking attacks, the attacker takes advantage of insecure session identifiers, finds a way to obtain them, and uses them to authenticate to the server and impersonate the victim. In this case, the attacker doesn't need an MITM attack to steal the cookie, since it can be obtained by using an XSSI (Cross Site Script Inclusion) attack. But in this scenario, both the attack vectors fail to exploit the target.

5.4 *Attacking the First Line of Defense: The Authentication Mechanism*

Reference [2]—As the URL which is leaking the tokens in a JavaScript file suggests that these tokens has something to do with the security challenge which is nothing but a captcha. So, the attacker tries to brute force the login form at *vuln-web.com/login* to examine the authentication flow.

After 5 incorrect attempts, if the user logs in at 6th attempt with correct login credentials. The web application prompts the user to fill the captcha. When the user completes the security challenge, a POST Request is sent to */auth/validatecaptcha* containing 4 parameters out of which two are leaked in the JavaScript file and the Response of this request from server is containing the username and password in plaintext (see Listing 14) which makes it vulnerable to Client-Side attacks.

In the above POST Request (see Listing 13), four variables are sent in the request body (_csrf, _sessionID, jse & recaptcha).

jse token is not invalidated. Upon further research, we get to know that the jse token is not invalidated meaning that the same jse token can be used more than once.

So, the attacker will use his own jse token while crafting the forged request to /auth/validatecaptcha.

Recaptcha can be calculated by any automated solving service. In the forged request, the recaptcha is obtained using google and it is not tied to any session.

Therefore, at this point, the attacker is able to perform a complete account takeover of the victim just by sending one login link to the victim.

5.5 *XSSI (Cross Site Scripting Inclusion) Attack*

Cross Site Script Inclusion (XSSI) vulnerability is a security issue that can lead to the exposure of sensitive information across different websites or domains [1]. If this JavaScript Code (see Listing 15) is executed in context of attacker.com by the victim, the attacker will be able to use the tokens present in recaptchav3.js file as global variables. Meaning that, the attacker.com will be able to complete the security challenge on behalf of the victim.

5.6 *Crafting the Phishing Exploit*

The attacker hosts a malicious web page called 'xssi.html' on his own server.

HTML File Structure

1. The attacker fetches the session id and csrf tokens of the victim by fetching the cross-domain resource at /recaptchav3.js through XSSI in context of attacker.com and declares global variables csrf and sessID within the html file xssi.html. This is happening because the SOP (Same-Origin Policy) is not able to stop XSSI as SOP is not applicable for HTML <script> tag inclusions [1]. This exception is necessary, as without it websites would not be able to consume third party services, perform traffic analysis, or use advertisement platforms, etc.
2. The attacker, aware of the 5-failed-login security challenge, exploits XSSI by automatically sending 5 authentication attempts to vulnerable-web.com/login using a JavaScript function triggered on 'window.onload' (see Listing 16). The victim, visiting 'http://attacker.com/xssi.html,' unknowingly logs in for the 6th time with correct credentials, as the login form appears normal to them.

As soon as the victim logs in, the endpoint */auth/validatecaptcha* is activated. Now the attacker has the complete POST data in order to send a server side request to */auth/validatecaptcha* and in response he will be able to see the plain text password and email of the victim.

3. Finally, the attacker completes the security challenge on behalf of the victim to make the attack more realistic and reduce the suspicion of victim (see Listing 17). Though the attacker can also complete the security challenge from his machine and needs only two conditions to get the credentials:

   i. The victim's session ID and csrf token.
   ii. The victim logs in and activates the endpoint *'POST /auth/validatecaptcha'*.

Note— *the csrf and sessID are declared globally within the XSSI code.*

5.6.1 Remediation and Root Cause of Vulnerability

Root Cause

1. Reuse of the tokens leaked in the recaptchav3.js file.
2. Not invalidating the jse token's value after continuing the authentication flow, thereby allowing the same jse token to be reused for different requests.
3. Storing the credentials in plaintext.

Remediation

- Implement additional controls on the security challenge request to prevent token reuse.
- The /auth/validatecaptcha endpoint should require an additional CSRF token, which cannot be leaked using cross-site script inclusion.
- Invalidate the jse token after replaying the authentication request.

6 Conclusion

Summary of Findings

This paper underscores that authentication mechanisms, despite possessing robust security, can be compromised due to weaknesses in their implementation. It highlights the significance of addressing vulnerabilities in the execution of these mechanisms, emphasizing that a single oversight can lead to successful exploitation.

Future Directions for Research

Biometric Integration: Explore advancements in behavioral biometrics for robust and user-friendly authentication.

Balancing Usability and Security: Develop methods to enhance user experience while maintaining strong authentication security measures.

Ethical Considerations: Address ethical implications and privacy concerns in the design and implementation of authentication systems.

Human-Centric Authentication: Investigate authentication methods based on human behavior, habits, and cognitive patterns for enhanced security.

References

1. Lekies S, Stocks B, Johns M (2015) The unexpected dangers of dynamic JavaScript. USENIX Security Symposium, pp 3–5
2. Report 739737. https://hackerone.com/reports/739737. Reported 18 Nov 2019
3. Mursi MFM, Assassa GMR, Aboalsamh HA, Alghathbar K (2009) A secure semi-fragile JPEG image authentication scheme based on discrete cosine transform. In: 2009 international conference on computing, engineering and information, Fullerton, CA, USA, pp 285–291. https://doi.org/10.1109/ICC.2009.58
4. CVE Record (2016) https://www.cve.org/CVERecord?id=CVE-2016-0783
5. WordPress Username Enumeration. https://melapress.com/wordpress-username-disclosure-vulnerability/

A Comprehensive Research Study on Evaluation of Intrusion Detection Datasets for DDoS Attack Detection

M. Raghupathi and V. Radhakrishna

Abstract During the past three decades, numerous studies have proposed various network intrusion and anomaly detection methods and techniques. The majority of these research studies are only limited to the performance evaluation of intrusion detection techniques by using benchmark datasets. The performance of any intrusion detection system mainly relies on the quality of IDS dataset used for discriminating normal traffic from attack traffic. In the present scenario, one of the most challenging issues for an intrusion detection system is to precisely detect modern day DDoS attacks. Existing IDSs for detecting network intrusions are not suitable for DDoS attack detection as the underlying datasets used for detection do not satisfy the evaluation criteria of a quality IDS dataset. In this research, we have considered the eleven benchmark IDS datasets between 1998 and 2022 widely used in various research studies and evaluated them by applying Gharib's IDS evaluation framework to gauge the quality of IDS datasets. We show in detail how various benchmark datasets can be evaluated with detailed computations carried for each benchmark dataset. The present study gains importance as it considers the attack diversity information recently published in the NetScout 1H 2023 DDoS threat report. The evaluation study proved that among all the eleven datasets, CICDDoS2019 dataset satisfied all eleven criteria defined in the evaluation framework for a quality IDS dataset to detect modern DDoS network attacks by learning algorithms.

Keywords Intrusion detection · Evaluation framework · Intrusion detection dataset · IDS · IPS · DDoS attacks

M. Raghupathi
Center of Excellence in Networks and Security, VNR VJIET, Hyderabad, India
e-mail: mraghu30@gmail.com

Department of Computer Science and Engineering, VJIET, Hyderabad, India

V. Radhakrishna (✉)
Department of Information Technology, VNR VJIET, Hyderabad, India
e-mail: radhakrishna_v@vnrvjiet.in

B. N. Gohil et al. (eds.), *Information Security, Privacy and Digital Forensics*,
Lecture Notes in Electrical Engineering 1423,
https://doi.org/10.1007/978-981-96-9443-3_11

1 Introduction

Modern day internet environment poses several significant attack threats to organizations and networks. Majority of the existing studies which have proposed various intrusion detection methods and techniques may not reliable as the IDS dataset used in those studies were not generated by following a systematic approach for capturing network traffic [1, 2]. When compared to various network attack threats, detection of distributed denial of service attacks is more challenging for detection algorithms [3]. Also, modern network attacks such as DDoS amplification and DDoS exploitation attack types are more complex [4], more diverse and thus throw more challenges to detection algorithms. The high complexity posed by modern DDoS traffic is mainly due to the close resemblance of DDoS traffic to normal traffic. This fact can be represented and understood visually by using Andrews plot. Consider Fig. 1 which represents Andrews's plot of DDoS and Benign traffic.

It can be seen that the DDoS traffic highly overlaps the benign traffic. The highly overlapping nature of DDoS traffic makes it challenging for detection methods and techniques to differentiate normal and attack traffic. Thus, there are two challenges because of this highly overlapping nature (a) detection algorithm could predict DDoS traffic as normal traffic and (b) normal traffic as DDoS traffic. Added to this, modern DDoS attacks are of two types (i) High-rate DDoS attacks and (ii) Low-rate DDoS attacks. When compared to high rate attacks, low rate attacks throw significant challenge to detection methods and techniques employed to detect DDoS attacks.

Figure 2 represents the plot of low-rate attacks, high rate attacks along with benign traffic by considering traffic flow from CICDDoS2019 dataset. It is visible from Fig. 2 that the low rate traffic closely resembles benign traffic (due to high overlapping of benign and low rate traffic). This high overlapping nature of low rate DDoS attacks is the main challenge faced by intrusion detection systems to detect these attacks. Due to this, the performance of detection algorithms and techniques is highly compromised.

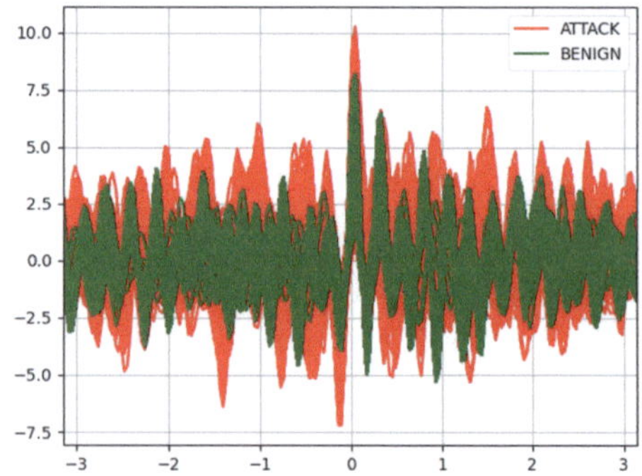

Fig. 1 Andrews plot depicting DDoS and Benign traffic

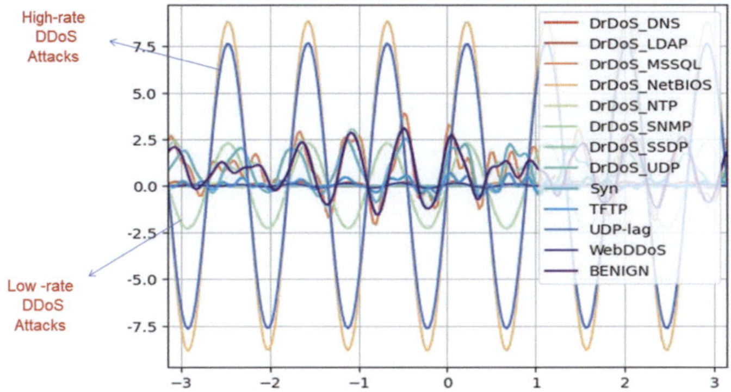

Fig. 2 Andrews plot depicting benign, low-rate and high-rate attacks

1.1 Motivation for the Present Study

Organizations require a comprehensive network security solution that shields their infrastructure, websites, applications, and DNS servers against Layer3, Layer4 and Layer7. DDoS attacks continue to surge in size, get more complicated, and increasingly target multiple vectors. For instance, in 2022, worldwide DDoS attacks increased by 115.1% to those observed in 2021 as per NetScout 2023 threat report [5]. In the last three decades, numerous techniques are proposed in various research studies to detect internet based attacks [6–8]. The detection techniques are based on statistical, knowledge-based, data mining, machine learning [8–10], and deep learning approaches [10, 11]. The detection algorithms employed require reliable input data to differentiate normal and attack traffic. Past studies on intrusion detection have two limitations. (i) Majority research studies on intrusion detection do not provide public access to the data they have used for experimentation. Such studies which do not make their experimentation data for future research studies cannot be considered as basis for evaluating new intrusion detection algorithms and techniques [1, 6, 12]. (ii) Benchmark datasets that are widely used in research studies do not satisfy the standard evaluation criteria of a quality IDS dataset mentioned by Gharib et al. [1]. Consequently, the widely used benchmark IDS datasets in various research studies are not suitable for evaluation and assessment of detection algorithms which are used to detect DDoS attacks.

In Sect. 2, we address various widely used IDS benchmark datasets for IDS evaluation. In Sect. 3, Gharib's framework for evaluating IDS datasets is described. In Sect. 4, evaluation and assessment of benchmark IDS datasets is discussed in detail and evaluation scores are computed for each dataset using Gharib's evaluation framework. Section 5 presents key findings and insights of present study.

2 Benchmark Datasets for IDS Evaluation

This section describes the eleven benchmark datasets that are widely used in various intrusion detection studies. In Sect. 4 of this paper, these datasets are evaluated by applying Gharib's evaluation framework for IDS datasets [1].

(i) DARPA 98—DARPA dataset was created by DARPA team in 1998 and the full dataset is available publicly. DARPA dataset contains 32 attacks and 9 features. These 32 attacks are divided into 4 categories (i) DoS, (ii) Probe, (iii) U2R and (iv) R2L. When compared to modern network attacks, these attacks are outdated. Originally, DARPA data is obtained by executing twenty four attacks on training day and an additional fourteen attacks are executed on testing day. The data is captured in two formats (i) Tcpdump file system and (ii) BSM file system. There are 287000 samples in train dataset. This dataset has several drawbacks (i) real time traffic is not represented by DARPA dataset because it was synthesized due to privacy policy (ii) there was no exact definition for attacks. This dataset does not satisfy complete traffic, anonymity, heterogeneity, and feature set evaluation criteria used for evaluating IDS datasets. The anonymity and complete traffic criteria are not satisfied because of the synthetic characteristics of the dataset. The heterogeneity criteria is not satisfied as operating systems logs or network equipment logs are missing. Also, about the feature set information not mentioned anywhere, which is helpful to inspect deeply about the attack behavior.

(ii) KDD 99—The KDD dataset is created from the DARPA dataset and it contains artificial attacks injected traces. So real time attack profiles are not represented in this dataset. The dataset is suggested to overcome drawbacks in DARPA. The dataset contains 52,094,580 records with 41 features and four attack diversities (DoS, Probe, U2R, and R2L). The train and test sets contains 4,898,431 (3925650 attack and 972,781 normal records) and 311,027 (25,436 attack and 60,591 normal records) samples respectively. The feature set information available with this dataset is helpful to inspect the attack behavior deeply. An important reason for its wide usage in various research studies is because of the high detection rate obtained by learning algorithms. Tavallaee et al. [13] has performed a detailed analysis on the KDD dataset and identified that train and test sets have 78% and 75% duplicate records respectively, which is one of the main drawback. Due to these duplicate records, the learning algorithms are more biased towards more frequent records which affects evaluation results. KDD dataset does not satisfy the anonymity, complete traffic, and heterogeneity criteria and it also does not contain the DDoS attack diversities that are listed in Tables 1 and 2.

(iii) NSL-KDD 2009—Another most widely used benchmark dataset is the NSL KDD dataset suggested by Tavallaee et al. [13] to overcome shortcomings of KDD. It does not contain duplicate records as KDD dataset and hence learning algorithms are not biased towards more frequent records. It was created by applying statistical analysis on KDD dataset and then filtering out distinct

Table 1 Eleven benchmark datasets and the properties satisfied

Eleven criteria	Sub factor	D1	D2	D3	D4	D5	D6	D7	D8	D9	D10	D11
Complete Network Configuration	_	✓	✓	✓	✓	✗	✓	✓	✓	✓	✓	✓
Complete traffic	_	✗	✗	✗	✓	✗	✗	✗	✗	✓	✓	✓
Labelled dataset	_	✓	✓	✓	✗	✗	✓	✓	✓	✓	✓	✓
Complete interaction	_	✓	✓	✓	✗	✓	✓	✗	✓	✓	✓	✓
Complete capture	_	✓	✓	✓	✗	✓	✓	✓	✓	✓	✓	✓
	HTTP	✓	✓	✓	_	✓	✓	✓	✓	✓	✓	✓
	HTTPS	✗	✗	✗	_	✗	✓	✗	✗	✓	✓	✓
Available protocols	SSH	✓	✓	✓	_	✓	✓	✗	✓	✓	✓	✓
	FTP	✓	✓	✓	_	✓	✓	✗	✓	✓	✓	✓
	EMAIL	✓	✓	✓	_	✓	✓	✗	✓	✓	✓	✓
	A1	✗	✗	✗	✗	✗	✗	✗	✗	✗	✗	✓
	A2	✗	✗	✗	✗	✗	✗	✗	✓	✗	✗	✓
Attack diversity	A3	✗	✗	✗	✗	✗	✗	✗	✗	✗	✗	✓
	A4	✗	✗	✗	✗	✗	✗	✗	✗	✓	✓	✓
	A5	✓	✓	✓	✓	✓	✓	✓	✓	✓	✓	✓
Anonymity	_	✗	✗	✗	✓	_	✗	_	✗	✓	✓	✓
Heterogeneity	_	✗	✗	✗	✗	✗	✗	_	✓	✓	✓	✓
Feature set	_	✗	✓	✓	✗	✗	✓	✗	✗	✓	✓	✓
Meta data	_	✓	✓	✓	✓	✗	✓	✗	✓	✓	✓	✓
Publicly available	_	✓	✓	✓	✗	✓	✓	✗	✓	✓	✓	✓

Table 2 Attack diversity information as per NetScout 1H 2023 DDoS threat report [6]

Serial number	Attack diversity	Number of attacks	Attack percentage
1	A1	2,51,417	7.20
2	A2	15,56,259	44.56
3	A3	5,10,820	14.63
4	A4	11,71,401	33.54
5	A5	2636	0.08

records in two folds. The first fold contains 125,973 records which represent the train set and second fold contains 22,544 records representing the test set. The distribution of test set is different from the train set which makes it helpful to improve anomaly detection of IDS systems. The dataset has four attack categories (DoS, Probe, U2R and R2L) but does not contain modern DDoS attack types. This dataset does not satisfy the complete traffic, anonymity and heterogeneity evaluation criteria of IDS datasets.

(iv) DEFCON—The initial published version of DEFCON8 dataset consisted the port scanning and buffer overflow attacks, the dataset is published in 2000. Later, in 2002, the DEFCON-10 dataset, covered (a) port scan and sweeps, (b) malformed packets, (c) administrative privilege, and (d) FTP by Telnet protocol attacks. The traffic generated during the "Capture the Flag (CTF)" competition is captured to obtain this dataset. It stands out from real world network traffic due to the fact that it consists primarily invasive traffic in contrast to typical background traffic. DEFCON dataset is used to test alert correlation algorithms and do not provide information about network, labelling, attack diversity.

(v) CAIDA 2007—The CAIDA dataset consists traces of one hour anonymized traffic from a DDoS attack performed on 4th August, 2007 split into 5-minute PCAP files. The benign traffic is removed from the anonymized traces and hence the anonymized traces contain only attack traffic to the victim and responses from the victim. The CAIDA 2016 dataset contains passive traffic traces from CAIDA's Equinix Chicago monitor on the high-speed Internet backbone. A large portion of CAIDA datasets are highly specific to specified attacks or events and are anonymized w.r.t payload, protocol, and destination. Due to these flaws, these are ineffective bench marking datasets [4, 12].

(vi) CDX 2009—CDX dataset is made available by United States military academy in 2009. CDX dataset includes network traffic such as web, email, DNS lookups, and other necessary services. The attackers executed reconnaissance and captured attack traffic automatically using attack tools (Nikto, Nessus, and Web Scarab). This dataset can be used to evaluate IDS alerting rules, although it lacks diversity and volume of traffic. For the present study, when evaluating this dataset, as the metadata is not available for this dataset, we considered the coefficient of complete network configuration, complete traffic, labelled dataset, heterogeneity criteria as 0. As they did not mention anywhere that they removed payload from the dataset, thus anonymity criteria coefficient taken as 0.

(vii) KYOTO (2006–2009)—Kyoto dataset was generated using honeypots to capture the real traffic. The data is publicly available in the form of sessions with labelled data at https://www.takakura.com/Kyoto-data/. The data is captured in 93,076,270 sessions. Out of these, 50,033,015 are normal sessions, 42,617,536 are known attack sessions and 425,719 unknown attack sessions. The dataset is defined over 24 features. As all these sessions data is collected from honeypots, because of this, the dataset does not satisfy the complete traffic, heterogeneity and anonymity evaluation criteria. Also, KYOTO dataset did not capture modern attacks and is not diverse.

(viii) UMASS 2011—UMASS dataset contains trace files (network packets, and some traces on wireless applications). The trace files are generated using a single TCP based download request attack scenario. UMASS 2011 is not useful to test IDS and IPS techniques due to lack of attack diversity [9].

(ix) ISCX2012—The ISCX2012 dataset was created by Ali Shiravi et al. [2] with the motive of a systematic approach to traffic generation. This dataset satisfies five criteria which includes (a) realistic network and traffic; (b) labeled dataset; (c) total interaction capture; (d) complete capture; and (e) diverse intrusion scenarios. The alpha and beta profiles used for traffic generation generated realistic benign and attack traffic to overcome the lack of realistic network traffic capture. The packet drop problem was addressed in this dataset, which was not properly addressed in the previous datasets. The dataset contains 2,450,324 flows (2,381,532 normal and 68,792 attack) captured in PCAP format. The dataset contains four types of attacks, thus infiltrating the network from inside: (a) HTTP (b) denial of service, (c) DDoS using an IRC botnet, and (d) brute force SSH. This dataset did not define the important features related to each attack type, which is helpful in discriminating against all the remaining attacks.

(x) CIC-IDS2017—The CICIDS 2017 dataset was created by Sharafaldin et al. [4] to overcome the shortcomings (traffic diversity, variety of attacks, feature sets, volume of dataset, and metadata) of previous benchmark datasets, which are available up to 2013. This dataset is available in PCAP and CSV format. Sharafaldin et al. [4] suggested important feature sets related to each attack type. Most of the datasets are available with removed payload, and anonymized packet information due to privacy concerns. To overcome this shortcoming, a separate testbed architecture network was created and used one mirror port to capture the complete traffic. To generate realistic network traffic, benign profiles and attack profiles are used to generate traffic. The CSV format dataset, which is available on their website contains 2830743 instances with 78 features and covers 7 different types of attacks (Heartbleed Attack (11), Brute Force Attack (13,835), Botnet (1966), DoS Attack (252,661), DDoS Attack (128,027), Web Attack (2180), Infiltration Attack (158,966) and Benign (2,273,097)). This dataset meets 10 out of 11 criteria completely and 1 criteria is partially satisfying because it does not cover all the 5 categories of DDoS attack diversity suggested by Sharafaldin et al. [4].

(xi) CICDDoS2019—The study by Sharafaldin et al. [12], generated the CICDDoS2019 dataset, has most recent and updated DDoS attacks which are classified into five categories. They have also proposed important feature sets for detecting specific DDoS attacks for machine learning. This dataset is available publicly in PCAP as well as CSV format. The dataset satisfies all the 11 criteria required by a quality IDS dataset.

The next section describes quality benchmark datasets available for IDS can be evaluated by using IDS evaluation framework proposed by Gharib et al. [1].

3 Framework to Evaluate Benchmark Intrusion Detection Datasets for Building Machine Learning and Deep Learning Models

The evaluation of benchmark datasets that are used in various research studies can help us to gauge the reliability of datasets and judge their suitability for designing new detection algorithms and techniques. In this section, we discuss how we can evaluate benchmark datasets used in various research studies to gauge their suitability for building new IDS.

3.1 Motivation

For building any machine learning based IDS, the dataset used to build the ma-chine learning model should be reliable. To evaluate the suitability of existing benchmark IDS datasets, in this paper, we have considered eleven benchmark IDS datasets which are generated between 1998 and 2022, and those that have been used in various research studies related to network intrusion detection. The idea to evaluate various IDS datasets used in the research literature is motivated from recent research contributions by Gharib et al. [1, 4, 12, 14].

3.2 Description of Evaluation Framework for IDS Datasets

Gharib et al. [1] proposed an evaluation framework to evaluate intrusion detection and intrusion prevention datasets. In this paper, we use the evaluation framework proposed by Gharib et al. [1] for evaluating IDS or IPS datasets. As per this framework, any dataset which is used to build IDS must strictly satisfy eleven criteria. Thus, any IDS dataset satisfying the eleven criteria or features defined in the framework can be considered as a well designed and reliable dataset. Such a dataset can be used to evaluate existing or newly designed IDS.

The eleven features comprised in the evaluation framework defined by Gharib et al. [1] are (i) Complete network configuration (ii) Complete traffic (iii) Labelled dataset, (iv) Complete interaction (v) Available protocols (vi) Attack diversity (vii) Anonymity (viii) Feature set (ix) Metadata (x) Data source heterogeneity (xi) Complete capture.

In the present study, we have used the framework suggested by Gharib et al. [1] and computed the evaluation score for each IDS dataset using equation (1) proposed by Gharib et al. [1].

$$\sum_{i=1}^{n} W_i \left(\sum_{j=1}^{m} V_i * F_j \right) \tag{1}$$

This equation can be used to measure the framework. In Eq. (1), the variable W_i is called as the flexibility coefficient which related to type of intrusion detection systems or Organization, i.e. W represents each feature weight. The value of W is defined based on either type of intrusion detection system chosen for test or organization request. The variables ‘n’ and ‘m’ represents number of features in the evaluation framework and number of coefficients for each factor. The variable ‘V’ denotes the coefficient of each sub factor. The value for coefficient of sub factor ‘V’ can be assigned based on distribution of sub-factors in various scenarios. The variable ‘F’ denotes the appearance of specific factor and sub factor in the considered dataset. F can be either binary or multi valued.

4 Assessment and Evaluation of IDS Datasets

In this paper, we have evaluated eleven (11) benchmark IDS datasets generated between 1998 and 2022. The benchmark datasets used for evaluation are (i) DARPA (ii) KDD (iii) NSL-KDD (iv) CAIDA (v) CDX (vi) KYOTO2009 (vii) UMAS2011 (viii) ISCX 2012 (ix) CICIDS 2017 (x) CSECICIDS 2018 and (xi) CICDDoS 2019. To evaluate benchmark IDS datasets, Gharib et al. [1] proposed a new evaluation framework with eleven (11) criteria which includes (i) Complete network configuration (ii) Complete traffic (iii) Labelled dataset, (iv) Complete interaction (v) Available protocols (vi) Attack diversity (vii) Anonymity (viii) Feature set (ix) Metadata (x) Data source heterogeneity (xi) Complete capture.

The above mentioned eleven criteria are considered by Sharafaldin et al. [4] to generate the CICDDoS2019 dataset which resembles real world network traffic. For this purpose, a test bed network is created which mimics real-time network configuration. The CICDDoS2019 dataset is generated by including all network interactions with the testbed consisting of an inside network (LAN) and an outside network (Internet).This dataset is publicly available at the Canadian Institute for Cyber Security. CICDDoS2019 dataset has upto date common DDoS attacks such as reflexive and exploitation attacks along with benign traffic. The attack diversity and huge number of attack traffic samples present in this dataset makes it significant and viable to evaluate new intrusion detection algorithms and techniques. The CICDDoS2019 dataset contains thirteen types of modern day DDoS attacks. Out of these 13 types of DDoS attacks, twelve attack types are executed on training day; and seven attack types are executed on testing day. To the best of our knowledge, CICDDoS2019 dataset is the only dataset which satisfies all the eleven criteria mentioned by Gharib et al. [1] which has diverse modern day DDoS attacks. Thus, this dataset can be considered worthy and quality dataset for design and development of new detection algorithms and techniques. This is evident from the scores computed for IDS datasets described in the next subsection.

4.1 Score Computation for IDS Datasets Using Gharib's Evaluation Framework

In this section, we show how to evaluate benchmark IDS datasets by computing the score for each dataset. The eleven datasets considered in this study and the details of various features for these eleven datasets is represented using Table 1. To compute scores for datasets, we must assign values for variables n, m, W, V and F. The evaluation framework for IDS dataset evaluation has 11 criteria. So, to obtain the dataset score for 11 datasets, the value for 'n' is chosen equal to 11. So, n=11. Among these 11 criteria, two criteria namely available protocol and attack diversity have sub criteria (or sub factors). The 'm' value for these two sub criteria are set as (i) five for available protocol and (ii) five for attack diversity.

We considered m = 5 for available protocol based on different types of protocols used in real time networks. The protocols considered for evaluation are HTTP, HTTPS, SSH, FTP and email protocols such as SMTP, POP, and IMAP. Since the evaluation framework has eleven criteria, we must define 11 values for W. The recent research by Gharib et al. [1] mentioned the weights vector for eleven criteria as W = [0.05, 0.05, 0.1, 0.05, 0.05, 0.25, 0.25, 0.05, 0.05, 0.05, 0.05] and the sub factor weights vector for available protocol as V1 = [0.1, 0.74, 0.04, 0.08, 0.04]. From Table 1, We have the attack diversity criteria categorized into five types. The five categories are (i) TCP based reflection/amplification attacks (A1), (ii) TCP/UDP based reflection/amplification attacks (A2), (iii) UDP based reflection/amplification attacks (A3), (iv) TCP based volumetric/exploitation attacks (A4), (v) UDP based volumetric/exploitation attacks and all other attacks (A5) mentioned in Sharafaldin et al. [12].

In Tables 1 and 3 eleven datasets are designated as D1: DARPA 98, D2: KDD 99, D3: NSL-KDD2009, D4: CAIDA2007, D5: CDX2009, D6: KYOTO (2006–2009), D7: UMASS2011, D8: ISCX2012, D9: CICIDS2017, D10: CSECICIDS2018, D11: CICDDoS2019.

Now, to obtain attack diversity vector, we must consider five attack categories in Table 1. The number of attacks, and the attack percentage of five attack categories A1, A2, A3, A4, and A5 are shown in Table 2. The information about the number of attacks for each attack category is obtained from the NetScout 1H 2023 DDoS threat report [5]. By using Table 1, we have computed the weight value for every attack diversity category. The weight vector representing the attack diversity information is denoted using V2 = [0.071987, 0.445596, 0.146261, 0.335402, 0.000755]. Table 3 shows the computations and evaluation scores for each benchmark dataset.

Out of the eleven benchmark datasets, the CICDDoS2019 dataset has obtained the highest evaluation score which is equal to 1.0. This is evident from the dataset score computed for IDS datasets as shown in Table 3. Hence, among all these datasets, we can consider the CICDDoS2019 dataset as worthy and quality dataset for design and development of new detection algorithms and techniques for DDoS attack detection.

5 Significant Findings and Key Insights of the Present Research Study

The performance of the machine learning and deep learning based network intrusion detection systems (NIDS) relies on the quality of IDS datasets which are used to train these systems. A quality IDS dataset helps NIDS to differentiate between benign and attack traffic with high accuracy and precision. So, for evaluating any detection algorithm for intrusion detection, it is important to choose the best IDS dataset to train the model as the quality of dataset plays an important role in learning and detecting not only existing but also new incoming network attacks.

Table 3 Benchmark dataset evaluation scores

S. No	Dataset	Computation carried using Gharib's framework and DDoS attacks information in NETSCOUT DDoS threat report 2023	Score
1	D1	0.05 * 1 + 0.05 * 0 + 0.1 * 1 + 0.05 * 1 + 0.05 * 1 + 0.25 * (0.1 + 0 + 0.04 + 0.08 + 0.04) + 0.25 * (0 + 0 + 0 + 0 + 0.000755) + 0.05 * 0 + 0.05 * 0 + 0.05 * 0 + 0.05 * 1	0.365189
2	D2	0.05 * 1 + 0.05 * 0 + 0.1 * 1 + 0.05 * 1 + 0.05 * 1 + 0.25 * (0.1 + 0 + 0.04 + 0.08 + 0.04) + 0.25 * (0 + 0 + 0 + 0 + 0.000755) + 0.05 * 0 + 0.05 * 0 + 0.05 * 1 + 0.05 * 1	0.415189
3	D3	0.05 * 1 + 0.05 * 0 + 0.1 * 1 + 0.05 * 1 + 0.05 * 1 + 0.25 * (0.1 + 0 + 0.04 + 0.08 + 0.04) + 0.25 * (0 + 0 + 0 + 0 + 0.000755) + 0.05 * 0 + 0.05 * 0 + 0.05 * 1 + 0.05 * 1	0.415189
4	D4	0.05 * 1 + 0.05 * 1 + 0.1 * 0 + 0.05 * 0 + 0.05 * 0 + 0.25 * (0 + 0 + 0 + 0 + 0) + 0.25 * (0 + 0 + 0 + 0 + 0.000755) + 0.05 * 1 + 0.05 * 0 + 0.05 * 0 + 0.05 * 1	0.200189
5	D5	0.05 * 0 + 0.05 * 0 + 0.1 * 0 + 0.05 * 1 + 0.05 * 1 + 0.25 * (0.1 + 0 + 0.04 + 0.08 + 0.04) + 0.25 * (0 + 0 + 0 + 0 + 0.000755) + 0.05 * 0 + 0.05 * 0 + 0.05 * 0 + 0.05 * 0	0.165189
6	D6	0.05 * 1 + 0.05 * 0 + 0.1 * 1 + 0.05 * 1 + 0.05 * 1 + 0.25 * (0.1 + 0.74 + 0.04 + 0.08 + 0.04) + 0.25 * (0 + 0 + 0 + 0 + 0.000755) + 0.05 * 0 + 0.05 * 0 + 0.05 * 1 + 0.05 * 1	0.600189
7	D7	0.05 * 1 + 0.05 * 0 + 0.1 * 1 + 0.05 * 0 + 0.05 * 1 + 0.25 * (0.1 + 0 + 0 + 0 + 0) + 0.25 * (0 + 0 + 0 + 0 + 0.000755) + 0.05 * 0 + 0.05 * 0 + 0.05 * 0 + 0.05 * 0	0.225189
8	D8	0.05 * 1 + 0.05 * 0 + 0.1 * 1 + 0.05 * 1 + 0.05 * 1 + 0.25 * (0.1 + 0 + 0.04 + 0.08 + 0.04) + 0.25 * (0 + 0.445596 + 0 + 0 + 0.000755) + 0.05 * 0 + 0.05 * 1 + 0.05 * 0 + 0.05 * 1	0.526588
9	D9	0.05 * 1 + 0.05 * 1 + 0.1 * 1 + 0.05 * 1 + 0.05 * 1 + 0.25 * (0.1 + 0.74 + 0.04 + 0.08 + 0.04) + 0.25 * (0 + 0 + 0 + 0.335402 + 0.000755) + 0.05 * 1 + 0.05 * 1 + 0.05 * 1 + 0.05 * 1	0.834039
10	D10	0.05 * 1 + 0.05 * 1 + 0.1 * 1 + 0.05 * 1 + 0.05 * 1 + 0.25 * (0.1 + 0.74 + 0.04 + 0.08 + 0.04) + 0.25 * (0 + 0 + 0 + 0.335402 + 0.000755) + 0.05 * 1 + 0.05 * 1 + 0.05 * 1 + 0.05 * 1	0.834039
11	D11	0.05 * 1 + 0.05 * 1 + 0.1 * 1 + 0.05 * 1 + 0.05 * 1 + 0.25 * (0.1 + 0.74 + 0.04 + 0.08 + 0.04) + 0.25 * (0.071987 + 0.445596 + 0.146261 + 0.335402 + 0.000755) + 0.05 * 1 + 0.05 * 1 + 0.05 * 1 + 0.05 * 1	1.0

From the detailed evaluation and assessment carried in Sect. 4, following are the various key insights derived from the present research study. (i) The widely used benchmark datasets such as DARPA98, KDD99, NSL-KDD, CAIDA 2007, CDX 2009, KYOTO 2009, UMAS 2011, ISCX 2012 datasets received low evaluation scores. Among these, the lowest score is obtained for CDX 2009, followed by CAIDA, UMASS, DARPA, KDD, NSL-KDD, ISCX datasets. (ii) KYOTO dataset received 60% score.(iii) CICIDS 2017 and CICIDS 2018 datasets received 83% score.(iv) CIC-DDoS2019 dataset obtained the highest score equal to 1.0 or 100%.

These insights receive prominence because the present research study has

(a) Applied Gharib's 2016 evaluation framework on the eleven benchmark IDS datasets widely used in most research studies.
(b) Benchmark datasets considered between 1998 and 2022.
(c) Considered NETSCOUT DDoS threat report 2023; which has the most recent information w.r.t DDoS attack diversity, the number of DDoS attacks that have been recorded globally.

6 Conclusions

In this research, we discussed in detail how to evaluate various benchmark IDS datasets to gauge their suitability to detect modern DDoS attacks. The dataset evaluation is done using Gharib's evaluation framework and NetScout 2023 first half global DDoS threat report. Specifically, our research is aimed at DDoS attack detection. Hence, in the present study, we have considered eleven benchmark IDS datasets which are widely used in various research studies to gauge their suitability for building machine learning models to detect modern DDoS attacks. Research study in this paper is limited to evaluation of various benchmark IDS datasets for DDoS attack detection. For this, widely used IDS datasets are considered between 1998 and 2022. After evaluation and assessment, it is observed that out of eleven benchmark datasets, the CICDDoS2019 dataset has satisfied eleven properties of a quality dataset with an evaluation score obtained as 1.0. To the best of our knowledge and detailed analysis carried on various benchmark datasets, we conclude that CICDDoS2019 dataset satisfied all the eleven criteria of a quality dataset as per Gharib's evaluation framework for IDS datasets. Hence, we conclude that CICDDoS2019 is the currently available best IDS dataset for DDoS attack detection. As a future work, the present study can be extended to evaluate performance of the existing and new classifiers for DDoS attack detection.

References

1. Gharib A et al (2016) An evaluation framework for intrusion detection dataset. In: 2016 International conference on information science and security (ICISS). IEEE, pp 1–6
2. Shiravi A et al (2012) Toward developing a systematic approach to generate benchmark datasets for intrusion detection. Comput Secur 31(3):357–374
3. Hussain F (2020) IoT DoS and DDoS attack detection using ResNet. In: et al (2020) IEEE 23rd international multitopic conference (INMIC). IEEE, pp 1–6
4. Sharafaldin I, Lashkari AH, Ghorbani AA (2018) Toward generating a new intrusion detection dataset and intrusion traffic characterization. ICISSp 1:108–116
5. https://www.netscout.com/threatreport/ddos-threat-intelligence-report/
6. Halladay J et al (2022) Detection and characterization of DDoS attacks using time-based features. IEEE Access 10:49794–49807

7. Hussain F et al (2021) A two-fold machine learning approach to prevent and detect IoT botnet attacks. IEEE Access 9:163412–163430
8. Jazi HH et al (2017) Detecting HTTP-based application layer DoS attacks on web servers in the presence of sampling. Comput Netw 121:25–36
9. Mohammed Y Aldarwbi, Arash H Lashkari, Ali A Ghorbani (2022) The sound of intrusion: a novel network intrusion detection system. In: Comput Electr Eng 104:108455
10. Mahdavifar S, Ghorbani AA (2019) Application of deep learning to cybersecurity: a survey. Neurocomputing 347:149–176
11. Mahdavifar S, Ghorbani AA (2023) CapsRule: explainable deep learning for classifying network attacks. In: IEEE Trans Neural Netw Learn Syst
12. Sharafaldin I et al (2019) Developing realistic distributed denial of service (DDoS) attack dataset and taxonomy. In: 2019 International carnahan conference on security technology (ICCST). IEEE, pp 1–8
13. Tavallaee M et al (2009) A detailed analysis of the KDD CUP 99 data set. In: 2009 IEEE symposium on computational intelligence for security and defense applications. IEEE, pp 1–6
14. Sharafaldin I et al (2017) Towards a reliable intrusion detection benchmark dataset. Softw Network 1:177–200

A Detailed Exploration to the Cloud Forensics Challenges and Solutions

Tanvi Modi, Dharvi Kotak, Om Patel, Yash Vasoya, Kaushal Shah, and Payal Chaudhari

Abstract In the area of digital forensics, the term "cloud forensics" has gained significant traction recently. This paper discusses the majority of the international standards bodies and their attempts to deal with both the current trend of cloud forensics in light of the growing influence of digital forensics on the standardization process and its requirement. It has been explained how to analyze the aforementioned categories in order to determine which regions require additional research. Cloud-based services have transformed the way many businesses operate. Businesses that embrace cloud migration can host their applications and software on low-cost server farms, and save them money and time by eliminating the need to manage hardware. These services also enable companies and individuals to safely store large amounts of data. However, before implementing these tactics into daily operations, businesses should consider problems such as cloud forensics. Cloud forensics has been made available. Cloud forensics was created to protect the security and integrity of data stored in the cloud and help forensic investigators find potential evidence against cloud criminals. This paper focuses on the methodological aspects of cloud forensics. It examines the advancements achieved to enable digital forensic procedures especially for investigating security incidents involving cloud computing and critically assesses the current issues and solutions for aiding investigations into such occurrences.

Keywords Forensics · AWS · Seizure · Decentralization

D. Kotak, O. Patel, Y. Vasoya, K. Shah and P. Chaudhari: These authors contributed equally to this work.

T. Modi (✉) · O. Patel · Y. Vasoya · K. Shah · P. Chaudhari
School of Technology, Pandit Deendayal Energy University, Gandhinagar, Gujarat, India
e-mail: tanvimodi297@gmail.com

D. Kotak
School of Engineering, RK University, Rajkot, Gujarat, India

B. N. Gohil et al. (eds.), *Information Security, Privacy and Digital Forensics*,
Lecture Notes in Electrical Engineering 1423,
https://doi.org/10.1007/978-981-96-9443-3_12

1 Introduction

Cloud security refers to research into crimes involving cloud services, such as data leaks or identity fraud. A cloud forensics strategy can help an organization protect itself from data loss by providing a system to preserve evidence from these types of incidents. There, without a, the holder could not have straightforward access to all relevant information about an infringement or aim on its cloud platform, especially if it was started by a third party or remote sites [1]. Cloud forensics, as opposed to traditional digital forensics, is an essential problem to consider when integrating cloud storage into your business. Cloud forensics, which can be done remotely, requires expertise in network security, network administration, and computer forensics techniques, as well as access to remote servers and storage areas.

Even though cloud hosting is recognized for its ease of use and low cost, it can still be a target of cybercrime [2]. In order to investigate a data leak or even other type of online violent act, you may also need direct exposure to all evidence. This evidence must also be admissible at trial in order for criminals to be charged. If your data is stored in a jurisdiction other than the one where it was stolen, it might not be admissible at trial. Users may also feel powerless about whether third party candidates tamper to their data on a cloud platform because they are not the rightful proprietors of that data. Since cloud-based innovation is convenient, it can also be risky if users don't select the right service or product for your business's needs. It's important to comprehend how cloud influence your company when you employ these services.

2 Literature Review

By using the cloud, digital forensics are getting better. The cloud makes a lot of technical, administrative, and legal problems even worse. Many of these difficulties are specific to cloud forensics, including data replication, location transparency, and multi-tenancy [3]. However, cloud forensics offers special possibilities that can greatly improve the effectiveness and efficiency of forensic investigations.

Developing reliable cloud forensics strategies is becoming more important as cloud computing usage grows. Researchers have examined the difficulties and suggested a few ways to lessen them [4]. Due to the fact that the location of the data and its replicas (which are kept as backups) are unknown, these circumstances present difficulties for digital forensics. Additionally, these data are kept in many countries where various laws surrounding data access may be in effect. Additionally, the copyright of the these information is in doubt as a result of the resource sharing (multi-tenancy). Because cloud technology is able to outperform traditional digital forensics, this new concept needs to be developed in a variety of ways, taking into account technical, legal, and structural aspects [5].

One of the crucial aspects of the field of cloud technology, which is still growing, is how researchers do studies to find out how a digital crime was done over the cloud. This is called "cloud spectroscopy." At the same time, the problems and issues that come dressed in fancy forensic evidence are different from those that come up in forensic investigation [6]. This paper talks about the problems with forensic investigation that were found in a review of the field and then moves onto a model that divides the problems into phases.

In addition to its obvious benefits, the complexities of cloud computing give unscrupulous individuals a haven to engage in a variety of illegal actions. Researchers have discovered methods, problems, and solutions that can be used to increase user security in cloud systems. First, a comprehensive overview of all the frameworks and approaches for digital and cloud forensics has been provided, along with a detailed assessment of their features, limitations, and complexity characteristics [7].

Cloud computing is widely recognised as one of the most important advancements in information and communication technology (IT) solutions that have occurred in recent years. Numerous cloud providers (CSPs) have made their services available, which has resulted in a variety of revolutionary shifts in computer activities and opened the door to a great number of exciting opportunities in the fields of technology and the economy. Despite this, many cloud clients are still hesitant to migrate their information technology (IT) requirements to the cloud, mostly because of their fears regarding the security of the cloud and the danger posed by the unknown [8]. Sadly, the conventional techniques to proof catalogue and recovering in a non-cloud (traditional) scheme are not feasible. This is because they depend on unfettered access to the pertinent systems and user data, a feature that is not available through the cloud due to the cloud's decentralised data processing. In the cloud, this is not an issue. In this article, we take a methodical look at the forensic challenges presented by cloud computing and investigate the most recent advances and solutions to these issues. In particular, in contrast to the other surveys that have been done on the subject, we highlight the problems with cloud computing by basing our explanation on the phases of conventional digital forensics [9].

The delivery and use of IT services have altered as a result of cloud computing. Cloud adoption has increased significantly, and experts anticipate that trend to continue. Consumers' worries about the privacy and security of data assets kept in the cloud are correspondingly growing. On the other hand Concern over the potential for cybercrimes to use the cloud as a platform is growing. The cloud's massive computational and storage capacity allows for the swift and affordable execution of major attacks [10].

The account can then be totally closed by the crooks, who can then vanish into thin air. The complexities and limitations of digital forensics in a cloud setting only serve to compound this. In this paper, we've offered a methodical study of the problems with cloud forensics, their potential fixes for various stages of the forensic procedure, and a thorough review of the suggested fixes. We have noted the level of maturity of the solutions and opportunities for more study and development. A concise explanation of forensics-asa-service models is also available from us [11].

3 Overview of Cloud Computing and Digital Forensics

Traditional digital forensics uses methods to solve cybercrimes, such as gathering evidence from software and data. To chase down hacking or start investigating an event, computer forensics advisors obtain data from resources like computers and networks. Cloud based services make this hunt for evidence more complex. While the investigator uses the same methodologies in cloud forensics just like in conventional computer forensics, the lines between who owns the proof and where it is admissible in court may blur. Data can be stored off and in multiple locations or on server possessed by a private entity when using cloud-based facilities [4]. The rules have been determined by the services provided.

3.1 Definition of Cloud Computing

Cloud computing refers to any service delivered over the internet. Cloud computing is a term used to describe the delivery of computer resources and IT services over the internet, rather than within an organization's own infrastructure.Cloud infrastructure consists the both software and hardware components required for classic cloud computing execution.

3.1.1 Types of Cloud Computing Services

Cloud computing services can be generally divided into Platform as a Service (PaaS), Software as a Service (SaaS), and Infrastructure as a Service (IaaS) are the three main types. These categories meet a range of corporate needs and applications while offering users differing levels of control and administration.

1. **IaaS**: Users are given a storage capacity and can begin, halt, connect directly, and configure their virtual machines and storage as needed. IaaS providers offer tiny, moderate, large, even more, memory or computer optimized instances, in addition to instance personalization for specific workload requirements. For example, Amazon Web Services (AWS)
2. **PaaS**: A PaaS (Platform-as-a-Service) model Is a cloudprimarily based totally software program platform that allows developers to access pre-built tools and services hosted on a provider's infrastructure. For example, APIs, portals, or gateway software.
3. **SaaS**: It is a software as a service distribution method that provides software over the internet; such applications are also known as web services [12]. SaaS provides users with subscription-based connectivity to application and database software. Microsoft 365, for example, offers efficiency and email services

3.1.2 Cloud Computing Deployment Models

The various methods that consumers and organizations can access cloud services and resources are referred to as cloud computing deployment models. Generally, there are four primary models for cloud deployment:

1. **Private cloud**: The company's data center provides private cloud storage for internal users. Cloud services are created and maintained in-house rather than by third parties. Private cloud technology includes VMware and OpenStack.
2. **Public cloud**: Public cloud services are delivered over the internet by third-party cloud service providers (CSPs), who sell their services on a pay-per-use basis. The most common examples of public cloud services include Amazon Web Services, Microsoft Azure, and IBM's Bluemix.
3. **community cloud**: The community Deployment Model is somewhat similar to the Private cloud. A single person or entity owns the cloud server in a private cloud Community Cloud server is shared by several businesses with similar histories.
4. **Hybrid cloud**: A hybrid cloud can be composed of both on-premises private and public cloud services, with configuration automation between them. The primary objective of a hybrid cloud would be to build an environment that can handle quest application forms while also enabling for resource consumption flexibility.

3.2 *Definition of Digital Forensics*

Digital forensics is the investigation and analysis of digital data, such as devices and data. Originally used to refer to the retrieval and investigation of computer-related material, it has since expanded to include all devices that store digital data. As society becomes more reliant on computer systems and the internet, digital forensics has become a critical component of both business and law enforcement [6].

3.2.1 Digital Forensics Investigation Process

A methodical approach called "digital forensics" is used for finding, preserve, investigate, and present digital evidence from electronic devices and data storage media in a way that is appropriate for court cases. The process of conducting a digital forensics investigation usually comprises multiple crucial stages:

1. **Seizure**: Prior to examination, digital media is seized in criminal cases as part of the chain of custody.
2. **Acquisition**: Following the seizure of assets, an investigative copy of the information is created. The original drive is once again secured to avoid tampering

and unauthorized access. To authenticate users' parties can access the evidence, a hash is used.

3. **Analysis**: Following the body of data, the files are studied to identify proof that might or might not confirm the hypothesis. Forensic investigators typically recover removed information by backing up from available disc space and also the OS cache.
4. **Reporting**: The document is presented in a manner that non-technical individuals can comprehend. It could contain audit data or other documentation (Fig. 1).

4 Overview of Cloud Forensics

When a crime or crime using the cloud as a medium occurs, cloud forensics professionals use their abilities and expertise to identify the individuals or organizations involved. Cloud investigators must follow strict rules to guarantee their work is permissible in court.

Cloud security is a subcategory of computer forensics that focuses specifically on cloud technology. Cloud forensic scientists, like digital forensic scientists, must work with a variety of computing assets such as servers, networks, apps, datasets, and storage, but they do not have accessibility to the explored systems and settings. This fact has a significant impact on how cloud investigative inquests have been carried out.

4.1 Cloud Forensics Process

This model is intended to make the process of analyzing and trying to associate challenges to forensic investigation as simple as possible. The model is comprised of four steps:

1. **Identification**: The first process in any occurrence investigation is to identify all potential evidence sources in a public cloud. It is critical because the subsequent processes rely on this evidence.
2. **Preservation**: It is the act of gathering evidence from various locations, including clouds, as well as the various types of media and tools used to do so. Researchers

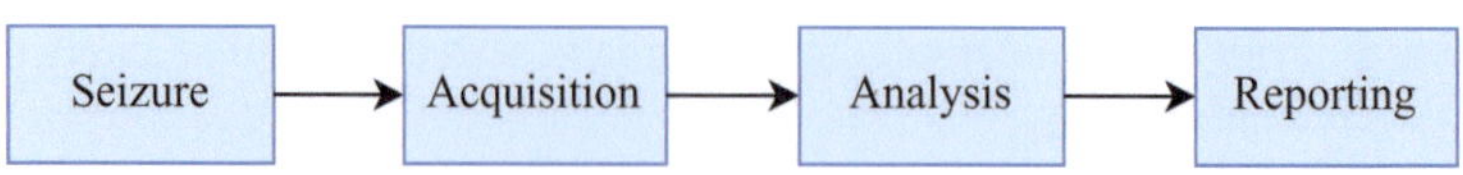

Fig. 1 Digital forensic investigation process

must isolate and collect evidence by prohibiting the use of digital devices and the duplication of digital evidence.

3. **Examinations**: are investigations that involve data extraction from earlier steps and the inspection of huge amounts of information to locate evidence regarding an incident.
4. **Presentation**: In the—phase of a trial, the evidence is presented in a legal court. Using expert evidence on the analysis of the evidence, a very well report with the conclusions should be compiled. Due to the complication of the cloud computing system for the average Internet user, evidence must be supplied so that all technical details can be comprehended by the average Internet user (Fig. 2).

4.2 Challenges of Cloud Forensics

1. Log access to evidence: Logs are essential to an inquiry. Obtaining access to log data will allow the investigators to locate an incident. Data are kept in unidentifiable locations due to systems spread in cloud environments, making log location a challenging and time-consuming process
2. Physical Inaccessibility: Because the hardware devices in a cloud system are dispersed geographically, data localization is difficult. The premise of the well-known digital forensic techniques and tools is direct access to the hardware.
3. Volatile Data: In the IaaS cloud model, data stored in a Virtualization instance is lost when the instance is powered down or restarted. This includes crucial evidence such as registry entries, active processes, and temporary internet files.
4. Service Level Agreement (SLA): The challenge for CSPs lies in their dependence on external parties. They form agreements with fellow CSPs to access their services, making it crucial to involve everyone with a direct impact on the chain of custody during investigations.
5. Synchronization of Time: The significance of time in handling data is consistent across all three service models. Ensuring accuracy demands effort, given the widespread geographical distribution of data across different time zones. Investigators must meticulously gather timestamps from various devices to establish an accurate timeline of events.
6. Chain of Custody: Ensuring the integrity of evidence in court requires strict adherence to the chain of custody, documenting every step from collection to presentation. If this chain is broken, the evidence's credibility is jeopardized.

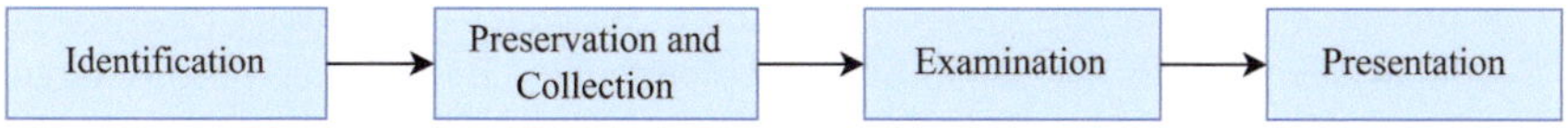

Fig. 2 Cloud forensic process

7. Multi-jurisdiction: Gathering evidence from cloud-based systems across various jurisdictions poses a significant challenge for investigators. Cloud systems inherently distribute their data globally, making it exceptionally challenging, if not entirely impossible, to collect evidence effectively. This complexity arises due to the divergent legal frameworks in different countries.
8. Insufficient Forensic Equipment: Analyzing data in cloud systems necessitates specialized forensic tools that are compatible with the distributed nature of these platforms. Digital forensic investigations rely on a variety of tools designed specifically for cloud inquiries.
9. Volume of Data: The data stored in Cloud Service Providers' (CSPs) data centers is vast and continually increasing. This surge poses a significant challenge when it comes to analyzing data to extract pertinent evidence for investigations.

5 Comparative Analysis of Cloud Forensic and Investigation Tools

In this section, we will explore several cloud forensics tools, highlighting their respective strengths and considerations. Conducting a nuanced analysis of these tools is crucial for discerning their suitability in various investigative scenarios.

1. **Magnet AXIOM Cyber**:
   - Strengths: Comprehensive cloud support, covering AWS, Azure, and Google Cloud. Noteworthy features include thorough evidence collection, detailed timeline analysis, and in-depth artifact examination.
   - Considerations: Users appreciate its versatility but note that a learning curve might exist due to its extensive feature set.
2. **AccessData FTK (Forensic Toolkit) Cloud**:
   - Strengths: An extension of the renowned FTK tool, FTK Cloud specializes in analyzing data from cloud services like Office 365 and Google Workspace. It stands out for its data extraction and analysis capabilities.
   - Considerations: Known for its reliability, FTK Cloud might be preferred for its seamless integration with traditional forensic workflows.
3. **Cellebrite UFED Cloud Analyzer**:
   - Strengths: Leveraging Cellebrite's mobile forensics expertise, UFED Cloud Analyzer extends its capabilities to cloud data. It supports various cloud platforms and enables the extraction and analysis of cloud-stored data.
   - Considerations: Widely recognized for its reliability, UFED Cloud Analyzer is often chosen for its seamless integration with mobile forensic workflows.

4. **Belkasoft Evidence Center**:

   - Strengths: Beyond cloud forensics, Belkasoft's Evidence Center covers computer and mobile forensic features. It supports multiple cloud services, providing robust data extraction, analysis, and reporting.
   - Considerations: Users appreciate its all-encompassing approach to digital forensics, making it a preferred choice for those requiring a comprehensive solution.

5. **X-Ways Forensics**:

   - Strengths: While not exclusively a cloud forensic tool, X-Ways Forensics is renowned for its powerful disk and filesystem analysis. It extends its capabilities to cloud investigations, supporting the examination of evidence obtained from cloud storage.
   - Considerations: Known for its speed and efficiency in traditional forensics, X-Ways Forensics offers a solid option for organizations requiring versatile capabilities.

When selecting a tool, factors such as the extent of cloud service support, ease of use, reporting features, and integration with existing forensic workflows should be carefully considered.

In conclusion, the selection of a cloud forensics tool should align with the specific requirements of an investigation, taking into account factors such as platform compatibility, ease of use, cost considerations, and the expertise of the investigative team.

6 Cloud Forensics Solution

Cloud forensics solutions encompass the tools, techniques, and methods employed in the examination and interpretation of digital evidence within cloud computing settings. These resources are vital for both organizations and experts in the field of digital forensics when conducting investigations within cloud environments.

1. Forensic Tool Testing: There are currently no filled cloud-specific forensic tools available. However, forensic investigators are still obtaining substantiation from of the cloud using existing tools. In one âL˜s inquests, forensic scientists employ the following tools:

   - Encase Enterprise: To gather data remote location from the cloud's guest OS layer. It is preferable to analyze IaaS data rather than a snapshot of data.
   - Accessdata FTK: To obtain information from the cloud compute clusters' guest operating system.

- UFED cloud analyzer: it is used to examine the metadata and data stored in the cloud.
- Docker Forensics Toolkit & Docker Explorer: These tools extract extra details from Docker hosting service images.

7 Optimal Solution

We suggested the Open Cloud Forensics Model in this (OCF). We developed a cloud services architecture based on this concept, and we verified the model with a research study drawn from a court case.

Data preservation in the cloud is one of the unresolved issues with the aforementioned suggested approach. A benefit of cloud computing is its quick elasticity, but this comes with the issue of protecting data in an examination until it can be located and retrieved.

Just the acquisition part of the investigation examination is implemented by FROST; the organisation, analysis, and presentation phases of the process, which are all impacted by cloud computing, are not addressed.

1. **FROST**:

   FROST, a forensic software designed for the OpenStack cloud computing platform, collects essential data for digital forensic investigations from guest firewall logs, virtual drives, and API logs. Operating within the cloud's Infrastructure-as-a-Service (IaaS) framework, FROST processes log data without directly interacting with the guest virtual machines' operating systems. Instead, it operates at the cloud management level, ensuring independence from the guest machines. The collected information is securely stored in hash trees and returned in cryptographic form, eliminating the need to rely on the integrity of individual machines. The framework presents a series of scientific goals that can be broadened in the future. These objectives encompass the advancement of additional information security techniques, disclosure strategies, validation procedures, metrics, and assessment abilities. The tool must align with the technical specifications of the cloud environment, leveraging its self-service, on-demand, scalable, and elastic features. To achieve this, the instrument being built should adhere to the following technical requirements:

   (a) Compatibility with established forensic file formats.
   (b) Ease of creation and generation.
   (c) Flexibility and open customizability.
   (d) Ability to scale and expand seamlessly based on demand.
   (e) with existing norms and standards.

FROST consists of three key components, each serving distinct functions:

(a) Image Retrieval and Integrity Verification: Users can utilize this feature to retrieve images of their virtual disks from their virtual machines. The program also allows for the verification of image integrity through cryptographic checksums.
(b) API Request Logging and Verification: Users can access and validate the integrity of logs detailing every API request they've initiated with their cloud provider, using their own authentication credentials.
(c) Virtual Machine Integrity Verification and Firewall Log Access: This tool empowers users to verify the integrity of their owned virtual machines and provides access to OpenStack firewall logs.

Architecture and Features

FROST, an integrated framework, incorporates Horizon and Nova from OpenStack's diverse components. Nova employs virtual servers akin to Amazon EC2, delivering the compute service through its compute API. Horizon, on the other hand, serves as OpenStack's web-based user interface and seamlessly connects with Nova using the Compute API. This integration is illustrated in Fig. 3, showcasing the seamless collaboration between Horizon, Nova, and the broader OpenStack environment.

The FROST suite for OpenStack can be described as a collection of forensic tools seamlessly integrated into the management framework of cloud architecture. These tools are valuable for law enforcement, cloud users, and forensic investigators in their pursuit of obtaining reliable forensic data independently of the cloud service provider. Additionally, FROST is capable of supporting tasks such as audits, real-time monitoring, and the generation of metrics, making its functionalities easily accessible to users.

The FROST tool is highly adaptable, allowing users to generate metrics, perform audits, and facilitate real-time monitoring. FROST provides users with practical functionalities and features tailored to their needs.

8 Conclusion

Based on the reviews of the literature, it is evident that Based on the reviews of the literature, it is evident that cloud forensics is more onerous than digital forensics. This is why we need new frameworks and methodologies to properly In all phases of an investigation, it is essential to preserve evidence and maintain the chain of custody. Cloud forensics is a new subject, thus approaches and frameworks were derived from digital forensics. No author has, to our knowledge, established and proposed a framework or methodology that encompasses every facet and step of a cloud forensic investigation. The majority of cloud forensics work focuses on obstacles, issues, and dangers associated with service models; these challenges apply to many phases and activities within an investigation.

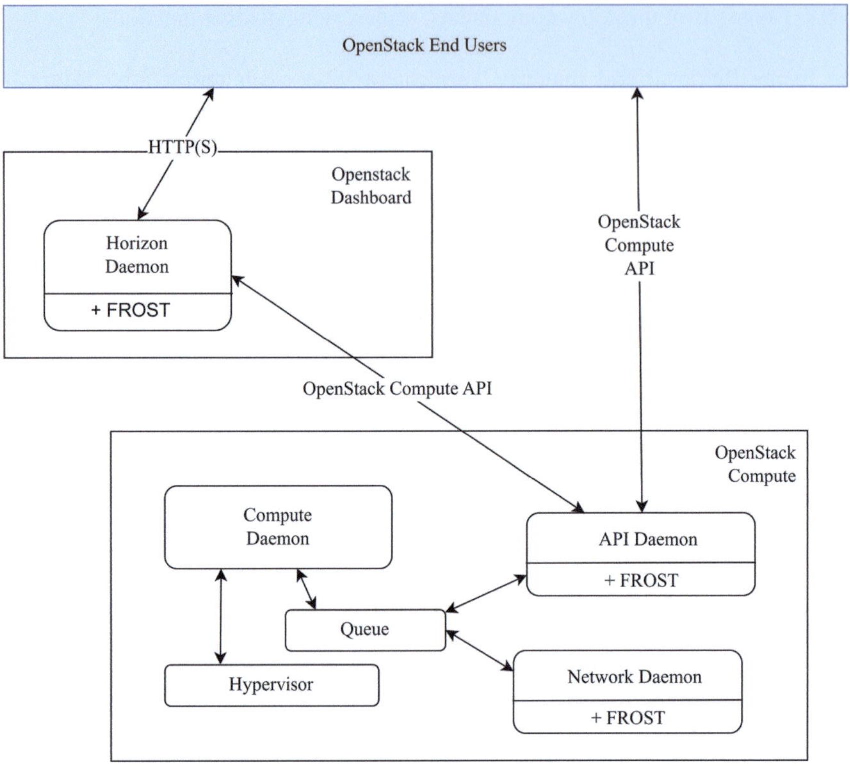

Fig. 3 Frost architecture

Cloud computing provides minimal-cost services through the utilization of massive data centers for storage in multiple countries and multitenant serving by virtual servers. The challenge for digital forensics specialists is that the Unknown is the source of information and its copies (for backup purposes). In addition, these data are maintained in jurisdictions where differing laws on data access may have been implemented. Also, sharing resources (multi-tenancy) creates ownership issues for digital forensic investigators.

References

1. Simou S, Kalloniatis C, Kavakli E, Gritzalis S (2014) Cloud forensics: identifying the major issues and challenges. In: Jarke M, Mylopoulos J, Quix C, Rolland C, Manolopoulos Y, Mouratidis H, Horkoff J (eds) Advanced information systems engineering. Springer, Cham, pp 271–284
2. Ruan K, Carthy J, Kechadi T, Crosbie M (2011) Cloud forensics. In: Peterson G, Shenoi S (eds) Advances in digital forensics VII. Springer, Berlin, Heidelberg, pp 35–46

3. Sharma BK, Joseph MA, Jacob B, Miranda B (2019) Emerging trends in digital forensic and cyber security- an overview. In: 2019 Sixth HCT information technology trends (ITT), pp 309–313 (2019). https://doi.org/10.1109/ITT48889.2019.9075101
4. Ahmed O, Haji L, Shukur H, Zebari R, Abass S, Sadeeq M (2020) Comparison among cloud technologies and cloud performance. J Appl Sci Technol Trends 1:40–47. https://doi.org/10.38094/jastt1219
5. Dillon T, Wu C, Chang E (2010) Cloud computing: issues and challenges. In: 2010 24th IEEE international conference on advanced information networking and applications, pp 27–33. https://doi.org/10.1109/AINA.2010.187
6. Lim N Cloud forensics and the digital CrimeScene
7. Shivam K 'Cloud forensics'. https://kumarshivam-66534.medium.com/cloud-forensics-be18e14230de
8. Zawoad S, Hasan R (2013) Cloud forensics: a meta-study of challenges, approaches, and open problems. ArXiv preprint arXiv:1302.6312
9. Zargari S, Benford D (2012) Cloud forensics: concepts, issues, and challenges. In: 2012 third international conference on emerging intelligent data and web technologies, pp 236–243. https://doi.org/10.1109/EIDWT.2012.44
10. Almulla S (2014) A state-of-the-art review of cloud forensics. J Digital Forens Secur Law https://doi.org/10.15394/jdfsl.2014.1190
11. Pichan A, Lazarescu M, Soh ST (2015) Cloud forensics: technical challenges, solutions and comparative analysis. Digital Invest 13:38–57. https://doi.org/10.1016/j.diin.2015.03.002
12. Ruan K, Carthy J, Kechadi T, Baggili I (2013) Cloud forensics definitions and critical criteria for cloud forensic capability: an overview of survey results. Digit Investig 10(1):34–43. https://doi.org/10.1016/j.diin.2013.02.004

Forensic Analysis of Internet Protocol Detail Record (IPDR) for Investigative Purposes: Techniques, Challenges and Future Directions

P. S. Viji, A. Aswathy, J. Anwer Reyaz, and A. Nandu

Abstract The rapid adoption of Internet-based messaging applications, such as WhatsApp, Facebook, Instagram etc. has revolutionized communications worldwide. However, these technological advancements have also created additional opportunities for criminals to engage in illicit activities. These messaging services pose challenges for law enforcement agencies while trying to intercept and identify potential actors involved in criminal activities. There is an urgent need to develop new techniques for analyzing internet communication logs and connecting potential criminals who exploit messaging services. Internet Protocol Detail Record (IPDR) contains information about IP-based service usage. Internet service providers store such information for billing, auditing and other purposes. Law Enforcement Agencies use these records as a source of evidence to solve cybercrimes. IPDR contains comprehensive information about internet activity including session details, data transfer volume, device & SIM identification numbers, timestamp of accessing an internet service and tower information. By conducting IPDR analysis, investigators can overcome the limitations of traditional approaches and extract meaningful insights to identify potential crimes and gather evidence for legal proceedings. This paper proposes leveraging IPDR as a valuable source of evidence for forensic investigation and tracking suspects. This paper also explores the benefits of IPDR analysis, the challenges faced by law enforcement agencies in analyzing encrypted messaging services, and the potential of IPDR analysis to enhance forensic investigations.

Keywords IPDR · Correlation · CDR · Filters · Link analyzer

P. S. Viji · A. Aswathy · J. Anwer Reyaz (✉) · A. Nandu
Centre for Development of Advanced Computing, Cyber Forensic Section, Thiruvananthapuram, Kerala, India
e-mail: anwer@cdac.in

A. Aswathy
e-mail: aswathy.a@cdac.in

A. Nandu
e-mail: nandu.a@cdac.in

B. N. Gohil et al. (eds.), *Information Security, Privacy and Digital Forensics*, Lecture Notes in Electrical Engineering 1423,
https://doi.org/10.1007/978-981-96-9443-3_13

1 Introduction

In recent years, the widespread adoption of Internet-based messaging applications has revolutionized interpersonal communication. However, the rise in criminal activities facilitated by encrypted platforms has raised concerns among law enforcement agencies globally. To address these challenges, this paper proposes leveraging IPDR (Internet Protocol Detail Record) analysis as a solution.

IPDRs, typically maintained by Internet Service Providers for billing and accounting purposes, offer a valuable source of cyber-forensic evidence beyond financial matters. The paper emphasizes the diverse content, structure, and file formats of IPDRs, presenting a challenge in their analysis using traditional tools.

While Adya Joshi et al. [1] introduced a method for user profiling using IPDRs and CDRs, it lacks a comprehensive approach for overall IPDR analysis in case investigations. The paper aims to fill this gap by underlining the importance of IPDR analysis in forensic investigations related to Internet communications. Lingaraju [3] explains the parameters within IPDR files and discusses their forensic significance, focusing on a comprehensive understanding of network activities, communication protocols and fundamental manual investigation techniques. The mandatory parameters to be preserved by the service providers in IPDR and their format are provided by the Telecom Regulatory Authority of India (TRAI) [2, 11].

The focus of the paper is on detailing IPDR's capacity to capture session information, data transfer specifics, device metadata, and location data. By employing IPDR analysis techniques, law enforcement can surmount limitations posed by log data files, gaining crucial insights into potential criminal activities. The paper advocates for automated techniques to enhance the efficiency and effectiveness of IPDR analysis, addressing the existing manual processes.

The subsequent sections of the paper are organized as follows: Sect. 2 delves into the current manual processes and the imperative need for automation in IPDR analysis. Section 3 explores various techniques in IPDR analysis. Section 4 outlines the system design and presents the results of the evaluation. Section 5 provides insights from a case study, while Sect. 6 encapsulates key findings and offers a comprehensive conclusion. Lastly, Sect. 7 outlines planned future works aimed at improving the system.

2 Existing Manual Process and the Need for Automation in IPDR Analysis

Existing manual processes involved in IPDR analysis using traditional data analysis tools are often time-consuming and labor-intensive. A significant challenge in the analysis of IPDR lies in the inherent diversity of log file formats employed by different service providers across different circles. Despite the provision of a format by TRAI [2] to ensure the preservation of mandatory information, service providers often deviate by utilizing their own field names, incorporating additional data, or omitting certain columns. Furthermore, the log data itself can exhibit variations subject to specific queries issued by law enforcement agencies (LEAs). IPDRs can be generated based on factors such as mobile numbers, source IP addresses, IMEI numbers, or IMSI numbers [3]. An IMEI-based IPDR means it is generated with records of a specific IMEI number for a period. Analysing and correlating these logs in multiple formats, without the help of a standardized importing tool is a cumbersome task.

Each individual is likely to generate a significant volume of IP data records based on their internet usage. Considering the number of individuals associated with a given case, the IPDR data linked to that case is expected to be substantial. Manual processing and analysing such a large amount of data becomes a tedious task and is prone to errors.

Automation can significantly enhance the efficiency and effectiveness of investigations by enabling faster data importing and standardization of IPDR data. Also, automated techniques can be incorporated into the identification of suspicious activities, tracking communication patterns, and pinpointing potential crimes, ultimately enabling law enforcement agencies to respond promptly and effectively. Traditional methods of analysis often lack standardized methodologies, leading to variations in data interpretation and analysis across different analysts. By implementing automated techniques, agencies can ensure a more consistent and reliable approach to IPDR analysis, reducing discrepancies and improving the overall quality of investigative findings. Additionally, automation enables the integration of multiple data sources, such as call logs, messaging data, and internet usage logs, providing a holistic view of suspects' activities and aiding in the generation of comprehensive investigative reports.

3 Techniques in IPDR Analysis

Automated tools and techniques can be employed to extract relevant information from the IPDRs and perform initial data processing techniques such as filtering, sorting, and aggregating the data. This automation reduces the manual effort required and improves efficiency in handling large volumes of IPDRs.

3.1 Complexity and Variety of Data

IPDR data consists of diverse information, including source and destination IP addresses, timestamps, session details, bandwidth usage, and more. The IPDRS from service providers comes in various file formats—Excel, CSV, HTML, MDB etc. Extracting meaningful insights and identifying relevant patterns within this complex and varied data can be difficult. Pre-sets can be incorporated to address this. A Pre-set is a predefined set of header texts and the values or synonyms it can have in real IPDR files. Preset can help in importing complex and various IPDR files with minimum user intervention.

3.2 Quicker Analysis and Decision Making

IPDR data can contain relevant information and relationships that may be challenging to identify and comprehend manually, leading to delays in analysis and decision-making processes. Implementing data visualization can help represent IPDR data in a visual format such as graphs, charts, or dashboards. Visual representations make it easier to identify patterns, trends, and anomalies, enabling quicker analysis and decision-making.

3.3 Destination IP Analysis

The destination IP to which a user had connected has prime importance in analysis. IP Address Analysis can be done using Domain Name System (DNS) lookup. DNS resolution allows analysts to map IP addresses to domain names. DNS logs can provide a record of domain names accessed by a particular device or user. This information can be used to reconstruct online activities, identify potentially malicious behaviour, or establish connections between different entities involved in an investigation.

Note that the DNS lookup may not always return a domain name for an IP address. The domain might have expired, the DNS records could be misconfigured, or the domain name might not exist. Also, DNS resolvers and local devices often cache DNS information to improve performance. However, if the cached data becomes outdated or corrupted, it can cause a failed DNS resolution.

3.4 Obtaining App Information

Obtaining Application-related information such as the App name, Organization Name, country, and region associated with a destination IP address can play a crucial role in the analysis. There are situations when the analyst needs to know the countries to which a specific user has communicated. Availability and accuracy of IP-Geo Location databases impact the correctness of the App information.

3.5 WhatsApp Communication

Analyzing IPDRs to determine probable WhatsApp communication can be a challenging task. WhatsApp, which is owned by Meta, falls under the umbrella of various public messaging applications like Facebook and Instagram [9]. These applications share common ownership which in turn causes them to share servers. It is challenging to differentiate and identify the specific IP addresses associated with WhatsApp communication.

WhatsApp may employ a pool of dynamically allocated IP addresses [8, 10], meaning that the IP addresses associated with WhatsApp communication can change frequently. Consequently, maintaining an up-to-date and comprehensive list of WhatsApp IPs becomes difficult, as the dynamic allocation of addresses requires continuous monitoring and updating.

3.6 CDR, SDR and Cell ID Correlation with IPDR

Call Detail Records (CDRs) are the log of records kept by the service provider which contains information about the communication between mobile numbers, timestamps, and other details. A subscriber Detail Record (SDR) is a record that contains information about subscribers including name, date of birth, address etc. Cell ID log is a record of the unique identifiers associated with towers that a mobile device connects to during communication. It can contain the address and geographic location of the towers.

Correlating CDR, SDR, Cell ID, and IPDRs enables law enforcement agencies to gain insights into the communication and online activities of individuals under investigation. They can determine call patterns, identify contacts, track locations, and analyze internet usage. This information helps in building a comprehensive profile of suspects and understanding their network of connections. By analyzing location data from CDRs and IPDRs, investigators can establish timelines, identify key locations, and track the movements of individuals. This can be crucial in solving crimes, apprehending suspects, and establishing their involvement in specific incidents. This analysis can help identify key individuals involved in criminal activities, establish links between suspects, and uncover potential co-conspirators.

3.7 IMEI Number Analysis

IMEI, or International Mobile Equipment Identity, is a unique 15-digit code assigned to every mobile phone. Various details about the device associated with the provided IMEI number can be obtained [5]. The commonly retrieved details from IMEI include:

- Device Manufacturer: The Company that manufactured the device.
- Device Model: The specific model or version of the device.
- Serial Number: Uniquely identifies the device.

By analyzing IMEI numbers and associated device information [4], an analyst can gain insight into the history of a particular device. For example, if the same IMEI number is associated with multiple phone numbers, it could suggest that the user is using more than one SIM card on the same device. This information can be valuable in cases related to phone theft or fraudulent activities, as it helps identify irregular device usage and potentially track stolen devices.

3.8 IMSI Number Analysis

IMSI stands for International Mobile Subscriber Identity. It is a unique identifier associated with a subscriber in a mobile network [6]. Unlike IMEI, the database for IMSI is not available publicly. The commonly retrieved details from IMSI [7] include:

- Mobile Network Operator: The telecommunications company providing services to the mobile device.
- Mobile Country Code: A numerical code representing the country where the mobile network is registered.
- Mobile Network Code: A numerical code identifying the specific mobile network within the country.
- Subscriber Identity: The unique identity assigned to the SIM card.

IMSI number analysis can be useful in the identification of service providers which in turn helps in identifying ported numbers.

4 System

Based on the above criteria and methodologies, we have developed a holistic solution for the in-depth analysis of IPDRs for cyber forensic crime resolution. The idea of the tool is to help the investigators get meaningful insights from the internet access information of a suspect and generate comprehensive reports that are producible to the court. The application consists of six main parts: Importer, Filters, Link Analyzer, Geo Distance, Probable Direct Communication, Commonality Analyzer, Customizable Search and Correlation. The overall architecture of the tool is given in Fig. 1.

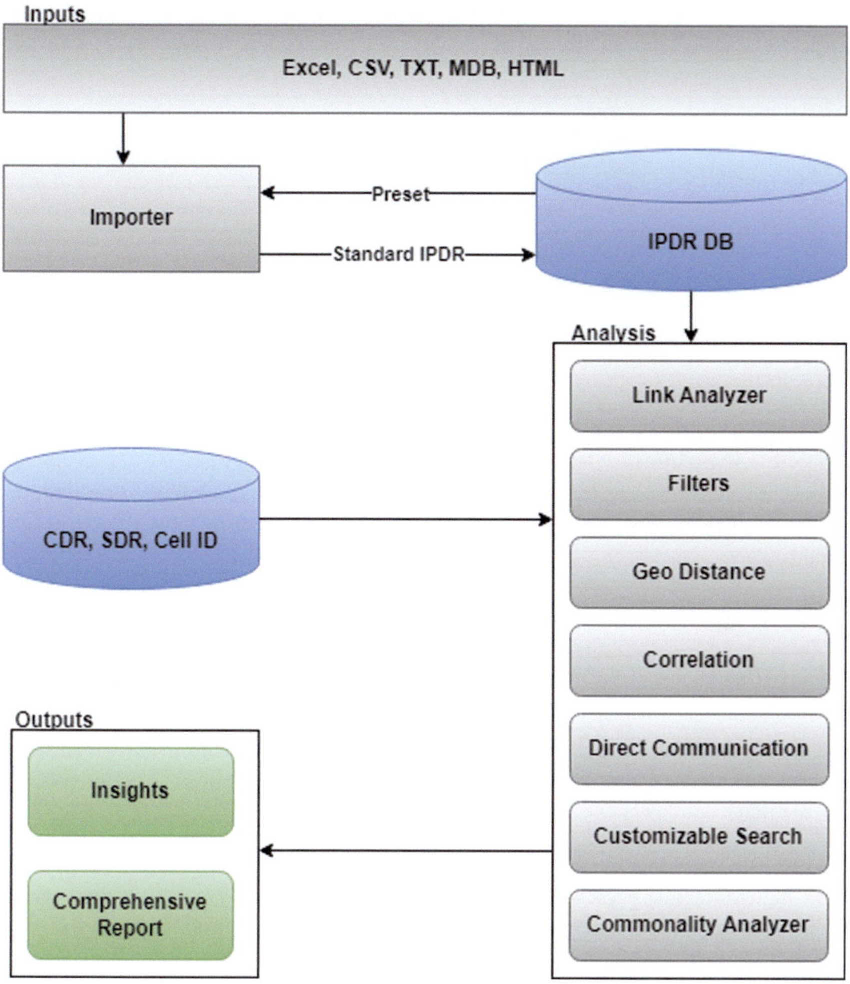

Fig. 1 Architecture diagram

4.1 Importer

The Importer module allows users to import single or multiple IPDRs into the system. It provides the capability to map IPDRs provided by service providers and convert them into a standard format for effective analysis. The Importer supports customizable pre-sets, enabling users to import IPDRs with a single click. In cases where pre-sets are not available, a pre-set management module can help to add pre-sets.

The tool automatically maps the required fields and converts user-provided IPDRs into the standardized format, simplifying the import process. Figure 2 shows the imported IPDR with some fields removed to preserve the privacy of the person.

ID	PhoneNumber	SourceIP	SourcePort	DestinationIP	DestinationPort	StartDateTime	EndDateTime	Duration	TowerID
1		5	36168	49.44.100.186	80	2017-05-11 19:10:11	2017-05-11 19:40:11	1800	405840007c410
2		5	57861	49.44.100.186	80	2017-05-11 19:10:11	2017-05-11 19:40:11	1800	405840007c410
3			35063	8.37.236.236	80	2017-05-11 19:11:15	2017-05-11 19:41:15	1800	40584001c0b30
4			40687	217.65.40.36	80	2017-05-11 19:11:15	2017-05-11 19:41:15	1800	40584001c0b30
5			41030	8.37.236.236	80	2017-05-11 19:11:15	2017-05-11 19:41:15	1800	40584001c0b30
6			53388	8.37.236.236	80	2017-05-11 19:11:15	2017-05-11 19:41:15	1800	40584001c0b30
7			43900	74.125.68.114	80	2017-05-11 18:29:59	2017-05-11 19:29:59	3600	4058400014125
8			55060	104.17.38.113	80	2017-05-11 18:49:01	2017-05-11 19:19:01	1800	40584000ca513
9			55061	104.17.38.113	80	2017-05-11 18:49:01	2017-05-11 19:19:01	1800	40584000ca513
10			55064	104.17.38.113	80	2017-05-11 18:49:01	2017-05-11 19:19:01	1800	40584000ca513
11			55065	104.17.38.113	80	2017-05-11 18:49:01	2017-05-11 19:19:01	1800	40584000ca513
12			42634	49.44.78.49	443	2017-05-11 18:48:33	2017-05-11 19:18:33	1800	405840016d612
13			35342	8.37.236.193	80	2017-05-11 18:50:21	2017-05-11 19:20:21	1800	4058400079230

Fig. 2 Imported IPDR with masked Phone Number and Source IP Address

DNS conversion is done on the destination IPs of imported IPDRs to get the domain information and App-related information. App-related information includes details like the app name, organization name, and country in which the server is hosted.

4.2 Filters

The module offers various filtering options to consolidate and organize the data for easier analysis. Common data analysis methods are combined to get answers to queries like,

- How much data is uploaded/downloaded to distinct websites by distinct users?
- Which website is used most by the individuals in the case?
- Which port/service is used most by the individuals in the case?
- Which website-port combination is used most by the individuals in the case?
- Under which tower, the individuals stayed most?
- Which App is used most by the individuals in the case?
- Which of the individuals accessed the website hosted in a specific country?
- Is there a chance that the two parties in the IPDRs have direct communication?
- Which of the parties used VPN or WhatsApp?

Filter results can be viewed in grid and chart format. Figure 3 displays the result of the country-based filter applied to the data in Fig. 2.

The tool has a search option to retrieve specific details based on phone numbers, IMEI, IMSI, cell ID, IP number, duration, upload/download data, and time. Search options can be customized to get any complex query result, such as getting the IP Records of an individual whose mobile number ends with 5604 to a specific website for more than 10 min between 8 and 10 pm.

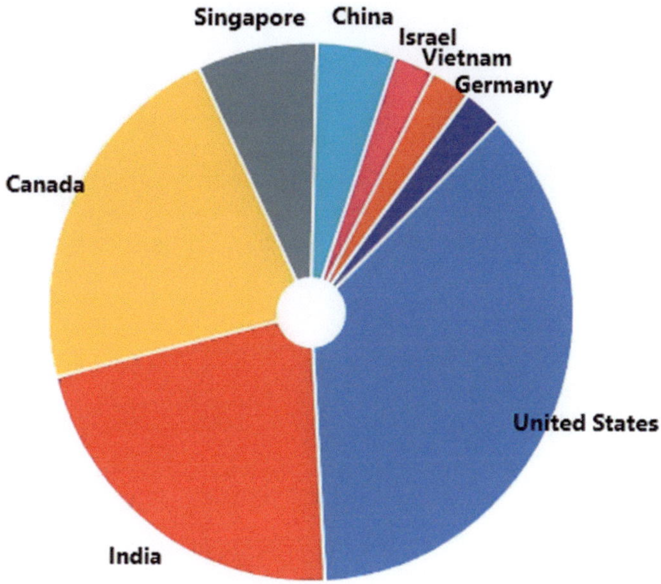

Fig. 3 Country-based filter results in pie-chart

4.3 Link Analyzer

The Link Analyzer module is used to identify relationships between IP addresses and mobile numbers imported to the tool. It analyses connections from different mobile numbers to IP addresses, generating a visualization of relationships between them as shown in Fig. 4. The graph can be manipulated to retrieve the specific data of interest.

Links are obtained by aggregating the internet session details of two or more mobile numbers by checking if they've connected to the same destination IP. An example of information gleaned using this feature is that if two persons access a website that is not commonly used by everyone, there is a high chance that they have planned something together or looked for some information together.

4.4 Geo Distance

The Geo Distance module is used to identify the distance between two individual IPDR data points. IPDR data point in this context is the individual record entry in the IPDR log.

Geo distance means the distance between the locations at which these individual internet sessions are recorded. The Geo Distance feature includes visualizations

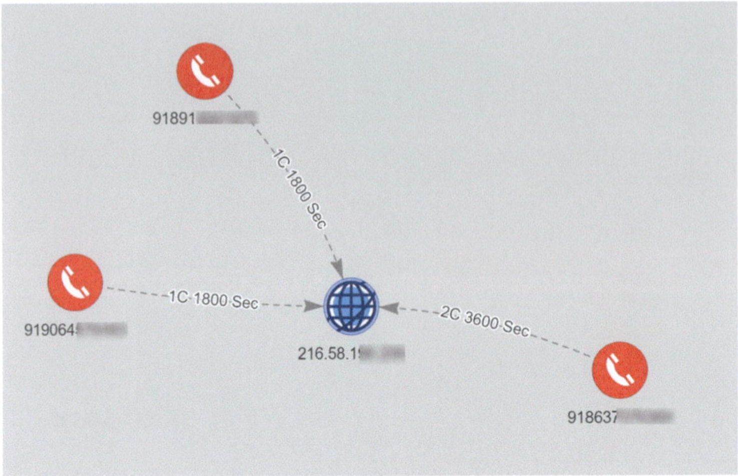

Fig. 4 Link analyzer

(Fig. 5) that showcase the identified distances between different IPDR data points, enabling investigators to gain insights into geographic correlations.

This is achieved by obtaining the tower details from the tower IDs of the two IP Detail Records. Tower details like geo-location and address are available in the Cell ID database kept by the service providers. This Cell ID database can be collected by law enforcement agencies on request. Latitude and longitude values in the tower details are then plotted using open street maps along with the distance between two towers and the mean time to travel from one location to the other. Geo Distance

Fig. 5 Geo distance

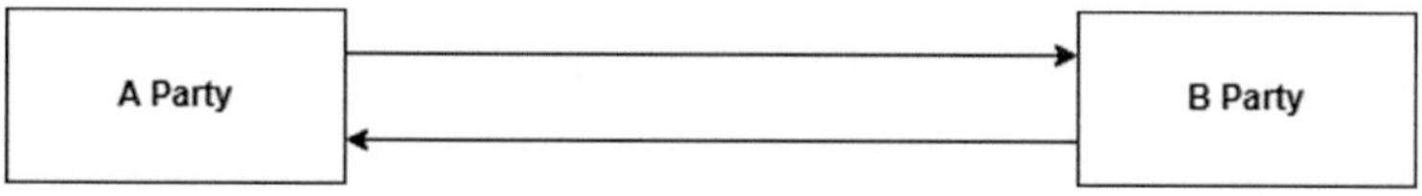

Fig. 6 Traditional cellular communication

Fig. 7 Internet communication

identification is useful to determine how long the suspect has travelled between accessing two internet sessions.

4.5 Direct Communication

Unlike traditional voice calls, Internet communication does not connect individuals directly. Instead, they both were connected to the application or website that supports internet communication. Figures 5 and 6 explain this difference. 'A party' in the figure is a person who has initiated the call. 'B party' is the person who has received the call. Because of this difference, IPDR does not contain called party information. So, it is difficult to identify whether the two parties communicated (Fig. 7).

One trick to identify probable direct communication is to check whether they have accessed the same website with time overlap. This can be achieved by aggregating the IPDRs. For two IPDRs with different Source IPs and mobile numbers, if the destination IP is the same, and the time of internet access overlaps, it can be a direct communication. For investigative purposes, this itself is an inference.

4.6 Correlation

The Correlation module focuses on correlating Call Detail Records (CDRs), Subscriber Detail Records (SDRs), Cell IDs and IPDRs to provide a comprehensive view of communication and online activities. By correlating these data sources, investigators can identify call patterns, track locations, analyze internet usage, and establish links between suspects. This correlation process helps build a comprehensive profile of individuals under investigation and facilitates the understanding of their network of connections. It also enables investigators to identify previous criminal activities or patterns related to the individuals involved.

Mobile number is the key to achieving the correlation between IPDR, CDR and SDR. IPDR gives the internet usage information of the mobile number user. CDR gives the details of the person's cellular calls and messages. SDR gives the present and permanent address, alternate mobile number and other KYC information of the person.

The tower ID information from IPDR can be used to correlate with the Cell ID database, to get track of the locations that person has travelled. Cell ID information contains the GPS location and address of a tower. So, tracking the address of each tower for each internet access can easily identify the travel history.

This way, by correlating these four types of logs we get the name, addresses, alternate number, cellular call usage information, internet usage information, where he stays most of the time and the travel history i.e. a 360-degree view of a person.

4.7 Commonality Analyzer

Commonality Analyzer identifies the common values from multiple IPDR files. Common values can be mobile numbers, Source IPs, IMEIs or IMSIs. This becomes useful when there are a number of IPDR files of different internet events. For Example, if the same phone number, appeared in multiple IPDRs related to a suspected online activity, it could be considered suspicious. In cases where a suspected mobile number cannot be identified directly, we can consider other parameters. If there is a common IMEI, the person might have used two different phone numbers on a single mobile device and got involved in the crime.

4.8 Report

The Report generation feature provides a summary of the entire case, consolidating the findings and analysis conducted throughout the investigation process. The report acts as a strong piece of evidence and helps streamline the investigation process by presenting relevant information in a concise and organized manner.

5 Case Study

A prototype of the tool was given to various cyber forensic and law enforcement agencies for analyzing cybercrimes. The tool was used to analyse a cyberbullying case. A person had received threatening messages from a fake profile four times in a month via Instagram's direct messaging service. The enquiry agency collected all the source IPs connected to Instagram during those four time periods. They fed the IPDRs of these Source IPs to the tool and identified the two suspected mobile numbers using the common number analyzer which otherwise would have taken a lot of labour and time.

Analyzing the internet usage reports of the numbers using filters and searches, it was found that one of the users started accessing Instagram only a day before the bullying started. The name, alternate number, contact list, the location at which the message was sent and the address of that person were identified using the correlation module which correlates information from CDR, SDR and tower location data. A 360-degree view of the person behind the fake profile was generated using this correlation. This case study is an example of the practical utility of the tool in cybercrime investigations, showcasing its ability to swiftly and accurately uncover crucial evidence.

6 Conclusion

The analysis of IPDRs plays a crucial role in digital forensic investigations involving Internet activities. The paper discussed the importance of automated techniques in enhancing the efficiency and effectiveness of IPDR analysis. The existing manual processes involved in IPDR analysis were identified, including the complexities of analyzing large volumes of data, the variety of data types and the need for quicker analysis and decision-making. The paper proposed solutions such as data mapping, pre-sets, predefined analysis templates, data visualization, and the standardization of different data from different sources to address these challenges. The features of our automated IPDR analysis system were also discussed. In response to the limitations of Joshi et al.'s method [1], this paper proposes a complete user profiling along with more analysis features. The automatic importing feature incorporating pre-sets effectively addresses the challenges associated with handling diverse IPDR data. By incorporating these refinements, this method underscores the potential for a more robust and versatile user profiling methodology in the context of telecommunications data analysis.

7 Future Scope

The above-mentioned system effectively automates a wide range of techniques in IPDR Analysis; however, there remains potential for further enhancements and advancements. Some areas of further enhancement are mentioned below.

Behavioural Analysis: Leveraging advanced data analysis algorithms and machine learning can uncover hidden patterns in IPDR data, providing insights into user behavior. This enables robust behavioral profiles, offering a comprehensive understanding of individuals' online activities. Analyzing IPDR data with other contextual information, like web browsing history and location data, helps build meaningful user profiles, aiding in anomaly detection and identification of suspicious activities.

Future efforts may focus on integrating IPDR analysis with advanced technologies, such as machine learning, natural language processing, and big data analytics, to enhance investigative capabilities for detecting and predicting suspicious activities.

Timeline Analysis: Timeline analysis involves examining IPDR data based on the time and date of each internet service access. This analysis can help detect patterns, identify trends, and understand the temporal dynamics of user behaviour. For example, by leveraging timeline analysis, one can determine the sequence of domains accessed by a user on a particular day.

Geo Analysis: Analysing the geographical locations of towers from internet records can offer a valuable perspective of the past movement of a user.

References

1. Joshi A, Oberoi M, Bose R (2018) Analyzing CDR/IPDR data to find people network from encrypted messaging services. In 2018 IEEE 4th International conference on collaboration and internet computing (CIC) [Online]. Available: https://ieeexplore.ieee.org/document/8537870
2. Department of Telecommunications, Government of India (2022) Compliance of revised IPDR format notified vide DOT letter no 8520–01/98LR/Vol. (IX) Pt. I dated 16.11.2021 [Online]. Available: https://dot.gov.in/sites/default/files/Compliance%20of%20IPDR.pdf?download=1
3. Lingaraju S IPDR Investigation [Online]. Available: https://www.scribd.com/document/640912200/IPDR-English
4. IMEI Information (n.d.) [Online]. Available: https://www.imei.info/. Accessed 14 July 2023
5. IMEI numbers could help track stolen mobiles. But how do you find it and what does it do? Indian Express 29 May 2019 [Online]. Available: https://indianexpress.com/article/technology/mobile-tabs/imei-number-india-track-stolen-mobiles-phones-how-to-find-imei-what-it-does-5790035/
6. International Mobile Subscriber Identity (n.d.) Wikipedia, The Free Encyclopedia. Retrieved 14 July 2023. From https://en.wikipedia.org/wiki/International_mobile_subscriber_identity
7. ITU-T Recommendation E.212, The International Identification Plan for Public Networks and Subscriptions
8. Facebook Developers (n.d.) Meta for Developers [Online]. Available: https://developers.facebook.com/docs/whatsapp/guides/network-requirements/. Accessed 14 July 2023
9. WhatsApp (n.d.) Netify Application Lookup. Retrieved 14 July 2023. From https://www.netify.ai/resources/applications/whatsapp
10. Ahmed W, Shahzad F, Javed AR, Iqbal F (April) WhatsApp network forensics: discovering the IP addresses of suspects. In: 2021 11th IFIP International conference on new technologies, mobility and security (NTMS). Paris, France
11. Department of Telecommunications (2018) Parameter of IPDR and SYS LOG of Network Address Translation (NAT). Retrieved 14 July 2023. [Online]. Available: https://dot.gov.in/sites/default/files/Authentication%20and%20Maintenance.pdf?download=1

Comprehensive Multi-modal Analysis for Enhanced Road Safety and Traffic Law Enforcement

Kesanam Ashinee, Simhadri Sevitha, Renukasakshi V. Patil, and Ram Mohana Reddy Guddeti

Abstract This research presents a comprehensive approach to enhancing road safety and Traffic Law enforcement through advanced multi-modal image analysis. The methodology encompasses three key components: Vehicle Traffic Signal Violation Detection, Pedestrian Counting, and Driver Identification, with an extension for Vehicle License Plate Recognition. When a vehicle violates traffic signal laws, the system intelligently assesses the situation. Initially, it checks for the visibility of the driver's face, and if obscured, it proceeds to detect and recognize the vehicle's license plate. Furthermore, pedestrian counting near zebra crossings is employed to ensure the safety of road users. The methodology leverages state-of-the-art object detection and recognition models, including Easy OCR, and YOLOv3, for robust and accurate results. The integration of these components creates a powerful system for traffic signal violation detection, pedestrian safety assessment, and driver identification.

Keywords Traffic signal violation · Pedestrian counting · License plate recognition · Object detection · Image analysis · Easy OCR · YOLOv3

1 Introduction

The enforcement of traffic regulations has long been a significant concern for public safety and law enforcement agencies. With the increasing volume of vehicles on the roads, monitoring and controlling traffic violations have become paramount in ensuring road safety and adherence to legal mandates. In light of this pressing need, our research endeavors to introduce an advanced system that combines the realms of vehicle traffic signal violation detection, driver identification, and pedestrian safety assurance.

Our primary motivation for this research is to address a critical gap in law enforcement. The proposed system seeks to revolutionize traffic regulation enforcement by harnessing the power of cutting-edge technologies. Through this endeavor, we

K. Ashinee (✉) · S. Sevitha · R. V. Patil · R. M. R. Guddeti
National Institute of Technology Karnataka, Surathkal, Mangalore, Karnataka, India
e-mail: ashineekesanam@gmail.com

B. N. Gohil et al. (eds.), *Information Security, Privacy and Digital Forensics*,
Lecture Notes in Electrical Engineering 1423,
https://doi.org/10.1007/978-981-96-9443-3_14

aim to enhance the ability to monitor and act upon traffic signal violations, thereby contributing to a safer and more orderly traffic environment.

The methodology employed is multifaceted, comprising a sequence of technologies, including YOLOv3 and Easy OCR. When a vehicle infringes upon traffic signal regulations, our system engages in a layered analysis. First, it checks for the visibility of the driver's face, ensuring compliance with regulations regarding the driver's presence and attention. If the driver's face is obscured, the system seamlessly transitions to license plate detection and recognition, allowing for efficient vehicle and driver identification. Furthermore, the system also counts pedestrians in the vicinity during signal violations, aiming to prioritize their safety.

Key components of this proposed system include:

1. **Traffic Signal Violation Detection**: Utilizing computer vision technology, the system identifies vehicles that breach traffic signal regulations. This detection is a crucial step towards improving road safety by discouraging reckless behavior and promoting adherence to traffic rules [2, 10].
2. **Driver Face Identification**: When a vehicle violating a traffic signal is captured with its driver's face visible, the system employs facial recognition techniques[9] to match the driver with a pre-existing database of driver information. This allows for swift identification and retrieval of pertinent driver details, such as license information and traffic violation history [1, 5].
3. **Vehicle License Plate Recognition**: In cases where the driver's face is not visible, the system switches to license plate recognition technology. By recognizing the vehicle's license plate, it accesses information associated with the vehicle and its owner, aiding law enforcement [7, 8].
4. **Pedestrian Count**: To enhance overall road safety, the system also incorporates pedestrian counting capabilities, especially around zebra crossings near traffic signals. Accurate counting of pedestrians helps in optimizing traffic signal timing and ensures safe passage for walkers, reducing the risk of accidents.

The integration of these functions into a unified system offers law enforcement agencies a powerful tool to curb traffic violations effectively, enhance road safety, and promote responsible driving behavior. An extension for Vehicle License Plate Recognition further strengthens the capabilities of the system. When a vehicle is detected violating traffic signal regulations, the system employs a smart approach. It first verifies the visibility of the driver's face; if detected then recognizes the driver but if the face is not detected, it proceeds to detect and recognize the vehicle's license plate, facilitating the identification process. Moreover, pedestrian counting is utilized near zebra crossings to ensure the safety of pedestrians. This paper details our methodology and presents the results of its application, underscoring the potential impact on road safety and traffic regulation enforcement.

2 Related Work

1. "**Intelligent Traffic Violation Detection**"
   Paper by Roopa Ravish, Shanta Rangaswamy, and S. N. Omkar proposes an algorithm called YOLOv3 to detect traffic violations using Artificial Intelligence and deep learning concepts. The authors propose the YOLOv3 algorithm to detect traffic violations such as jumping red signals, riding vehicles without helmets, driving without seat belts, and vehicles stepping over the stop line during red signals. The YOLOv3 algorithm uses Convolutional Neural Networks (CNN) to detect an object and Darknet-53 as a feature extractor. The paper discusses the implementation details, results, and analysis of the proposed algorithm. The authors claim that the algorithm offers a precision of 97.67% for vehicle identification and an exactness of 89.24% to identify the speed of a moving vehicle [6].
2. "**A novel Squeeze YOLO-based real-time people counting approach**"
   Paper by Peiming Ren, Lin Wang, Wei Fang* and Shulin Song addresses the critical task of real-time people counting in the context of smart cities and intelligent building systems. The paper introduces the YOLO (You Only Look Once) framework as an effective real-time object detection [3]approach, emphasizing its advantages in accuracy and speed. To tackle the challenge of large model sizes, the authors propose Squeeze YOLO-based people counting (S-YOLO-PC), which optimizes the network structure using the fire layer of SqueezeNet. This optimization significantly reduces model parameters while maintaining high accuracy. S-YOLO-PC is presented as a promising solution for practical applications in intelligent systems.
3. "**License Plate Recognition System Based on Improved YOLOv5 and GRU**
   Paper by Hengliang Shi and Dongnan Zhao presents an end-to-end deep learning model for license plate location and recognition in natural scenarios. The proposed model is based on the YOLOv5-LSE architecture and includes an improved channel attention mechanism to enhance accuracy and speed. The model is trained on a large-scale dataset of license plate images and tested on the CCPD dataset. The experimental results show that the proposed method outperforms other state-of-the-art license plate recognition algorithms in terms of accuracy and efficiency. The paper also includes a detailed comparative analysis with other cutting-edge recognition algorithms.
4. "**Face Transformer for Recognition**"
   In paper by ,Yaoyao Zhong and Weihong [11] Deng explore the application of Transformers in face recognition, extending beyond their prevalent use in NLP and delving into computer vision. They address the question of whether Transformers can outperform CNNs. The authors modify the patch generation

Table 1 State-of-the-art comparison table

Paper name	Technique	Limitations	Acurracy (%)
Squeeze YOLO-based real-time people counting	S-YOLO-PC	Comparison made with only three YOLO techniques	72
Intelligent traffic violation detection	Yolo V3, CNNs	Traffic violation detection in late night	99.18
License plate recognition system	YOLOV5-LSE	Not applicable to embedded systems	96.94
Face transformer for recognition	Transformers, CNNs	Employed on a dataset rather than real-time	95.96

process to enhance inter-patch information, utilizing sliding patches with overlaps. Training on CASIA-WebFace and MS-Celeb-1M databases and evaluating on prominent benchmarks, their Face Transformer models exhibit comparable performance to CNNs with similar parameters and MACs. The paper contributes to the field by providing openly accessible Face Transformer models and codes, for further research at the intersection of Transformers and face recognition (Table 1).

3 Problem Statement

The current state of traffic management is marked by widespread signal violations, limited means of swiftly identifying violators, and inadequate pedestrian safety monitoring. This research addresses these issues by developing an integrated traffic management system to detect signal violations, identify drivers, and count pedestrians for enhanced road safety and responsible driving behavior.

Objectives

- Develop a robust Traffic Signal Violation Detection System using computer vision and AI.
- Implement Facial Recognition for swift driver identification when the driver's face is visible.
- Integrate License Plate Recognition technology for identification when facial recognition is not possible.
- Create pedestrian counting mechanisms near zebra crossings to enhance pedestrian safety.

4 Proposed Work

4.1 Vehicle Traffic Signal Violation Detection

- **Data Collection**: We collected a diverse set of images featuring vehicles within a real-world traffic environment. These images served as the foundation of our database.
- **Object Detection**: Utilizing the YOLO (You Only Look Once) version 3 algorithm, we conducted object detection to identify and extract vehicles within the collected images. The extracted vehicle images were then organized and stored in a designated folder, constituting our database of vehicle images.
- **Defining Violation Boundaries**: In order to differentiate between vehicles following traffic signal regulations and those violating them, we established a boundary within each image. If a vehicle crosses this predefined boundary, it is considered to have committed a traffic signal violation.
- **Collection of Violation Images**: We also gathered a separate set of images that exemplify instances of vehicles violating traffic signal laws. These images were used to train and evaluate our detection system (Fig. 1).
- **Hopcroft-Karp Algorithm**: The Hopcroft-Karp algorithm, a powerful method for bipartite graph matching, was utilized to efficiently search for matches between the features of the vehicles in violation images and those in the database. This algorithm helped us identify the vehicles involved in traffic signal violations (Fig. 2).

4.2 Pedestrian Count

- **People Detection and Annotation with YOLOv3**: Utilize the YOLOv3 model to perform real-time object detection [4] on image frames from a specified source.Annotate the detected objects with bounding boxes and labels using the Supervision library. Refer (Fig. 3) This process helps identify and mark the pedestrians near the zebra crossing, classifying them as needed.Implement any additional steps or filtering criteria, such as focusing on a specific class (e.g., classid 0, representing pedestrians), to refine the annotations as required.Use polygon zones to define regions of interest (e.g., the zebra crossing area) for tracking pedestrians. Annotate frames accordingly using the defined polygon zones to highlight pedestrian movements in the specified area. Repeat these steps for multiple frames to ensure consistent and accurate annotation. Refer (Fig. 3)

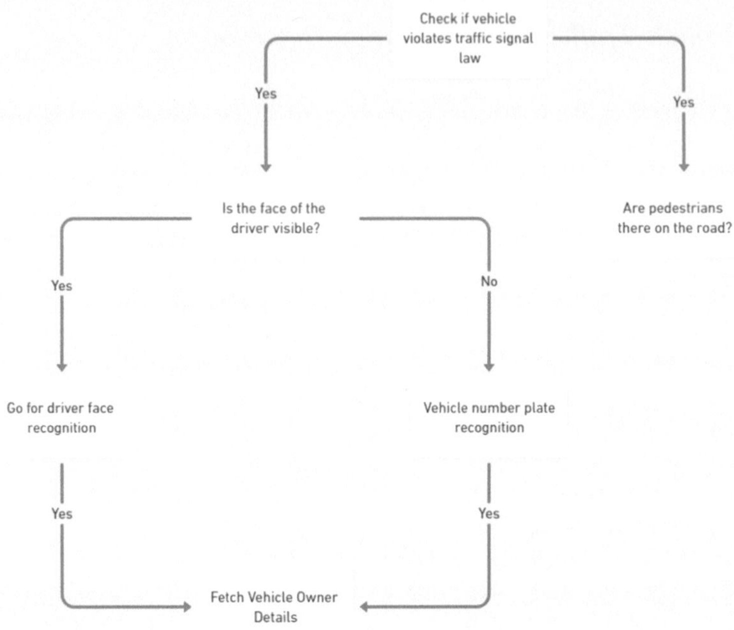

Fig. 1 Methodology

4.3 *Driver Face Identification*

- **Data Collection and Preprocessing**: This experiment involves obtaining and using a diverse dataset of driver face images, capturing them under varying lighting conditions, angles, and levels of blurriness. The method initializes video capture and a face detection classifier using OpenCV. Users input a label (e.g., driver's name) for the collected facial data. The system continuously captures frames, detects faces, and stores cropped and resized facial images in the faces data list. The code checks for existing data storage files; if absent, it creates and saves files with the user's label and facial data. For existing files, the code appends new data, maintaining a comprehensive, labeled facial data database. Simultaneously, the Vision Transformer (ViT) model training uses a comprehensive dataset of labeled facial images from the web
- **Model training**: This experiment provides a methodology for face recognition and driver face tracking. It initiates by setting up the system to capture and detect the image using the OpenCV. Pre-trained facial data and associated labels are loaded from dataset and a K-Nearest Neighbors classifier is trained for face recognition. The code continuously processes the webcam feed, detecting faces and predicting

```
FOR EACH violating_img_name IN violating_image_names:
  img2 = READ_IMAGE(violating_img_name)
  Initialize empty lists key1, key2, features
  max_val = 0
  max_img = None
  matchings = []

  FOR EACH img_name IN image_names:
    img1 = READ_IMAGE(img_name)
    img1, img2 = RESIZE_IMAGES(img1, img2, desired_width)
    key_pnt1, descrip1, key_pnt2, descrip2 = DETECT_AND_COMPUTE_FEATURES(img1, img2)
    matches = FEATURE_MATCHING(descrip1, descrip2)
    matchings.append(LENGTH(matches))
    IF LENGTH(matches) > max_val:
      max_val = LENGTH(matches)
      max_img = COPY_IMAGE(img1)
      features.append(matches)
      key1.append(key_pnt1)
      key2.append(key_pnt2)

  im1_gray, im2_gray = CONVERT_TO_GRAYSCALE(img1, img2)

  IF max_img is not None:
    DISPLAY_OUTPUT(max_img, key1[-1], img2, key2[-1], features[-1])
```

Fig. 2 Vehicle traffic signal violation detection model algorithm

identities. Recognized names and timestamps are used to mark the time, which is then logged in a file for record-keeping. To adapt this code for driver face recognition, driver names and their corresponding facial data can be stored in files, respectively. The code would then enable driver identification and tracking, making it a versatile tool for applications such as driver monitoring, access control, or security. [Fig. 4] Coming to the ViT model, it initiates the identification process by capturing the facial features of the driver. This step is crucial for establishing a foundation for subsequent comparisons and verifications. Once the facial data is obtained, it undergoes a meticulous recognition process using the processing model based on the Vision Transformer (ViT) architecture, specifically the ViT-B-16-plus-240 variant. The processing model is optimized for efficiency and speed, leveraging GPU acceleration through PyTorch. Then the comparison of facial features between the captured driver's face and the registered dataset, producing cosine similarity scores is done. We also observe that this model performs better.

```
FUNCTION process_frame(frame, _):
  results = DETECT_OBJECTS(frame)
  detections = FILTER_DETECTIONS(results)
  TRIGGER_ZONE(detections)
  frame = ANNOTATE_BOXES(frame, detections)
  frame = ANNOTATE_ZONE(frame)
  RETURN frame

FUNCTION transform_image(array):
  normalized_image = TRANSFORM_IMAGE(array)
  RETURN normalized_image
norm_image, unnorm_image = transform_image(test_output)

FUNCTION detect(network, data):
  pred = network(data)
  class_ids, scores, bounding_boxes = EXTRACT_PREDICTIONS(pred)
  RETURN class_ids, scores, bounding_boxes

FUNCTION count_object(network, class_ids, scores, bounding_boxes, object_label,
threshold=0.75):
  idx = GET_CLASS_INDEX(network, object_label)
  scores, class_ids = FILTER_DETECTIONS(scores, class_ids, idx, threshold)
  num_people = COUNT_PEOPLE(scores)
  RETURN num_people

FOR EACH object_label IN ["person", "sports ball"]:
  count = count_object(network, class_ids, scores, bounding_boxes, object_label)
  PRINT_COUNT(count, object_label)

FOR EACH threshold IN thresholds:
  num_people = count_object(network, class_ids, scores, bounding_boxes, "person", threshold)
  PRINT_COUNT(num_people, threshold)
```

Fig. 3 Pedestrain count model algorithm

4.4 Vehicle License Plate Recogniton

- **License Plate Detection**: To extract license plate information from violating vehicles, the YOLOv5 model was implemented. This model effectively identified and localized license plates within the images.
- **License Plate Recognition**: For the recognition of license plate characters, we employed the Easy OCR system. It provided accurate text extraction from the detected license plates.
- **Driver Database Matching**: The extracted license plate numbers were then compared to the entries in the driver database, where driver information such as name, contact details, and license details were stored.
- **Driver Details Retrieval**: In cases of a successful match between the detected license plate and the database, driver details were retrieved, providing essential information about the vehicle's owner (Fig. 5)

```
WHILE True:
  ret, frame = READ_FRAME(video)
  gray = CONVERT_TO_GRAY(frame)
  faces = DETECT_FACES(facedetect, gray, scaleFactor=1.3, minNeighbors=5)

  FOR EACH (x, y, w, h) IN faces:
    crop_img = CROP_IMAGE(frame, (x, y, x + w, y + h))
    resized_img = RESIZE_IMAGE(crop_img, (50, 50))

    IF LENGTH(faces_data) <= 100 AND i % 10 == 0:
      APPEND_TO_FACES_DATA(faces_data, resized_img)

    i = i + 1
    DRAW_TEXT(frame, str(LENGTH(faces_data)), (50, 50))
    DRAW_RECTANGLE(frame, (x, y), (x + w, y + h), color=(50, 50, 255))

  SHOW_FRAME("Frame", frame)
  k = WAIT_KEY(1)

  IF k == ord('q') OR LENGTH(faces_data) == 100:
    BREAK
```

Fig. 4 Driver face identification model algorithm

```
FOR EACH image_path in images
   yolo = LOAD_YOLO_MODEL(yolo_model_path)
   input_image = READ_IMAGE(image_path)
   results = yolo(input_image)

   ocr_reader = INIT_OCR_READER(ocr_reader_languages)
   output_image = PROCESS_RESULTS(results, input_image, ocr_reader, confidence_threshold)
   SAVE_OR_DISPLAY_OUTPUT(output_image, output_image_path)
```

Fig. 5 Vehicle license plate recognitonn model algorithm

5 Experimental Results

5.1 Vehicle Traffic Signal Violation Detection

- The Hopcroft-Karp searches for matches between the features of the vehicles in violation images and those in the database
- The image with the highest count of matched features was considered the best match. The lines in the images shows the features matched by the feature matching Hopkroft Karp Algorithm Refer (Fig. 6)
- A visual representation of the matching was generated using Matplotlib, displaying the number of features matched in each case. Refer (Fig. 7)
- The overall accuracy is 74.5%, Comparison results are given in (Table 2)

Table 2 Comparision between YoloV3 and hopcroft-Karp integrated Yolo V3 models

Model name	Accuracy	Precision
Yolo V3 model	0.701	0.81
Yolo V3 with hopcroft algorithm	0.745	0.89

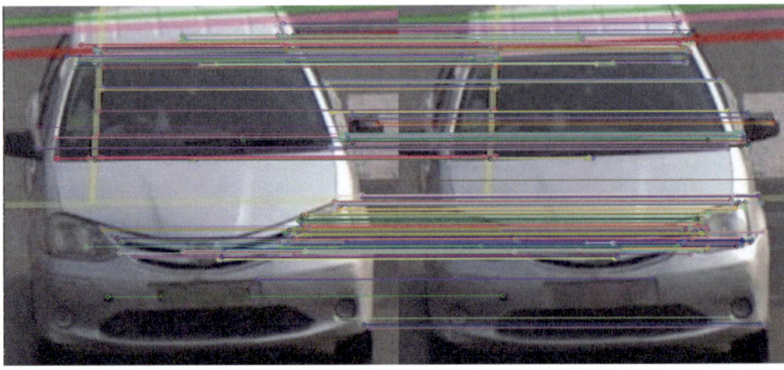

Fig. 6 Vehicles matched by lines using feature matching Hopcroft Karp Algorithm

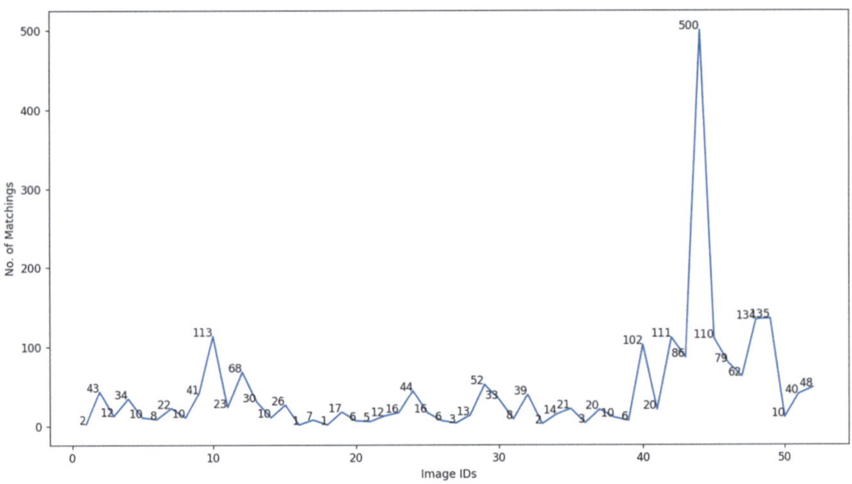

Fig. 7 Line plot to show the number of features matched

5.2 *Driver Face Identification*

- By Utilizing the Vision Transformer (ViT) model (ViT-B-16-plus-240) with GPU acceleration via PyTorch, our experiment achieved a good performance in facial feature recognition. Comparison results are given in (Table 3)

Table 3 Comparision between vision transformer and KNN classifier

Model name	Accuracy	Precision
Vision transformer	94.8	0.927
KNN classifier	81.02	0.735

- The ViT model showcased efficiency and speed, making our system a reliable tool for various applications.
- The model which used OpenCV and detected images in various diverse conditions enabling face recognition using the K-Nearest Neighbors classifier. This contributed to enhanced road safety and traffic law enforcement.
- It allows for versatile Driver Face Recognition. The system gives an approach for storage of driver names and facial data in necessary situations, facilitating applications such as driver monitoring, access control, and security.

5.3 Pedestrian Counting

- Dataset was compiled from a wide array of internet images, including those captured in urban settings like busy streets, parks, and transit stations. It deliberately includes scenes with overlapping pedestrians and a range of crowd densities, mirroring the complexities of real-world urban environments.
- Yolo finds the person in the background with an amazing 86.7 confidence, despite the fact that they are fuzzy, as you can see above. This makes YOLO extremely popular despite its issues with overlapping objects.
- Some of the individuals are absent from Fig. 8. This is due to Yolo's subpar performance with overlapping objects. This is YOLO models' primary drawback.But because this algorithm is quick and memory-efficient, it's highly recommended.

5.4 Vehicle License PLate Recognition

- The model trained in 15 training epochs
- the model achieved a box loss of less than 10%, signifying its proficiency in localizing objects accurately within the images.
- the model attained an image loss of less than 2%, demonstrating its ability to minimize errors in image recognition and classification.
- The final output images featured license plate numbers annotated above the detected license plates. Refer Fig. 9

Fig. 8 Zebra cross

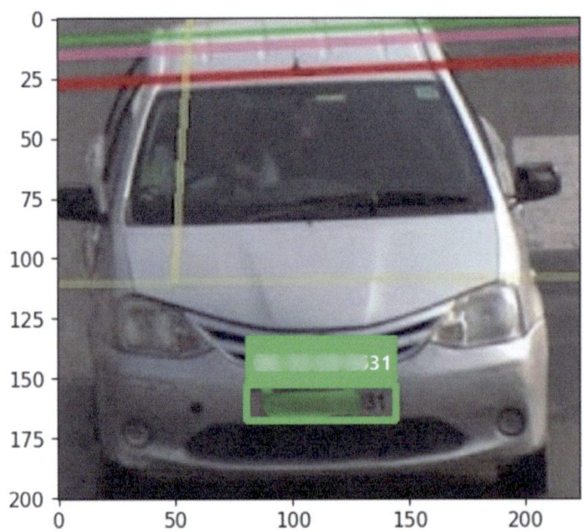

Fig. 9 License plate detected

6 Contributions

- A novel approach is being discussed in the paper that ensures law enforcement
- Enhanced YOLO v3 with Hopcroft Karp algorithm for traffic violation detection and it performs better compared to the base YOLO v3 model.

- The Vision Transformer (ViT) model demonstrated a better performance in facial recognition compared to the K-Nearest Neighbors classifier, achieving higher accuracy and precision in our Driver face recognition in diverse environments experiment.
- Additional to people counting in general crowded places here pedestrian counting is performed. To improvise the safety of the pedestrians.

7 Conclusion and Future Work

This paper introduces an integrated system for improving road safety and traffic law enforcement. It incorporates components such as Traffic Signal Violation Detection, Driver Identification, Vehicle License Plate Recognition, and Pedestrian Counting. This system combines advanced computer vision and AI technologies to detect violations and, when possible, identify drivers for more effective law enforcement.

In Future we aim to:

- **Video and Real-Time Implementation**: We plan to extend our models to process videos and implement real-time object recognition and tracking. This advancement will enable us to detect and track objects, such as vehicles and pedestrians,
- **Integration with CCTV Cameras**: We intend to integrate our models with real-time camera, we can actively monitor and enforce traffic regulations, identify violations, and contribute to improved traffic safety and law enforcement.

Acknowledgements Our sincere thanks to Springer for publishing our paper. We extend our heartfelt gratitude to NIT Karnataka, Prof. Ram Mohan Reddy Guddeti for their invaluable guidance and support. Additionally, we appreciate the contributions of past researchers and the essential tools utilized in this research.

References

1. Dinalankara L (2017) Face detection and face recognition using open computer vision classifies. ResearchGate
2. Dissanayake D, Aluvihare W, Rajapaksha KD et al (2022) Smartgo"–intelligent traffic controlling system with violators detection. In: 2022 4th international conference on advancements in computing (ICAC). IEEE, pp 304–309
3. Lin T-Y, Goyal P, Girshick R, He K, Dollár P (2017) Focal loss for dense object detection. In: Proceedings of the IEEE international conference on computer vision, pp 2980–2988
4. Ma H, Lu H, Zhang M (2008) A real-time effective system for tracking passing people using a single camera. In; 2008 7th world congress on intelligent control and automation. IEEE, pp 6173–6177
5. Nazira FA, Uddin MI, Raju MH, Hossain S, Rahman MN, Mridha MF (2021) Face recognition based driver detection system. In: 2021 international conference on data analytics for business and industry (ICDABI). IEEE, pp 572–577

6. Ravish R, Rangaswamy S, Char K (2021) Intelligent traffic violation detection. In: 2021 2nd global conference for advancement in technology (GCAT). IEEE, pp 1–7
7. Redmon J, Divvala S, Girshick R, Farhadi A (2016) You only look once: unified, real-time object detection. In: Proceedings of the IEEE conference on computer vision and pattern recognition, pp 779–788
8. Shi H, Zhao D (2023) License plate recognition system based on improved yolov5 and gru. IEEE Access 11:10429–10439
9. Singh G, Gupta I, Singh J, Kaur N (202) Face recognition using open source computer vision library (opencv) with python. In: 2022 10th international conference on reliability, infocom technologies and optimization (Trends and Future Directions)(ICRITO). IEEE, pp 1–6
10. Tonge A, Chandak S, Khiste R, Khan U, Bewoor LA (2020) Traffic rules violation detection using deep learning. In: 2020 4th international conference on electronics, communication and aerospace technology (ICECA). IEEE, pp 1250–1257
11. Zhong Y, Deng W (2021) Face transformer for recognition. ArXiv preprint arXiv:2103.14803

A Brief Overview on Different Approaches of Image Manipulation and Detection

Monisha Mohan, Anjali Diwan, and Parth Parmar

Abstract In today's digital age, the authenticity and trustworthiness of images play a pivotal role in a multitude of domains, ranging from journalism and law enforcement to art authentication and social media content validation. The increasing accessibility of image editing tools and the widespread prevalence of manipulated visual content have underscored the urgency of developing robust techniques for image manipulation detection. It can be quite difficult to detect whether or not a digital image has been altered from its original form. Finding signs of tampering in a digital image is a difficult undertaking to complete. This survey paper provides a comprehensive overview of the state-of-the-art methods for detecting image manipulation, including contrast enhancement detection, the major image tampering detection methods using copy-move, splicing, retouching and others. Also, the advances in the field of image manipulation detection. A comparison of all the methods reveals the most effective strategy for further research.

Keywords Image manipulation · Copy-move · Splicing · Tampering · Detection techniques

1 Introduction

The ubiquitous nature of digital imagery and the ease with which it can be manipulated have given rise to new challenges and opportunities in the realm of image forensics. The development of image manipulation techniques possesses two sides. While photo editing software allows for the enhancement of images and promotes artistic expression, it also presents a challenge in detecting manipulated content,

M. Mohan (✉) · P. Parmar
Department of Computer Engineering, Marwadi University, Rajkot, India
e-mail: monisha.mohan@marwadieducation.edu.in

A. Diwan
Department of Computer Engineering—AI and Big Data, Marwadi University, Rajkot, India
e-mail: anjali.diwan@ieee.org

B. N. Gohil et al. (eds.), *Information Security, Privacy and Digital Forensics*, Lecture Notes in Electrical Engineering 1423,
https://doi.org/10.1007/978-981-96-9443-3_15

making it easier for individuals to disseminate misleading information. The detection of image manipulations is paramount to ensure the integrity and reliability of visual content used as evidence, conveyed in news, or shared through online platforms. The consequences of failing to verify the authenticity of images can be profound, affecting public perception, legal proceedings, and the overall trustworthiness of digital communication.

The major purpose of this survey study is to present a comprehensive examination of the different aspects of image modification detection, spanning methodologies, problems, and emerging trends. This will be accomplished by providing a broad look at all of these factors. It is extremely beneficial to have a full awareness of the existing landscape as researchers, practitioners, and technologists work to expand our capabilities in this subject. Numerous image alteration techniques exist with the objective of misleading people or altering the veracity of visual content. A frequently employed method in image manipulation is known as" Copy-Move Forgery," when a certain portion of an image is duplicated and subsequently inserted into another region, typically with the intention of concealing or replicating items within the confines of the same image. The act of" splicing" entails the combining of various components from different images to produce a singular composition that deceives the viewer. Conversely, "cloning" refers to the duplication of items or regions with the intention of introducing undesirable aspects or eliminating pre-existing ones. The method known as" information and Logo Addition" is a technique employed to overlay misleading information or corporate branding onto an existing image. The detection of alterations in visual content is of utmost importance in preserving its integrity, necessitating the use of digital forensics and image analysis to identify subtle or complex image manipulation techniques employed for forgeries.

Image manipulations are recognized in recent works employing feature descriptors, color filtering array differences, uneven shadows, misaligned JPEG blocks, double JPEG compression, and EXIF feature inconsistencies [1]. Image tampering detection entails looking into altered images for any correlations that might have been introduced during tampering operations. Digital image forgery detection is a developing research area with significant consequences for maintaining the reliability of digital images. It is very important to come up with new ways to spot picture fraud because the number of cases and the damage they cause are growing. To do this, it is necessary to look at current tampering detection methods in order to come up with the new methods.

2 Literature Survey

Image manipulation detection research is an active area of study in digital forensics and computer vision. The goal is to create methods and tools for detecting and analyzing modified or falsified photographs. To overcome the issues given by ever-evolving image alteration tools, researchers employ a range of methodologies. Advanced picture editing software has made digital image alteration simple and invisible to the naked eye. To assist beginners, comprehend, appreciate, and identify research gaps in digital picture forensics, this study examines its development and obstacles [2].

An attention mechanism for processing and improving feature maps for the classification problem. The learnt attention maps emphasize the informative regions to improve the binary classification (genuine vs. fake face), as well as visualize the altered regions. To support our research on altered face identification and localization, we a massed a big library of various forms of facial forgeries. We conduct a thorough investigation of data-driven phony face detection using this dataset. Using an attention mechanism improves face forgery detection and localization of modified regions [3]. Various models have been constructed using deep learning techniques for various applications like object detection; similar models can also be utilized for tamper detection. Because models giving precise results on tampering detection are not yet available, nevertheless better accuracy can be expected from deep learning ideas [4].

Using the "Energy Deviation Measure" is another thought-provoking technique. Gupta et al. introduces the Energy Deviation Measure as a metric for quantifying energy deviation in pixel neighborhoods inside manipulated and re-compressed images [5]. Employing camera settings was once a viable approach. However, with the proliferation of diverse camera models, this method is now discouraged and deemed unacceptable [6]. The dimensionality reduction feature of PCA makes it less suitable for lossy compression. Block-based approaches are used in one effective way of detecting copy-move forgeries. Zhang et al. [7] adopted the Discrete Wavelet Transform (DWT) where a synthetic image is broke into four frequency sub-bands and these sub-band into overlying blocks [7]. Most of the research on detecting retouching has been conducted using machine learning or deep learning approaches.

Several strategies provided by prominent scholars in this field have been examined by writers, who have identified a select few algorithms that are most suitable for their specific requirements, taking into consideration the optimal time complexity [8]. Based on the foundational algorithms, the researchers have developed an algorithm capable of processing image files of any format and producing output regardless of the specific tampering techniques employed.

The digital era has brought about a revolution in the way we capture, share, and consume visual content. Photographs and images serve as powerful tools for communication, documentation, and artistic expression. However, the rise of sophisticated image editing software and the widespread availability of such tools have opened the floodgates to image manipulations, both subtle and glaring. These manipulations can be used to deceive, misinform, or perpetrate hoaxes, making it imperative to develop techniques and technologies that can discern authentic images from manipulated ones. The prevalence of image alteration in the digital age has led to serious worries about the reliability and authenticity of visual output. In forensics, media integrity, and content verification, detecting picture tampering is a crucial challenge.

3 Common Image Tampering Tools

McKemmish defined digital forensics as" the process of identifying, preserving, analyzing, and presenting digital evidence in a manner that is legally acceptable by court of law". Image forensics is characterized by the following definition:" The identification, acquisition, analysis, and reportage of digital mark pertaining to photographs in a way that satisfies legal requirements in a court of law [9] (Fig. 1).

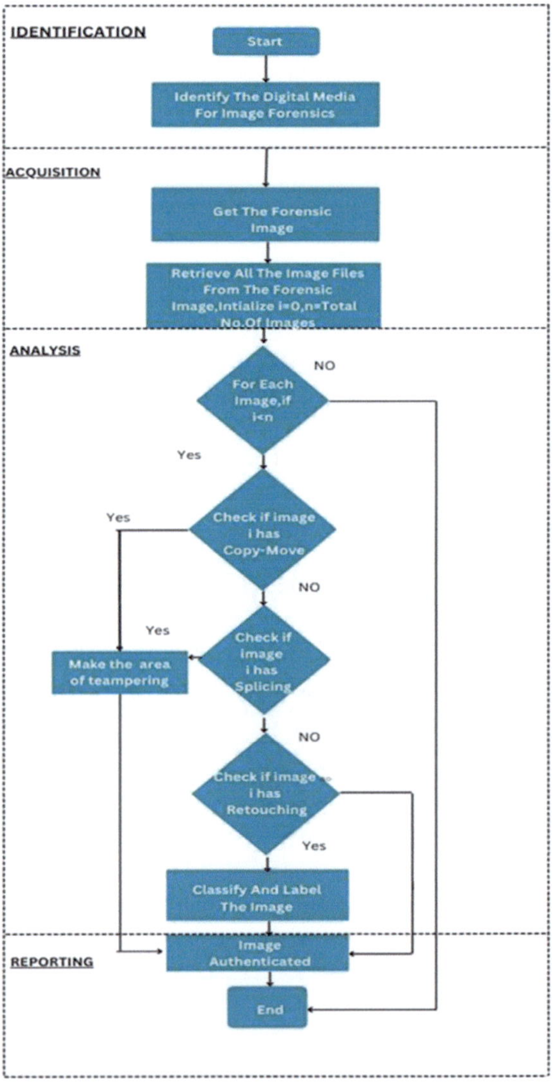

Fig. 1 Control flow diagram of image forensic tool [10]

There are four stages to the model. The digital device that has to be inspected into will be recognized during the identification process. Its forensic image, or bit-by-bit copy of the digital device, is created for forensics purposes during the collection stage. There are four stages to the model. The digital device that has to be inspected into will be recognized during the identification process. Its forensic image, or bit-by-bit copy of the digital device, is created for forensics purposes during the collection stage. The writers must use a process known as file carving to extract all picture files (.jpg,.png,.bmp, etc.) from the obtained forensic image. The process of recovering files using file format analysis, or" file carving," typically involves looking at meta-data such as the file size, header, and footer. Upon retrieval of all the image files, the analysis phase involves the detection of image tampering. The authentication (originality verification) of the photo files in the reporting phase marks the final step in the procedure [10] (Table 1).

4 Common Tampering Methods

With the emergence of strong graphics editing software such as Deepfake generators, Image Magick, Adobe Photoshop, GIMP, Corel Paint Shop, and others, the process of making fake images has become tremendously simple. Some of them are completely free. Photoshop is an incredible tool for modifying reality. It, like any other instrument, can be utilized by both good and evil forces. GIMP is a cross-platform image editor that is available for GNU/LINUX, OSX, Windows, and other platforms. It is open-source software. Deepfake Generators are software or tools that use deep learning and artificial intelligence to create convincing fake videos or images. Some examples include Face Swap and DeepArt.io. Also, there is ImageMagick which is a command-line tool for batch processing and manipulating images. Apart from these, photo editing software like as pictures cape, creative cloud, Picasa, paint shop pro, pixir, Aperture, ACD see, serif, affinity, snap seed, and so on are accessible for altering an image.

Image tampering, also known as image manipulation or image forging, is the deliberate alteration of the content or appearance of a digital image in such a way that the image misrepresents the reality represented by the image. Image tampering can be accomplished through the use of a variety of techniques and software tools to create fraudulent or misleading images. These manipulated images can be used for different purposes, like deception, Image enhancement or retouching for aesthetic objectives, such as erasing flaws, changing colors, or using artistic filters. Photo editing for periodicals, commercials, and social media is frequently done in this manner. Also, in malicious activities by using modified images to engage in fraudulent or malevolent acts such as making bogus identification documents, propagating hoaxes, or impersonating someone.

Table 1 Details of image tampering techniques

Sr. No.	Classification	Technique	Algorithm	Pros	Cons
1	Active method	Watermarking	Robust watermarking algorithm for digital images using discrete wavelet and probabilistic neural network [11]	The algorithm based on PNN in the wavelet domain can maintain the quality of the watermarked image after embedding	Extraction feature sometimes won't give better accuracy
2	Active method	Watermarking	Texture analysis in Watermarking paradigms [12]	The efficiency of embedding/extraction of a watermark from a still image depends from the applied watermarking method and detection of preferable areas for embedding	Enclose values in textural area detection and significant differences in time consuming
3	Passive method	Copy-move detection	Block-based Copy Forgery Detection [13]	Detects accurately tampering much	Time complexity Not invariant to ascending and variation
4	Passive method	Copy-move detection	Key points-based Copy Move Forgery Detection [14]	Very fast in computation	Accuracy depends upon the key points
5	Passive method	Copy-move detection	DCT Based Copy Move forgery detection [15]	Use of clustering algorithm speeds up the detection of tampering	An optimal result cannot be identified
6	Passive method	Copy-move detection	Wavelength based Copy Move forgery detection [16]	Detect manipulated regions by analyzing the wavelet coefficients	Feature process extraction can be lengthy
7	Passive method	Copy-move detection	CNN based Copy Move Forgery Detection [17]	Can be used for both active and passive tampering detection	Cannot distinguish source and target location of copy move region
8	Passive method	Splicing	Image Splicing Detection based on Deep Convolutional Neural Network and Transfer Learning [18]	Model can successfully detect spliced images with advanced accuracy without very high training data and time	

(continued)

Table 1 (continued)

Sr. No.	Classification	Technique	Algorithm	Pros	Cons
9	Passive method	Splicing	Image-Splicing detection using camera response function consistency and Automatic segmentation [19]	A novel spliced image detection approach based on camera response function estimation, consistency checking and image segmentation	Images with similar objects and backgrounds tend to suffer from in accurate segmentation
10	Passive method	Splicing	Efficient image splicing detection algorithm based on markov features [20]	Achieves much higher detection accuracy but also reduces the total running time significantly in comparison with state-of-the-art methods	
11	Passive method	Splicing	Image Splicing Forgery Detection Using Local Binary Pattern and Shift Vector [21]	Automated method based on the relative consistency of noise parameters throughout an unaltered image	Results are promising but not convincing yet because of the lossy compression characteristic of JPEG
12	Passive method	Retouching	Demography-based Facial Retouching Detection using Subclass Supervised Sparse Autoencoder [3]	Robust to the input given. Categorizes altered images precisely	Cannot identify the area of tampering

(continued)

Table 1 (continued)

Sr. No.	Classification	Technique	Algorithm	Pros	Cons
13	Passive method	Retouching	Detecting GANs and Retouching based Digital Alterations via DAD-HCNN [22]	A hierarchical approach termed as task: DAD-HCNN which performs two-fold (i) it differentiates between and digitally retouched images digitally generated images and digitally retouched images from the original unaltered images, and (ii) to increase the explain ability of the decision, it also identifies the GAN architecture used to create the images	It is not pragmatic to assume this kind of apriori knowledge so, accuracy can be less
14	Passive method	Retouching	Differential Detection of Facial Retouching: A Multi-Biometric Approach [23]	A weighted sum-rule-based score-level fusion of detection scores obtained from separately between trained SVMs revealed good detection performance in challenging cross database evaluations	Results may vary in single image-based facial retouching detection schemes

5 Digital Image Forensics for Tampering Detection

The intentional addition, deletion, or concealment of some significant features from an image without leaving overt signs of the alteration is known as image tampering. Digital photographs are typically tampered with through region duplication, image splicing, or image retouching. Region duplication is also known as copy-move attack, in which specific portions of a image are duplicated, sometimes modified, and then pasted to other positions inside the image itself, with the goal of obscuring some of the original image elements.

Image tampering detection methods can be generally classified into two main categories: active and passive methods. These categories are based on their approaches and the timing of the detection process:

5.1 *Active Image Tampering Detection*

Active methods involve detecting image tampering at the time of image acquisition or shortly afterward, often in real-time or near real-time scenarios. These methods aim to prevent or flag tampered images as they are captured or uploaded. Active detection methods include:

(1) Real-Time Image Authentication: These methods focus on verifying the authenticity of images as they are being captured. They often involve checking metadata, sensor data, and cryptographic signatures to ensure the image's integrity.
(2) Blockchain-Based Authentication: Using blockchain technology to record and verify the provenance and editing history of images, which helps ensure their authenticity.
(3) Forensic Watermarking: Embedding digital watermarks or invisible signatures in images at the time of capture, which can later be used for authentication.
(4) Secure Camera Apps: Mobile applications and camera software that provide real-time tampering detection features to alert users to potential image manipulations.

5.2 *Passive Image Tampering Detection*

In contrast to active methods, passive approaches identify image alteration after the image has been acquired and subsequently shared. These technologies, which frequently function offline, focus on analyzing photos without any prior knowledge of tampering.

(1) Post-capture analysis techniques that study an image's content, metadata, and other artefacts to find discrepancies or indications of tampering are known as digital forensics and image analysis.
(2) Steganalysis: Detecting the presence of concealed information within images using statistical or deep learning techniques.
(3) Copy-Move Forgery Detection: Identifying regions in an image that have been duplicated and pasted within the same image.
(4) Blur Analysis: Detecting unnatural blurring in images, which can be a sign of tampering.
(5) Deep Learning-based Image Forgery Detection: Utilizing deep neural networks to identify image forgeries based on learned patterns and features, which can be applied after image capture [24].
(6) Splicing Detection: Identifying spliced regions in an image where one part is copied from another source.
(7) Detecting inconsistencies in the semantic content of an image, such as unnatural object placements or lighting conditions.

5.3 Classification of Passive Forgery Detection

(1) Pixel Based Technology: Pixel-based techniques in image forgery detection involves analyzing the individual pixels of an image to identify signs of manipulation or forgery. These techniques focus on examining pixel values, colors, and the relationships between neighboring pixels to detect inconsistencies or irregularities that may indicate tampering. Pixel-based methods are particularly useful for uncovering various types of image forgeries, such as splicing, retouching, and copy-move manipulation
(2) Format Based Technology: Format-based technology in image forgery detection examines an image's digital format to detect indicators of tampering or counterfeit. It entails inspecting the image file structure and attributes specific to a format, such as JPEG or PNG. This method seeks discrepancies or anomalies in format-specific features such as compression artefacts, marker segments, or color profiles. It can, for example, detect differences in JPEG artefacts, suggesting modifications or tampering. Format-based technology is useful for detecting forgeries that exploit format-specific weaknesses, and it is frequently used in conjunction with other image forensics techniques to improve overall forgery detection accuracy.
(3) Camera Based Technology: Camera-based picture fraud detection focuses on analyzing intrinsic camera sensor or imaging process properties and artefacts to detect traces of image modification. It entails investigating elements such as the Photo-Response Non-Uniformity (PRNU) noise pattern, sensor pattern noise (SPN), and other camera-specific characteristics that leave different fingerprints on images. Camera-based technology can detect irregularities or anomalies in an image that may indicate fabrication, such as splicing or retouching, by comparing these sensor-based patterns. This method is especially useful when forgers attempt to trick viewers by modifying image content but fail to account for the tiny traces left by the camera's hardware. Camera-based technology complements existing forgery detection approaches and improves total forensic analysis accuracy.
(4) Source camera Identification Based Technology: In image forensics, source camera identification-based technology is a method that uses the unique traits and defects inherent in individual camera sensors and optics to identify the precise camera that produced a picture. This method provides a camera" fingerprint" that can be used to match photos with their source cameras by analyzing components such as the Photo-Response Non-Uniformity (PRNU) noise pattern, chromatic aberrations, and lens distortions. This technique is useful for checking image authenticity and establishing whether an image was captured with a specific camera. It is useful in forensic investigations, particularly when seeking to determine the origin of photographs in legal disputes, and it aids in the detection of image forgeries by determining whether the reported source camera information corresponds with the inherent camera features discovered in the image.

(5) Physical Based Technology: Physical-based technology in image forgery detection involves the analysis of physical characteristics present in the image data, such as lighting, shadows, and reflections, to uncover signs of manipulation or forgery. By assessing how light interacts with objects within the image, this approach can identify inconsistencies or irregularities that may indicate digital tampering. It plays a crucial role in verifying the authenticity of images by examining the physical properties that are challenging to replicate artificially. This technology is particularly useful in forensic investigations where verifying the real-world context and conditions of an image is essential, aiding in the detection of forgeries that may alter or misrepresent the physical reality captured in the image.

(6) Geometrical based Technology: Geometric-based image forgery detection system analyses a picture's geometric features, structures, and relationships to detect signs of alteration or counterfeit. This method can detect abnormalities that may indicate manipulation by examining the consistency of geometric components such as object alignment, perspective, and distortion. Geometric analysis is critical for finding differences in photos caused by splicing, retouching, or other changes that impact the alignment and proportions of objects or scenes. This technology is critical in determining the validity of photographs, and it is especially useful when geometric distortions reveal concealed forgeries or adjustments intended to trick viewers.

6 Overview of the Major Image Forgery Detection Technique

6.1 Copy-Move Forgery Detection Technique

Copy-move forgery detection is one of a crucial image forensics technique used to identify and locate duplicated or manipulated regions within an image. This technique is commonly employed to detect if a portion of an image is copied and pasted into another part of the same image to manipulate [25].

An overview of a basic copy-move forgery detection technique is given:

Algorithm Overview:

- Divide the image into overlapping blocks.
- Calculate feature vectors for each block (e.g., using algorithms like SIFT, SURF, or others [26]).
- Compare feature vectors within the same image to identify similar regions.
- Apply a similarity threshold to determine potential copied regions.
- Validate suspected regions through additional analysis or refinement techniques.
- Mark or highlight detected forged regions for further examination or processing.

The Copy-Move Forgery Detection Technique involves several steps to identify duplicated regions within an image. First, the image is separated into overlying blocks. Then, feature extraction methods such as Scale-Invariant Feature Transform (SIFT) or Speeded-Up Robust Features (SURF) are applied to generate unique descriptors for each block [27]. These descriptors are compared to identify similar or matching patterns. After identifying potential copied regions, geometric transformations like translation and rotation are employed to verify the forgeries. Finally, the detected duplicated areas are highlighted, revealing the copied portions within the image.

6.2 Splicing Detection Technique

Splicing detection is a technique used in image forensics to find areas in an image where distinct sections have been blended or" spliced" together. This method is critical for detecting picture forgeries, which are created by combining pieces of one or more photographs to generate a false image. An overview of a basic splicing detection technique follows:

Algorithm Overview:

- Image pre-processing is done to convert the input image to grayscale and partition the image into overlapping
- For each block in the image, extract distinctive features that can be used for comparison.
- Feature matching is done on extracted features between all pairs of blocks to identify potential inconsistencies that may indicate spliced regions.
- Analyze any compression or format-specific artifacts introduced by splicing, such as block artifacts in JPEG images or inconsistencies in color profiles.
- Noise analysis on between different regions of image are done, especially looking for inconsistencies in noise patterns.
- Metadata and Exif Analysis to identify discrepancies in timestamps, camera information, or other metadata that may indicate splicing.
- Visualization or Mask Generation for the detected splicing regions to visualize the manipulated areas in the image.
- Report the results, including the location and extent of the detected splicing forgeries, as well as any additional relevant information.

The algorithm first separates the image into overlapping sections. Color histograms, noise patterns, and edge information are computed within these blocks. Next, the program seeks irregularities or disparities in these attributes across image regions. Correlation analysis evaluates similarity measurements across neighboring blocks or throughout the image to identify sudden variations or inconsistencies that may suggest splicing. Finally, the system can classify and highlight regions suspected

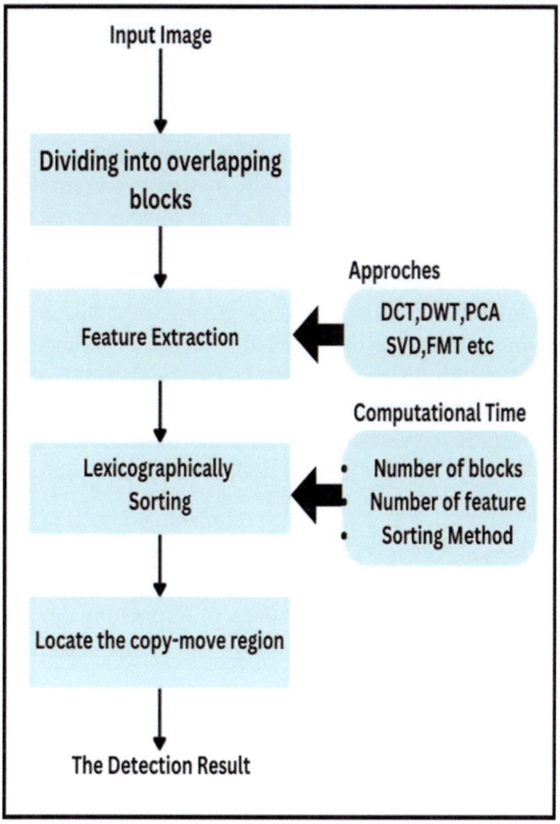

Fig. 2 Block diagram of copy-move forgery detection [2]

of being spliced by assessing these disparities and using machine learning or statistical models trained on splicing datasets. Splicing detection may require multiple algorithms and feature extraction techniques to enhance its accuracy, and the effectiveness of these methods can vary depending on the complexity of the forgery and the quality of the manipulated image (Fig. 2).

6.3 Retouching Detection Technique

Retouching detection is a key image forensics technique used to discover and analyses digitally altered or retouched areas in photographs. This method aids in determining image authenticity and whether any unauthorized changes have happened. Here's a quick rundown of a basic retouching detection technique:

Algorithm Overview:

- Divide the image acquired into overlapping blocks.

- For each block in the image, extract features that are indicative of image tampering.
- Analyze the extracted features to identify anomalies or inconsistencies that may indicate retouching.
- Examine the image for signs of resampling or compression, which may leave tell-tale artifacts and can indicate retouching.
- Detect and analyze blurring applied to certain areas of the image, which may be indicative of retouching attempts to smooth out details or imperfections.
- Analyze the geometry of the image to check for distortions or inconsistencies in the retouched areas.
- Investigate Exif metadata to identify discrepancies in timestamps, camera information, or other metadata that may indicate retouching.
- Highlight or generate masks for the detected retouched regions to visualize the manipulated areas in the image.
- Report the results, including the location and extent of the detected retouching forgeries, as well as any additional relevant information.

To improve their accuracy, retouching detection systems may involve the usage of various algorithms and feature extraction techniques. The efficiency of these procedures varies depending on the forgery's sophistication and the quality of the modified image. To increase the accuracy of retouching detection, researchers are constantly creating sophisticated algorithms, including deep learning-based techniques.

7 Conclusion

In summary, this survey study work has presented a thorough examination of the current advancements in approaches for detecting image alteration. The research has shed light on the progression of techniques, starting from conventional forensic procedures to advanced deep learning-based solutions. Developing systems capable of real-time detection and prevention of the spread of manipulated images across various online platforms and social media networks. This could involve collaboration between tech companies and researchers to implement automated detection algorithms at scale will likely pave the way for more effective and comprehensive image manipulation detection techniques in the future. Some novel approaches involve utilizing blockchain technology for image authentication and verification. Upon examination of the various tools and methodologies discussed, it becomes apparent that the field of image manipulation detection remains dynamic and indispensable. It presents promising opportunities for bolstering the credibility and reliability of digital visual content in diverse domains, including but not limited to law enforcement and journalism.

References

1. Ratnarajah A (2020) Survey on image manipulation detection.https://doi.org/10.13140/RG.2.2.24131.22560
2. Singh MN, Joshi S (2015) Digital image forensics: progress and challenges
3. Bharati A, Vatsa M, Singh R, Bowyer KW, Tong X (2017) Demography-based facial retouching detection using subclass supervised sparse autoencoder. In: 2017 IEEE International joint conference on biometrics (IJCB), Denver, CO, USA, pp 474–482. https://doi.org/10.1109/BTAS.2017.8272732
4. Roy A, Dixit R, Naskar R, Chakraborty RS (2020) Digital image forensics theory and implementation. Stud Comput Intell 755
5. Gupta S, Mohan N, Sandhu P (2018) Energy deviation measure: a technique for digital image forensics. Int J Electron Secur Digit Forensics 10:401. https://doi.org/10.1504/IJESDF.2018.10015333
6. Ferna´ndez EG, Ana LSO, Luis JGV, Hernandez-Castro J (2018) Digital image tamper detection technique based on spectrum analysis of CFA artifacts. Sensors (Basel) 18(9):2804
7. Zheng L, Zhang Y, Vrizlynn LL (2019) Thing, a survey on image tampering and its detection in real-world photos. J Vis Commun Image Represent 58:380–399 ISSN 1047–3203. https://doi.org/10.1016/j.jvcir.2018.12.022
8. Bayram S, Avcibas I, Sankur B, Memon N (2006) Image manipulation detection. J Electronic Imaging 15:041102. https://doi.org/10.1117/1.2401138
9. Salim MZ, Yildirim R, Abboud AJ (2021) Comparison of copy-move image forgery detection techniques
10. Pawar D, Gajpal M (2021) Image forensic tool (IFT): image retrieval, tampering detection, and classification. Int J Digit Crime Forensics 13:1–15. https://doi.org/10.4018/IJDCF.287606
11. Yahya ALN, Jalab HA, Wahid A, Noor RM (2015) Robust watermarking algorithm for digital images using discrete wavelet and probabilistic neural network. J King Saud University—Computer Inf Sci 27(4):393401 ISSN13191578. https://doi.org/10.1016/j.jksuci.2015.02.00
12. Favorskaya M, Pyataeva A, Popov A (2017) Texture analysis in watermarking paradigms. Procedia Comput Sci 112:1460–1469 ISSN 1877-0509. https://doi.org/10.1016/j.procs.2017.08.019
13. Megha K et al (2023) A comprehensive review of media forensics and deepfake detection technique. In: 2023 10th International conference on computing for sustainable global development (INDIACom), pp 392–395
14. Moussa AM (2015) A fast and accurate algorithm for copy-move forgery detection. In: 2015 Tenth international conference on computer engineering & systems (ICCES), Cairo, Egypt, pp 281–285. https://doi.org/10.1109/ICCES.2015.7393060
15. Alahmadi A, Hussain M, Aboalsamh H et al (2017) Passive detection of image forgery using DCT and local binary pattern. SIViP 11:81–88. https://doi.org/10.1007/s11760-016-0899-0
16. Hashmi MF, Anand V, Keskar AG (2014) Copy-move image forgery detection using an efficient and robust method combining un-decimated wavelet transform and scale invariant feature transform. AASRI Procedia 9:84–91 ISSN 2212-6716. https://doi.org/10.1016/j.aasri.2014.09.015
17. Abdalla Y, Iqbal MT, Shehata M (2019) Convolutional neural network for copy-move forgery detection. Symmetry 11:1280. https://doi.org/10.3390/sym11101280
18. Das D, Naskar R (2022) Image splicing detection based on deep convolutional neural network and transfer learning. In: 2022 IEEE 19th India council international conference (INDICON), Kochi, India, pp 1–6. https://doi.org/10.1109/INDICON56171.2022.10039789
19. Chen C et al (2017) Image splicing detection via camera response function analysis. In: 2017 IEEE Conference on computer vision and pattern recognition (CVPR), pp 1876–1885
20. Pham NT et al (2018) Efficient image splicing detection algorithm based on markov features. Multimed Tools Appl 78:12405–12419
21. Julliand T et al (2015) Automated image splicing detection from noise estimation in raw images. In: International conferences on imaging for crime detection and prevention

22. Jain A et al (2020) Detecting GANs and retouching based digital alterations via DAD-HCNN. In: 2020 IEEE/CVF Conference on computer vision and pattern recognition workshops (CVPRW), pp 2870–2879
23. Rathgeb C et al (2020) Differential detection of facial retouching: a multi-biometric approach. IEEE Access 8:106373–106385
24. Salih ZA, Thabit R, Zidan KA, Khoo BE (2022) A new face image manipulation reveal scheme based on face detection and image watermarking 1–6. https://doi.org/10.1109/IICAIET55139.2022.9936838
25. Abrahim AR et al (2017) Literature review: detection of image splicing forgery
26. Yusoff N, Alamro L (2019) Implementation of feature extraction algorithms for image tampering detection. Int J Adv Comput Res 9:2277–7970. https://doi.org/10.19101/IJACR.PID37
27. Jung K-H (2016) Block-based authentication scheme for forgery attacks on digital images. Adv Sci Lett 22:2583–2587. https://doi.org/10.1166/asl.2016.7784

An Application of Analytical Hierarchical Process to Measure Money Laundering

Priyanka Yadav and Siva Krishna Golla

Abstract Money laundering is a deliberate and serious crime of financial nature and refers to the process of making illegally earned money look legitimate. Such illegal activities may include drug trafficking or terrorist funding. The money has its origins from criminal activity and is illegal, however the process of laundering makes it look clean as if earned legally. Developing countries like India have been extremely vulnerable to terrorism and financial scams over the past several decades which are financed by laundered money. Despite the establishment of several regulators at different levels, this problem continues to be a national threat and jeopardize the formal economic system. Therefore, examining indicators of money laundering activities in the Indian economy is necessary. This study aims to propose an index to measure money laundering and assign weights to individual parameters to assess the extent of money laundering prevalent in an economy. The study is based on primary data gathered by seeking experts' opinions on money laundering and its parameters of measurement. The results show that the most significant indicator for money laundering in a developing economy is terror funding. The study further highlights the need for enhanced vigilance and integrated security measures by enforcement agencies to combat money laundering across the world economies. This study would be helpful for academicians and policymakers to understand the key indicators of money laundering in an economy.

Keywords Money laundering · Analytical Hierarchical Process · Multi-dimensional index · Illegal · FDI

P. Yadav (✉) · S. K. Golla
School of Management Studies, National Forensic Sciences University Gandhinagar, Gandhinagar, Gujarat, India
e-mail: priyanka.yadav@nfsu.ac.in

S. K. Golla
e-mail: sivakrishna.golla@nfsu.ac.in

B. N. Gohil et al. (eds.), *Information Security, Privacy and Digital Forensics*, Lecture Notes in Electrical Engineering 1423,
https://doi.org/10.1007/978-981-96-9443-3_16

1 Introduction

The battle against money laundering in recent years is getting intense each passing day and preventing money laundering activities is among the top priorities of top world leaders be it a developed nation or a developing one. At the outset, money laundering was not considered any kind of crime and hence it did not invite any criminal liability in majority of the nations. However, in recent times perhaps each economy has started considering it a crime inviting prosecution. Even several international committees have adopted a large number of specialized procedures designed to overcome this peril. It is well established that criminal organizations that wish to use the illegally sourced money effectively make use of money laundering method to deceive regulating authorities. Being aware that dealing with transactions involving large amounts of cash could be dangerous, the criminals intend to find some way to transfer illegal money in legal financial institutions. The process of laundering money typically involves three steps: placement, layering, and integration [1]. However, sometimes in reality all the three steps need not necessarily be there.

Money laundering is a procedure to ensure the functioning of crime as a financial/monetary phenomenon. It is the safest way for criminals to legalize their illegally earned money. They usually invest the illegal money outside the state/country where it was actually earned. An estimate by International Monetary Fund (IMF) experts suggests that more than 2% of the total world GDP is illegally laundered on an annual basis. Hence it is important to keep a check on money laundering be it a developed or a developing economy. There have been rising concerns that money laundering leads to the spread of unaccounted dirty money around the world, leads to uneven functioning of the otherwise smooth running financial systems, promotes instability of national currencies and thereby triggering major exchange rate fluctuations. Thus, money laundering is dangerous to not only the state/country of origin but has turned into one of the most significant threat worldwide.

Money laundering can happen through a number of ways—from the most fundamental ones to the very complex ones. Most commonly a legal formal and cash-based business owned by a criminal firm is used to facilitate money laundering. Although banks are directed to report huge transactions involving huge cash and/or suspicious activities of criminal nature that might signal money laundering, this could not stop the active ongoing criminal money laundering activities. The reasons for it can be many ranging from lack of competent staff to inadequate number of investigators to lack of proper investigative support system. The motive of Money laundering is also attained through the use of several currencies/derivative products, wired or wireless transfers, cash smuggling to nations where money-laundering enforcement laws are relatively liberal. Other money-laundering methods include investing in costly commodities and metals such as gems, gold and diamond that can be easily be transported to other jurisdictions. Investment in real estate, expensive vehicles, boats; gambling, casinos, using shell companies are also used as avenues for money laundering.

In today's world with highest use of advanced technology, the electronic money transfer has become even easier and in a bit of seconds funds get transferred in a click of mouse only. With advanced use of internet, the rise in number of online banking institutions with instant funds transfer options, unidentified online payment services, and P2P transfer of funds/resources with the help of mobile phones have indeed made the task of differentiating between legal and illegal money very difficult if not impossible. With the help of proxy servers and almost unidentifiable software, money laundering becomes almost impossible to trace.

In the Indian context, to alleviate money laundering, Indian government has taken several initiatives to ensure that it is effective in battling illegal transactions; however the progression faced by the economy is in line with the change theory. In accordance with implementation, it is also the responsibility of relevant parties to ensure their effectiveness in following the regime. Several competent regulatory authorities, banks and most importantly their employees play a vital role in alleviating money laundering.

Money also can be laundered through several ways like e-auctions and sales transactions, web-based gambling, web-based virtual gaming sites/play stores, where illegal money is willfully converted into gaming money and thereafter converted again into real money which is readily usable. The increasingly used and newest frontier involves use of crypto currencies, such as Bit coin and distributed ledger to launder money. There is no denial to the fact that globally governments and regulators have geared up their endeavors to fight money laundering, with such laws that require systems in place for detection, tracing and reporting of suspicious activities to be used by financial institutions; however it cannot be further contradicted that the amount of money involved is too huge. The ways and means to launder money have increased many folds putting huge challenges in front of regulators. Money laundering does not only have financial consequences but it has social consequences as well. Besides giving rise to illegal transactions and a parallel economy thereby jeopardizing the formal setup; it also paves way for illegal activities which may be of dangerous nature, such as drug trafficking, smuggling, human trafficking, funding of terror activities, extortion and fraud thereby putting millions of people at risk. Therefore, combating money laundering may have the benefits of reduced crimes and may benefit the society significantly.

This study aims to determine the factors indicative of the prevalence of money laundering activities in an economy. In a way they are proxies for identifying the magnitude of money laundering in an economy. This study proposes a multi-dimensional index involving multiple criteria to measure money laundering in an economy. With such inputs, several economies/states can be compared with one another and/or over same/different time horizons to assess the level of money laundering activities in a nation. It may be of great use to policy makers as it may help them to ascertain the magnitude of effect of their efforts to combat money laundering. Further, the results may help policy makers to plan next level of activities to combat money laundering in case if the previous efforts were unsuccessful.

2 Literature Review

Money laundering, its economic and social effects have been studied by past numerous researchers. Buchchan asserts that given the complex nature of money laundering, the paper trail formed through the layering procedure further complicates the legal bodies' task to ascertain which funds within the legitimate economy are legal and which ones are not.

Araujo [2] shows that merely creating a formal agreement with the aim to persuade banks and other similar financial institutions to cooperate is not simply fruitful and it faces the limitation of hidden information/facts which can lead to the problem of hidden selection.

Veiga et al. [3] identify the effects of anti-money laundering regulations on FDI and found that the banks' duty to report suspicious transactions was inversely related to growth thereby indicating that the effective implementation of laws to prevent money laundering policies can reduce growth in the countries where the regulation is in place. On similar lines, Masciandaro [4] concludes that in case if a country decides to be a "non-cooperative country" based on its historical characteristics, then it is viewed as a suggestion of path dependence in the fight of money laundering.

Araujo [5, 6] follows an evolutionary approach to counter money laundering by throwing light on how with the help of mutative game between financial institutions and their employees, it is possible to establish that the final decisions of banks and its several employees to cope against money laundering is determined internally, however it may be affected by the structure of the regulatory institution itself. The study concludes that the success of any anti-money laundering regulation is subject to regulatory design, intention of banks and employees working there to cope against money laundering.

Barone and Masciandaro [7] in their study on money laundering propose a real-time dynamic model to simulate inter-relationships among earnings from of organized crime, money laundering, and legal investments. The model tries to capture the situations under which money laundering causes a favorable predictable trend in class of assets which are held lawfully for which criminal business houses are owners. The model simulates the total legal wealth which has been earned by organized crime through trafficking of banned substances like drugs in several parts of the world with special reference to Europe.

Unger et al. [8] examine the perils of money laundering and classify them into three categories i.e. price distortions, ruining integrity and political effect of intrusion.

Enofe et al. [9] employ cross-sectional data to examine the relationship between the practice of money laundering and its impact on the economy of Nigeria. The results of the study confirm that money laundering has a negative and causal relationship with real GDP which is used to proxy the Nigerian economy.

Takats [10] investigates the relation between the incidence of money laundering and corporate tax avoidance using a sample of US firm observations over the period 1995–2014 and documents a strong positive relation between money laundering and tax avoidance. Bartlett [11] states that an economy cannot reach its optimal level of development if money laundering activity proceeds unchallenged and no action is taken to prevent them. The possible reasons for this could be the damage it makes to otherwise smoothly running financial institutions which happen to be crucial for prosperity and economic growth.

The Indian government enacted Prevention of Money Laundering Act in the year 2002 to protect the economy from the net of money laundering. Further, amendments have been made to Information Technology Act (2000) to contain crimes of digital nature. Several committees in the past were formed to identify extent of money laundering in India, the most important ones were-Rangnekar and Chopra committees which pointed towards huge under-reporting of income and its sources by wealthy businessmen. In the global context, similar to India, China has Anti money laundering laws where any failure to comply can invite a huge penalty for defaulters. Further, in Malaysia, an anti money laundering mechanism is there in place but relatively lower number of prosecutions and penalties points towards the mechanism inefficiency. Some researchers have also pointed towards the threat posed by money laundering and terror funding on financial as well as overall integrity of a nation.

On the basis of a comprehensive review of relevant literature, it was found that although previous researchers have highlighted the measures of money laundering that are used to identify the extent of money laundering across the world; no singly study has focused on multi-dimensional aspects of money laundering. Studying money laundering with the help of several dimensions is the key research gap that has been addressed by this study.

3 Objective of the Study

The objective of this study is to propose a multi-dimensional index to measure money laundering activities of a nation. One of the steps in constructing such index requires assignment of weights to individual parameters. This study adopts a scientific and rational approach to assign weights to the parameters which can be used to identify the extent of money laundering in a nation. Basis a detailed review of literature, the study proceeds as follows. First, the parameters to identify the level of money laundering have been identified. Experts' opinions was then sought to identify weight to be assigned to each parameter to compose a composite indicator of money laundering.

4 Data and Research Methodology

Data

The variables that comprise the index of money laundering have been carefully selected by reviewing relevant literature. After identifying variables, experts' opinion was sought to assign weights to individual parameters which consist the index of money laundering. Experts were professionals from banking sector, academicians, heads of financial institutions and practicing lawyers.

Research methodology

Analytical Hierarchical Process (AHP)

It is a structured method of analyzing complex decisions with multiple criteria in group decision making. This technique was developed by Saaty [12]. Under this technique, the broad-criteria are first decomposed into sub-criteria and then each sub-criteria is analyzed independently. AHP can be used for both quantitative as well as qualitative data [13]. The step-wise procedure for AHP can be described as follows:

In the first step, define the problem under consideration and then determine goals of the analysis. Here, the goal has to be divided in criteria and then criteria are further decomposed into sub-criteria. In the subsequent step, hierarchy is structured from top to bottom through intermediate levels by considering all objectives and outcomes. In the third step, pair-wise comparison matrices ($n * n$) are constructed for each of the lower levels by use of relative scale measurement as presented in Table 1 and each element in the corresponding level is compared with $n(n-1)/2$ comparisons where n is the total number of elements with the considerations that diagonal elements are going to remain equal and other elements will be reciprocal of earlier comparisons.

In the fourth step, hierarchical synthesis is used to weight eigenvectors by taking weights of the criteria and the sum total is taken over all weighted eigenvector entries relevant to those which are in the next lower level of the hierarchy. In the fifth step, the consistency is determined by using the eigenvalue, λmax, to calculate the consistency index (CI) such that

$$CI = (\lambda \max - n)/(n - 1)$$

where n is representative of matrix size.

To check consistency in judgment, CI is used and consistency is measured taking the consistency ratio (CR) of CI with the appropriate value in Table 2. According to [15] the CR is acceptable, if it does not exceed 0.10 where

Table 1 Pair-wise comparison scale for AHP preferences

Numerical ratings	Verbal judgment of preferences
9	Extremely preferred
7	Very strongly preferred
5	Strongly preferred
3	Moderately preferred
1	Equally preferred
2,4,6,8	Intermediate preference values

Source[14]

Table 2 Average random consistency table

Size of matrix	1	2	3	4	5	6	7	8	9	10
Randomness index (RI)	0.00	0.00	0.58	0.90	1.12	1.24	1.32	1.41	1.45	1.49

$$CR = CI/RI$$

where *RI* is the randomness index value

If it is more than 0.10, the judgment matrix is inconsistent. To obtain a consistent matrix and to avoid vogue results, judgments should be reviewed and improved till consistency is achieved. Table 2 presents the random index values for different matrix size.

5 Results of AHP

The AHP is a technique under MCDM which was originally developed by [12]. This technique is a decision making technique which breaks down complex problems into different levels which are useful in the process of decision-making. This technique is effective in handling large number of criteria and sub-criteria in complex decision making. For the purpose of this study, AHP has been employed to assign weights to eight parameters which have been used to study the extent of money laundering. This technique has been used by several past researchers in problem-solving which require multiple criteria. Therefore, this technique has been used to assign scientific weights to individual indicators of money laundering. The technique starts with the identification of goal. For the study, the goal is to assign weights to parameters. Next step is to assign relative importance to each criteria. With inputs from experts, the parameters have been assigned importance values relative to each other. Table 3 shows coding of variables. Table 4 presents the pair wise comparison matrix for all criteria. In Table 5, the pair-wise comparison values have been summed up. Table 6 shows normalized matrix with weights to individual parameters and Table 7 indicates weighted normalized decision matrix.

As shown in Table 8, the CR is found to be 0.087 which is less than 10 percent. It shows that the judgment matrix is consistent and there is no internal inconsistency in pair-wise comparisons, hence there is no need for revision of decision matrix. If it is found to be more than 0.10, the judgment matrix is assumed to be lacking consistency. To obtain a consistent matrix and to avoid vogue results, judgments should be reviewed and improved till consistency is achieved.

Table 3 Coding of variables

Variable code	Variable name
V1	Terror funding
V2	Drug trafficking
V3	Fostered crime and corruption
V4	Suspicious real estate transactions
V5	Decreased tax revenues
V6	Illicit financial flows
V7	Cross border illegal operations
V8	Mal invoicing

Table 4 Criteria comparison matrix

Variable (s)	V1	V2	V3	V4	V5	V6	V7	V8
V1	1.00	7.00	3.00	9.00	3.00	5.00	3.00	9.00
V2	1/7	1.00	1.00	3.00	1/3	3.00	1/3	3.00
V3	1/3	1.00	1.00	1.00	1/3	1.00	1/7	3.00
V4	1/9	1/3	1.00	1.00	1/5	1/3	1/7	5.00
V5	1/3	3	3.00	5.00	1.00	5.00	1.00	7.00
V6	1/3	1/3	1.00	3.00	1/5	1.00	1/2	3.00
V7	1/3	3.00	7.00	3.00	1.00	2.00	1.00	9.00
V8	1/9	1/3	1/3	1/5	1/7	1/3	1/9	1.00

Table 5 Criteria comparison matrix with Eigen vectors

Variable (s)	V1	V2	V3	V4	V5	V6	V7	V8
V1	1.00	7.00	3.00	9.00	3.00	5.00	3.00	9.00
V2	0.14	1.00	1.00	3.00	0.33	3.00	0.33	3.00
V3	0.33	1.00	1.00	1.00	0.33	1.00	0.14	3.00
V4	0.11	0.33	1.00	1.00	0.20	0.33	0.33	5.00
V5	0.33	3.03	3.00	5.00	1.00	5.00	1.00	7.00
V6	0.20	0.33	1.00	3.00	0.20	1.00	0.50	3.00
V7	0.33	3.00	7.00	3.03	1.00	2.00	1.00	9.00
V8	0.11	0.33	0.33	0.20	0.14	0.33	0.11	1.00
Sum	2.57	16.03	17.33	25.23	6.21	17.67	6.42	40.00

Table 6 Normalized matrix

Variable (s)	V1	V2	V3	V4	V5	V6	V7	V8	Weights
V1	0.390	0.437	0.173	0.357	0.483	0.283	0.467	0.225	0.352
V2	0.056	0.062	0.058	0.119	0.053	0.170	0.052	0.075	0.081
V3	0.130	0.062	0.058	0.040	0.054	0.057	0.022	0.075	0.062
V4	0.043	0.021	0.058	0.040	0.032	0.019	0.051	0.125	0.049
V5	0.130	0.189	0.173	0.198	0.161	0.283	0.156	0.175	0.183
V6	0.078	0.021	0.058	0.119	0.032	0.057	0.078	0.075	0.065
V7	0.130	0.187	0.404	0.120	0.161	0.113	0.156	0.225	0.187
V8	0.043	0.021	0.019	0.008	0.023	0.019	0.017	0.025	0.022

Table 7 Weighted normalized decision matrix

Variable (s)	
V1	0.903
V2	1.292
V3	1.077
V4	1.227
V5	1.137
V6	1.142
V7	1.200
V8	0.877
Λmax	8.854486

Table 8 Consistency ratio

Consistency index (CI)	0.122
Randomness index (RI)	1.41
Consistency ratio (CR) = CI/RI	0.087

6 Conclusion

In the wake of rising criminal activities around the world, money laundering has taken a lead role in crime prevention and control in the modern economic setting. By combating money laundering, other activities which are systematically to money laundering can be controlled. Interestingly when researchers are coming up with ideas that foreign direct investment promotes growth and carbon emissions and as a result lead to black money, it is important to identify various aspects which directly/indirectly measure money laundering. At a time when financing of criminal activities from illegal money has become a tradition of intense fully expanding criminal business thereby representing higher danger level to public, the question that whether money laundering and subsequent crimes are correlated needs an answer. This article has proposed an index to measure the extent of money laundering prevalent in an economy. Based on opinions from experts, this study has proposed eight parameters to measure the magnitude of money laundering activities and assign weight to each parameter. Future researchers may propose an index of money laundering with inputs from this study. The weights so assigned in this study to individual parameters will be of great use and several nations/states can be compared with one another across same/different time periods to identify whether the measures to combat money laundering are bringing in fruitful results or not. Since assigning equal weights to all parameters of measuring money laundering prevalent in an economy may be irrational and unscientific, this study has tried to bridge this gap by proposing a multi-dimensional measure of money laundering.

References

1. Masciandaro D (1999) Money laundering: the economics of regulation. Eur J Law Econ 7:225–240
2. Araujo RA (2008) Assessing the efficiency of the anti-money laundering regulation: an incentive-based approach. J Money Laund Control 11(1):67–75
3. Veiga L, Andrade J, Rossi A (2006) Money laundering, corruption and growth: an empirical rationale for a global convergence on anti-money laundering regulation. In: Proceedings of the 34th Brazilian economics meeting
4. Masciandaro D (2008) Offshore financial centres: the political economy of regulation. Eur J Law Econ 26(3):307–340
5. Araujo RA (2010) An evolutionary game theory approach to combat money laundering. J Money Laund Control13(1):70–78. https://doi.org/10.1108/13685201011010236
6. Araujo RA (2010) An evolutionary game theory approach to combat money laundering. J Money Laund Control 13(1):70–78
7. Barone R, Masciandaro D (2011) Organized crime, money laundering and legal economy: theory and simulations. Eur J Law Econ 32(1):115–142
8. Unger B, Rawlings G, Siegel M, Ferwerda J, de Kruijf W, Busuioc EM, Wokke K (2006) The amount and effects of money laundering. Dutch Ministry of Finance Report
9. Enofe AO, Aliu AK, Ombu A (2018) Money laundering and the Nigerian economy. Int J Adv Acad Res Soc Manag Sci 4(4):185–201
10. Takats E (2007) A theory of "Crying Wolf": the economics of money laundering enforcement, IMF Working Paper. Last accessed on 2023/02/20
11. Bartlett B (2002) The negative effects of money laundering on economic development. The Asian Development Bank Regional Technical Assistance Project No. 5967
12. Saaty TL (1980) Multi criteria decision making: the analytic hierarchy process. McGraw-Hill, New York
13. Kahraman C, Cebeci U, Ulukan Z (2003) Multi-criteria supplier selection using fuzzy AHP. Logist Inf Manag 16(6):382–394
14. Saaty TL (1994) How to make a decision: the analytic hierarchy process. Interface 24(6):19–43
15. Partovi FY, Burton J, Banerjee A (1990) Application of analytical hierarchical process in operations management. Int J Oper Prod Manag 10(3):5–19. https://doi.org/10.1108/01443579010134945

File System Artefacts Generator (FSAGen): Towards Faster Forensic Tool Testing

Gaurav Gogia and Parag Rughani

Abstract Software testing is one of the most fundamental steps in any software development lifecycle. The larger the scale, the more testing is required to ensure the correctness and reliability of the software. In the case of digital forensics, one of the main problems that researchers face is the availability of datasets for testing the reliability of the product they are evaluating. Different forensic tools with similar features may present different results even with similar inputs. This makes it extremely important to have standardised and reproducible datasets. This research explores synthetic dataset generators and introduces a novel command-line interface (CLI) tool for generating file system artefacts. The tool aims to facilitate the quick and convenient creation of synthetic datasets to aid in the validation of file system forensic tools. By offering a simplified and cross-platform solution, this tool addresses the need for standardised datasets in digital forensics research and enhances the reliability and accuracy of forensic tool evaluations.

Keywords File system forensics · Forensic artefacts · File system artefacts · Dataset generation · Artefacts generation

1 Introduction

File systems are one of the most important sources of evidence. This significance stems from the fundamental requirement of electronic devices to store and organise data across power cycles. Consequently, the organisation of data requires at least one file system to be present in the secondary storage of these electronic devices, making file systems a highly valuable source of digital evidence [1]. Several digital forensics tools have been developed to parse file systems, extract data, and carve deleted content out of them when required [2–6].

G. Gogia · P. Rughani (✉)
National Forensic Sciences University, Gandhinagar, Gujarat, India
e-mail: parag.rughani@gmail.com

B. N. Gohil et al. (eds.), *Information Security, Privacy and Digital Forensics*,
Lecture Notes in Electrical Engineering 1423,
https://doi.org/10.1007/978-981-96-9443-3_17

Thanks to the wide range of available file system analysis tools, investigators have access to a variety of solutions to address their specific challenges with relative ease. However, the same variety of solutions can be a double-edged sword. Testing & verifying the correctness of digital forensics tools is a complex task. Tools with similar features may present different output for the same dataset [7–9]. Validation of digital forensics tools and methodologies is one of the most important, yet, complex tasks. Testing requires a huge corpus of reproducible and reliable source of test data [10].

1.1 Motivation

The primary motivation of this research is the absence of standardised datasets for testing file system forensics tools. Poor quality datasets can degrade the reliability of the tests performed to validate the tools [11]. To this date, Grafinkel's dataset is the largest and one of the most common datasets used for forensic testing [12]. While this approach has been effective, recent research indicates that the use of synthetic or generated datasets can facilitate the verification of digital forensics software [13]. However, there's an absence of file system artefact generation tools that work across multiple platforms and file systems. The "Literature Review" section discusses existing tools for generating file system artefacts and the gaps this research fills; in more detail.

1.2 Contribution

In this paper, we introduce a lightweight, cross-platform tool for generating file system artefacts. This Command Line Interface (CLI) tool offers investigators and researchers a simple and efficient means of generating datasets of varying sizes. The tool serves the purpose of testing the reliability and correctness of file system forensics tools. The tool generates five types of files with randomised data everytime it is run, ensuring high-entropy datasets are generated every-time. All the files are generated in a multi-threaded way. This multi-threading and algorithm for data generation is better explained in the Methodology section. The following list shows all the file types generated:

- Text
- DOCX
- PNG
- PDF
- MP4

As a POC, only the five most common file types were selected. These types of files can later be expanded. As an auxiliary effect, due to the way these files are generated, more file system artefacts like Shell Bags and Shell Bags MRU [14] are populated in Windows based operating systems. Similarly, in MacOS, .DS_Store [15] file is generated as a secondary artefact when the FSAGen tool is run.

1.3 Paper Structure

The remainder of this paper unfolds across five principal sections, each contributing distinct dimensions to the overall study. The Literature Review establishes a theoretical framework and identifies gaps in current research. The Methodology section explains the implementation of the tool along with an algorithm to explain how it works. In the Experiments section, empirical results are presented, accompanied by detailed analyses. The Discussion critically interprets findings in the context of existing literature, addressing implications and limitations. Finally, the Conclusion synthesizes key findings and proposes avenues for future research, providing a comprehensive endpoint to the study.

2 Literature Review

In recent years, the development of various software tools for generating datasets has significantly contributed to the field of digital forensics. These tools have been explored in the literature, offering valuable insights into their functionalities and applications. FADE, a disk image generator designed for Android device education, leverages Android API tools to populate rooted mobile devices with artefacts, enhancing the educational experience [16]. TraceGen, another notable tool, maintains a list of actions directed to a specific tool and executes them within a virtual machine. This process records network activity to create a network image and generates a disk image as well [17]. EviPlant, on the other hand, is an extensive framework aimed at generating forensic artefacts for educational purposes. It incorporates diffing and injection components, enabling users to identify differences between existing and newly generated artefacts within a base virtual machine [18]. iGen employs Convolutional Neural Networks (CNN) to generate Indicators of Compromise (IoC), showcasing the application of machine learning techniques in dataset generation [19]. Additionally, Hystck follows a server-client approach, simulating user activity to generate network and disk images, similar to TraceGen [13]. The literature also explores other approaches, such as TREDE and VMPOP, which combine curated artefact lists with automated framework-based artefact population in virtual machines. Lastly, ForTrace adopts a comprehensive client-server model to generate disk images by populating virtual machines with artefacts, sharing similarities with TraceGen and Hystck [20]. SysGen, on the other hand uses a pre-seeded corpus of dataset to re-generate the dataset for validaton testing of software [21]. Through an extensive literature review, these tools and frameworks offer diverse approaches to dataset generation, providing researchers and practitioners with valuable resources for digital forensics experimentation and evaluation.

An underlying commonality observed among the aforementioned forensic artefact generation tools is the extensive setup required for their environment. These tools often involve configuring multiple virtual machines and software components to generate the desired datasets. While these tools demonstrate the capability to generate various types of artefacts and emulate user activity, they still rely on initial user inputs or predefined lists of artefacts that are regenerated repeatedly.

While fake dataset and file generators exist for software testing, they seem to be generating files for more general purpose use-cases. These file generator software do not create disk images required for testing file system forensics tools [22–28].

Addressing above limitations, the present research endeavour aims to bridge two significant gaps in the field: environment setup and user input. This study proposes a novel solution by introducing a single executable binary that enables the generation of an infinite number of file system artefacts without the need for user guidance or input at any given point in time.

3 Methodology

This section outlines the research methodology employed in the development of the file system artefact generation tool. The tool is implemented using Google's Go programming language [29]. Go was chosen as the programming language for its beneficial features, such as easy concurrency, green threads, memory safety, and cross-compilation capabilities [30].

The file system artefact generation tool, FSAGen, follows a straightforward algorithm for generating artefact files. The process begins by taking user inputs, including the absolute path for file generation, the desired number of folders, and the depth limit for sub-folders. The tool heavily makes use of goroutines to optimise for high performance subfolder and file generation. Goroutines [31, 32] are user mode scheduled threads, also known as green threads. These threads are scheduled in the user mode by Go runtime without switching into the Kernel mode for faster context switching. The tool utilises goroutines (green threads) to spawn a new goroutine for each folder creation, another goroutine for each sub-folder creation, and yet another goroutine for writing files to the disk. These goroutines are synchronised using channels to ensure proper coordination. The number of goroutine spawned is limited by the available CPU cores on the host computer. The maximum number of goroutine allowed is determined by the number of CPU cores, preventing excessive resource consumption. An Algorithm explaining the process is defined in Algorithm 1.

Algorithm 1 FSAGen Artefact Generation Algorithm

```
procedure GENERATEARTEFACTS(absolutePath, numFolders, depthLimit)
    input: absolutePath, numFolders, depthLimit

    Spawn goroutine for each new folder
    for i ← 1 to numFolders do
        createFolder(absolutePath + "/Folder" + i)
    end for

    Spawn goroutine for each new sub-folder
    for i ← 1 to numFolders do
        for j ← 1 to depthLimit do
            createSubFolder(absolutePath + "/Folder" + i + "/SubFolder" + j)
        end for
    end for

    Spawn goroutine for each file
    for i ← 1 to numFolders do
        for j ← 1 to depthLimit do
            writeFile(absolutePath + "/Folder" + i + "/SubFolder" + j + "/file")
        end for
    end for
end procedure
```

4 Experiments

To evaluate the performance and resource utilisation of FSAGen, a series of experiments were conducted. All these experiments were profiled using a python [33] script that uses psutil [34] library to monitor max RAM use and execution time of the software.

This library helps in profiling system events like memory use, execution time, thread count, processor use, disk reads/writes etc. Current version of the library is v5.9.5. The library has a proven record and is being actively maintained on GitHub by many contributors. Results of the experiments are presented through tables and graphs in upcoming sections.

4.1 Environment Setup

The experiment setup involved creating an environment conducive to conducting the file system artefact generation experiments. This section outlines the hardware and software configurations. FSAGen tool was tested across 5 different test environments: Windows Subsystem for Linux 2 (WSL-2) [35], Anarchy Linux [36], Windows 10 Professional [37], Windows 11 Professional [38], and Kali Linux [39]. All these environments were used created within VMWare Workstation Pro 17 [40]. Windows

Table 1 User options: number of folders and subfolders

Files	Breadth	Depth
5	1	1
10	1	2
15	1	3
30	1	6
60	2	3
120	2	6
250	5	2
500	10	1
1000	10	1

10, Windows 11, Anarchy Linux, & Kali Linux environments were created with 4 vCPUs and 6 GB RAM. A 12 TB 7200RPM external HDD was used for storage.

4.2 Experiment Details

To assess the performance and reliability of the file system artefact generation tool, experiments were conducted using sampling rate 100ms. Table 1 presents the details of the files used and the user-selected options for each scenario. These experiments were repeated for every platform mentioned in the previous sub-section, ensuring a comprehensive evaluation across different operating systems.

Number of files were calculated using a simple formula: 5 $\times$ BREADTH $\times$ DEPTH where BREADTH is the number of folders and DEPTH is the number of sub-folders per folder. Figure 1 presents a line chart showing maximum RAM usage in megabytes (MB) against file count for different virtual machines and WSL-2. The x-axis represents file count, ranging from 0 to 1000, and the y-axis represents max RAM use, ranging from 0 to 400 MB. The chart includes five lines: WSL-2 (redcircles), Anarchy Linux VM (blue squares), Kali Linux VM (green triangles), Windows 10 VM (orange diamonds), and Windows 11 VM (purple pentagons). Each line shows varying trends in RAM usage as file count increases.

Figure 2 is another line chart comparing execution time in seconds against file count for different virtual machines and WSL-2. The x-axis represents file count, ranging from 0 to 1000, and the y-axis represents execution time in seconds, ranging from 0 to 25. The chart includes five lines: WSL-2 (red circles), Anarchy Linux VM (blue squares), Kali Linux VM (green triangles), Windows 10 VM (orange diamonds), and Windows 11 VM (magenta pentagons). WSL2 shows a significant increase in execution time as file count increases, while other VMs have relatively lower execution times.

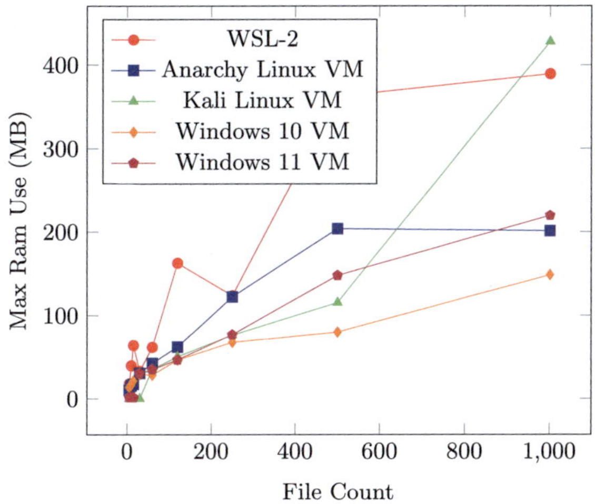

Fig. 1 FSAGen Profiling: RAM Use

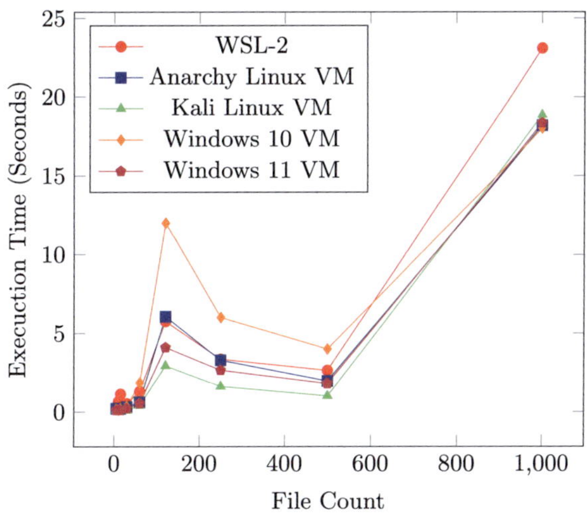

Fig. 2 FSAGen Profiling: Execution Time

5 Discussion

This section presents the outcomes and notable observations derived from the conducted experiments. The experiments aimed to evaluate the performance and resource consumption of the file system artefact generation tool (FSAGen) on five platforms: Windows Subsystem for Linux 2, Anarchy Linux, Windows 10, and Windows 11. These platforms employed a diverse range of file systems to assess FSAGen's cross-platform compatibility. As FSAGen does not rely on external user seeds or platform-specific configurations, it operates seamlessly across major operating systems, including but not limited to Windows, Linux distributions, Windows Subsystem for Linux, and macOS. Additionally, FSAGen's independence from the latest glibc libraries ensures its compatibility with older operating systems, such as CentOS 7. Graphical representations of the experimental data provide valuable insights into resource utilization and performance across different environments.

It is important to note that while FSAGen may not scale up to generating several thousand files in a single run on consumer-grade electronics, it remains a suitable tool for high-end forensic workstations. Lower-end computers can still utilise FSAGen by running it multiple times, generating a smaller number of files in each run to complete the disk image generation process. The observed inverse relationship between performance and memory usage indicates that, in this iteration of FSAGen, performance prioritisation was emphasised, as evident in Fig. 2.

While FSAGen may not be designed for generating thousands of files simultaneously on consumer-grade hardware, it remains an invaluable tool for high-performance forensic workstations. On lower-end systems, users can employ FSAGen by executing multiple instances, generating a smaller number of files per run, enabling the completion of disk image generation tasks. The identified inverse relationship between performance and memory usage highlights the focus on optimising performance in this iteration of FSAGen, as exemplified in Fig. 2.

6 Conclusion

In conclusion, this study presents a novel and cross-platform file system artefact generation tool designed to facilitate the rapid and effortless generation of synthetic datasets for the validation of file system forensic tools. The tool offers a convenient solution for creating various file system-level artefacts, enabling researchers and investigators to efficiently test and evaluate the performance of file system forensic tools.

The experimental results demonstrate the tool's ability to generate thousands of files swiftly. With the aid of this tool, advancements in the validation and testing of file system forensic tools can be made, leading to improved capabilities in digital investigations and ensuring the integrity of evidence extracted from file systems. However, it is important to note that resource consumption increases as the number of files grows, highlighting the need for further research and development in optimising resource utilisation. Future research will focus on resource use optimisation to increase the compatibility of FSAGen.

References

1. Mohammad RMA, Alqahtani M (2019) A comparison of machine learning techniques for file system forensics analysis. J Inform Secur Appl 46:53–61 https://doi.org/10.1016/j.jisa.2019.02.009, https://www.sciencedirect.com/science/article/pii/S2214212618307579

2. Bhat WA, AlZahrani A, Wani MA (2021) Can computer forensic tools be trusted in digital investigations? Sci Just 61(2):198–203. https://doi.org/10.1016/j.scijus.2020.10.002, https://www.sciencedirect.com/science/article/pii/S1355030620303002
3. Ghosh A, Majumder K, De D (2021) Android forensics using Sleuth Kit Autopsy. In: Giri D, Buyya R, Ponnusamy S, De D, Adamatzky A, Abawajy JH (eds) Proceedings of the sixth international conference on mathematics and computing. Advances in Intelligent Systems and Computing. Springer, Singapore, pp 297–308. https://doi.org/10.1007/978-981-15-8061-1_24
4. Nayak SC, Tiwari V, Samanthula BK (2023) Review of ransomware attacks and a data recovery framework using autopsy digital forensics platform. In: 2023 IEEE 13th annual computing and communication workshop and conference (CCWC), pp 0605–0611. https://doi.org/10.1109/CCWC57344.2023.10099169
5. Plum J, Dewald A (2018) Forensic apfs file recovery. In: Proceedings of the 13th international conference on availability, reliability and security. ARES 2018. Association for Computing Machinery, New York, pp 1–10. https://doi.org/10.1145/3230833.3232808, https://doi.org/10.1145/3230833.3232808
6. Wani MA, AlZahrani A, Bhat WA (2020) File system anti-forensics–types, techniques and tools. Comput Fraud Secur 3:14–19. https://doi.org/10.1016/S1361-3723(20)30030-0, http://www.magonlinelibrary.com/doi/10.1016/S1361-3723%2820%2930030-0
7. Bhat WA, AlZahrani A, Wani MA (2021) Can computer forensic tools be trusted in digital investigations? Sci Just 61(2):198–203. https://doi.org/10.1016/j.scijus.2020.10.002, https://www.sciencedirect.com/science/article/pii/S1355030620303002
8. Horsman G (2018) I couldn't find it your honour, it mustn't be there!–tool errors, tool limitations and user error in digital forensics. Sci Just 58(6):433–440. https://doi.org/10.1016/j.scijus.2018.04.001, https://www.sciencedirect.com/science/article/pii/S1355030617301508
9. Horsman G (2019) Tool testing and reliability issues in the field of digital forensics. Digit Invest 28:163–175. https://doi.org/10.1016/j.diin.2019.01.009, https://www.sciencedirect.com/science/article/pii/S1742287618303062
10. Hughes N, Karabiyik U (2020) Towards reliable digital forensics investigations through measurement science. WIREs Forens Sci 2(4):e1367. https://doi.org/10.1002/wfs2.1367, https://wires.onlinelibrary.wiley.com/doi/10.1002/wfs2.1367
11. Horsman G, Lyle JR (2021) Dataset construction challenges for digital forensics. Forens Sci Int Digit Invest 38:301264. https://doi.org/10.1016/j.fsidi.2021.301264, https://www.sciencedirect.com/science/article/pii/S2666281721001815
12. Nordvik R, Stoykova R, Franke K, Axelsson S, Toolan F (2021) Reliability validation for file system interpretation. Forens Sci Int Digit Invest 37:301174. https://doi.org/10.1016/j.fsidi.2021.301174, https://www.sciencedirect.com/science/article/pii/S2666281721000822
13. Göbel T, Schäfer T, Hachenberger J, Türr J, Baier H (2020) A novel approach for generating synthetic datasets for digital forensics. In: Peterson G, Shenoi S (eds) Advances in digital forensics XVI. IFIP advances in information and communication technology. Springer International Publishing, Cham, pp 73–93. https://doi.org/10.1007/978-3-030-56223-6_5
14. Mbatha MP (2016) Windows registry forensic artifacts; shellbags for computer security. Thesis, University of Nairobi. http://erepository.uonbi.ac.ke/handle/11295/99644
15. Jordan S (2016) Chapter 7—OS X El Capitan forensics. In: Sammons J (ed) Digital forensics. Syngress, Boston, pp 99–118. https://doi.org/10.1016/B978-0-12-804526-8.00007-1, https://www.sciencedirect.com/science/article/pii/B9780128045268000071
16. Ceballos Delgado AA, Glisson WB, Grispos G, Choo KR (2022) FADE: a forensic image generator for android device education. WIREs Forens Sci 4(2). https://doi.org/10.1002/wfs2.1432, https://onlinelibrary.wiley.com/doi/10.1002/wfs2.1432
17. Du X, Hargreaves C, Sheppard J, Scanlon M (2021) TraceGen: user activity emulation for digital forensic test image generation. Forens Sci Int Digit Invest 38:301133. https://doi.org/10.1016/j.fsidi.2021.301133, https://www.sciencedirect.com/science/article/pii/S2666281721000317
18. Scanlon M, Du X, Lillis D (2017) EviPlant: an efficient digital forensic challenge creation, manipulation and distribution solution. Digit Invest 20:S29–S36. https://doi.org/10.1016/j.diin.2017.01.010, https://www.sciencedirect.com/science/article/pii/S1742287617300397

19. Panwar A (2017) iGen: toward automatic generation and analysis of indicators of compromise (IOCs) using convolutional neural network. Technical report. Arizona State University. https://keep.lib.asu.edu/items/155561
20. Göbel T, Maltan S, Türr J, Baier H, Mann F (2022) ForTrace–a holistic forensic data set synthesis framework. Forens Sci Int Digit Invest 40:301344. https://doi.org/10.1016/j.fsidi.2022.301344, https://www.sciencedirect.com/science/article/pii/S2666281722000130
21. Lenard B, Wagner J, Rasin A, Grier J (2020) SysGen: system state corpus generator. In: Proceedings of the 15th international conference on availability, reliability and security. ARES '20, Association for Computing Machinery, New York, pp 1–6. https://doi.org/10.1145/3407023.3409202, https://dl.acm.org/doi/10.1145/3407023.3409202
22. Mockaroo—Random data generator and API mocking tool | JSON/CSV/SQL/Excel. https://mockaroo.com/
23. Download & Generate Test Files (2023). https://fastest.fish/test-files
24. Fake File Generator—The easy way to generate files (2023). https://www.fakefilegenerator.com/
25. Datahappy1 (2022) Dummy-file-generator: dummy csv, flat, json text file generator, typical usage scenario can be load/stress/performance testing of file-processing data tools. https://github.com/datahappy1/dummy_file_generator
26. LaxmanSingh@TWC (2021) Best free dummy file generator software for Windows 11/10. https://www.thewindowsclub.com/dummy-file-generator-software
27. Muller MM (2023) dummyfilescreator: desktop & CLI tool to generate dummy files. https://github.com/matuzalemmuller/dummy-files-creator
28. MyNikko (2023) MyNikko.com—dummy file creator. http://www.mynikko.com/dummy/
29. Google (2023) The go programming language. https://go.dev/
30. Dilley N, Lange J (2019) An empirical study of messaging passing concurrency in go projects. In: 2019 IEEE 26th international conference on software analysis, evolution and reengineering (SANER), pp 377–387. https://doi.org/10.1109/SANER.2019.8668036. ISSN: 1534-5351
31. Chabbi M, Ramanathan MK (2022) A study of real-world data races in Golang. In: Proceedings of the 43rd ACM SIGPLAN international conference on programming language design and implementation, pp 474–489. PLDI 2022, Association for Computing Machinery, New York, NY, USA. https://doi.org/10.1145/3519939.3523720, https://doi.org/10.1145/3519939.3523720
32. Shmelov O, Gubareva O (2023) Usage and implementation of parallelism in go. Scientia 94–97. https://previous.scientia.report/index.php/archive/article/view/1086
33. Welcome to Python.org (2023). https://www.python.org/
34. psutil: Cross-platform lib for process and system monitoring in Python. https://github.com/giampaolo/psutil
35. Barnes H (2021) Pro Windows Subsystem for Linux (WSL): powerful tools and practices for cross-platform development and collaboration. Apress Berkeley CA. https://doi.org/10.1007/978-1-4842-6873-5, https://link.springer.com/10.1007/978-1-4842-6873-5
36. Anarchy Installer (2023). https://anarchyinstaller.gitlab.io/
37. Download Windows 10 (2023). https://www.microsoft.com/en-in/software-download/windows10
38. Download Windows 11 (2023). https://www.microsoft.com/en-in/software-download/windows11
39. Kali Linux | Penetration Testing and Ethical Hacking Linux Distribution (May 2023). https://www.kali.org/
40. Download VMware Workstation Pro (2023). https://www.vmware.com/products/workstation-pro/workstation-pro-evaluation.html

Exploring Digital Forensics Tools and Techniques in Money Laundering Investigations Involving Virtual Assets

Kaushik Thinnaneri Ganesan

Abstract Digital Forensics has now come to occupy a central role in investigations, irrespective of the nature of crime. From murder to theft to smuggling to duty evasion to money laundering, there is a strong likelihood of there being some kind of digital trail present in every crime. Conviction in the court of law is the ultimate objective of every investigator and such evidences are crucial for building a watertight case. While law enforcement agencies the world over have started waking up to the critical role of digital forensics in investigations, the world of crime has moved ahead significantly. Before investigators could settle down with standard templates for how digital forensics could be used in investigations, the proliferation of cryptocurrencies (officially referred to as "virtual assets", which is the official term used by the Financial Action Task Force) in money laundering has thrown up a new set of challenges. This paper attempts to take a holistic look at how virtual assets have begun to be used in money laundering, the extent of their proliferation, what solutions digital forensics currently has, for aiding anti money-laundering (AML) investigations, specifically money laundering involving usage of virtual assets. Thereafter, this paper examines what challenges law enforcement agencies face with the current tools and finally, how law enforcement agencies can reorient themselves to tackle the ever-evolving scenarios involving usage of virtual assets in money laundering.

Keywords Anti money-laundering · AML · Virtual assets · Cryptocurrency · Digital forensics · Financial Action Task Force · FATF · Money laundering

1 Introduction

Digital Forensics has now come to occupy a central role in investigations, irrespective of the nature of crime. From murder to theft to smuggling to duty evasion to money laundering, there is a strong likelihood of there being some kind of digital trail present

K. T. Ganesan (✉)
Indian Revenue Service, Ministry of Finance, Government of India, Mumbai, India
e-mail: kaushik.tg@gmail.com

B. N. Gohil et al. (eds.), *Information Security, Privacy and Digital Forensics*,
Lecture Notes in Electrical Engineering 1423,
https://doi.org/10.1007/978-981-96-9443-3_18

in every crime. It is these digital trails that become the holy grail for investigators to uncover to help establish their case in a foolproof manner. Conviction in the court of law is the ultimate objective of every investigator and such evidences are crucial for building a watertight case.

While law enforcement agencies the world over have started waking up to the critical role of digital forensics in investigations, the world of crime has moved ahead significantly. Before investigators could settle down with standard templates for how digital forensics could be used in investigations, the proliferation of cryptocurrencies (officially referred to as "virtual assets", which is the official term used by the Financial Action Task Force [1] or FATF, the global watchdog for anti-money laundering) in money laundering has thrown up a new set of challenges. This paper attempts to take a holistic look at how virtual assets have begun to be used in money laundering, the extent of their proliferation, what solutions digital forensics currently has, for aiding anti money-laundering (AML) investigations, specifically money laundering involving usage of virtual assets. Thereafter, this paper examines what challenges law enforcement agencies face with the current tools and finally, how law enforcement agencies can reorient themselves to tackle the ever-evolving scenarios involving usage of virtual assets in money laundering.

It may be noted that this paper restricts itself to the post-crime stage of forensic investigation, i.e. usage of digital forensics techniques to investigate usage of virtual assets in for money laundering after the crime has occurred and not the preventive aspects. Hence, this paper does not explore some of the work global agencies have been doing to prevent such crimes from happening, which deserves a separate analysis in itself.

2 Money Laundering

"Money laundering" is a commonly-used phrase, sometimes used in multiple contexts. At its core, however, it refers to attempts at whitewashing or disguising the proceeds of crime with the intention to conceal their illicit origins. Article 6 of the United Nations Convention against Transnational Organized Crime [2] defines money laundering as follows—

Criminalization of the laundering of proceeds of crime—

(1) The conversion or transfer of property, knowing that such property is the proceeds of crime, for the purpose of concealing or disguising the illicit origin of the property or of helping any person who is involved in the commission of the predicate offence to evade the legal consequences of his or her action;
(2) The concealment or disguise of the true nature, source, location, disposition, movement or ownership of or rights with respect to property, knowing that such property is the proceeds of crime;

Considering the global nature of money laundering, the Financial Action Task Force (FATF) was established in 1989 by the Group of 7 (G7) to examine and develop measures to combat money laundering. Today, the FATF is the pre-eminent global body responsible for examining money laundering techniques, drafting policies to combat money laundering, reviewing action taken by various countries and setting out measures to effectively tackle money laundering. In 2001, the FATF included combating terrorist financing under its mandate. Today, the FATF comprises 38 members including India and has drafted Standards which have the commitment of more than 200 countries.

2.1 How Money Laundering Works

While money laundering is essentially a singular activity, it is accomplished through multiple stages. A report on "Money Laundering and Terrorist Financing Typologies—2004–2005" [3] prepared by FATF in 2005 was one of the first to lay down, in detail, the stages that money laundering comprises of. Money laundering is done in the following three stages (Fig. 1).

1. Placement—This is the first stage in which "dirty" money or proceeds of crime are pumped into the financial system. This serves dual purposes—one, of getting the criminal rid of a huge amount of cash obtained illegally and two, infusing the illegally-obtained money into the legitimate financial system. This stage is generally considered to be the most vulnerable stage for criminals since the likelihood of getting caught is highest here, considering that global financial systems are designed today to capture such activities specifically.
2. Layering—The second stage in money laundering is the layering stage, sometimes also referred to as "structuring". In this stage, the proceeds of crime are moved as far away as possible from the source and multiple layers are established in-between. This is generally the most sophisticated step since the layers need to be created in such a way that back-tracing to arrive at the source of the funds is as difficult as possible.
3. Integration—In this final stage of the money laundering process, the money, after traversing through multiple layers, now returns to the perpetrator disguised as

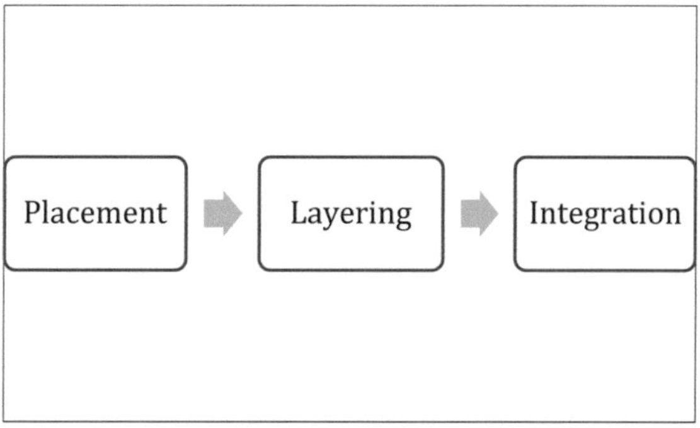

Fig. 1 The 3 stages of money laundering

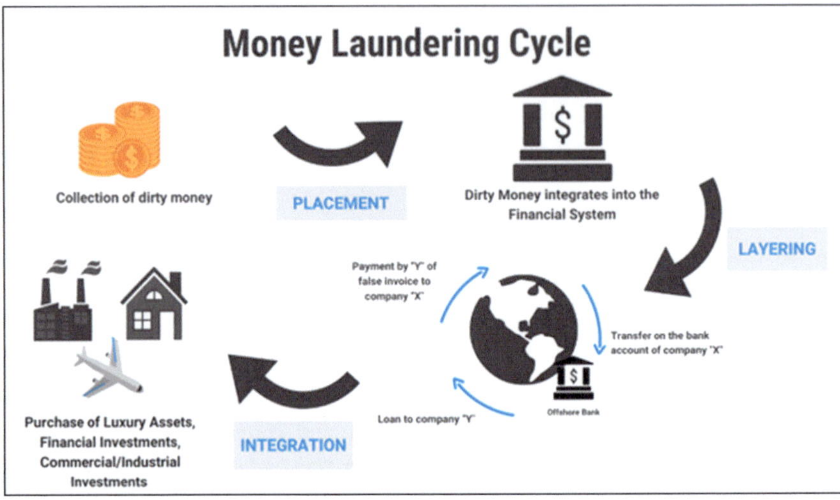

Fig. 2 The money laundering cycle. *Source* UNODC

legitimate money that is integrated into the financial system. This money can now be utilized as legal currency for legitimate purposes.

According to the United Nations Office on Drugs and Crime (UNODC) [4], the estimated amount of money laundered globally in one year is 2–5% of global GDP, which works out to an amount ranging from $800 billion—$2 trillion. Given the nature of the activity of money laundering, however, it is difficult to state with certainty the exact quantum of funds laundered globally. The picture below gives a visual depiction of the cycle of money laundering (Fig. 2).

3 How Money Laundering is Tackled in India

The Federation of Indian Chambers of Commerce and Industry (FICCI) recently released a report titled "Hidden Streams: Linkages between Illicit Markets, Financial Flows, Organized Crime and Terrorism" [5] in which, based on UNODC estimates, a tentative estimate of the quantum of money laundered in India has been reported to be in the region of $150 billion.

The Prevention of Money Laundering Act, 2002 (PMLA), forms the cornerstone of India's anti money laundering framework. The law, which came into effect on 1 July 2005, provides a framework for dealing with money laundering as a crime and a legal basis for tracing, seizing and confiscating the proceeds of crime. The three main objectives of PMLA are—

1. To prevent and control money laundering;
2. To confiscate and seize the property obtained from the laundered money; and

3. To deal with any other issue connected with money laundering in India.

The law was also instrumental in setting up two organizations to oversee money laundering-related intelligence and investigations. A brief description of the two organizations and their respective roles in tackling money laundering in India are given below—

a. The Directorate of Enforcement—Established in 1956, the Directorate of Enforcement is responsible for enforcement of the Foreign Exchange Management Act, 1999 (FEMA) and certain provisions under PMLA. Work relating to investigation and prosecution of cases under the PMLA has been entrusted to the Directorate of Enforcement.
b. The Financial Intelligence Unit—The Financial Intelligence Unit or FIU is India's central, national agency responsible for receiving, processing, analyzing and disseminating information relating to suspicious financial transactions. The FIU is also responsible for coordinating and strengthening efforts of national and international intelligence, investigation and enforcement agencies in pursuing the global efforts against money laundering and related crimes.

As per statistics published by the Directorate of Enforcement [6], provisional attachment orders worth $13.85 billion have been issued as of January 2023, based on approximately 6000 cases of money laundering booked by the agency.

3.1 Traditional Digital Forensics in Money Laundering Investigations

Section 17 of PMLA provides investigators powers to search and seize any record or property found as a result of such search when the officer has reason to believe that any person—

(1) has committed any act which constitutes money-laundering, or
(2) is in possession of any proceeds of crime involved in money-laundering, or
(3) is in possession of any records relating to money-laundering, or
(4) is in possession of any property related to crime

Section 18 of PMLA dealing with search of persons also provides officers the power to seize records or documents during the course of the search.

It is these two sections which are primarily used when investigating money laundering offences in India, to gather evidence. Using the power vested through these two sections, investigators can seize electronic devices including smartphones, laptops, hard drives, servers, etc.

A typical investigation ensues as follows (Fig. 3).

Further, Section 21 of PMLA contains a provision which enables officers to retain records seized during the course of investigation either under Section 17 or Section 18 of PMLA.

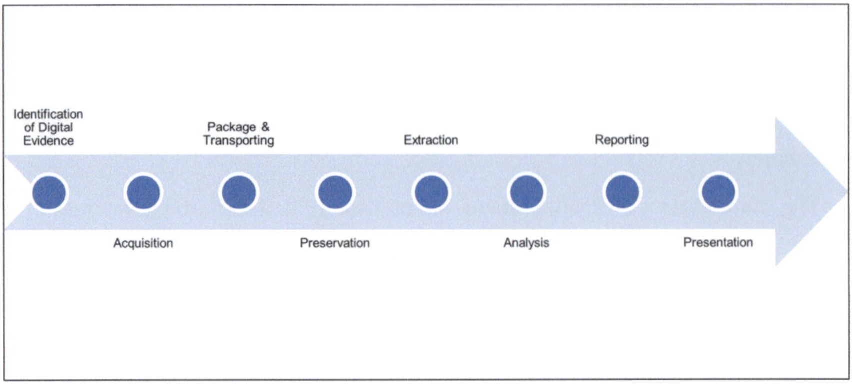

Fig. 3 Lifecycle of digital forensics in investigations

4 Virtual Assets in Money Laundering

The primary reason for usage of virtual assets in money laundering is the anonymity which virtual assets offer. One of the emerging trends is the usage of private channels between transacting parties to transfer virtual assets without the creation/usage of any public ledger to reflect individual transactions. Records would exist only for the final settlement and not for individual transactions.

Laundering of virtual assets has steadily been increasing over the last decade, despite a brief blip during the pandemic year of 2020. The chart below shows the progression of cryptocurrency laundered from 2015–2022, with a staggering $23.8 billion worth of cryptocurrency estimated to have been laundered in 2022 (Fig. 4).

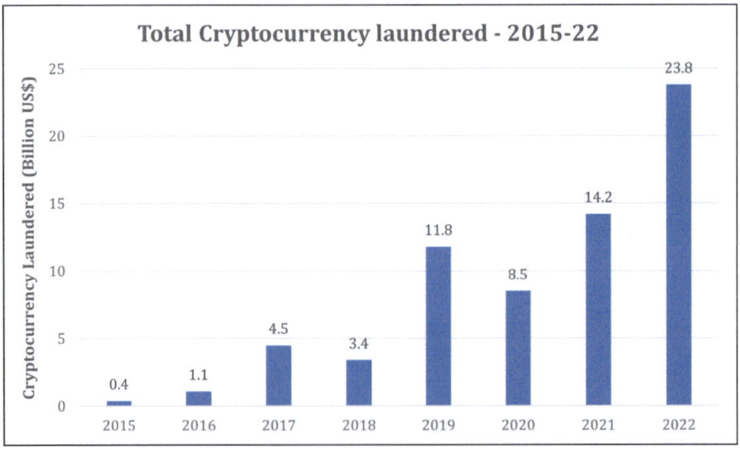

Fig. 4 Total cryptocurrency laundered by year. *Source* Chainalysis [7]

The Narcotics Control Bureau, India's national nodal agency for drug law enforcement, had recently reported [8] that the use of dark net and cryptocurrency in drug trafficking had been observed in 38 cases during the time period from 2020–2022. However, given the increased convenience and rapid proliferation of virtual assets service providers (VASPs), there exists a real threat of this quantum increasing significantly in the coming years. It is therefore incumbent on investigating agencies to be adequately prepared to face this challenge. Further, Indian law enforcement agencies have started unearthing the usage of cryptocurrency in crimes such as fraud and illegal gaming in addition to drug smuggling and money laundering. Cryptocurrency usage appears especially prevalent in the dark net, which has emerged as a major hub for drug smuggling activities in recent years.

4.1 Investigating Virtual Assets in Money Laundering

Currently, investigation of virtual assets involves the following steps—

i. Law enforcement agency (LEA) detects virtual assets during the course of investigation;
ii. LEA seizes the virtual assets;
iii. LEA identifies any virtual accounts or wallets linked to the virtual assets;
iv. LEA seeks data from the associated VASP to try and link any transactions associated with the virtual accounts/wallets. LEA also explores if any other VASPs are linked to the chain of transactions and attempts to uncover real-world identities of all accounts associated with the account under investigation.

The following data are crucial for any investigation into virtual assets—

a. Account information
b. Transaction details (including virtual currency transaction hash and information on the originator and the recipient)
c. Login information (including IP addresses)
d. Device information (such as device IMEI, IP Address, etc.)
e. Information obtained from analysis of the customer's public online profile and communications.
f. Cryptocurrency wallets/addresses and associated blockchain records

A typical law enforcement investigation unearths a wallet during the course of a search operation. Once a virtual asset is encountered, the associated exchange is contacted. Wallets are broadly of two kinds –

1. Public Wallet—Such a wallet is usually used as a public identifier to which funds (in the form of virtual assets) are sent/received. These are more popular since they help establish the idea of anonymous public accounts which can be used to send and receive currency (in whatever form) with the benefits that a blockchain provides, in terms of security and authentication. Such a wallet is

relatively easier for law enforcement to investigate, since all transactions of such wallets are available in the open source.

2. Private Wallet—These are wallets which are used in P2P (peer-to-peer) transactions and cannot be found publicly. They provide added security and are similar to cash transactions since it is a one-to-one transaction with the exception that instead of cash, a virtual currency is used. These are extremely hard for law enforcement to crack, since there is no record publicly available.

Some of the techniques used in analyzing transactions involving virtual assets [9] are given below -

a. Transaction Analysis—This is generally the most common action taken by investigators when analyzing virtual asset transactions. The aforementioned tools are used to identify the players involved in the transactions of virtual assets.
b. Address Clustering—This may be considered to be a subset of transaction analysis wherein addresses appearing similar based on some parameters are grouped together to get a broad overview of the movement of virtual assets.
c. Taint Analysis—This method is used to trace the flow of funds in the blockchain, covering the entire gamut from illicit sources to grey ones to legitimate sources.
d. Wallet Identification—The ultimate goal of every blockchain analysis is to uncover the identity behind a wallet. This is also often the most challenging step in blockchain investigations.

4.1.1 Tools Used to Investigate Virtual Assets

Forensic Tools used to investigate virtual assets fall under two broad categories—open-source tools and proprietary tools.

A brief summary of some of the tools explored for the purpose of this paper are given below.

(1) GraphSense [10]—This is an open-source tool developed under the stewardship of the Austrian Institute of Technology GmbH as a cryptoasset analytics platform for viewing monetary flows of virtual assets and performing advanced analytics.
(2) CipherTrace Inspector [11]—This is a proprietary tool designed for tracking blockchain transactions and following digital money trails related to different kinds of crimes, including the ability to attribute crypto addresses to real-world organizations, a key requirement for investigators worldwide.
(3) Elliptic Investigator [12]—This is a proprietary tool which provides features to visualize the flow of crypto funds through wallets, entities and transactions link crypto addresses to real-world actors across blockchains and assets.
(4) Chainalysis [13]—Chainalysis is a US-headquartered blockchain analysis company offering a solution "Chainalysis Reactor" which maps crypto addresses to real-world entities, discover related addresses and an interface which allows users with minimal training to create powerful visualizations of cryptocurrency flows.

(5) TRM Labs [14]—Labs is also a US-headquartered blockchain analysis company whose tool enables a user to view comprehensive risk profiles for wallets, addresses and entities, build graphs to trace the flow of funds and also enables a user to view connections across blockchains to trace the flow of funds.

The key difference between open-source tools and proprietary tools is that while the latter (in this case GraphSense) are freely available to download, modify and add further value in terms of capabilities, while the proprietary tools are managed and governed by the companies which developed them.

The tools discussed above broadly help answer the following questions—

- Who/which are the entities behind an address?
- What is the source and destination of funds?
- Are there any patterns to the transactions/activities of the accounts?
- Provide a visual depiction of the flow of assets across entities over a period of time.

However, there are certain key challenges that exist in investigating money laundering cases involving virtual assets. These challenges are examined in detail in the next section.

4.2 Challenges in Money Laundering Investigations Involving Virtual Assets

While the extent of proliferation of virtual assets used in money laundering varies across the globe, the challenges faced by law enforcement are largely uniform. Some of these challenges are outlined below—

(1) Lack of standardization—Virtual assets gained prominence as a reliable utility using the blockchain framework, however, over a period of time, different VASPs have come to develop different templates and frameworks, with there being no standardization in the virtual assets being used. This has proved to be a major roadblock for law enforcement the world over.

(2) Anonymity—While the concept of anonymity is likely blockchain's biggest selling point, it is also law enforcement's biggest nightmare. The transition from fiat currency to virtual assets is the most crucial step in the laundering process, post which the cloak of anonymity aids laundering significantly.

(3) Prohibitive Cost of Software—Technological solutions to explore blockchains and virtual assets are limited globally, with only a handful of established players currently in the market. Moreover, the costs of the software in the market currently are prohibitively expensive and beyond the reach of most law enforcement agencies, which are bound by tight budgets as well as procedural constraints which prevent them from acquiring such expensive tools.

(4) Lack of Expertise—The current tools available require a substantial level of expertise to operate—both on the technological front as well as on cryptocurrencies. Given the nascent nature of crimes in this field, it would require specialized investigators to use these tools.
(5) Limitation of public blockchain data—While a large quantity of blockchain data is available in open source, there is a slowly but steadily increasing private blockchain.
(6) Legal Conversion of Virtual Assets to Fiat Currency—The current legal framework in India does not pose any challenges for confiscation/seizure of virtual assets, as can be evidenced by the fact that such seizures have taken places over the past few years. However, the challenge arises when such seized proceeds of crime are required to be attached as property and the proceeds need to be realized to the Government, after conclusion of legal processes.
(7) Scarcity of Indian-made technological tools—This is a key area of concern. The existing tools available in the market for exploring virtual assets are not Indian and even if the tools are procured and installed in servers in India, the service providers and underlying technology powering the tool are developed abroad. Moreover, considering the market for such tools is only bound to increase, both in India and globally, the development of such tools in India would, in addition to addressing any potential security concerns, would be a boost to the Make in India initiative of the Government of India. India does not have any dearth of talent in the technology sector. With adequate R&D support, such hi-tech tools need to be developed in India going forward.

The Committee of Experts on the Evaluation of Anti-Money Laundering Measures and the Financing of Terrorism (also known as MONEYVAL) is a permanent monitoring body of the Council of Europe and an FATF-Style Regional Body (FSRB) entrusted with the task of assessing compliance with the principal international standards to counter money laundering and the financing of terrorism and the effectiveness of their implementation. In its 2023 typologies report [15] on money laundering and terrorist financing risks in the world of virtual assets adopted by the MONEYVAL Committee, several of the above observations were made about technological tools used by law enforcement agencies carrying out virtual assets-related investigations, indicating that the issues listed above are of a larger global nature, requiring solutions.

5 Concluding Remarks

While there have been papers looking at the digital forensics processes to investigate blockchain and cryptocurrency such as Mas'ud et al. [16]; Sahil Dudani et al. [17], such papers, appear more specifically from a purely technological standpoint rather than exploring the challenges faced by law enforcement agencies. This paper attempts to bridge that gap, while also presenting some factual scenarios regarding the quantum of crimes involving virtual assets and cryptocurrencies.

The field of digital forensics is, by its inherent nature, highly technical. Taking into account the sophisticated nature of virtual assets, blockchain and cryptocurrencies, an already-technical field is rendered even more complex.

This begets an important question—are current legal procedures involved in investigation of money laundering hindering effective detection, attachment and confiscation of proceeds of crime especially when it comes to virtual assets? While no legal lacunae have come to the fore so far, it is, however, a pertinent point to note and will depend on the variety, quantum and nature of investigations carried out by law enforcement agencies involving virtual assets in criminal activities.

In India, as is the case the world over, law enforcement agencies have slowly begun unravelling the complex world of frauds involving virtual assets and cryptocurrencies. The field is ripe for unravelling and further challenges in addition to the ones listed above, are bound to come up only when the number of cases under investigation increase substantially. A useful development that would hugely benefit the Indian law enforcement landscape as well as bolster the Indian technology startup ecosystem is if Indian technology entities started getting into developing tools providing solutions for exploring crimes involving virtual assets and cryptocurrencies.

Parallely, it is also imperative for law enforcement to nurture and develop specialists adept at investigating virtual assets used in money laundering—this will require a rather challenging amalgamation of technical proficiency, legal awareness and knowledge of money laundering activities.

Chapter IX of PMLA deals with Reciprocal Arrangement for Assistance in Certain Matters and Procedure for Attachment and Confiscation of Property, which empowers FIU to get into Memoranda of Understanding with FIUs of other countries to exchange intelligence. Since most virtual assets are 'situated' abroad, it is an area worth exploring further. This also goes to show that with the truly global nature of money laundering and virtual assets, increased global cooperation is the need of the hour.

Acknowledgements This author would like to thank Salil Bijur, Additional Director, National Academy of Direct Taxes, Ministry of Finance, Government of India for his valuable inputs during the preparation of this paper.

References

1. Virtual Assets FATF Website. https://www.fatf-gafi.org/en/topics/virtual-assets.html. Last accessed 2023/11/30
2. United Nations Convention Against Transnational Organized Crime and the Protocols Thereto UNODC Website. https://www.unodc.org/documents/treaties/UNTOC/Publications/TOC%20Convention/TOCebook-e.pdf. Last accessed 2023/11/30
3. Money Laundering and Terrorist Financing Typologies 2004–2005 FATF Website. https://www.fatf-gafi.org/en/publications/Methodsandtrends/Moneylaunderingandterroristfinancingtypologies2004-2005.html. Last accessed 2023/11/30
4. Overview of Money Laundering UNODC Website. https://www.unodc.org/unodc/en/money-laundering/overview.html. Last accessed 2023/11/30

5. Hidden Streams: Linkages between Illicit Markets, Financial Flows, Organized Crime and Terrorism, FICCI CASCADE Website. https://www.ficcicascade.in/wp-content/uploads/2023/06/illegal-economy-report.pdf. Last accessed 2023/11/30
6. Statistics of the Directorate of Enforcement. https://enforcementdirectorate.gov.in/statistics-0. Last accessed 2023/11/30
7. The 2023 Crypto Crime Report by Chainalysis
8. Ministry of Home Affairs, Government of India website. https://www.mha.gov.in/MHA1/Par2017/pdfs/par2023-pdfs/RS08022023/693.pdf. Last accessed 2023/11/30
9. Investigating Blockchain Crimes using Blockchain Forensics, Merkle Science Website. https://blog.merklescience.com/general/investigating-blockchain-crimes-using-blockchain-forensics. Last accessed 2023/11/30
10. Haslhofer B, Stütz R, Romiti M, King R GraphSense: a general-purpose cryptoasset analytics platform. arXiv:2102.13613v1[cs.CR]
11. Ciphertrace Inspector. https://ciphertrace.com/wp-content/uploads/2023/05/Inspector_rev05222023.pdf. Last accessed 2023/11/30
12. Elliptic Investigator. https://www.elliptic.co/solutions/crypto-investigations. Last accessed 2023/11/30
13. Chainalysis Reactor Webpage. https://www.chainalysis.com/chainalysis-reactor. Last accessed 2023/11/30
14. TRM Forensics Webpage. https://www.trmlabs.com/products/forensics. Last accessed 2023/11/30
15. Money Laundering and Terrorist Financing Risks in the World of Virtual Assets. https://rm.coe.int/moneyval-2023-12-vasp-typologies-report/1680abdec4. Last accessed 2023/11/30
16. Mas'ud MZ et al (2021) A review of digital forensics framework for blockchain in cryptocurrency technology. In: 2021 3rd International cyber resilience conference (CRC), Langkawi Island, Malaysia, pp 1–6. https://doi.org/10.1109/CRC50527.2021.9392563
17. Dudani S, Baggili I, Raymond D, Marchany R (2023) The current state of cryptocurrency forensics. Forensic Sci Int: Digit Investig 46:301576 ISSN 2666-2817

Application of Blockchain Technology in Malware Detection

Niharika Pagare and Mukti Padhya

Abstract As technology advances, there is an increase in devices connected to the internet. Malware infections are evolving in accordance with technological trends. Although the existing malware detection methods are advanced, there is a further need to increase its detection efficiency. Traditional detection techniques use emulated environments like virtual machines and sandboxes that lower malware's ability to reveal its true behavior during run-time. The existing detection methods lack traceability. The source of malware in a targeted network remains unknown. Further, the existing malware detection techniques have a centralized database. Such databases serve as single points for various attacks. Research studies suggest blockchain technology as a probable solution to most of the lacunae in the existing malware detection techniques. Blockchain provides a ledger system that allows a record of all digital events. This provides traceability. Additionally, blockchain provides distributed decentralization that allows shared processing and updating of databases. This paper proposes a model that utilizes a trust model for malware detection using blockchain technology. This proposed model consists of two phases: The data Generation phase and the Consensus phase. In the data generation phase, blocks containing file data are created and after further analysis are added to the existing blockchain. In the consensus phase, the files are processed for malware detection. Additionally, the proposed model is enhanced with a trust model that is based on three parameters (1) Behaviour history (2) Risk associated with behaviour (3) Feedback of behaviour. The proposed work aims to enhance the overall performance of malware detection.

Keywords Malware detection · Blockchain · Trust model

N. Pagare (✉) · M. Padhya
National Forensic Sciences University, Gandhinagar, Gujarat, India
e-mail: niharika.phdcs22@nfsu.ac.in

M. Padhya
e-mail: mukti.padhya@nfsu.ac.in

B. N. Gohil et al. (eds.), *Information Security, Privacy and Digital Forensics*,
Lecture Notes in Electrical Engineering 1423,
https://doi.org/10.1007/978-981-96-9443-3_19

1 Introduction

Many areas of our lives have transformed due to new and faster technological innovations. Significant changes are seen with the emerging technologies such as artificial intelligence/machine learning, 5G, Internet of Things (IoT), etc., as they impact everything that is internet-connected. Although the introduction of the aforesaid technologies make communication and overall living easier, they have implications on cybersecurity. Further their primary challenge is keeping humans and data safe. With 5G services been introduced, faster downloads require faster and real-time monitoring for cyber-attacks such as the malware attacks.

Traditional malware detection approaches use centralized databases. Signature-based method compares the malicious signature of a malware to known malware signatures databases. Signature based detection methods are incapable of detecting zero-day malware or new variants of malware. Behavior-based malware detection analyses the behavior of a file on the API calls, sequence of function calls, etc., to further classify it as malicious or non-malicious. Even though latter is good at detecting polymorphic malware, it produces high false positive ratio (FPR). This is because benign files also makes use of system calls similar to malware but do not classify as malware. Advanced malware detection make use of machine learning (ML) and its combination with other methods like data mining and other methods [11].

Distributed ledger technology (DLT) uses ledgers stored on separate but connected devices in a network. Blockchain evolved from distributed ledgers to address concerns of third parties being involved in several transactions. Studies suggest blockchain technology has potential solution for existing lacunae in detection systems. Its distributed ledger system that allows a record of all digital events. Distributed decentralization allows more security. Distributed database feature provides shared processing and updation of databases. Further, blockchain provides better malware detection as it is based on peer-to-peer sharing of suspected malware files signatures. This allows simultaneous updation of databases which further reduces false positive rates (FPRs) in detection [11].

Figure 1 shows some of the overall drawbacks of traditional malware detection techniques and databases. additionally the figure provides some related solutions adjacent to them as blockchain technology based solution.

1.1 Motivation

Conventional malware detection methods are based on signature generation and behaviour patterns or heuristic methods [4]. Malware indicators that are collected and stored after analysis by the antivirus and anti-malware solutions providers (vendors). According to studies, considerable amount of time is required for signature generation or dynamic sequence detection of malware patterns. Thus the antivirus or anti-malware vendor alone cannot respond adequately to malware that is rapidly

Fig. 1 Drawbacks of traditional Malware detection methods and database and blockchain as a solution

increasing [4]. Along with the antivirus vendors, if the users also collect malware indicators, information can be shared with other users or nodes as well. In conclusion, the traditional antivirus system which uses known virus signature databases require time to update the signature

Blockchain is based on distributed ledger. It uses ledger comprising of blocks for transactions. It is a digital ledger different from centralized networks and ledger systems. In two ways this digital ledger advantageous over the traditional ones. Firstly, with the change in the information stored on a network of nodes, the changes in ledger are reflected simultaneously to all holders. Secondly, using encryption or digital certificates, the information is authenticated. Together, these systems provide a transparent and verifiable record of transactions [2].

Lets consider a case scenario in an organisational network, most of the hosts have a some antivirus solutions on their systems. Apart from the intrusion detection systems (IDS) and intrusion prevention systems (IPS), the servers can have real-time antivirus solutions hosted on them. This allows continuous monitoring of the systems and networks. On analysing a malware, its signature is generated. It is a unique piece of code with malicious intent that identifies as malware. Sequence of dynamic function calls are also a part of its identity. All of the process are seen to work on one network itself. Also the database maintained is centralized. The continuous monitoring along with malware signature generation will consume time to show the efficient results.

Lets consider a case with blockchain-based malware detection. To start with, the use of blockchain enables layered architecture. Jingjing et al. [7] in CB-MDEE framework presented how each layer can function simultaneously to provide better results than the traditional detection systems. The architecture consists of network layer for peer-to-peer communication; storage layer for malicious feature storage;

support layer for consensus, encryption, authentication, etc.; and application layer for user interaction. This case also makes use of multiple chains for public and private user interactions. Public blockchain (PB) as application chain that is open to users and Consortium blockchain (CB) as the core chain for consensus members.

With blockchain, the analysis, detection, updation and storing of malware indicators is possible in decentralized form. The traditional centralized system were prone to single point failure. But with blockchain, decentralized sharing of signatures and simultaneous updation can enhance the detection process.

1.2 Our Contribution

In this paper we explore the application of blockchain technology for malware detection. We propose a model aiming at identifying the maliciousness of a file. The model consists of two phases: (A) The Data Generation Phase and (B) Consensus Phase. The trust model gives a decision to add the block to chain, quarantine the block or to terminate the block. This is based on three parameters: (1) Behaviour History (2) Risk associated with behaviour and (3) Feedback based on the behavior.

Overall, this paper makes the following contributions:

- This paper proposes a novel approach for blockchain-based malware detection based on a trust factor.
- The model consists of two phases **(A) Data generation** and **(B) Consensus phase**.
- Data generation phase: creates data blocks containing required file information. After further analysis of the file, it is added to the existing blockchain.
- The consensus phase the file are analysed for malware based on three parameters **(1) Behaviour history (2) Risk associated with behaviour (3) Feedback of behaviour**.

1.3 Outline

The outline of the paper is as follows: Sect. 1 is the introduction to our work. This section further contains motivation of the research, authors contribution and overall outline of the paper. Section 2 contains related work in the research area, specifically: malware, blockchain based malware detection and trust in peer-to-peer systems. Section 3, we explain our Proposed framework. Discussion related to the proposed model is provided in Sect. 4. It presents the advantages, scope and limitation and future work of the proposed model. Finally, in Sect. 5 we conclude our work.

2 Related Work

2.1 Malware

Malware refers to malicious code that violates a computer system's confidentiality, integrity, or availability security policy [13]. Malware or malicious software can be found in a wide range of forms such as virus, worms, bots and botnets, Trojan horse, ransomware, rootkits, backdoor, and spyware, etc. These malware families are mutually inclusive, thus a specific malware may share the qualities of various classes simultaneously [5].

Traditional malware had simpler codes and could be identified comparatively faster, unlike the current evolved malware [6]. Next-generation malware are equipped to execute direct on kernel, they are persistent in a network or system [1]. Thus, malware detection tools, anti-virus, threat detection tools are implemented in security companies as a defense to cyber-attacks such as malware, intrusion. etc. Malware Analysis types:

- Static Malware analysis: Sharp et al. [13] stated static malware analysis as analyzing malicious software without executing it is called static analysis The static analysis approach has been widely utilized by exploring the source code without running the executable files to extract a unique signature which is used to represent the file under investigation.
- Dynamic analysis or behavioral analysis: Sihwail et al. [14] mentioned dynamic malware analysis as analyzing the behavior of a malicious code (interaction with the system) while it is being executed in a controlled environment (virtual machine, simulator, emulator, sandbox etc.) is called dynamic analysis.
- Hybrid analysis: Gandotra et al. [5] stated hybrid malware analysis as a technique which is a combination of static and dynamic analysis. First it analyses the signature for presence of malicious code. It combines analysis with other behavioral parameters such as network connections, API calls sequences, etc. This combination of approaches overcomes the limitations of both static and dynamic analysis.

Currently several malware detection are based on advanced technology such as machine learning, deep learning. Sundarkumar et al. [15] used API call sequences with topic models and machine learning for malware detection. Yoo et al. [20] uses combination of random forest technique and deep learning for malware classification.

2.2 Blockchain Based Malware Detection

Fundamentally blockchain is a distributed or linked database. It is based on a consensus algorithm that ensures agreement on certain data or predefined criteria among distributed nodes. A consensus algorithm is the core component that directly dictates how such a system behaves and the performance it can achieve [3]. In contrast to traditional database architectures, blockchain has a decentralized network. It holds information of all events and transactions in a ledger entered on to it, and the data stored on the network is verified from all other users available on the network.

Gupta et al. [8] describes types of blockchain viz Public that is accessible to all users, Private that is accessible to limited users and Consortium that is permissioned by government or a organizational group. Blockchain consists of consensus algorithms that required mathematical computation to participate in the consensus. Xiong et al. [18] describes some of the algorithms include such as Proof of Work (PoW), Proof of Stake (PoS), Byzantine fault tolerance (BFT) etc.

Gu et al. [7] presented framework of Consortium Blockchain for Malware Detection and Evidence Extraction (CB-MDEE) in mobile devices. They used two chains, public chain for all users and private chain for test users. To analyse the malware families, they used statistical analysis for feature modeling. They also adopted fuzzy comparison method named multi-feature to reduce false-positive rate and improve the detecting ability of malware variants. Further their experimental results showed higher detection accuracy in limited time with lower false-positive and false-negative rates as compared to previous studies.

Gupta et al. [8] developed a decentralized and distributed database-oriented intrusion detection framework powered by three malware detection frameworks. The framework utilizes three malware detection frameworks viz. signature-based, behavior-based and multi-antivirus-based engines. It uses blockchain technology to maintain distributed database. The framework classifies portable executable (PE) files as malicious or non-malicious. The advantage of the proposed framework is that it uses low-end resources to achieve better results in terms of detecting and quarantining malware.

Fuji et al. [4] proposes a system that can share the signatures of suspected files between users. It uses decentralized and distributed database feature of blockchain that allows them to respond to rapid malware threats. The proposed system used both signature-based and heuristic methods or behavior-based methods thus yielded better results as compared to heuristic methods alone. Evaluation results of the experiments on the prototype created show 4% improvement in false negative results and 2.5% in false positive results.

Talukder et al. [16] propose a distributed framework of anti-malware database management. The framework uses customized blockchain by decentralizing the detection process by initiating distributed malware prevention program. The model proposed to ensure better data management with no requirement of relying on single database.

2.3 *Trust Models Based Peer-to-Peer Computing*

Shalini et al. [12] proposes a trust model for consensus in blockchain. The proposed system forms trust nodes based on practical fault tolerance (pBFT) consensus algorithm. This makes more reliable verification of nodes in the blockchain. The model calculates trust factor (TF) based on of three parameter namely history factor, risk factor and feedback factor. This trust factor helps eliminate un-trusted nodes from the mining process. This further enhances the reliability and security of the blockchain according to the proposed model.

Xiong et al. [19] proposed PeerTrust model. This trust framework is based on reputation. Authors propose an adaptive trust model for quantifying and comparing the trustworthiness of peers. This is based on a transaction-based feedback system. They further implement it on a decentralized structured P2P network.

Xiaoyong et al. [17] presents a novel feedback based trust aggregating mechanism. This trust model is based on Direct Trust Tree (DTT). For every peer, DTT is based on its last direct interaction experience. Further the feedback of trust information is searched by using DTT rather than broadcasting it in others reputation system. Additional two parameters namely quality and distance factor are introduced. These are used to adjust the scale of aggregation computing automatically.

Li et al. [10] proposed an innovative trust model. In this model the peers are divided as service provider (SP), service requester (SR), and feedback rater (FR). The proposed P2P trust management system monitors entity behavior. This is done by collecting, aggregating, and further distributing trust rating values.

Li et al. [9] presents an access control model based on trust. In this model the trust value is assessed based on history and peer recommendations. This ensures how much a requester or user is reliable. Additionally the model handles mutability and uncertainty using dynamically re-evaluating and revoking the access granted on non-compliance of the defined access control rules.

3 Proposed Framework

In this section, we explain the proposed system. This work proposes a blockchain-based malware detection method using trust enabled consensus algorithm. An overview of the proposed system is shown in Fig. 3.

The proposed is divided into two phases: (A) Data Generation and (B) Consensus Model. Additionally the model shall function using two separate chains. A Public blockchain for the Data Generation phase. A Private or Consortium chain for Consensus phase as this chain is envisioned to provide access to authorized and trusted nodes. This phase will majorly comply with the trust calculation and decision making in the proposed model.

Fuji et al. [4] used Ethereum platform for their proposed model for sharing suspected signatures using blockchain. Ethereum platform can be used for building decentralized applications (DApps) in an open-source development environment. As Ethereum platform uses blockchain platform in many decentralized applications such as uPort, it is envisioned to be applied in the proposed model. This will allow various applications to be developed by executing a smart contract that is programmed to function on agreed terms.

(A) Data Generation Phase

There are various sources from where a user can receive files on their system. It could be from the internet, by device transfer, bluetooth, etc. Malware can invade user system from the internet via email, by accessing malicious websites or downloading files or applications from un-trusted sources and so on. In the proposed model, once the file is received, it is envisioned to go through the following process.

Hashing and comparison

When a file gets into the users system, it will be a part of public blockchain. The proposed system will generate a hash of that file and share it to the distributed ledger to check whether the hash is already stored or not stored. This comparison is signature-based detection.

- On comparing the hash if the signature exists in the ledger or database, an alarm will broadcast on the distributed database about the file containing malicious indicators. Additionally, the system will send an alert to the user system to discontinue the file usage. This can save computing power.
- On comparison if the file hash does not exist in the database, its hash will be broadcast-ed to the users or nodes for further analysis. After analysis if found malicious, it will be quarantined and blocked. If found non-malicious, it will be added to the public blockchain.

(B) Consensus Phase

If the file hash is not present in the distributed ledger or distributed database, on comparison in the data generation phase, it enters the private or consortium blockchain. The hash is broadcast to all the nodes in the chain. Once it is broadcasted, the incoming file is scanned and analysed through the anti-malware present at the respective nodes.

Gupta et al. [8] used three anti-malware detection engines in their proposed system to develop blockchain-Based and distributed database multi-malware detection engine.

The proposed system envisions to incorporate behavior-based detection that uses dynamic analysis. Here port scanning, process analysis, sequences of function calls, etc. will be examined to determine if the file is trying to manipulate any system process or trying to gain root access or trying to open an unnecessary network port. This is done as malware harms system processes or modifies them, gains root access for backdoor entries or remote communication.

Trust Model

The addition of trust model in blockchain-based malware detection envisions to enhance the overall malware detection. Shalini et al. [12] proposed the concept of trust model for effective consensus in blockchain. But it has not yet been applied for blockcahin based malware detection. In the proposed model the file is further assessed on trust model that is based on three factors. The new trust model verifies the node before getting into the consensus group based on three characteristic parameters: (1) Behaviour History (2) Risk of behaviour (3) Feedback of Behaviour. Trust factor in the proposed model can be considered as the overall assessment and normalization of the three factors.

- Behaviour History (BH): The behavior history of a file: It can be the past connections to blacklisted IPs, Malicious API call sequences, macro-enabled documents that communicates to system APIs like CreateProcess(), etc.
- Risk of Behaviour (RB): It is the risk associated with the file behaviour.
- Feedback Behaviour (FB): Based on the level of maliciousness and risk associated with it, feedback of the file behaviour.

This phase will calculate the trust value for nodes on private blockchain (trusted chain) based on the aforesaid factors and a normalised trust value will be computed based on assessment of the three factors.

After the trust assessment on each node, the file is stated as either malign (Malware) or benign (Non-malware). If the file is malign, then its malicious indicators are updated to distributed databases. Once the entry is made in the database, it will be further updated for each and every user along with its probability of being malicious.

On the other hand, if the file is assessed as non-malicious, the system will be notified as the file is safe and will be added as a block to public blockchain.

Figure 2 gives a basic idea of data contained on blocks and chain formation. It represents the contents of a block in proposed model.

The workflow of the proposed trust enable blockchain based malware detection system is depicted in the Fig. 3. In the given figure, two components are shown in boxes viz. the Data Generation phase and the Consensus Phase.

4 Discussion

4.1 Advantages of the Proposed Model

Existing literature of malware is specific to signatures [5, 13], behaviours[5, 14], generating data-sets to train learning models for using machine learning in combination of various techniques [5, 15, 20]. Recent but few studies use advanced technology such as blockchain for malware detection [4, 7, 8, 16]. To enhance trust in peer-to-peer computing studies [9, 10, 12, 17, 19] depict the use of various trust factors.

Our proposed model incorporates each of the aspects. It consists of distributed layered architecture for distributed databases. This ensures simultaneous updation of databases. It uses two blockchains for data generation and analysis for malware. This allows multiple detection to be used like the signature and behaviour databases.

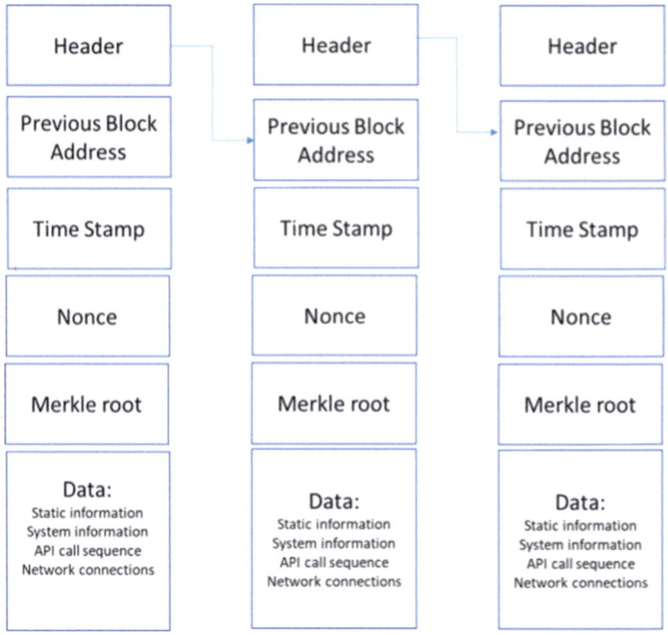

Fig. 2 Data-block contents in the proposed work

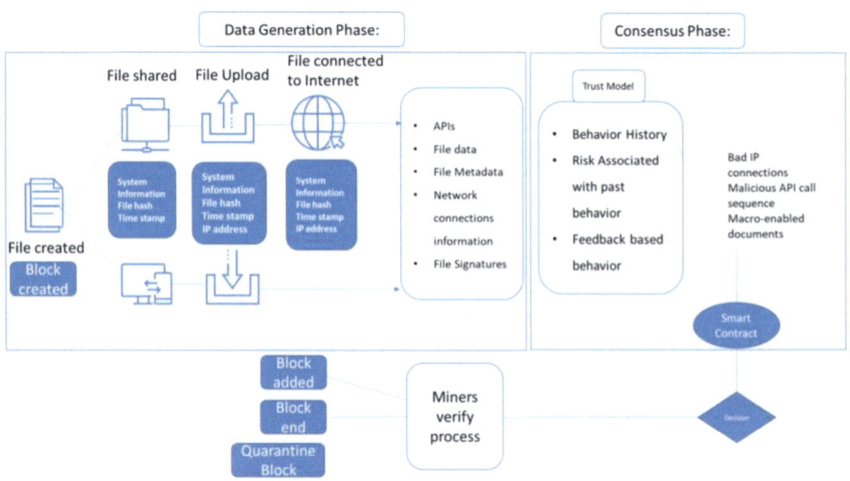

Fig. 3 Proposed model of blockchain based Malware detection using trust model

To reduce the false positives existing in several studies, trust factor is proposed based on file behavior. This trust factor enhances the overall detection system as it is based on behaviours history, risks associated with file behaviour and feedback of the file behaviour. The final assessment based on these factors decide on if the file is malicious or non-malicious for its further path.

4.2 Scope and Limitations

The primary scope of this proposed system is blockchain based malware detection in general platforms. There are limited studies that show use cases and applications in malware detection using blockchain. The existing studies have drawbacks such as scalabilty, lack of implementation and application in real-time cases. Selection of blockchain platform, type of blockchain, creating a blockchain requires though research and trials to work further. Utilizing existing blockchains will also need to be customized according to requirement. Since there is limit to storage on blocks, research is required on the type of data, such as File hash, PE header information or other file meta-data (different indicators of Compromise (IOCs)), to be added in the blocks.

4.3 Future Work

After successful implementation of this proposed work, our future work aims to provide security for personal computers and servers and further for smart IoT devices as well. This can further be extended to Operational Technology (OT) platforms as well. The proposed work currently considers portable executable (PE) files. Future work can be extended to non-PE files in data-block of blockchain, as malware authors also use non-PE files as malware vectors.

5 Conclusion

Several research studies exists for malware detection. Blockchain technology being relatively new still has uncovered application. Although studies show the use of blockchain in supply-chain management and in security such as intrusion detection, IoT security, research is still in infancy. Recent studies have also been extended to detection of malware but are limited. More over the existing blockchain based malware detection methods revolve around data generation and comparison with databases. This paper adds on the trust factor which can enable better performance and efficiency in the detection system. In this paper, we propose a model based on blockchain technology for malware detection. This proposed model consists of two phases: Data Generation phase and Consensus phase. In the data generation phase, block containing file data is created. In the consensus phase the file are analysed for malware based on three parameters (1) Behaviour history (2) Risk associated with behaviour (3) Feedback of behaviour. The proposed work aims to enhance overall performance of malware detection. This work further aims to extend to multiple platforms such as Internet of things (IoT) and Operational technology (OT). Additionally this work aims to consider non-PE files as well in future work.

References

1. Aslan ÖA, Samet R (2020) A comprehensive review on malware detection approaches. IEEE Access 8:6249–6271
2. Deshpande A, Stewart K, Lepetit L, Gunashekar S (2017) Distributed ledger technologies/blockchain: challenges, opportunities and the prospects for standards. In: Overview report The British Standards Institution (BSI), vol 40
3. Ferdous MS, Chowdhury MJM, Hoque MA, Colman A (2020) Blockchain consensus algorithms: a survey. arXiv preprint arXiv:2001.07091 (2020)
4. Fuji R, Usuzaki S, Aburada K, Yamaba H, Katayama T, Park M, Shiratori N, Okazaki N (2019) Investigation on sharing signatures of suspected malware files using blockchain technology. In: International multi conference of engineers and computer scientists (IMECS), pp 94–99
5. Gandotra E, Bansal D, Sofat S (2014) Malware analysis and classification: a survey. J Inf Secur
6. Gopinath M, Sethuraman SC (2023) A comprehensive survey on deep learning based malware detection techniques. Comput Sci Rev 47:100529
7. Gu J, Sun B, Du X, Wang J, Zhuang Y, Wang Z (2018) Consortium blockchain-based malware detection in mobile devices. IEEE Access 6:12118–12128
8. Gupta S, Thakur P, Biswas K, Kumar S, Singh AP (2021) Developing a blockchain-based and distributed database-oriented multi-malware detection engine. In: Machine intelligence and big data analytics for cybersecurity applications, pp 249–275
9. Li M, Wang H, Ross D (2009) Trust-based access control for privacy protection in collaborative environment. In: 2009 IEEE international conference on e-business engineering. IEEE, pp 425–430
10. Li X, Zhou F, Yang X (2011) A multi-dimensional trust evaluation model for large-scale p2p computing. J Parall Distrib Comput 71(6):837–847
11. Ndukwu C (2022) How blockchain has improved detection of malware. https://hackernoon.com/how-blockchain-has-improved-detection-of-malware
12. Shalini R, Manoharan R (2022) Trust model for effective consensus in blockchain. EAI Endors Trans Scalable Inform Syst 9(5)
13. Sharp R (2009) An introduction to malware
14. Sihwail R, Omar K, Ariffin KZ (2018) A survey on malware analysis techniques: static, dynamic, hybrid and memory analysis. Int J Adv Sci Eng Inf Technol 8(4-2):1662–1671
15. Sundarkumar GG, Ravi V, Nwogu I, Govindaraju V (2015) Malware detection via API calls, topic models and machine learning. In: 2015 IEEE international conference on automation science and engineering (CASE). IEEE, pp 1212–1217
16. Talukder S, Roy S, Al Mahmud T (2019) An approach for an distributed anti-malware system based on blockchain technology. In: 2019 11th international conference on communication systems & networks (COMSNET). IEEE, pp 1–6
17. Xiaoyong L, Xiaolin G (2007) Engineering trusted p2p system with fast reputation aggregating mechanism. In: 2007 IEEE international conference on robotics and biomimetics (ROBIO). IEEE
18. Xiong H, Chen M, Wu C, Zhao Y, Yi W (2022) Research on progress of blockchain consensus algorithm: a review on recent progress of blockchain consensus algorithms. Fut Internet 14(2):47

19. Xiong L, Liu L (2004) Peertrust: supporting reputation-based trust for peer-to-peer electronic communities. IEEE Trans Knowl Data Eng 16(7):843–857
20. Yoo S, Kim S, Kim S, Kang BB (2021) Ai-hydra: advanced hybrid approach using random forest and deep learning for malware classification. Inf Sci 546:420–435

Process of Creating Custom Linux Kernel with Boot Time Integrity Check Using U-Boot for Embedded Devices

Parth Ghughriwala, Nilay Mistry, Sourav Kunal, and T. Sukumara

Abstract Protecting the system against malicious code being loaded and executed early in the boot process is necessary for the era where cyber security incidents are at their peak and still more to come. Usually, embedded devices do not come with any kind security that checks kernel integrity before booting. Therefore, a method like Secure boot in embedded devices is essential to prevent such attacks. In critical infrastructure too firmware level security is essential. In the world of embedded devices resources are very limited and hence there is a need to create a custom kernel that is stripped down to serve specific purpose. In this paper we are showing a standard method of creating custom kernel and do integrity verification while booting using custom built u-boot bootloader that have TPM support. The complete process in embedded devices is quite complex and involves several complicated steps. Purpose is to eliminate that complexity and make generalized method that can work for almost any type of embedded board.

Keywords Custom kernel · Embedded devices · u-boot · Kernel integrity verification

P. Ghughriwala (✉) · S. Kunal · T. Sukumara
Electrification Products, ABB Ability Innovation Center GISPL, Bengaluru, India
e-mail: parth.ghughriwala@in.abb.com

S. Kunal
e-mail: souraviiitnr@gmail.com

T. Sukumara
e-mail: sukumara.t@in.abb.com

N. Mistry
School of Cyber Security and Digital Forensics, National Forensic Sciences University Gandhinagar, Gandhinagar, Gujarat, India
e-mail: nilay.mistry@nfsu.ac.in

B. N. Gohil et al. (eds.), *Information Security, Privacy and Digital Forensics*, Lecture Notes in Electrical Engineering 1423,
https://doi.org/10.1007/978-981-96-9443-3_20

1 Introduction

As the field of cyber security is growing day by day, the raise in cyber-attacks can also be seen. With the top-level applications and protocols introduce new security mechanisms attackers also finds new ways to infect the system and to seek persistence [1] in critical infrastructure [2] and SCADA devices. One of the most prominent ways to achieve that is by infecting system from level below OS that is kernel, bootloader, etc. Hence Secure Boot provide the key role to defense the systems against such attacks.

Today's modern world shows an inclination towards being more and more digital. Embedded systems prove to be very helpful in achieving this goal. Embedded systems are present everywhere around us. Single Board computers are also a type of embedded devices. The name "Single Board" [3] is because they have a processor, ram, device interfaces and memory integrated on to the same board. Hence, these are a great option for using in projects. The rise of "IoT" has also been a big reason for the rise of Single Board computers.

One such series of hardware is Raspberry Pi Series. These follow the general characteristics of embedded devices as they have a very limited resource and are designed to consume less power. Now, Raspberry Pi run a very generic Debian based OS, called Raspberry Pi OS. The agenda is to build a customized light weight Linux based OS and customized boot loader [4] with security implementations and for Pi boards that will be customized according to the requirement and to provide a complete generalized process that can be followed by any embedded board.

2 Methodology

2.1 *Objectives*

The higher-level objective of this project is to introduce a simplified and standard way to implement a method like secure boot in embedded devices with custom Linux kernel that can verify the kernel integrity before booting using cryptographic operations.

Creating procedure to build a custom platform which constitutes of custom Linux based OS and a custom open-source boot loader with additional layer of security that verifies kernel integrity. Both of them should be tweaked according to the target board, i.e., RPi (raspberry pi). Also, to support various devices on the RPi we need to provide an appropriate Device Tree Blob [5]. To store necessary files related to both, system and user application, a Root File System is required. A configuration file has to be generated to configure the environment before boot loader is handed control. Also, it will tell the RPi's boot loader to hand control to U-Boot [6].

Objectives in nonabstract manner are listed below:

1. To create a custom Linux based Kernel
2. To build a rootfs with necessary packages like networking
3. To create a second stage custom boot loader using U-Boot
4. Applying base device tree blob and patching required device tree overlays
5. Cryptographically sign Linux kernel and device tree
6. Increasing security robustness by creating FIT image with hashes as well as signature of components.

3 Lab Setup

For the purpose of POC we have used Raspberry pi 4. As this is one of the most widely available and used embedded board with large community support. Raspberry pi needs to be powered up using the adapter. In the initial stages of the boot up, USB-TTY converter can be connected to monitor and enter commands. Mainly, this will be handy while passing commands to the hush shell (U-Boot). There are two machines here, i.e., Build Machine and Target Device. Build Machine is the computer running Ubuntu OS, which will be used to build the components of the target platform. The Target Device here will be the Raspberry Pi for which the platform is being developed. The Raspberry Pi 4 only supports mini HDMI—HDMI cable can be used to connect an external monitor with the Pi. This step might not be required throughout the application.

As part of Lab setup, first for ease of applying the procedure, it is best to have a monitor and USB keyboard attached to the RPi4. Setup broadly includes two components, build machine and target device. The build machine has Ubuntu 18.04 LTS running on Virtual Machine (VMWare/VirtualBox) with 4 GB RAM and 20–30 GB of ROM. This VM is allocated 4 cores of processor. There have been multiple errors encountered while building using Buildroot if less number of cores or RAM is allocated. Going beyond 4 cores and 4 GB of RAM is not tested due to limitations in the developer machine, but this seems to be bare minimum. An unrestricted internet connection is provided to the VM for satisfying various dependencies to run Buildroot and U-boot. Although a dedicated system with Ubuntu can be used instead of a VM for this purpose. As far as the setup is considered for the target device, i.e., Raspberry Pi 4, is straight forward. Mini HDMI to HDMI cable is connected between the board and monitor. After the procedure is finished and all the required components are present on the SDcard, it is plugged in the sdcard slot on the Pi. To perform set some configurations/debug it is best to connect USB to TTY converter (RS232—Adafruit, with female cable), from the GPIO pins [7] to the USB port of the Build Machine. This gives a serial communication to interact with U-Boot's Hush Shell and Linux CLI. To pass commands when the Linux has booted up, alternatively, a usb keyboard can also be used. As well as a LAN cable can be attached into the RPi and a router for SSH connection.

3.1 Proposed System

Broadly, two different open-source programs will be utilised. One, Buildroot for the kernel and rootfs and U-Boot for the boot loader. The final procedure to be proposed consists of the following important points:

1. Applying defconfig (Rpi4—Buildroot)
2. Adding/Removing Packages (Buildroot)
3. Building Linux kernel, rootfs and dtb
4. Applying defconfig (Rpi4—UBoot)
5. Enable config for FIT support
6. Building FIT image from Existing Buildroot Kernel and dtb (mkimage)
7. Building Boot Script for U-Boot (mkimage)
8. Burning sdcard.img from Buildroot on sdcard
9. Sign FIT image using public–private keypair.
10. Add public key to device tree blob of u-boot
11. Copying signed FIT Image, u-boot.bin and boot script to sdcard
12. Editing Config file to point u-boot.bin (Fig. 1)

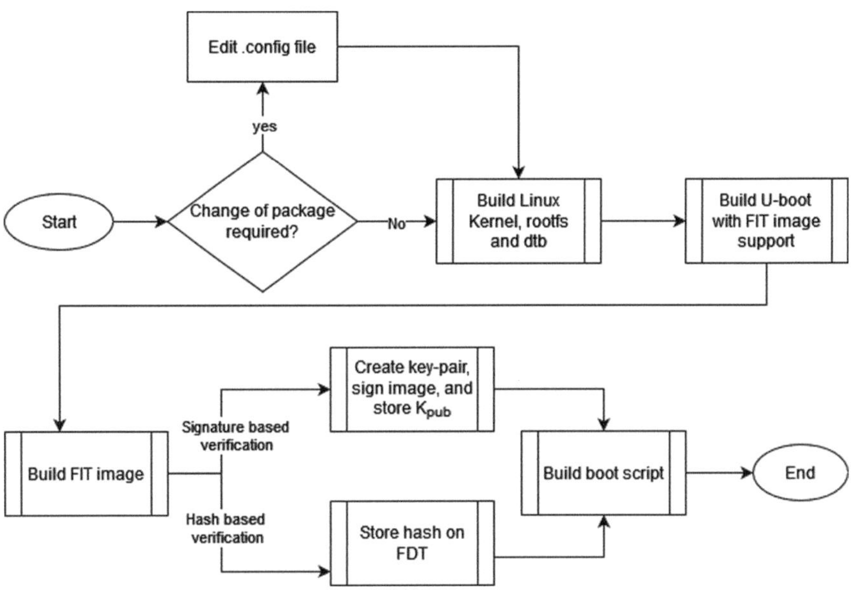

Fig. 1 Methodology process flow

4 Custom Linux Kernel Using Buildroot

To begin with building using Buildroot, must install it by satisfying a few dependencies. An Ubuntu system can be a good choice for Build system. Dependencies which need to be installed are as follows:

```
which
sed
make (version 3.81 or any later)
binutils
build-essential (only for Debian based systems)
gcc (version 4.8 or any later)
g++ (version 4.8 or any later)
bash
patch
gzip
bzip2
perl (version 5.8.7 or any later)
tar
cpio
unzip
rsync
file (must be in /usr/bin/file)
bc
wget
python (version 2.7 or any later)
ncurses5
qt5
glib2
gtk2
glade2
git
```

4.1 Configuring and Customizing Linux

The Linux kernel can be customized to suit the target board, i.e., Raspberry Pi 4. After which a bunch of customizations needs to be done to achieve the set target of enabling basic networking. Basic configuration that needs to be applied to base Linux for RPi 4 is provided by Buildroot in the form of defconfigs. The list of such defconfigs can be found under/configs directory. Using grep utility to find Pi4 config. make command needs to be issued from the Buildroot root directory. The response confirms that required changes are written to config. After this, issuing make menuconfig to do necessary customizations. This menu-based interface will be very key to making customizations.

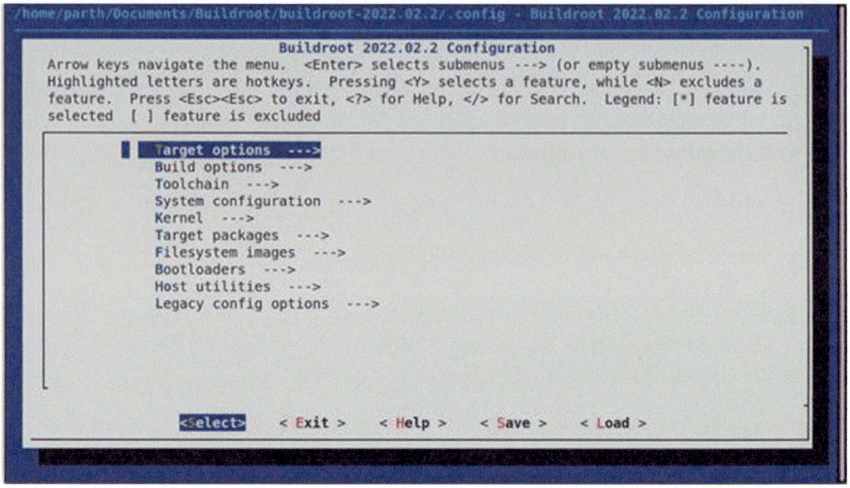

Fig. 2 Buildroot menuconfig

```
make raspberrypi4_64_defconfig
make menuconfig
```

Menuconfig present us with a command line application that allow us to modify configuration of Linux kernel with the help of a menu like interface, where pressing up down key allow us to go up and down enter to select and pressing double escape to go back (Fig. 2).

Some more options that need to be based on the type of kernel required. There are different high-level sections available on the home screen of menuconfig starting from Target options to Legacy config options. Each section is self-explanatory consists of relevant settings. Some of the options that we have changed for our POC is shown below. Apart from that user can change default shell, add or remove tools and utilities as per requirement, change and configure bootloader, filesystem format size, etc.

```
Target Options
  Target Architecture -> AArch64
Build Options
  Enable compiler cache -> y
System Configuration
  System hostname -> "YourHostname"
  Root password -> "rootpassword"
  Kernel binary format -> Image
```

4.2 Buildroot Output

After all the above configurations and other required changes are made. We now need to start building the target environment components based on our config and customization. For this we need to hit make command in the buildroot's root directory. This step will take a while to complete. Depends on the config of the build machine. A rough estimate on a 4 core 64-bit CPU with 4 GB of RAM will be of 2–3 h.

Once the make is complete, a dir under buildroot directory will be created called as '/output'. This directory basically contains all the components required to run the custom OS on the target. The major components that are to be focused here are—kernel image, rootfs, Device Tree Blob, Cross—Compiler, config.txt and sdcard.img. We need to write sdcard.img into SD card to make it bootable. dd command or disks utility can be used for that.

5 Build Custom U-Boot Bootloader

Das U-Boot is an open-sourced boot loader program. This program supports majority of platforms including ARM and $\times$ 86 platform. U-Boot source code can be fetched using git clone commandThere are various kernel image formats supported by U-Boot. There images have different applications and uses. They can be listed as—

- Legacy (Image/zImage)
- uImage
- FIT Image

Here FIT stands for Flattened Image Tree. This owes to the fact that FIT is a tree like structure. This tree like structure is very similar to Device Trees. FIT images support multiple images and also configurations. One image can be included in multiple configurations.

Like Buildroot, U-Boot does contain pre-built config files to support U-Boot on various boards like Beaglebone, RPi, etc. These are present under/configs dir. under root directory. Apply defconfig using make command.

FIT support is not present on the rpi4 defconfig provided. This configuration needs to be enabled via menuconfig. Inside this menu, "Boot Images" submenu contains image related configs. Enabled FIT support by toggling "Support Flattened Image Tree" option. Along with that Enable signature verification of FIT uImages. Now after doing all necessary and other board specific changes U-boot has to be finally built according to this.config using make utility. As a result, we get u-boot.bin and config.txt file which can be loaded onto SD card.

```
git clone https://gitlab.denx.de/u-boot/u-boot.git
make CROSS_COMPILE=aarch64-linux-gnu- rpi_4_defconfig
make CROSS_COMPILE=aarch64-linux-gnu- all
```

6 Build Kernel FIT Image

At this stage, U-Boot is customised to support booting FIT images. We have our custom kernel and rootfs built with buildroot. This kernel is in legacy format This section is, focused on how to convert the legacy format image to FIT image. Important thing to notice here is the fact that legacy image contain only the kernel image whereas FIT image contains kernel all other booting related files like dtb, dtbo, intird, etc. as a single image. When booting legacy images on RPi using second stage as U-Boot, only the legacy image is booted with the help of U-boot. All other necessary files like dtb and overlays are loaded by the Raspberry Pi's first stage bootloader. Once, U-Boot is handed the control, fatload operation on the hush shell is performed to copy legacy image from SD Card and booted using bootz or bootm command. But when booting FIT images, this process isn't the same as the FIT image will be containing the dtb and overlays.

Now to generate FIT image an Image Tree Source (.its) file is required. Image Tree Source file is a tree type format where each nodes contains description of the target FIT and leaf nodes contains attributes and its corresponding values. The nodes in Image Tree Source file have two main parts. One containing the images (kernel and dtb) and the other part containing the configuration. Image node includes description of the kernel, description of the kernel architecture, where to load it in memory, hash and/or signature usage, etc. Configuration node contains which kernel and fdt in combination will be loaded while booting along with signature/hashing usage. For us hashing/signature is the main attribute that enables U-Boot to do the integrity verification prior to boot the OS. This source file has to be written according to the requirement. The source file for this project is as follows:

```
/dts-v1/;
/ {
    description = "Rpi4 FIT Image";
    #address-cells = <1>;
    images {
        kernel-1 {
            description = "Rpi4 Custom Linux kernel";
            data = /incbin/("Image");
            type = "kernel";
            arch = "arm64";
            os = "linux";
            compression = "none";
            load = <0x00200000>;
            entry = <0x00200000>;
            hash {
                algo = "sha256";
            };
        };
        fdt-1 {
            description = "FDT Blob";
            data = /incbin/("bcm2711-rpi-4-b.dtb");
            type = "flat_dt";
            arch = "arm64";
            load = <0x2180000>;
            compression = "none";
            hash {
                algo = "sha256";
            };
        };
    };
configurations {
        default = "config-1";
        config-1 {
            description = " Kernel+FDT blob";
            kernel = "kernel-1";
            fdt = "fdt-1";
            signature-1 {
                algo = "sha256,rsa2048";
                key-name-hint = "key-name";
                sign-images = "fdt", "kernel";
            };
        };
    };
};
```

Issue mkimage command to create fit image from given .its file.

```
mkimage -f image.its image.fit
```

6.1 Sign FIT Image

Now next step is signing of FIT image. For that first need to generate a RSA keypair. Generating private half of the can be easily done using openssl utility with genpkey option. It is preferred to use RSA algorithm with 2048 bits of key length as it suite the best for u-boot with adequate level of encryption strength. To generate public half openssl with req and × 509 option can be use. It takes private key as input.

Using the mkimage utility and generated keypairs, FIT image can be signed. In the command -F takes input FIT image, -k is the location of the folder where RSA keypairs are stored, -r stands for required keys, -c for comments and -K is the control dtb where public key certificate will be added. Here it is somewhat confusing but this control dtb and dtb used in fit image are different. Sole purpose of control dtb to store public key certificate which U-Boot while booting can use using to check integrity of FIT image.

```
mkimage -F image.fit -k keys -K bcm2711-rpi-4-b.dtb -c
"signed fit" -r
```

6.2 Building Boot Script

While booting, U-boot runs the autoboot program, The autorun has some pre-programmed schedule that on every boot it runs, which also includes finding a script with of commands defined by user for booting called as boot script. Following code with setenv, fatload and bootm commands can be created in "boot.scr" file. U-Boot needs encoded script file which can be done using mkimage utility.

```
setenv bootargs root=/dev/mmcblk0p2 rootwait console=tty1
console=ttyAMA0,115200
fatload mmc 0:1 10000000 image.fit
bootm 10000000

mkimage -T script -A arm64 -n "U-Boot boot script" -d
boot.scr boot.scr.uimg
```

In config.txt generated by Buildroot, it is required to mention kernel as u-boot.bin. So that internal bootloader of Raspberry pi will call u-boot for booting and u-boot can do signature and/or hash verification of kernel FIT image. To enable serial output from Raspberry pi set 1 to enable_uart [8] attribute in the same config.txt. In the end, copy all files to SD card boot partition and make boot partition read-only to make SD card ready to boot.

7 Summary

An easy to adapt procedure has been developed to take command of the platform. The traditional OS to be used here would have been Raspberry Pi OS which uses much more RAM and ROM than the custom OS built using the proposed procedure. Also, this procedure verifies measurements (hash and signature) for kernel and dtb before booting them. Although, RPi and most of the Single board embedded devices do not fundamentally support boot level verification without hardware root of trust. Simply replacing the SDcard with a malicious platform can compromise the entire project. However, it needs physical access to the device. That being said, here the agenda was to demonstrate the possibility of implementation of such security measures in a generalized manner that is applicable to majority of embedded devices.

8 Conclusion

A procedure has been developed with a working proof of concept to deploy custom platform on specific embedded devices. Here, building custom platform refers to paring a custom Linux kernel along with custom boot loader program from Raspberry Pi 4 B. This provided great command on pre kernel boot up portion of the boot up procedure. The custom platform has helped in reducing the usage of resources on the platform than traditional Raspbian OS hence can be helpful when used to run heavy application on Pi. The introduction of a second stage bootloader has not only provided with the control of which dtb and dtbo to load but also on added a security layer by measuring the kernel and dtb present in the FIT image before booting it. This demonstrates a use case for security critical projects using similar boards. This proposed solution will ease the adaption of such custom platforms for project in various fields as well help in employing boot level security concepts.

As part of future scope of work, it can be considered using security of dedicated hardware crypto processor TPM [9] in signing process. TPM is a physical hardware chip with various modules combined and one of them is persistent NVRAM. By utilizing NVRAM of TPM to store public key certificates that can provide hardware Root of Trust. Additionally, some parts of the process i.e., process of keypair creation and FIT image signing can be automated using bash or python like scripting languages.

References

1. Michael Sikorski AH (2012) Practical malware analysis. In: Michael Sikorski AH OREILLY
2. CISA.org Cybersecurity and Infrastructure Security Agency https://www.cisa.gov/critical-infrastructure-sectors. Last accessed 2023/10/31
3. PCmag (n.d.) PC Mag. Retrieved from https://www.pcmag.com/encyclopedia/term/single-board-computer. Last accessed 2023/10/31
4. Beningo J (2015) Bootloader design for microcontrollers in embedded systems. In: Embedded systems conference, Rev A
5. Likely G, Boyer J (2008) A symphony of flavours: using the device tree to describe embedded hardware. In: Proceedings of the linux symposium, vol 2, pp 27–37
6. Community A (n.d.) OSS Platforms. (ARM Community). Retrieved July 2022 from https://community.arm.com/oss-platforms/w/docs/523/u-boot
7. White J (2016) Raspberry Pi—the complete manual, 7th edn. Imagine Publishing, Bournemouth, p 36
8. Arthur WC (2015) Chapter 1: History of the TPM. In: A practical guide to TPM 2.0: using the new trusted platform module in the new age of security, p 392. Springer Nature
9. Peña E, Legaspi MG (2020) Uart: a hardware communication protocol understanding universal asynchronous receiver/transmitter. Analog Dialogue [online] 4:1–5

Securing Critical Infrastructure with On-Premise Lightweight Certificates

Sourav Kunal, Digvijaysinh Rathod, Parth Ghughriwala, and T. Sukumara

Abstract Embedded systems play a critical role in various applications, where software and hardware work together to perform dedicated tasks. Their constrained nature, involving factors like power, size, and performance, presents significant security challenges. As the demand for more functionality in smaller devices rises, security often takes a backseat. This paper addresses the increasing vulnerability of embedded systems to attacks and emphasizes the need for robust security measures. It presents the development of a secure communication method for embedded devices and offers comparisons of available open-source tools.

Keywords Embedded systems · Attacks · Security · Communication · SSL · Openssl · Bash · Certificate authority · Certificate signing request · Validation · Expiry

1 Introduction

In the world of technology today, critical infrastructure security has emerged as a critical issue. Because systems using in these environments are being used in more and more industries and are being given more and more important duties, bad actors find them to be appealing targets. There has never been a greater need to protect these systems against cyber attacks and guarantee the integrity of the firmware.

Effective security measures are still hard to come by in the embedded market, despite this crucial requirement. Daily advisories are a frequent approach to exposing

S. Kunal · P. Ghughriwala · T. Sukumara
Electrification Products, ABB Ability Innovation Center GISPL, Bengaluru, India
e-mail: sukumara.t@in.abb.com

S. Kunal (✉) · D. Rathod · P. Ghughriwala
National Forensic Sciences University (NFSU), Gandhinagar, Gujarat, India
e-mail: souraviiitnr@gmail.com

D. Rathod
e-mail: digvijay.rathd@nfsu.ac.in

B. N. Gohil et al. (eds.), *Information Security, Privacy and Digital Forensics*,
Lecture Notes in Electrical Engineering 1423,
https://doi.org/10.1007/978-981-96-9443-3_21

vulnerabilities in embedded systems and emphasizing the possibility for exploitation. The abundance of research papers and articles outlining distinct firmware zero-day exploits further emphasizes how prevalent these vulnerabilities are. The urgent necessity for enhanced safety precautions has been made clear by these attacks.

A number of community-driven efforts emerged in response to these issues, all aimed at improving the security of communications between embedded devices and reducing security vulnerabilities within firmware. These open-source initiatives are an attempt to solve the current security gaps and a proactive response to the growing risks in the embedded environment.

Embedded systems have become mainstream as technology develops, becoming essential to smart devices, industrial automation, as well as critical infrastructure. These systems form the foundation of essential operations, and the dependability of numerous applications is dependent on their security. The modern world is interconnected, which highlights the need for reliable and secure embedded devices even more. The security constraints of embedded systems must be addressed because of the dynamic nature of threats and the swift growth of the Internet of Things (IoT). In an increasingly connected and digitally dependent world, this paper attempts to offer a thorough examination of the security issues that exist today and the open-source solutions that have the potential to improve embedded systems' safety and resilience.

2 Organisation and Contributions of the Paper

Section 3 includes the background study, Sect. 4 of open source tools undertaken by authors in this manuscript. Section 5 discusses the proposed methodology which includes, certificate generation and validation of Lightweight Certificates. Section 6 is the overall discussion which highlights the key points required to keep the critical infrastructure secure along with the use of certificates and then concluding remarks in Sect. 7.

Following are the major contributions discussed in the following study:

- Overview of open source tools by implementing them and discussing the design choices as per the tight resource constraints.
- In recent times, people are working remotely. So, to use embedded devices securely, such architectures becomes even more important.
- Full implementation of end-to-end security architecture for highly constrained embedded device through scripts.

3 Preliminaries

Ravi et al. [1] discussed the increasing number of attack techniques encountered in embedded Devices as they are resource constrained, so it is challenging to implement security in the face of limited memory, capacities, flexibility issues, etc.

They classified these challenges into few categories namely, user identification, availability, secure content (usage restriction), secure storage (confidentiality and integrity), secure communications and secure network access. SSL combines public key cryptography for key distribution and authentication with symmetric key cryptography for data encryption and integrity.

Gupta et al. [2] developed a tool named Sizzle, that completes full SSL handshake in less time and allows the user to monitor or control remotely via web server.

Young and Hudson [3] introduced the concept of OpenSSL project as Cryptography and SSL/TLS Toolkit in 2009. Ghafoor et al. [4] analysed OpenSSL and discussed about the heartbleed vulnerability in it. Heartbeat is a process of signaling, "I am Alive" to the client by a server or server by a client. Heartbleed vulnerability was discovered by Neel Mehta in March 2014 from Google. Carvalho et al. [5] discussed that how the vulnerability was disclosed and patched by April 7, 2014.

Li Gui et al. [6] discussed a technique for building a secure website with Apache and OpenSSL was looked at and the two distinct Telecom effects were compared in order to determine whether or not to launch the safety module to ensure safe communication.

Coruh et al. [7] introduces a lightweight authentication scheme for secure remote work, designed for Lightweight Portable Security (LPS) devices. It employs Two-Factor Authentication (2FA), combining user possession of a mobile phone and USB dongle with a mobile PIN for enhanced security, while also implementing geofencing for added protection.

Costin et al. [8] conducts the first large-scale analysis of firmware images, revealing 38 previously unknown vulnerabilities in over 693 images, impacting at least 140,000 internet-accessible devices, emphasizing the significance of embedded device security.

Nikolov on his research [9] discusses on firmware updates for IoT embedded systems highlights the importance of secure update processes, with potential implications for PKI and SSL/TLS in ensuring authentication, trust, and data integrity during over-the-air updates.

Mtetwa [10] focuses on IoT device security, emphasizing the importance of PKI in securing firmware updates. It addresses vulnerabilities in IoT devices, particularly those in low-end IoT devices and LPWANs. The research aims to enhance security and trust in IoT through PKI-backed firmware updates.

Costin [11] addresses the challenges in managing diverse embedded system firmware. The study employs two key strategies: firmware classification and embedded web interface fingerprinting. These approaches aid in identifying web-enabled devices running specific firmware, which is crucial for security. The use of PKI and SSL can enhance the security of firmware updates and communications in these devices.

4 Overview of Open-Source Tools

Authors have tried to use several open source tool for secure creation and validation of certificates. Below are the list of a few of the widely used open-source tools.

4.1 Mkcert

A simple and quick utility to generate reliable SSL certificates for local development environments known as mkcert [12]. It enables the creation of legitimate SSL certificates for localhost and local domain names, enabling easier use of HTTPS while developing. A sample certificate generated by mkcert can be seen in Fig. 1.

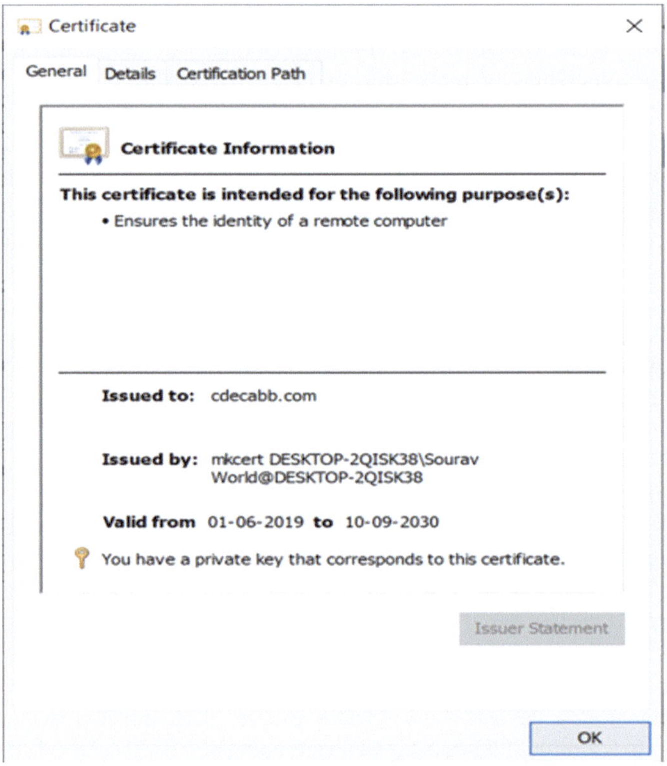

Fig. 1 Sample mkcert certificate

Lab setup and usage of mkcert

- Valid HTTPS Certificate; Pre-compiled Go Library;
- Use Chocolatey https://chocolatey.org/ to install in windows with the command: **choco install mkcert**
- Use Powershell for further generation of certificates: **mkcert—key-file key.pem—cert-file cert.pem example.com *.example.com**

Finally, Export the certificate to the Trusted Root Store of Windows. The Certificate is OK! But, their documentation says that the problem is that it should not be used in the production environment.

4.2 *Let's Encrypt*

The Automatic Certificate Management Environment protocol is a communications protocol for automating interactions between certificate authorities and their users' web servers, allowing the automated deployment of public key infrastructure at very low cost.

You can only get publicly trusted certificates (from Let's Encrypt [13]) for publicly registered domains as per their documentation.

4.3 *CloudFlare SSL*

CFSSL [14] is written in Go and are kept as open-source. But, the thing is it only has creation phase not the validation phase. Sample CFSSL Certificate can be seen in Fig. 2.

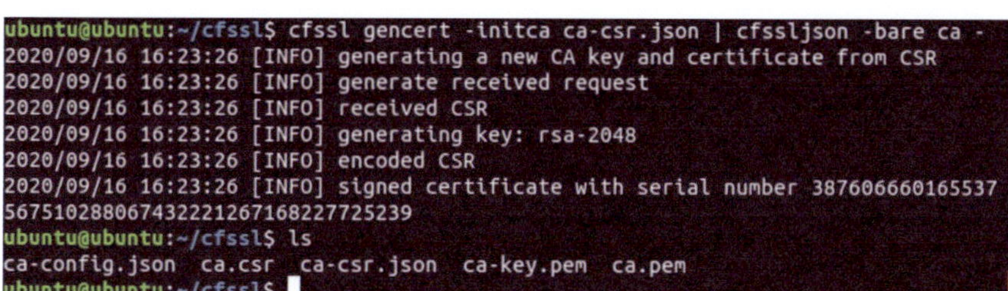

Fig. 2 Sample CFSSL certificate

4.4 Enterprise Java Beans Certificate Authority (EJBCA)

EJBCA [15] comes in two versions namely, Community and Licensed. It is executed under the supervision of an application server (JBOSS). We can see how to handle and administered the certificates generated by EJBCA in the Fig. 3. But, an important thing to note is that, EJBCA does not support renewal process.

5 Proposed Methodology

In this study, we highlight the significance of lightweight certificates for OT devices with limited resources. This covers methods for certificate revocation and shorter lifetimes, as well as an offline Certificate Authority (CA) for secure certificate issuance and two-way device authentication. To ensure a thorough approach to certificate administration in OT environments, it also covers automated management, time synchronization, security policies, network segmentation, monitoring, backup planning, penetration testing, and regular audits.

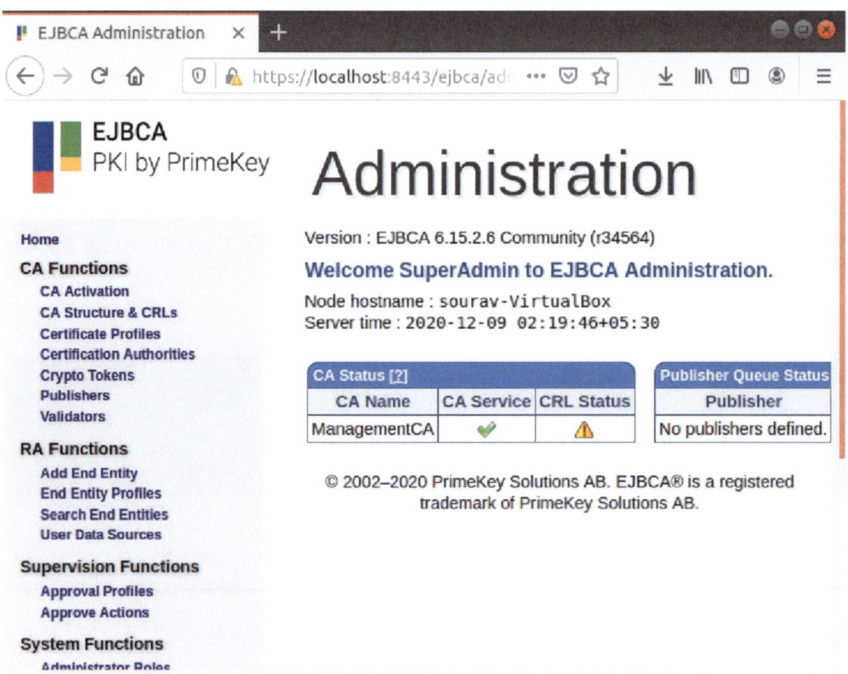

Fig. 3 Handling EJBCA certificate

OpenSSL project is managed by OpenSSL Software Foundation (OSF). This project is a software library for applications with SSL/TLS protocols, which can secure communication against man-in-the-middle kind of attacks. It supports many cryptographic algorithms. OpenSSL is available for most of the Linux or Windows operating systems.

Bash Script is used to run a series of commands one by one on the command line. Bash Scripts need to be given proper permission while running and these scripts starts with Shebang (#!) that is hash exclamation mark which is a path to the interpreter that runs the next lines.

In this manuscript, we have used the concepts of OpenSSL and Bash Script for the realization of the proposed methodology.

Process flow of whole process are consolidated in the form of flowchart as seen below in Figs. 4 and 5.

In this paper, to build a PKI using OpenSSL, we need the following five bash scripts:

1. For CA Generation
2. For CSR Generation of client and server respectively on each device accordingly.
3. CA has separate scripts for signing certificates based on server's/client's request.
4. Validation Checking script for Server, Client and CA Server
5. For Renewal, CA has to again sign using 3rd script.

Note: So all the server and client machines will have two scripts each while CA server machine will have four scripts.

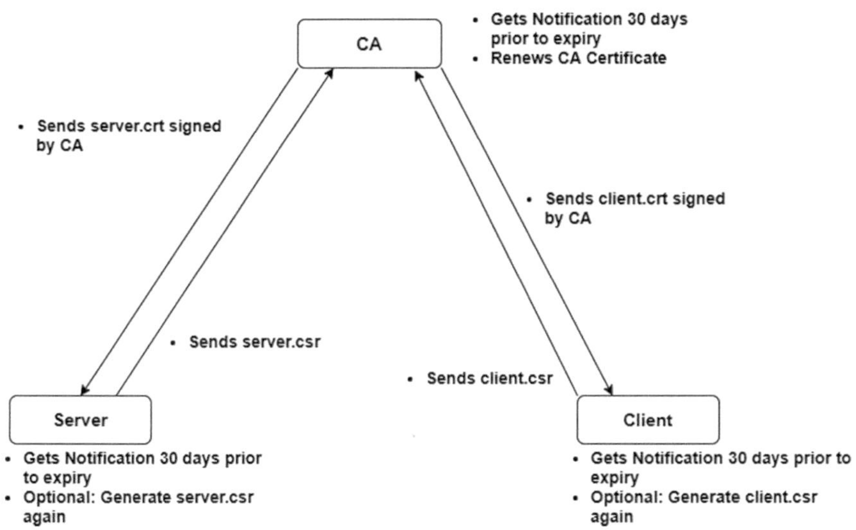

Fig. 4 Generation phase

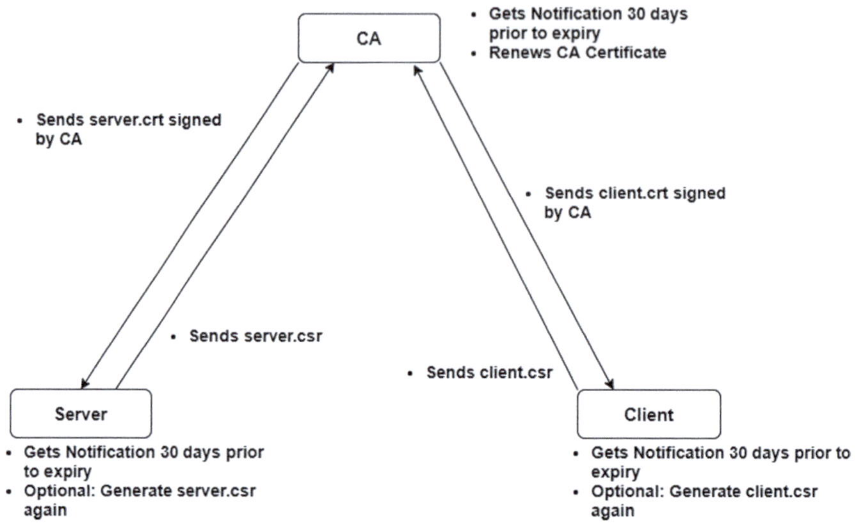

Fig. 5 Validation phase

5.1 Generating the CA Certificate

Creating a CA (Certificate Authority) certificate with OpenSSL begins with the creation of a self-signed root certificate which is then used for signing other certificates, like server or client certificates. First a key is generated as seen in Fig. 6 and then certificate can be generated as seen in Fig. 7.

```
#Generate the CA Key
openssl genrsa -out /etc/ssl/certs/ca.key 2048
openssl rsa -in /etc/ssl/certs/ca.key -out /etc/ssl/certs/ca.key
```

Fig. 6 Generate the Key for CA

```
#Generate the CA Certificate
openssl req -x509 -new -key /etc/ssl/certs/ca.key -sha256 -days 3650 -out /etc/
ssl/certs/ca.crt -nodes \
        -subj "/C=$country/ST=$state/L=$locality/O=$organization/
OU=$organizationalunit/CN=$commonname/emailAddress=$email"
```

Fig. 7 Generate the certificate for CA

5.2 Generating the Server Certificates

Once you have generated the CA (Certificate Authority) key and CA certificate using OpenSSL, you can proceed to generate server certificates signed by your CA. Below, are the steps to generate a server certificate. Generating Private Key for a server certificate as seen in Fig. 8, then generating Certificate Signing Request (CSR) can be seen in Fig. 9 and finally, genearting Certificate for Server or Domain can be done as in Fig. 10.

5.3 Generating the Client Certificates

To generate the client certificate, similarly we need to generate the key and then create the Certificate Signing Request and then finally generate the certificate. The process for the key generation can be seen in the Fig. 11 and the CSR generation can be seen in Fig. 12. Finally, the client certificate can be generated as seen in Fig. 13.

```
#Generate a Private key of domain
echo "------------------Generating a $domain private key---------------------"
openssl genrsa -out /etc/ssl/certs/$domain.key 2048
openssl rsa -in /etc/ssl/certs/$domain.key -out /etc/ssl/certs/$domain.key
```

Fig. 8 Generate the private key of domain

```
#Create the Certificate Signing Request
echo "-------------------Creating CSR----------------------------------"
openssl req -new -key /etc/ssl/certs/$domain.key -out /etc/ssl/certs/$domain.csr
-nodes -subj "/C=$country/ST=$state/L=$locality/O=$organization/
OU=$organizationalunit/CN=$commonname/emailAddress=$email"
```

Fig. 9 Generate the CSR of domain

```
openssl x509 -req -in /etc/ssl/certs/$domain.csr -CA /etc/ssl/certs/ca.crt -
CAkey /etc/ssl/certs/ca.key -CAcreateserial -days 3650 -out /etc/ssl/certs/
$domain.crt -sha256
```

Fig. 10 Generate the certificate of domain

```
openssl genrsa -out /etc/ssl/certs/client.key 4096
openssl rsa -in /etc/ssl/certs/client.key -out /etc/ssl/certs/client.key
```

Fig. 11 Generate the key for client

```
# Create a certificate signing request (CSR)
echo "------------- Creating CSR for client -----------------------"
openssl req -new -key /etc/ssl/certs/client.key -out /etc/ssl/certs/client.csr -
nodes -subj "/C=$country/ST=$state/L=$locality/O=$organization/
OU=$organizationalunit/CN=$commonname/emailAddress=$email"
```

Fig. 12 Generate the CSR for client

```
openssl x509 -req -in /etc/ssl/certs/client.csr -CA /etc/ssl/certs/ca.crt -
CAkey /etc/ssl/certs/ca.key -set_serial 101 -days 3650 -out /etc/ssl/certs/
client.crt -sha256
```

Fig. 13 Generate the certificate for client

5.4 Validation Phase

This script needs to be added to the crontab for checking the validity of the certificates and will prompt 30 days before for validation. The same can be done as seen in Figs. 17 and 14.

5.5 Output

A private key generated using OpenSSL is typically stored in a file in PEM (Privacy-Enhanced Mail) format. The content of the private key file will look like as seen in Fig. 15. The base64-encoded data within the "BEGIN PRIVATE KEY" and "END PRIVATE KEY" delimiters is the actual private key. This private key is to be stored securly and should not be shared to unknown parties. It is used to encrypt and decrypt data in SSL/TLS connections and to sign and verify digital signatures in many security

```
#! /bin/sh

CertExpires=`sudo openssl x509 -in /etc/ssl/certs/cdecel.com.crt -text -noout -
enddate | grep "Not After" | gawk '{print $4, $5, $7}'`

echo "Certificate Expires on: $CertExpires"

echo "Today's date is: `date`"

TodayPlus30=`date -ud "+30 day" | gawk '{print $2, $3, $6}'`

echo "Today Plus 30: $TodayPlus30"

if [ "$CertExpires" = "$TodayPlus30" ]
then
        echo "Certificate is Expiring Soon!!"
        exit 99

fi
```

Fig. 14 Certificate validation

```
-----BEGIN RSA PRIVATE KEY-----
MIIEpAIBAAKCAQEAqQwN3vTuuhuUHHnJBJOcQki+NmBPR90I2rTLvwyrJqXEWgQp
znZUa8xx3TmrHaPIuI93bxgD1go14Nsl97mby4sNkJLnAx+56fKAFyzpjmZEb/do
np6S9HwVJhwt6OP2/XxR4Hi9tAZ9oDuLB2GFNh+QRK6G0WR5onk54sO+lV4P9y2t
K2olKKl/PzSAYsZ/sGtP8bZB+1SLP09y5w9X52RfIqkcB1UavL6BnluteEkF4tKX
1ZhbKqdsZjddh9+kK/BKLjeGao80NIb3wBt7i2E6bW/4YCAKAH/11x5jNZK/tQcP
03KllB3JA81FiPkdkY37VO+BnZc3x/7u4u3qoQIDAQABAoIBAQCkPInda6nkNpcX
c1rRj3fpDjN/MOLVrbbwhWbOHsjJq5OwwQq9BEnQ0bhubnDJQy7n4LrwvCw9732Z
EFE69KFgh6COLaszZceCe4/m9EOVjdY/0eda9EViMot5kzcnZRO6AuapZ6UnGodC
/ZZ9fUmm49OOZuGk3jEuoQiUQAkRo9TonCFRHdw1toMNKLGFWMGG6IC7IVYOQtiL
rup7zJNAwhzj58+drsT1/pJDnDS6Fco9h7Kyr1EV4DNtjl45tbGdkIxrg3XgY41h
gBjl7k4OvNqyPVZZd+iwLhGjsM/+tDw6kncVChL3Oj5BwUVQJY29G0DoweN/WSH1
lPNMJkoBAoGBANg25sTTezT6jR7jXRowvRnfPZs/pRlZlgseSa8sP8Fm4uXPJgwA
C5UP4ONOJ6tHOn91Gc7lQdOwqg3Dc856SqkdBdx7kW4V8SjZUcQLhWg3hmGsqZU8
wK3ULUgtc8zgebmoPVh8SPTx4CfQwDB4xWLN1pqEJeivNZqEfX3Kzsh5AoGBAMgn
Q79ooVXOgYghxNAvvm0OOCDypU4jPHZ8Rr6zeyizsMxBUeaLv57wCzokqHniRmDI
Skw55BJPsBKCuHJcmGB1/tAjWtsa+OMIjecpOBsfk0YudPnFXJXP6xmqTL9gb1ef
8obWf7LhS4j2lUWgYrLfmWiVVepeGnXd7vWkIPlpAoGBAIzh4SZZIovXwkJhJdYd
8em8w7i4FMzayeC+wIZqz7QmZSwW+RSSpvle2ktiLoj1JZHNbJ6aVXUpRPUo6Pme
R62/4oTS42UW2Qej6xpR44CPxXk5d1pttqLNgR/pte3GSqqFjEtu2F76h/OJmuE6
oGsL8ozGFKl0GPpw4BAqKOkJAoGAXSbRA/NJKus6I8Y7l/ywbobwnnzvbEc/65D5
R+W2SwIeJWG9IUQnAWyMfRn0gw1JXd+5nHJQ8CjANE08VJU9oZ8o4Wui7FhIPzmK
+WuYnh765u3WKSyuY1bp/v7gSy0xhKF/OTv5IKJ0CiFg5Y+4f7FK736ZBsOXIwYQ
IaiqZAkCgYBDBbz8ChcwAvzMFKbDlpv+jIDn6ry2GcOUR4XRsRdTac4cARgGXzhA
CWwQjS7sipC1BJBAif5WTIkWyfz9HhykED5wE5F74Rd/QEkQQV5qM30oeyurQSKm
8cAtIj/PympE8b/e8D0B0/ptKLNdFIF1C+WK1DxNXZzAPlnRvT56Pg==
-----END RSA PRIVATE KEY-----
```


Fig. 15 Sample private key

processes. Sample certificate generated using OpenSSL, stored in PEM format and consists of several sections. Also, a sample certificate can be seen in the Fig. 16.

When the validity script is ran, user can see the certificate Expiry date as seen in the Fig. 17.

6 Overall Discussion

In Operational Technology (OT) systems, certificate management plays a critical role in guaranteeing security and reliability. Here, we discuss the different facets of certificate management and offer a condensed list of important points:

- **Use of Lightweight Certificates**: Selecting cryptographic algorithms and small certificate formats appropriate for devices with limited resources is crucial in off-the-shelf (OT) scenarios. While maintaining security, lightweight certificates reduce the need for memory and processing power.
- **Device Authentication**: Implementing two-way authentication methods, making sure that servers and devices use certificates to authenticate one another. Through the confirmation of each party's identity, this bidirectional verification improves security.

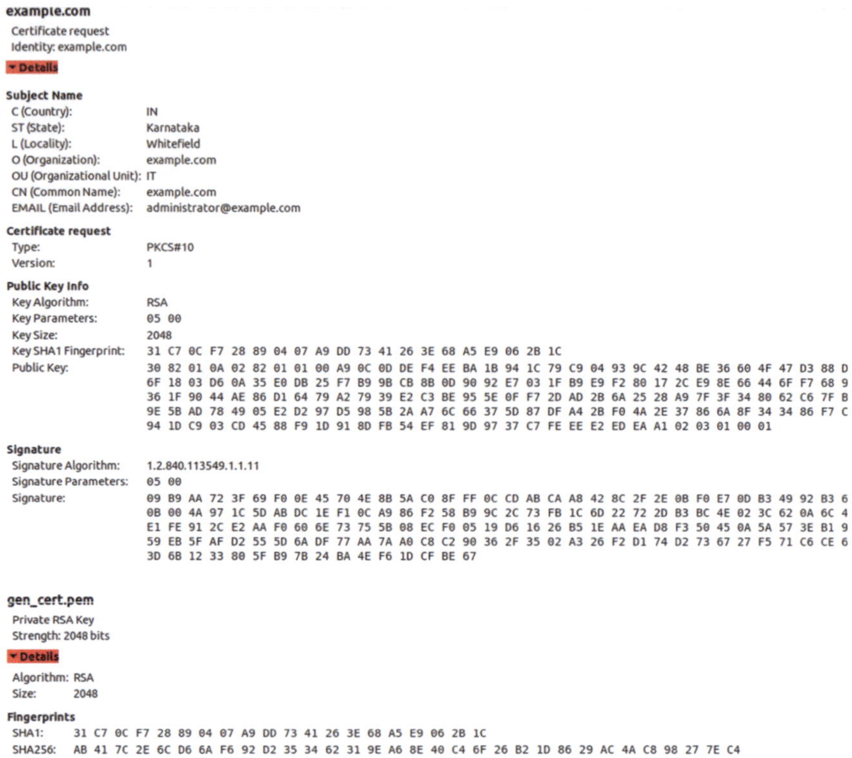

Fig. 16 Sample certificate

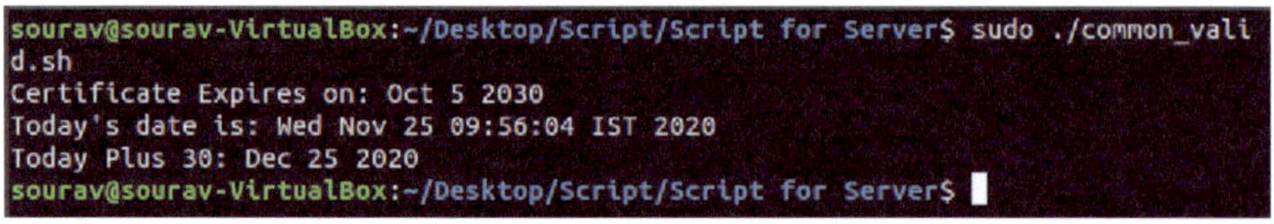

Fig. 17 Checking validity of certificate

- **Offline CA and Certificate Distribution**: To securely handle and issue certificates, create an offline Certificate Authority (CA) inside the OT network. An offline CA lessens vulnerability to outside threats. In the context of OT, distribute certificates using safe techniques.
- **Certification Revocation**: Providing a way to revoke certificates in the case that a device is compromised. For handling this procedure, offline Certificate Revocation Lists (CRLs) are a useful tool. Develop a safe procedure for distributing and updating CRLs in the OT environment. System security must be maintained by regular upgrades.

- **Certificate Lifetimes**: Limiting the amount of time you are exposed in the event of a security breach by setting short certificate lifetimes. Shorter lives mean that certificates need to be updated more frequently, but this improves security by reducing the amount of time that a compromised certificate can be used maliciously.
- **Automated Certificate Management**: Putting in place automated procedures for provisioning and certificate renewal. In certificate management, automation eliminates the chance of human error and reduces administrative effort.
- **Local Time Sync**: Ensuring that the OT environment's devices remain in sync with respect to time even when there is no internet connection. For the security and validity of certificates, accurate time synchronization is essential.
- **Security Policies and Training**: Establishing strict security guidelines that control certificate management procedures. Additionally, train certificate management personnel to guarantee adherence to security guidelines.
- **Network Segmentation**: Splitting important OT networks from less important ones, and implement stringent access restrictions. Segmenting a network reduces the amount of possible attack surfaces and prevents unwanted access.
- **Monitoring and Intrusion Detection**: Deploying reliable intrusion detection and monitoring systems to quickly spot and address any suspicious activity in the OT environment. It takes continuous monitoring to identify threats early.
- **Backup and Recovery**: Developing thorough backup and recovery strategies for certificate data and the Certificate Authority (CA). In the event of system malfunctions or data corruption, these policies lessen the possibility of data loss.
- **Penetration Testing**: Conducting penetration testing on a regular basis to proactively find weaknesses and vulnerabilities in the Public Key Infrastructure (PKI) installation. Penetration testing facilitates prompt mitigation by assisting in the discovery of possible security flaws.
- **Regular Audits**: Planning recurring audits to make sure the PKI is operating effectively and that stated security policies are being followed. An independent assessment of security protocols and policy compliance is offered by audits.

7 Conclusion

The necessity of deploying secure lightweight certificate management in operational technology (OT) environments is brought up in the current research. Through the utilization of an offline Certificate Authority, safe distribution strategies, and careful attention to important certificate validation factors, our study presents a strong architecture that greatly strengthens the security of critical OT infrastructure.

Our method not only successfully addresses the resource limitations that OT devices inherently present, but it also offers a scalable and adaptable solution that thwarts possible threats. Our ongoing effort in placing up comprehensive security measures, precise certificate life-cycle management, and seamless offline operation guarantees the best level of protection while preserving uninterrupted functioning of critical systems.

This research makes a substantial contribution to the pool of knowledge about OT environment defense against new threats and puts us in a stronger position to support the implementation of improved security procedures. Our work provides a solid foundation for bolstering the resilience and ensuring the security of critical infrastructure as the threat landscape continues its continuous evolution. The objective we seek in disseminating these results is to stimulate and encourage more study and cooperation in this crucial field. As we collaborate, we can consistently improve the security of operational technology environments, which are the vital foundation of numerous critical infrastructure based industries.

References

1. Ravi S, Raghunathan A, Kocher P, Hattangady S (2004) Security in embedded systems: design challenges. ACM Trans Embedded Comput Syst (TECS) 3(3):461–491
2. Gupta V, Wurm M, Zhu Y, Millard M, Fung S, Gura N, Shantz SC et al (2005) Sizzle: a standards-based end-to-end security architecture for the embedded internet. Pervas Mob Comput 1(4):425–445
3. Young EA, Hudson TJ (2009) OpenSSL: cryptography and SSL/TLS toolkit
4. Ghafoor I et al (2014) Analysis of OpenSSL heartbleed vulnerability for embedded systems. In: 17th IEEE international multi topic conference 2014. IEEE
5. Carvalho M, DeMott FR, Wheeler DA (2014) Heartbleed 101. Security and Privacy iEEE 12(4):63–67
6. Gui-hong L, Hua Z, Gui-zhi L (2010) Building a secure web server based on OpenSSL and Apache. E-Business and E-Government(ICEE), 2010 International conference on, vol, no, pp 1307–1310
7. Coruh U, Khan M, Bayat O (2021) Lightweight offline authentication scheme for secure remote working environment. In: 2021 International conference on electrical, computer and energy technologies (ICECET), Cape Town, South Africa, pp 1–9. https://doi.org/10.1109/ICECET52533.2021.9698586
8. Costin A, Zaddach J, Francillon A, Balzarotti D (2014) A large-scale analysis of the security of embedded firmwares. In: 23rd USENIX security symposium (USENIX Security 14), pp 95–110
9. Nikolov N (2018) Research firmware update over the air from the cloud. In: 2018 IEEE XXVII international scientific conference electronics-ET. IEEE, pp 1–4
10. Mtetwa NS, Tarwireyi P, Abu-Mahfouz AM, Adigun MO (2019) Secure firmware updates in the internet of things: a survey. In: 2019 international multidisciplinary information technology and engineering conference (IMITEC). IEEE, pp 1–7
11. Costin A, Zarras A, Francillon A (2017) Towards automated classification of firmware images and identification of embedded devices. IFIP international conference on ICT systems security and privacy protection. Springer, Cham, pp 233–247
12. npm: mkcert (nd) Npm. https://www.npmjs.com/package/mkcert
13. Let's encrypt (nd) https://letsencrypt.org/
14. Sullivan N (2023) Introducing CFSSL–CloudFlare's PKI toolkit. The Cloudflare Blog. https://blog.cloudflare.com/introducing-cfssl/
15. EJBCA (2023) EJBCA–The open-source certificate authority (CA) https://www.ejbca.org/

Study of Blockchain Technology from Law Enforcement and Investigator's Perspective

A. Y. V. Krishna, Naveen Kumar Chaudhary, and Ravirajsinh S. Vaghela

Abstract Blockchain technology, renowned for its revolutionary impact on virtual currency transactions, is poised to transform various industries, including the realm of law enforcement. In a world yearning for trust and transparency, blockchain technology emerges as a beacon of hope. Governments and top bureaucratic bodies worldwide recognize the immense potential of blockchain to enhance public welfare and streamline law enforcement investigations. This study delves into the myriad benefits of blockchain, including transparency in investigations, secure evidence storage, and fostering public trust in the system. It meticulously examines various use cases and evaluates diverse blockchain-based concepts tailored for law enforcement applications. Additionally, the study explores the intricacies of implementing blockchain technology and verifying the validity of evidence stored on its immutable ledger.

Keywords Blockchain · Law enforcement investigation · Chain of custody

1 Introduction

Blockchain is a decentralized system that spreads the maintenance and preservation of digital records across numerous nodes. Each node in blockchain contains entire data as well as the entire software that operates on the data [1]. Data once written onto blockchain, cannot be updated or deleted. Behaviour of software programs (aka Smart Contracts) deployed on blockchain can't be altered, not even by the administrator or creator of the software [2]. Blockchain is at that stage of regulation catching up. Governments across the world are framing their own blockchain policies [3,

A. Y. V. Krishna · N. K. Chaudhary · R. S. Vaghela (✉)
School of Cyber Security & Digital Forensic, National Forensic Science University, Gandhinagar, India
e-mail: ravirajsinh.vaghela@nfsu.ac.in

N. K. Chaudhary
e-mail: naveen.chaudhary@nfsu.ac.in

B. N. Gohil et al. (eds.), *Information Security, Privacy and Digital Forensics*,
Lecture Notes in Electrical Engineering 1423,
https://doi.org/10.1007/978-981-96-9443-3_22

4]. Central and state governments in India encourage blockchain technology. Indian Prime minister's tweet on 19th Feb18 about blockchain and several states going live with blockchain storage for land registry, farm insurance and ration distribution are few examples. In 2019, around 15% of the blockchain applications in India are used by PSUs and Government Sector [5]. Blockchain allows for the tracing of all transactions involving a given address, providing law enforcement with the ability to track the movement of funds in a way that was not previously possible [6, 7]. Blockchain does not present the problem of data retention. It knows no borders and is available from anywhere [8].

Blockchain technology offers a comprehensive solution to various law enforcement challenges by ensuring evidence integrity, enhancing transparency, facilitating cross-border investigations, and enabling secure intelligence sharing [9]. Make current systems more effective, transparent and easy to control for the information holder, sharing of Id documents data real-time—not raw data but its hash value, provides foolproof audit trail logs [6, 7], finally for investigation of Crypto currency frauds as crypto currencies are powered by Blockchain technology [10].

Paper comprise 3 section first section cover use cases of the blockchain in Law Enforcement Agencies second section cover Literature review of the Existing solution in Law enforcement agencies and third section cover solution in detail chain of custody and verification process.

1.1 Use Cases of Blockchain Technology by Law Enforcement Agencies

Use Case 1: Sharing id documents data real time:

Current Problem: Even at restricted and highly secured areas like airports, immigration desks, there is no way for law enforcement to verify if the photo identity card presented by entering individual is genuine one or a fake one. So fraudsters can potentially get away with producing fake document or cancelled document as id proof [11, 12]. Can be accomplished using Zero Knowledge proof method so that data confidentiality, privacy are not compromised. All the identity issuing government agencies like following host a node of the proposed blockchain [13] (Fig. 1).

Use Case 2: Leveraging tamper proofness feature of blockchain as evidence:

In any non-blockchain software system there will be data tampering vulnerability of a malicious administrator that has super user passwords, bypassing the application layer and directly updating the datastore layer. Even if audit trailing is enabled for the datastore layer, the admin has access to delete those audit trail logs as well removing any traces of the tampering. So, data in a non-blockchain software system cannot be relied on [14] (Fig. 2).

But data on a public blockchain is absolutely tamperproof (even system administrator/hacker/malicious insider cannot alter the data). So, if data on public blockchain

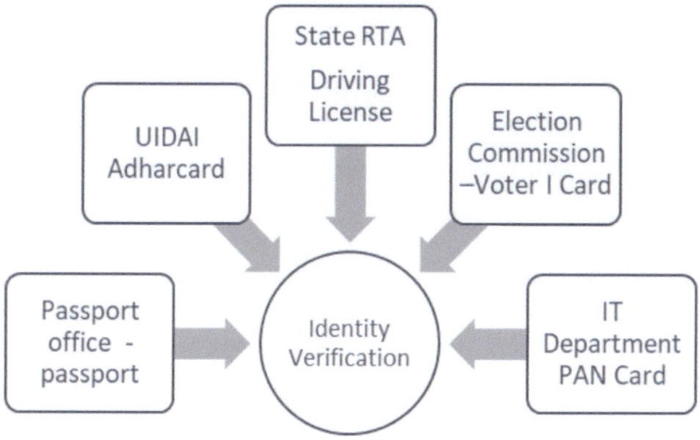

Fig. 1 Proposed blockchain to verify identification from different stack holder [13]

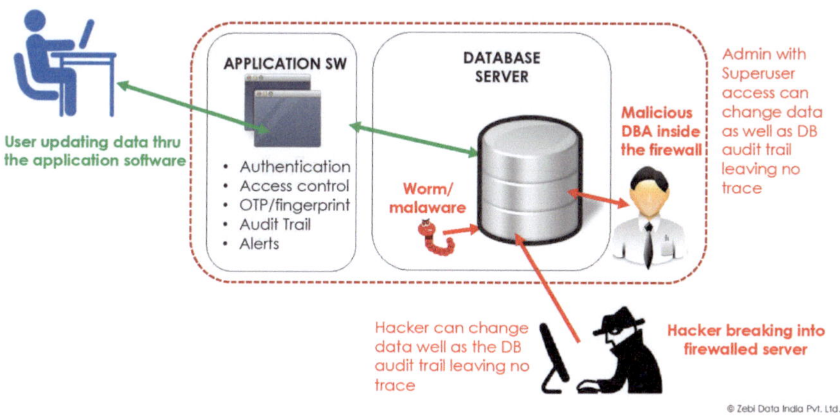

Fig. 2 Tamper vulnerability without blockchain

is treated as legal evidence in courts of law that will speed up resolution of many disputes/cases [14]. At present there are more than 2.1 crore pending cases in Indian courts for property ownership matters [15]. Storing the land registry data on blockchain and treating that record as evidence will automatically resolve many disputes [16]. Any cryptography experienced person from industry or academia can easily verify the hash and cumulative has of the involved blocks and can testify in courts about authenticity of the data.

Use Case 3: Audit trail log on blockchain:

In a well-designed software critical actions by users will be logged into a log file called Audit trail log. That log file is like a CCTV camera in a bank cash room and has crucial information of "what did what" when some fraud is being investigated. Malicious system administrators or hackers that do fraudulent data tampering delete the audit trail log entries of that period to remove traces of their wrongdoing. Those with super user credentials will have permission to delete the audit trail log entries. So, storing the audit trail log on blockchain will make it undeletable even by malicious system administrators and retains the content of the audit trail which helps law enforcement in investigation of cybercrimes [6, 7].

Use Case 4: Inter Agency Data Sharing:

In most countries there will be multiple departments/agencies for intelligence and law enforcement. Each of them is privy to information of suspects, crimes and other intelligence which is stored in their respective software systems. But sharing of this data with fellow agencies is always a big challenge given the bureaucracy and sensitive nature of the data. Solution for this is to use a private blockchain. Each agency would have a node of the blockchain and puts in the data it wants to share into the blockchain. From the same node the agency also can read the data put in by other agencies. In this way without compromising on confidentiality and data leak risk critical data is shared between the agencies in near real time [17].

Use Case 5: Record chain of custody of non-digital evidence:

Evidence collected from crime scene and elsewhere during an investigation is a very critical input to resolve cases. Many investigations are long running and sometimes change hands from one agency to another and from one officer to another. Many times, evidence is collected by a different person and case is investigated by different person. So, there is risk of losing evidence or ignoring evidence. Solution is to record details of each piece of evidence obtained onto a private blockchain as soon as it is collected. It should be done by person that collected the evidence itself. So whenever any officer or agency queries for evidence related to the case, it is available in the blockchain. Maintaining chain of custody of the evidence occurs automatically on the blockchain. In some cases, defense counsels are entitled to view evidence available to prosecution. Blockchain facilitates that as well. This builds up trust as well and preempts allegations of evidence suppression or tampering [18, 19].

Use Case 6: Storage and sharing of digital evidence:

Of late digital evidence is very common: files from confiscated computer, camera footage, CDs content etc. storing this evidence without tampering and proving to the courts that evidence hasn't been tampered is a challenge. Solution is to store the digital evidence on blockchain as soon as it is collected and access it from blockchain thereafter. Given the tamper proofness of blockchain, all parties trust that evidence hasn't been tampered [19].

Use Case 7: Use of Blockchain in evidence Handling:

Blockchain technology, the foundation of cryptocurrencies, enables secure and transparent data management. By leveraging its decentralized and immutable nature, blockchain can facilitate open data submission, automated verification, and tamper-proof record-keeping. This eliminates the need for intermediaries, enhances transparency, and fosters cross-jurisdictional collaboration. Blockchain's role in maintaining the integrity of evidence bolsters public trust in the authenticity of data [20]. Educate decision-makers about blockchain's benefits and its potential to address public safety challenges [21].

2 Related Work

Blockchain forensics helps investigators track stolen assets and identify criminals using the blockchain. A community-based approach can enhance efforts to combat financial crimes on the blockchain [6]. Data marketplaces face challenges like unauthorized data resale and dishonest data ownership claims. TrailChain, a novel blockchain framework, addresses these issues using watermarking and fair payment sharing [7]. This paper proposes a decentralized evidence management framework that utilizes blockchain, IPFS, and smart lockers to ensure evidence security, integrity, and accessibility [10]. LEChain is a blockchain-based evidence management scheme that ensures witness and juror privacy throughout the entire evidence lifecycle. It utilizes short randomizable signatures, fine-grained access control, and a secure voting method to protect privacy [14]. The paper proposes using a blockchain ledger to ensure the authenticity and integrity of investigative actions in security incident response [18]. The paper proposes a permissioned blockchain system based on Hyperledger Fabric for storing and sharing case records, enhancing chain of custody and case data protection [19]. Blockchain technology can help African governments reduce bureaucratic inefficiencies, but its implementation requires institutional readiness and investment in soft and technical skills [20]. This project investigates using blockchain technology to improve the chain of custody in law enforcement evidence management [21].

3 Need of Blockchain Model

Evidence tampering encompasses any act that alters, conceals, or destroys evidence, potentially leading to a breakdown of trust between the criminal justice system and the public.

A chain of custody is necessary to ensure the validity and integrity of the evidence, which is necessary for the successful prosecution of offenders in court [21, 22]. Managing the preservation and collection of digital evidence is challenging due to its fragile nature. Blockchain offers a promising solution to ensure immutability and traceability, but its application in law enforcement requires careful consideration of security.

3.1 BEST Application Using Private Blockchain

BEST (Blockchain based evidence securing & tracking) solution has been developed using a Hyperledger Sawtooth framework which is a private blockchain network as a proof of concept. This application stores all the data on the blockchain from Case creation followed by Seizure/Crime scene management and seized object location tracking.

3.1.1 Updating Seized Objects and Crime Scene

In the BEST app, Investigation officers take a photo of a seized object in crime location and submit it along with Metadata to the app, where the system generates the SHA-256 hash in the backend and is updated in the blockchain for a specific Case ID, while the image will be stored in the AWS S3 bucket. The authorized person also has provision to cross-check and trace evidence from the blockchain network whether it is manipulated or not. By ensuring thorough accountability, blockchain will eliminate the possibility of tampering with criminal records data, effectively preventing misconduct.

3.1.2 Tracking Seized Item Location in Blockchain

In the existing application the timestamp (latitude & longitude) is automatically captured for seized objects and the item movement will be traced by selecting values provided in dropdown (Malkahana, Forensic science lab, Court, Police station & Others (for manual entry)). The BEST application majorly came into the picture, when we talk about allegations like data modifications, exploitation and destroying of evidence or evidence tampering by unauthorized channels. This application safeguards data from malicious attempts to tamper with evidence, ensuring the integrity of information crucial for investigations.

In BEST App, the information is gathered (investigated evidence) in the form of seized objects and crime scenes i.e., digital files and images are stored in a private blockchain network (Sawtooth Hyperledger). Here users have an option to verify the confidential information in the form of proof with the object details. All the details provided in this screen are represented in the form of 'Hash Codes'. The hashcode is generated for digital files, Latitude-longitude values and images. In blockchain technology, distributed ledger databases are replicated and stored across multiple nodes in a peer-to-peer network, ensuring data integrity and consistency.

The primary objective of this application is to improve integrity, trust on evidence gathered during investigation by ensuring transparency on chain of custody and storing the evidence in an immutable (tamper-proof) way and providing convenient 24×7 query access of case evidence to all stakeholders.

In BEST APP internal Blockchain plays an important role in securing Criminal Data. BEST APP with integrated Blockchain technology focuses on five major elements in securing the evidence gathered.

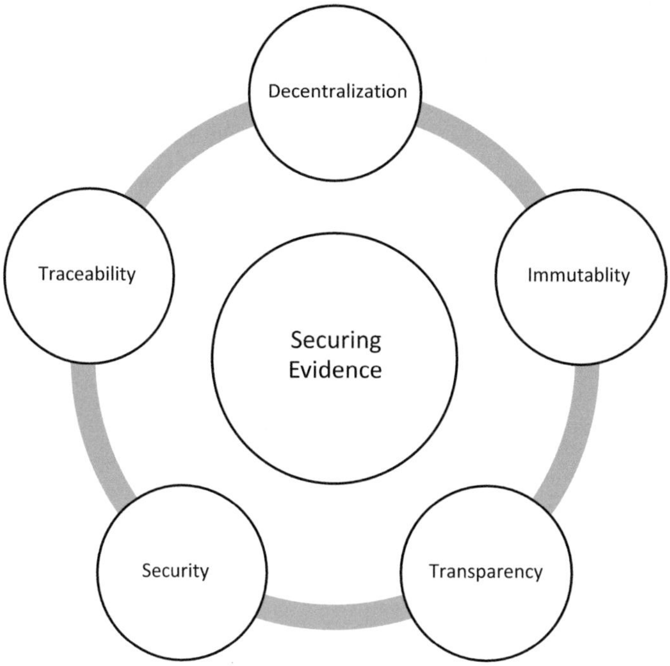

Verification Process

Upon clicking the "verify" button for each file, the system performs the following steps:

- The system checks the Seizure ID associated with the file.
- It then compares the file's Seizure ID with the stored Seizure IDs and calculates hashes in the backend at the storage location.

For the verification process:

- The transaction ID (Committed transaction) is linked to each Seizure ID.
- Using this transaction ID, the system retrieves file hashes from the blockchain.
- The retrieved hashes are compared with the hashes calculated for the files stored in the storage location.

The verification result is as follows:

- If the hashes of the files stored in the storage location have been modified, the verification fails, indicating potential evidence tampering.
- If the hashes match between the blockchain and the storage location, the verification is considered successful.

4 Conclusion

The current evidence management systems used by law enforcement agencies are often paper-based, inefficient, and prone to errors. This can lead to the loss of evidence, contamination, and challenges in establishing a chain of custody. A blockchain-based solution can address these challenges by providing a secure, tamper-proof, and transparent way to store and track evidence. Thus use of Blockchain Technology has a very vast potential for the LEAs in its day to day applications.

5 Future work

Developing standardized blockchain protocols for evidence management checking efficiency and accuracy by comparing with existing evidence management system.

References

1. Ramachandran LS, Bashir MI (2023) A peek into the blockchain technology developments
2. Balcerzak AP et al (2022) Blockchain technology and smart contracts in decentralized governance systems. Adm Sci 12(3):96
3. Shin D, Rice J (2022) Cryptocurrency: a panacea for economic growth and sustainability? A critical review of crypto innovation. Telematics Inform 71:101830
4. Miranda SM, Wang DD, Tian CA (2022) Discursive fields and the diversity-coherence paradox: an ecological perspective on the blockchain community discourse. MIS Q 46:3
5. Kumar P, Sangal AL (2020) Blockchain-based chit fund system: a financial inclusion tool. In: 2020 International conference on smart electronics and communication (ICOSEC). IEEE
6. Salisu S, Filipov V (2023) Blockchain forensics: a modern approach to investigating cybercrime in the age of decentralisation. International conference on cyber warfare and security, vol 18(1)
7. Gupta P et al (2022) TrailChain: traceability of data ownership across blockchain-enabled multiple marketplaces. J Netw Comput Appl 203:103389
8. Pujiyono P et al (2022) The role of blockchain in strengthening indonesia's economic stability. In: International conference for democracy and national resilience 2022 (ICDNR 2022). Atlantis Press
9. Dandurand Y, Colombo G, Passas N (2007) Measures and mechanisms to strengthen international cooperation among prosecution services. Crime Law Soc Chang 47:261–289
10. Onyeashie B et al (2023) An auditable framework for evidence sharing and management using smart lockers and distributed technologies: law enforcement use case
11. Salter MB (2004) Passports, mobility, and security: how smart can the border be? Int Stud Perspect 5(1):71–91
12. Ashbourn J (2014) Biometrics: advanced identity verification: the complete guide. Springer
13. Sengupta A, Saha D (2022) Digital identity: application of blockchain in public data
14. Li M et al (2021) LEChain: A blockchain-based lawful evidence management scheme for digital forensics. Futur Gener Comput Syst 115:406–420
15. Sharma M (2023) India's courts and artificial intelligence: a future outlook. LeXonomica 15(1):99–120

16. Lemieux VL (2017) Evaluating the use of blockchain in land transactions: an archival science perspective. Eur Prop Law J 6(3):392–440
17. Joshi AP, Han M, Wang Y (2018) A survey on security and privacy issues of blockchain technology. Math Found Comput 1:2
18. Olukoya O (2021) Distilling blockchain requirements for digital investigation platforms. J Inf Secur Appl 62:102969
19. Nischitha TS, Shrinivasacharya P (2023) Blockchain-based cyber forensics chain of custody management with hyperledger fabric. Grenze Int J Eng Technol (GIJET) 9(1)
20. Shava E, Mhlanga D (2023) Mitigating bureaucratic inefficiencies through blockchain technology in Africa. Front Blockchain 6:1053555
21. Sudhakar MM et al (2023) Blockchain based evidence management system. J Surv Fish Sci:2631–2636
22. D'Anna T et al (2023) The chain of custody in the era of modern forensics: from the classic procedures for gathering evidence to the new challenges related to digital data. Healthcare, vol 11(5). MDPI

Advanced Home Security Management System Using Raspberry Pi

Charanarur Panem, Kavita Ponnuraj, Naveen Kumar Chaudhary, Lokesh Chouhan, Laishram Hemanta Singh, and Gundu Srinivasa Rao

Abstract With the advent of IoT, rapid technological advancements in the realm of smart systems are now the norm. The goal of the IoT is to create a world where it is possible to operate any gadget from afar. The adoption of this strategy may likely increase home safety. As part of this project, we designed a system that would send an email to the property owner as well as any authorized users whenever a human incursion detector observes motion in the region of a door. An Internet of things (IoT) equipped home security system will generally consist of a Raspberry Pi 3 computer, Pi camera, PIR sensor, microphone, and an internet connection. When it detects motion, the system will snap a photo, which it will then upload to a database for subsequent analysis to identify whether the person or entity in the image is a recognized one. If neither the user nor any other registered members identify the person, the system will send an email to the user with a photo, video, and audio recording of the unknown person. If the system is successful in identifying the individual, a photo of them will be taken and added to the database. If the system finds any activity that is out of the norm in the neighborhood of the door, it will inform the user by email. The design of the solution safeguards the IoT platform against unwanted access.

Keywords Embedded system · Raspberry PI · Surveillance system · Motion detection · Tracking · Video processing

---

C. Panem · K. Ponnuraj (✉) · N. K. Chaudhary · L. Chouhan · L. H. Singh
Department of Cyber Security and Digital Forensic, National Forensic Sciences University, Goa Campus, Ponda, Goa, India
e-mail: ponnuraj.kavita@gmail.com

G. S. Rao
Department of Digital Forensics, School of Science, Malla Reddy University, Hyderabad, India

B. N. Gohil et al. (eds.), *Information Security, Privacy and Digital Forensics*,
Lecture Notes in Electrical Engineering 1423,
https://doi.org/10.1007/978-981-96-9443-3_23

1 Introduction

The Internet of Things has made lightning-fast innovations in smart systems the standard, rather than the exception. The ultimate aim of the Internet of Things is to make remote control of any device a reality. The adoption of this strategy may likely increase home safety. The need for video surveillance systems is only going to become more urgent as we go further into the twenty-first century. People are naturally interested in the possibilities of remote watching via the use of the internet in connection with any particular surveillance gadget. In the past, a guard's job consisted mostly of sitting alone in a room and watching over the various security systems. Even if it had been possible to view the movie many more once, doing so may not have been the best use of one's time. Researchers and scientists must establish techniques for doing so, which will ultimately result in an improvement in world safety [1].

Having a video-capturing system that can both alert staff in the event of an invasion and record footage of the intruder is crucial in settings as diverse as commercial buildings, schools, hospitals, casinos, and storage facilities. Thanks to recent developments in video surveillance technology, you can now access your remote security camera from any internet-connected computer or smartphone, no matter where you happen to be in the world [2].

This is the category that includes things like IP cameras and closed-circuit television (DVR) systems. Even though this technology is incredible, it has been found that the expenses associated with its implementation are too expensive, especially for low-volume residential applications [3].

For new technologies to develop and mature, they must be financially and logistically accessible. This will help their growth. The Raspberry Pi can fulfil both criteria since it is both affordable and powerful, and it can be customized with a variety of modules. Possible applications include motor speed control, automated lighting, security systems, and VPN servers [4–6].

2 Related Work

Modern home alarms need electricity to set up. Since 1853, wealthy individuals and businesses protected themselves with electromagnetic alarms. Electromagnetic cable signals triggered the alarm. This signal was conveyed via window and door magnetic contacts. Creativity among security officers stopped more break-ins.

Situational security matters now. Home security systems are being installed by more homes to deter burglars. A security system may make business and leisure travelers feel safer. CCTV is restricted geographically [7]. Control room operators must observe cameras. Since the administration provider must preserve the recorded video even when no human activity is detected, current anti-robbery security systems are expensive. Because administration is needed. An intelligent surveillance system that only records when it senses human movement is one option. Thus, storage capacity is reduced, making the system cheaper over time. The design improves internet security and saves space and money. Closed-circuit television cameras are used for "surveillance" [8, 9]. Internet of Things (IoT) automatically connects everyday events to the Internet, allowing people, things, and things to interact. Actuators like smartphones, sensors, and Internet TVs may be appliances [10]. These devices' electrical components, software, hardware, and system communication allow data collection and sharing.

In addition to providing a higher degree of security over the web, the proposed architecture requires less storage space and costs less money. In the study, a variety of various approaches to population counting have been developed [10, 11]. A variety of image processing methods and approaches for human counting have been proposed in the literature [12, 13], however all of these techniques and approaches have faults that present themselves, such as shadows, overlapping, and occlusion. To alleviate some of these issues, Rossi and Bozzoli [10] and Sexton et al. [14] developed a method in which the camera is positioned vertically, as if on a floor plane. Researchers in the literature [15] presented an adaptive background mixing approach for enhancing visual tracking in real time while also detecting shadows. The proposed framework provides an intelligent and comprehensive home security system. When unauthorized individuals approach, this system sends text and email alerts to permitted users. It also performs pre-programmed human inspections and has the capacity to turn off power-hungry items using appliance-specific coding. The proposed system is capable of a range of tasks, including motion and person detection, video recording to local storage, email notifications, and the provision of brief video services.

This company was founded to provide a cost-effective, effective, and cutting-edge monitoring solution. This project will establish a microcomputer-based security system. System CPU will be Raspberry Pi. An unauthorized person on the premises will be recorded. Building management should get a photo-attached email.

Video intrusion detection is another project component. This improves security. The camera quickly recognizes new items and tracks body parts. When something new emerges, the camera watches.

The initiative is constructing a security system that detects movements, examines photos, and emails and SMSes building owners. It will employ the Raspberry Pi, a single-board computer.

To learn how a Raspberry Pi can email a mail hub.

This project will construct a Raspberry Pi surveillance system.

Building a real-time moving object video analysis system.

This project sends a snapshot of the affected area to an administrator's device via the internet for real-time remote monitoring. System requires Raspberry Pi, camera, motion sensor, and internet. A remote monitoring surveillance system model is their goal. The system is visible worldwide.

This project's security system lets owners monitor their homes. Property owners need worldwide monitoring. It reduces minimum-security system expenses but is less effective than CCTV. Cheap and simple locking is now accessible for smaller homes. The basic real-time monitoring system will include a motion detector, camera, Raspberry Pi devices, and a dependable computer program.

3 Proposed System

Motion and image-based security systems that receive alerts may be made using Raspberry Pi computers. This device records and monitors images and motions. The message must be online and include a time graph. After installation, consumers may monitor their homes almost anywhere. Talent will be theirs.

Its security mechanism will be constructed using microcomputers. Soon, this mechanism will be implemented. If these conditions are met, the Raspberry Pi becomes the CPU. If an unauthorized person enters, a camera will start recording. Both will activate simultaneously. Plans call for emailing the building management. This email will include content and a photo.

The graphic above depicts five separate system components. Building these modules requires Raspberry Pi, Pi Camera, PIR Sensor, LED, Bread Board, Resistor (1k), Connecting wires and Power supply.

Many concerns were examined before implementing surveillance equipment. Given its cost, this technology is concerning. Everything is possible with the Raspberry Pi. The system may include a proxy server, temperature control, and automatic lighting. All these features are possible. Why is a Raspberry Pi-based home security system necessary? Internet-connected Raspberry Pi security and IP camera systems may warn. Custom systems are possible. This may happen. Conversations occur concurrently. IP cameras are too expensive for many. Because they're costly. Now we'll stick to these boundaries. They may work in industrial goods firms, the military, law enforcement, and other organizations, according to the material.

Arduino security systems are cheaper than Raspberry Pi ones, but they may fail. In certain cases, connecting cameras, displays, motion detectors, mice, and keyboards is challenging. SD cards allow Raspberry Pi customization. Arduino microcontrollers use GSM modems to send internet data. The internet allows this. Raspberry Pi connects online. Buying and installing CCTV costs more than other items. To make things worse, TNP/IP requires a DVR. DVRs may be costly. Low-income families may not be able to afford this approach in the present economy.

Helping design, build, and install a home security system may reduce burglaries. It will reduce burglaries. The setup involves a GSM modem and Arduino. Both parts are listed. Home use is possible. Intruder detection and reaction using microcontrollers. Even minor room movements may be detected by PIR/PIR sensors. The sensors detect complete motions. The system may SMS the property owner or a user-selected number after a break-in.

Security alarm systems include several parts. Examples include PIR sensors, Arduino Uno microcontrollers, and SIM900A GSM/GPRS modems. The system works on 12 VDC and 2 A, so any battery or power source will work. The system runs on these specifications.

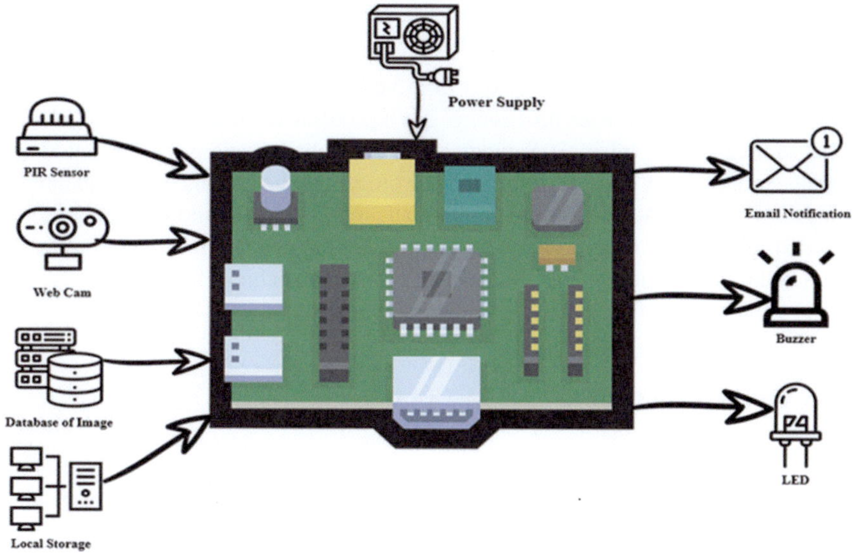

Fig. 1 Raspberry Pi based home security system

Figure 1 demonstrates a block-based system. A operating computer may sleep. "Shorting" the Arduino microcontroller's PIR terminals sends warning signals to mobile devices. This may reassure the customer. This device can't transmit trespasser photos. A warning is issued. Monitoring monitors receive surveillance footage. The device supports public, private, mesh, and public networks.

A camera and monitor are connected by coaxial cable in the simplest arrangement. Most simple setup. A display powers the camera. After shooting so many images quickly, it may be impossible to recognize them. Because the camera takes several photographs. A safe computer may receive data via optical fiber or coaxial cable. Computers receive data both ways. These systems are continuously monitored by security. Searching for strange conduct. These systems alert parties of security breaches.

Security video is recorded on VCRs and DVRs. A DVR may transmit digital video over a data network. Simplify remote management and monitoring. IP surveillance permits CCTV networking. IP surveillance cameras. These cameras record and share video. DCC systems may be seen and managed remotely over the internet. All network users can see camera footage. Since everyone can see videos.

IP-based storage may reduce a company's physical archive demands. Authorities often share mugshots shortly after production due of their ease of distribution. The ease of diffusion led to this conclusion. Warning systems enable timely notifications.

The new technology will help low-income households monitor their houses, but it won't replace CCTV and IP security cameras in big business settings. This aids multi-site enterprises. The camera used here is affordable compared to others. The low cost of Raspberry Pi-compatible hardware is another factor. Simple security system wiring is straightforward.

Picture parameters may be derived from an image or video frame. Some photo attributes may remain after processing. My approach is “image processing,” and “image processing” explains it. Seeing or comprehending previously hidden qualities is image processing’s purpose. Digital image processing has advanced human motion analysis. This work advances human motion analysis. Human emotions are detected in video clips using movements analysis and person detection. Human motion is compared to other components. Sequence analysis can achieve this.

3.1 Image Processing

Image processing may improve the quality of raw photos from satellite, spacecraft, and space probe cameras and sensors, as well as ordinary photography. This technique is widely used in surveillance. Two techniques to image processing exist:

Image blurring using a Gaussian Function, often known as Gaussian smoothing or Gaussian blur, is popular. Several names are used for this procedure. Noise and finer characteristics are decreased. This approach creates smooth blur, like a translucent screen, unlike the bokeh effect, which is made by an out-of-focus lens or an object’s shadow under normal illumination shown in Fig. 2.

This contrasts with the bokeh effect of an out-of-focus lens. Computer vision algorithms may enhance the look of variable-sized visual components using Gaussian smoothing. One-dimensional Gaussian equation:

$$G(x) = \frac{1}{\sqrt{2\pi\sigma^2}} e^{-\frac{x^2}{2\sigma^2}}$$

“Grayscale” is a range of non-color tones. Black emits and reflects no light. White absorbs or reflects every visible wavelength equally. For transmitted light, artists use varied intensities of red, green, and blue; for reflected light, cyan, magenta, and yellow.

Each of the three color channels in transmitted light is represented by a number between 0 and 255, or in binary, between 00000000 and 11111111. A computer screen shows this. R = G = B establishes the relationship between grayscale RGB pixel red, green, and blue values. The brightness of primary colors correlates to grey lightness. R = G = B = 0 and 00000000 symbolizes black and white. 8 bits are used to represent the grey level in binary; hence this imaging method is called 8-bit grayscale.

By settling on a suitable threshold, grayscale pictures may be transformed into binary representations. By using a threshold, we may choose just the picture pixels that belong to the photographed topic (either text or other line image data such as graphs, or maps). Even though the data are in binary form, each pixel has its distinct

Fig. 2 Video analysis

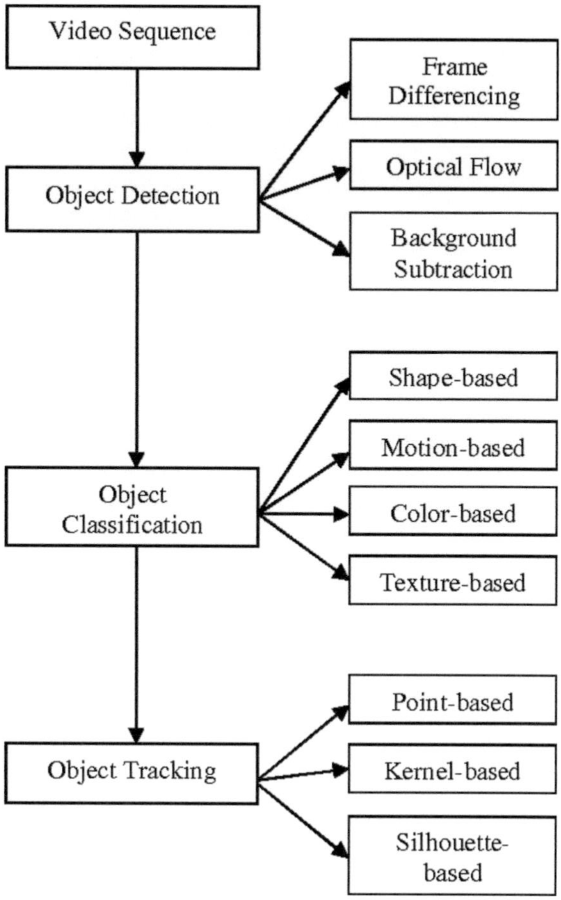

brightness value associated with it. When an image is binarized, its foreground and background pixels are assigned separate values.

The above can be achieved through the implementation of the algorithm.

3.2 *Resources*

It is very necessary to have three monitoring and alerting components at the same time in order to guarantee that integrated real-time surveillance performs in the suitable manner. There is a possibility that you will find out that this place has photo processing software, hardware, notifications, and a method for addressing items that have vanished without a trace. There are two characteristics of Raspberry Pi that are regarded to be the most important benefits, and the following quick overview will concentrate on those two characteristics. The production of both digital and physical material at the same time is required for both of these processes.

The modules of the system are comprised of seven distinct components, of which the following are examples: A Raspberry Pi B+ model is referring to proposed work. A Raspberry Pi camera module, an infrared motion detector, a MicroSD card, and an RJ45 Ethernet cable are all components that are included in the kit. These components are all included in the package. Additionally, for your convenience, the packaging includes a USB power chord attached to the device.

For the purpose of bringing this project to a successful end, the Raspberry Pi B+ will be used. The earlier versions featured a bigger number of GPIO pins, however this specific version has a greater number of USB ports than the previous versions had. The marketing of the product was the responsibility of this individual division.

In order to produce the images that were developed, the Raspbian "Wheezy" operating system was used. ARM is the foundation upon which Raspberry Pi's operating system is constructed, which is the reason why it is compatible with Raspberry Pi. This operating system is not only compatible with a wide variety of platforms, but it also comes with tools that may be used to create applications.

The Raspberry Pi was first linked to the computer that was running Putty via the use of RJ45 Ethernet before the system was turned on. Following that, the Micro SD card was likewise inserted into the slot. At last, the system was activated and started up. The Raspberry Pi may be remotely controlled by Windows PCs by using Putty, which is a Secure Shell client. This allows for the Raspberry Pi to be controlled remotely. It was suggested that Putty take use of the intellectual property that Raspberry Pi has as a result of this event. An alternative that was available was the ability to manually enter an IP address into Windows. This was one of the options. One of the effects was a delay in response. The Raspberry Pi was productive, which takes us to the last statement of our discussion.

You will learn how to connect your Raspberry Pi to the internet, including the methods that are listed below: To add insult to injury, in order for the Raspberry Pi to be able to communicate with other network devices and execute Python applications, it was essential for it to be connected to the internet. For the purpose of accomplishing this goal, a structure that is comparable to the one that is explained below was used and shown in Fig. 3.

Because the broadcast router assigns IP addresses using Dynamic Host Configuration Protocol (DHCP), you'll have to change the IP address on the Pi. The command sudo nano /etc./network/interfaces has to be used in order to make the changes to the file.

Pi Camera is only compatible with Raspberry Pi systems. Connected to the Raspberry Pi's high-speed port using the CSI-2 electrical interface. The camera was turned on and set up using the command line interface (CLI) of the Raspberry Pi. Do a "sudo apt-get upgrade" to install the latest changes from APT-get-update to "anything."

System restart was necessary to complete the reconfiguration. Consequently, the camera is capable of capturing both still and moving images. You can get up to 1080p recording from the 5-megapixel sensor. It was confirmed by the subsequent command that the camera was functioning properly. Using the image.png file is as

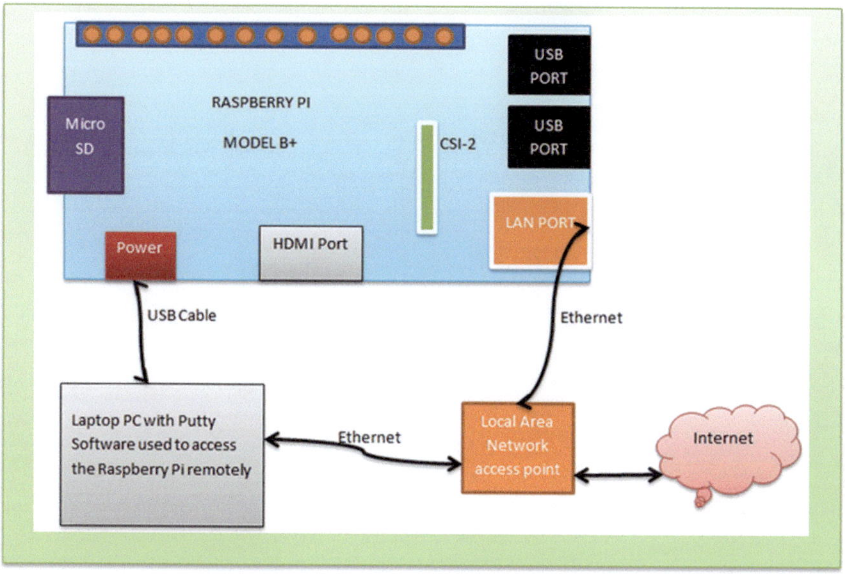

Fig. 3 Internet setup architecture

simple as running sudo raspistill -o. The image.png file will have a three-second movie automatically saved to it by using this command.

The principal motion detector in the building was a passive infrared (PIR) sensor. Within the structure, the sensor was set up. Applied to the overall management of the system. We utilized an HC501SR passive infrared sensor for this investigation. Seven meters is the detection range from a 140° vantage point. The amount of time spent waiting may be adjusted anywhere from 0 to 16 s. The temperature range that is considered acceptable is 253–323 K. It got all of its power from the Raspberry Pi itself since it was connected to the 5 V DC supply port on the Pi. The result of it was wired up to the input on the GPIO.

4 Technical Information

A passive infrared (PIR) sensor was meant to control its operation. This device's connection to GPIO was accomplished with the use of a resistor (1k). As can be seen in the picture below, all of the components of the system were connected shown in Fig. 3, 4.

The following flowchart was used in the process of documenting the project plan for the security systems. The warning is the last step in a series of actions that starts with an invasion of privacy and ends with a warning. Python was used for the coding of this method. The fundamental flowchart of the whole system is shown in Fig. 5.

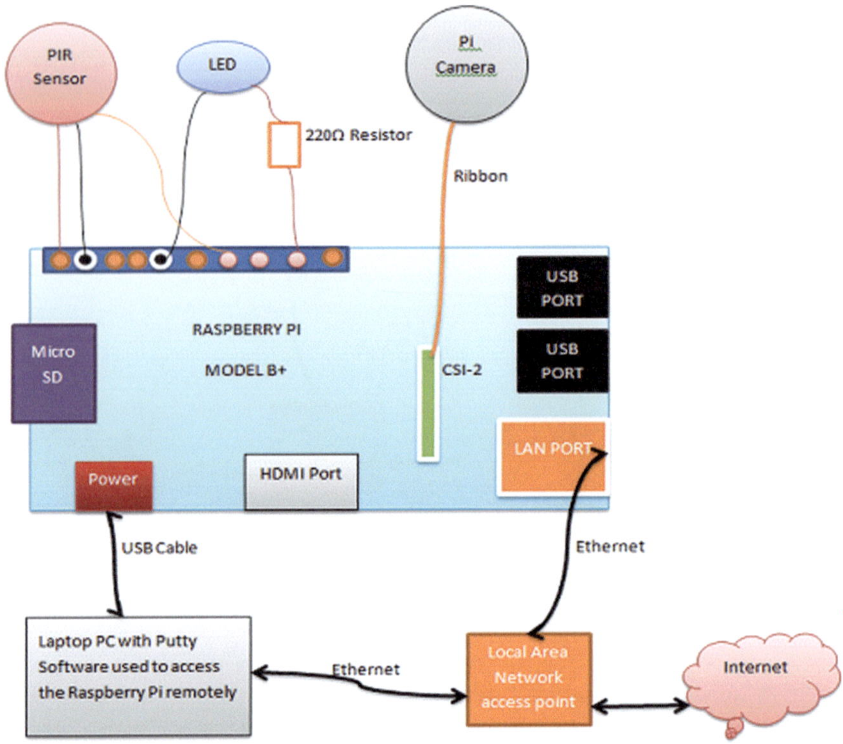

Fig. 4 Hardware architecture of the security systems based on raspberry Pi

Specifically, you had to do the actions that are listed below: importing already-created Python packages and libraries into the project. The appropriate operation of the interconnected pieces is helped to be guaranteed by these precompiled libraries.

Configuration and fine-tuning of the Raspberry Pi Camera.

The channel numbering of the BCM was used in the process of configuring the GPIOs and initializing their pins. While the passive infrared pin channel was utilized for reading, the LED channel was configured for drive and write operations.

Simply type GPIO. Input into the terminal will allow you to read the status of any GPIO pin or channel.

To provide a command to a particular GPIO pin channel, you need to type GPIO. output (channel, status).

After the system was designed to send an email notification to a subscriber, the letter could be sent. The MIME (Multipurpose Internet Mail Extension) software was used in the creation of the attachment. MIME enables you to convey and receive non-textual material such as music, video, and applications in addition to text. Change the settings for your email. The Raspberry Pi communicated with the main hub over SMTP to transmit an email.

Pseudocode:

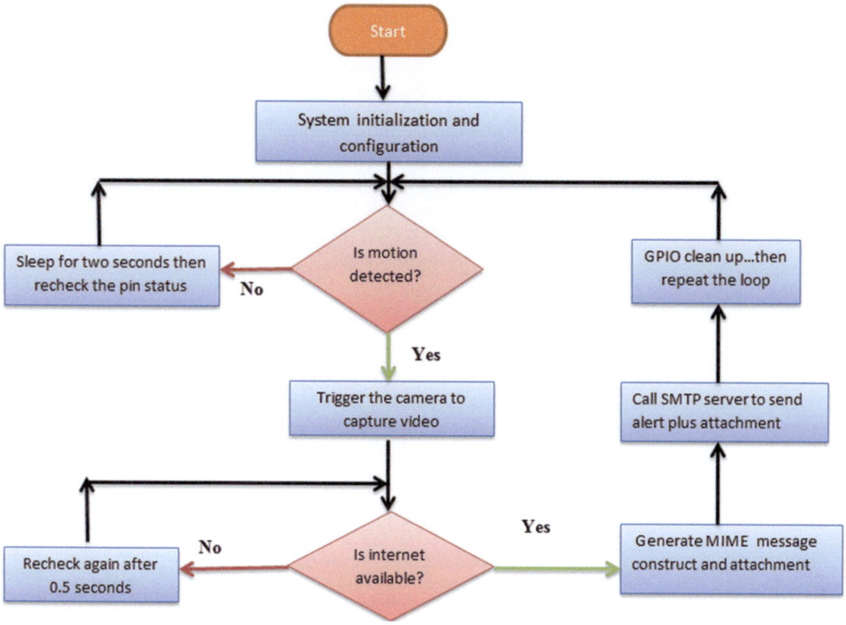

Fig. 5 Flowchart implementation of the security system

After the machine has been restarted, the boot IP should be used to establish a connection to a mail host.

Determine the state of the GPIO pins. The inactive status for the system is indicated by GPIO pin 13 being low. Unless the pin is at a HIGH level. It comes as a nice shock.

When the input GPIO is HIGH, pin 13 will be HIGH (interrupt event). LED flickers. Start Pi Camera.

A 10 s video clip is recorded and saved by the camera.

The Raspberry Pi's internet connectivity is investigated by the system.

When conversing with others online, be sure to send emails to your mail host. Check back in 5 s to see whether you're connected to the internet again.

After setting the pin on the PIR sensor to LOW, wait 2 s before checking the sensor's output. Come back to the main loop.

Therefore, Through the accumulation of codes,

The Python script that runs the flowchart algorithm was written when the Raspberry Pi was powered up and the mkdir program was used to establish a directory on the device. The directory received a new file after being touched and used sudo chmod +x to make the file executable (filename).

After the editor was prepared, the Python script was written with the help of the nano command. Enter Python followed by the sudo prompt to run the script.

OpenCv is a robust software tool that can analyze both video and still photos. Check out the flowchart for a breakdown of the processing phases. Image thresholding makes it possible to recognize and follow motion in video streams. OpenCv-Python

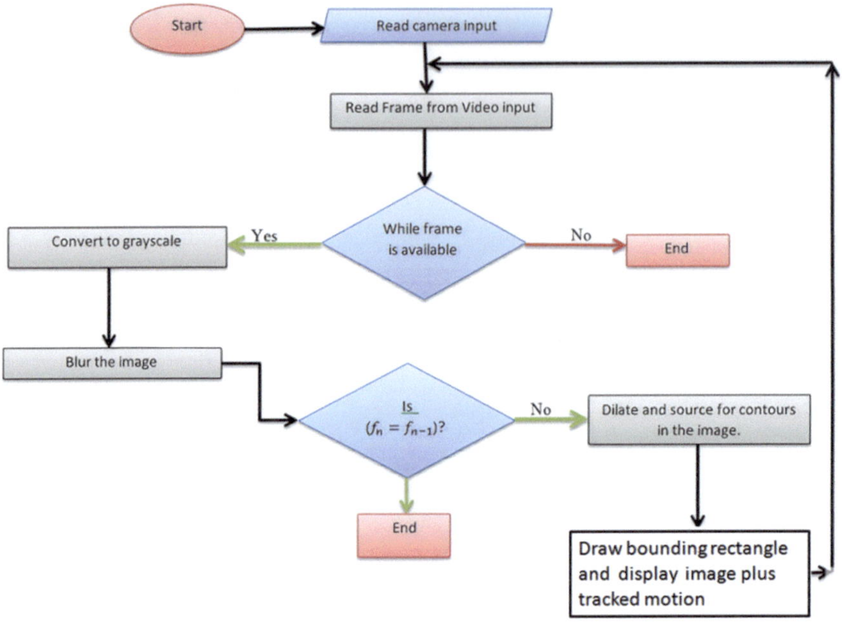

Fig. 6 Flowchart of motion detection and tracking algorithm

was the solution for us since Python does not support video processing. Up until recently, Python did not have a video library. We were provided with a framework for managing images via OpenCV. The flowchart that may be seen below was used and shown in Fig. 6.

Final Pseudocode as follows,

i. Turn on the camera and adjust its settings so that it may capture live video feeds.
ii. Select a single frame from the motion picture that is now playing. If the photo is taken, you should go on as before.

    Providing directions on how to carry out the steps.

    If that's not the case, come to a complete stop. Try something completely out of the question and turn that image into the one you're looking at right now.

    Create a black-and-white rendition of the picture that was taken. Applying a Gaussian blur to the grayscale picture is the next step that has to be taken. In order to continue with Step 2, snap another picture.
iii. Check to see that you have at least the required number of moving pixels.
iv. Draw a box that contains the active area in its entirety.

It is possible to approximate motion as either discrete or instantaneous displacements in pictures by using sequences of ordered photographs. This may be achieved by using the sequences in the appropriate order. One of the procedures that are used for optical flow characterisation is the calculation of the change in voxel position between two photographs that were acquired at intervals t and δt. When differential methods are used, local Taylor series approximations of the visual signal and partial derivatives with respect to spatial and temporal coordinates are utilised. All of these methods are employed in order to carry out measurements.

5 Result and Discussion

After adjusting the sensitivity of the PIR sensor, we discovered the following: Maximum sensitivity.

Screen shot 1 Distance in (m) Alert sent OFF

After the Python script was executed successfully, the data presented in Tables 1, 2 and 3 was obtained. It would be possible to demonstrate how variations in the sensitivity level of the PIR sensor cause a corresponding shift in its detection range. The enhanced sensitivity of the sensor permits it to observe a more extensive area of the surroundings.

Based on the data presented in Tables 1, 2 and 3, it is conceivable to suggest that the PIR sensor functioned as the primary motion detector and, therefore, the initial barrier. Simply put, for the correct operation of the other modules, the PIR GPIO pin must be in the HIGH state. Should this sensor malfunction, the overall operation of the security system would be compromised.

The email message that was transmitted to a mail host via the SMTP protocol is displayed in the sent notifications section of the website.

We developed a potential security solution with the assistance of Raspberry Pi processors. The system is comprised of three distinct components: an email alert platform, a Raspberry Pi camera, and a passive infrared (PIR) motion detector. Due to its inadequate central processing unit (CPU) capabilities, the Raspberry Pi was incapable of performing any type of image processing. Further sensor installations are planned in the event that it is determined that they are required. Thus far, we have only been able to successfully link PIR motion sensors and temperature sensors, and as a consequence, we are only able to see data that pertains to these two categories. We plan to deploy more sensors to monitor atmospheric conditions, smoke levels,

Table 1 Results for maximum sensitivity of the PIR sensor

Distance in (m)	L.E.D. (ON/OFF)	Alert sent	Reference
15	OFF	NO	–
10	OFF	NO	–
8	OFF	NO	–
6	ON	YES	Screen shot 1
5	ON	YES	Screen shot 1
4	ON	YES	Screen shot 1
3	ON	YES	Screen shot 1

Sensitivity = Medium

Table 2 Results for medium sensitivity of the PIR sensor

Distance in (m)	L.E.D. (ON/OFF)	Alert sent	Reference
15	OFF	NO	–
10	OFF	NO	–
8	OFF	NO	–
6	ON	YES	–
5	ON	YES	Screen shot 1
4	ON	YES	Screen shot 1
3	ON	YES	Screen shot 1

	L.E.D. (ON/OFF)	Alert sent	Reference
15	OFF	NO	–
10	OFF	NO	–
8	OFF	NO	–
6	OFF	NO	–
5	ON	YES	Screen shot 1
4	ON	YES	Screen shot 1
3	ON	YES	Screen shot 1

Sensitivity = Low

Table 3 Results for the low sensitivity of the PIR

Distance in (m)	L.E.D. (ON/OFF)	Alert sent	Reference
15	OFF	NO	–
10	OFF	NO	–
8	OFF	NO	–
6	OFF	NO	–
5	OFF	NO	–
4	OFF	NO	–
3	ON	YES	Screen shot 1

and other variables. A keypad that controls the alarm's on/off status is something we're considering installing. Once we have pinpointed the intruder's position, we will likely notify the proper authorities by text message.

6 Conclusions and Further Scope

A Raspberry Pi-based security solution was developed by the group. A passive infrared (PIR) motion detector, a Raspberry Pi camera, and an email alert system are all included in the system. Unfortunately, the Raspberry Pi's limited CPU capability meant that image processing was out of the question. To complete this part, we will explore potential additions that may be made to subsequent editions of the report. The capabilities that have been established are the very minimum of what a customer should be able to expect reasonably. In the future, the use of new circuit boards will make it possible for us to store photographs in a database and boost the processing speed. We may choose to set up more sensors. We have only succeeded in connecting PIR motion sensors and temperature sensors at this point, and as a result, we are only able to see data that is relevant to these two categories. We aim to increase the number of sensors that we employ to collect data on the weather, air quality, smoke, and other factors. There is a possibility that we may install a keypad that can be used to activate and deactivate the alarm. After we have determined the intruder's precise location, we will likely send a text message to the appropriate authorities. In addition, the cost of these products is quite near to two thousand dollars (USD). But to make it accessible to a large number of people, we will have to reduce the price.

References

1. Tekilu D, et al. (2021) Implementation of Iot based smart surveillance security system using face recognition. Adaliya J 10(1). https://doi.org/10.37896/aji10.1/013
2. Sanjay A, et al. (2018) Security surveillance and home automation system using IoT. EAI Endorsed Trans Smart Cities:165963. https://doi.org/10.4108/eaij.21-7-2020.165963
3. Stolojescu-Crisan C, et al. (2022) Access control and surveillance in a smart home. High Confid Comput 2(1):100036. https://doi.org/10.1016/jn.hcc.2021.100036
4. Stolojescu-Crisan C, et al. (2021) An IoT-based smart home automation system. Sensors 21(11):3784. https://doi.org/10.3390/si21113784
5. Taiwo O, Ezugwu AE (2021) Internet of things-based intelligent smart home control system. In: Aman MN (ed) Security and communication networks, vol 2021, pp 1–17. https://doi.org/10.11556/2021/9928254
6. Sefat MS, Khan AAM, Shahjahan M. Implementation of vision based intelligent home automation and security system. In: 3rd international conference on informatics, electronics and vision 2014
7. Domb M (2019) Smart home systems based on internet of things. IoT and smart home automation [working title]. IntecheOpen. https://doi.org/10.5772/intecheopen.84894
8. Rani R, Lavanya S, Poojitha B (2018) IoT based home security system using raspberry pi with email and voice alert. Int JS Adv Res Comput Sci Softw Eng ISSN 2277-128X, vol 8(4)
9. Prashad S, et al. (2014) Smart surveillance monitoring system using raspberry PI and PIR sensor. Int J Comput Sci Inf Technol 5(6):7107–7109
10. Govinda K, Prasad SK, Susheel SR (2014) Intrusion detection system for smart home using laser rays. Int J Sci Res Dev (IJSRD) 2(3):176–178
11. Karri V, Daniel Lim JS (2005) Method and device to communicate via SMS after a security intrusion. In: 1st international confernce on sensing technology Palmerston North New Zealand, pp 21–23
12. Jayashri B, Arvind S (2013) Design and implementation of security for smart home based on GSM technology. Int J Smart Home 7:201–208
13. Jyoti N, Vardhan KV (2016) Design and implementation of real time security surveillance system using IoT. In: Communication and electronics systems (ICCES), international conference. IEEE
14. Tiwari S (2012) Comparison of face recognition algorithms on dummy faces. Int J Multimed Its Appl
15. Wang Q (2017) Face detection for privacy protected images. Institute for Electrical and Electronic Engineers

Review on Dark Secrets of Practical iOS Malware Analysis

Jay Gajjar and Ramya Shah

Abstract As iOS devices become more common in both personal and professional settings, targeted attacks and sophisticated iOS malware have increased in frequency. In order to improve knowledge, investigate practical detection methods, and suggest mitigation strategies to protect iOS users' privacy and security, this review paper provides a thorough analysis of iOS malware. It covers a range of topics related to iOS malware, including types, methods of propagation, and security issues that analysts encounter as a result of Apple's strict regulations. In addition, the review paper analyses real-world examples, explores sophisticated detection techniques, and offers helpful suggestions for reducing the risk of iOS malware. This paper will be providing security experts and researchers with crucial insights to tackle the growing threat of iOS malware by providing this thorough analysis.

Keywords iOS · Malware · Attacks · Threats · Classification · Analysis

1 Introduction

iOS malware detections have surged by 57% in Q1 2023, according to McAfee, indicating a growing threat landscape for iOS devices. Symantec's research revealed that 88% of iOS malware in 2022 used sophisticated obfuscation tactics, demonstrating the complexity of malware. This highlights the need for comprehensive malware analysis to stay ahead of evolving threats. The sophistication of iOS malware presents a significant challenge for conventional security solutions. Furthermore, 83% of iOS devices in 2022 had at least one harmful app, highlighting the need for comprehensive research to identify and mitigate risks. Overall, the complexity of iOS malware poses a significant threat to iOS devices. iOS devices are a prime target for malware, which can pose significant threats to users' privacy. A survey by Bitdefender revealed that

J. Gajjar (✉) · R. Shah
Cyber Security Researcher at School of Cyber Security & Digital Forensics, National Forensic Sciences University, Gandhinagar, Gujarat, India
e-mail: jaygajjar93@gmail.com

B. N. Gohil et al. (eds.), *Information Security, Privacy and Digital Forensics*,
Lecture Notes in Electrical Engineering 1423,
https://doi.org/10.1007/978-981-96-9443-3_24

42% of iOS users are concerned about malware compromising their privacy. This includes sensitive data like financial information, personal contact details, and login credentials. To safeguard users, it is crucial to analyze the features and actions of these apps to identify and stop their installation. The average cost of a data breach in the US is $9.5 million, and businesses can mitigate risks by proactively detecting and mitigating risks through in-depth malware analysis. By proactively detecting and mitigating risks, security professionals can create plans to safeguard user data on iOS devices. iOS and Android are widely used smartphone systems, but both are susceptible to malevolent attackers. Android is more vulnerable to malware assaults and security lapses compared to iOS. As a result, Android is the top choice in the study sector. To address these issues, researchers should focus on device integrity, application privacy, hardware security, source code, and authentication techniques.

Robust compliance with CCPA and GDPR regulations is crucial for organizations to ensure data protection and privacy standards. By analyzing iOS malware, organizations can identify and mitigate threats, demonstrating their commitment to data protection and avoiding fines.

2 iOS Security Model with its Background

iOS is a secure operating system that unifies hardware, software, and services into a single entity, providing optimal security. The iOS secure boot chain ensures the integrity and unaltered execution of underlying software. The boot ROM, or hardware root of trust, executes unchangeable code and contains the Apple Root CA public key. The next-generation bootloader, iBoot, verifies and launches the iOS kernel. Applications are crucial components of iOS devices, as digital signing and verification are done on both firmware and hardware before execution.

- **Apple-issued certificates**: iOS requires executable code and apps over three years old to be signed with an Apple-issued certificate, which developers must authenticate through the iOS Developer Experience Programme before submitting to the app store for final testing.
- **App sandbox**: No other software can access or modify the data that any third-party programme stores because each one operates separately from the others. These programmes run on the privileged user mobile, and the OS partition is read-only during their operation.
- **Other security mechanisms**: iOS's OS and hardware features include file execution protection and address space layout randomization to prevent memory corruption and prevent injection. Apple's App Review Guidelines apply to all apps released through the App Store, categorized into over 100 policies. These policies cover areas like location, advertising, functionality, metadata, violence, privacy, and religion. Apps may be rejected for violating rules, having hidden functionality, using private APIs, reading or writing data outside the container, or downloading external code. Vulnerabilities such as misusing services, hiding private API calls,

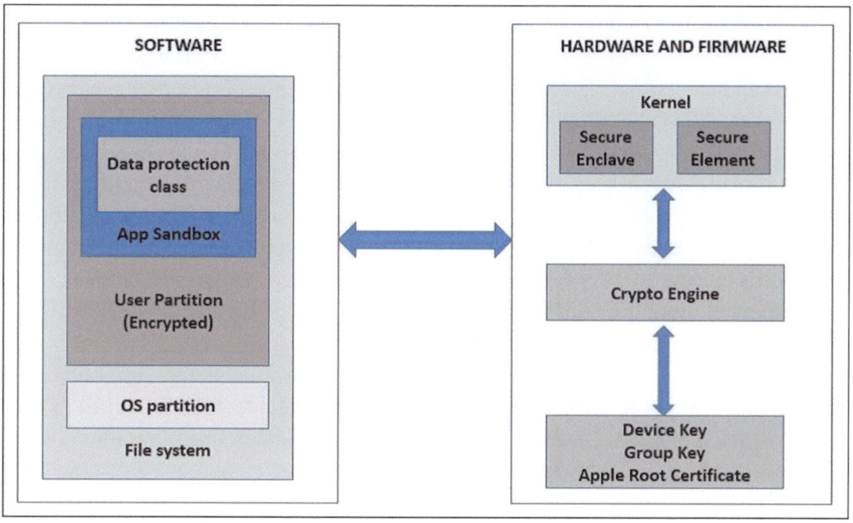

Fig. 1 iOS security model

and illegally distributing the official Apple SDK (Xcode) have been verified during the review process. The iOS Security Model Background provides a comprehensive and robust system for securing Apple's portable devices. Established in a combination of hardware and computer program security measures, it guarantees data protection, app judgment, and client privacy. Key components include secure boot, hardware-based encryption, app sandboxing, and code-signing. This multi-layered approach is designed to protect iOS devices against malware, unauthorized access, and data breaches. It has been instrumental in creating a reputation for iOS as a secure and privacy-centric platform [1]; (Fig. 1).

3 Evaluation and Classification of iOS Malware

Malware families have been a significant factor in malware sales, with several families emerging in the past. State-sponsored malware families first surfaced in 2012, 2014, and 2015. However, the number of malware families has significantly grown since 2014, with subterranean malware families having the highest number in 2015. This study highlights the importance of understanding the distribution of malware families in the industry [1, 2].

- **Devices**: The majority of malware targets jailbroken devices, with non-jailbroken devices being affected by 30.5%. The likelihood of malware infection increases with jailbreaking. However, only 8.3% of malware targets iOS devices, compared to 5.5% for non-jailbroken devices. To protect against threats, users should have non-jailbroken iOS devices, install appropriate apps, and double-check permissions. The number of devices infected varies depending on the malware family, with AdThief estimating 75,000 compromised machines. KeyRaider successfully took over 225,000 authentic iCloud accounts, while the App Store contained 39 XcodeGhost apps and 256 Youmi Ad SDK-infected apps [3].

- **Distribution**: Apple bans apps that transfer sensitive personal information without prior agreement, resulting in active and state-sponsored malware from legitimate and unknown sources. Under-ground malware, which is distributed differently, is found to be safe in 13.9% of the App Store. The other underground virus, Ikee, is dispersed among Cydia repositories. Due to lack of review procedures, these stores are not unusual.
- **Infection**: Most malware families rely on harmful user behaviors, but only 8.3% exploited iOS device weaknesses, including jailbroken devices' inability to reset passwords, intercepted transactions, temporary certificates, and malicious attacks, despite two types of malwares from underground sources and one from the state.
- **Attack Goals**: Malware underground targets a wide range of individuals, with 17.6% engaging in surveillance, 52.9% committing data theft, 23.5% infecting devices with spam, and 35.3% being fraudsters. Despite changing targets, 35.3% of malware families have a single objective.
- **Attack Vector**: Cydia Substrate and state-sponsored malware use attack vectors targeting non-jailbroken smartphones, targeting credentials with dubious methods. These malware families cover only non-jailbroken devices, with 52.9% using CS, 11.8% using private APIs, and 29.4% evading Apple's monitoring system. Forgery of certificate credentials is a significant issue in business/certificate creation crimes.

The text advises against jailbreaking iOS devices as it can affect performance and allow malware to continue its infection process. It suggests installing apps from reliable sources, keeping iOS updated, and using the iOS procedure to add or remove licenses. New malware families target non-jailbroken devices using unexplored methods to bypass Apple's layer standard review [1]; (Fig. 2).

4 Challenges for Dynamic Analysis of iOS Applications

The article discusses a method for analyzing system calls made during a program using dynamic analysis techniques for the iOS platform. It works with the Stoner interface function to create a system that performs an alternative monitoring function. Some analysis techniques, available on x86 ARM, are not available on iOS. Call monitoring is considered a useful initial step for providing specific usage behavior information, although other dynamic analysis techniques are available.

Thus, here are some Approaches for Dynamic Analysis are:

1. Objective-C functions
2. Monitoring the dispatcher.

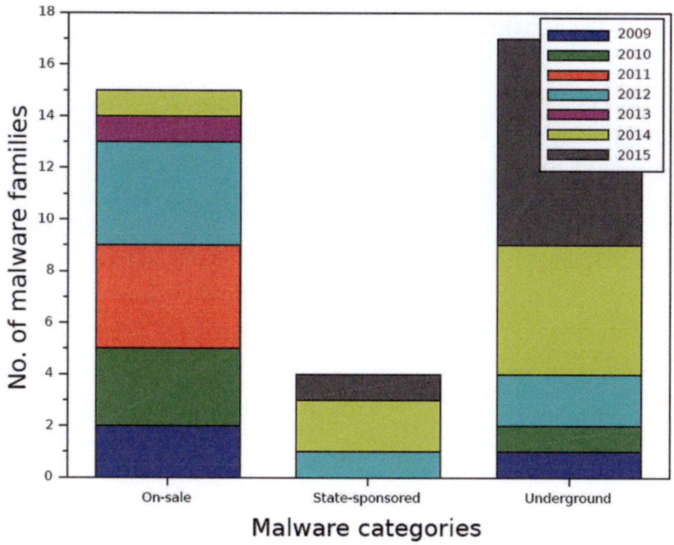

Fig. 2 Evaluation of malware families

3. Identifying method call sites.

Apple's iOS and App Store attract privacy-compromising malicious entities extracting sensitive data like phone numbers and GPS locations. Despite standard detection methods, attackers employ obfuscation tactics, posing challenges. This cited article introduces a dynamic iOS analysis tool, showcasing prototypes for system call tracing and operational interface testing. It addresses challenges and unresolved issues, emphasizing the significance of dynamic analysis amid Apple's stringent security measures. The discussion underscores the surge in mobile app significance and the imperative need to address security and privacy risks. Additionally, it delves into the complexities of dynamic analysis, notably the runtime app execution required to pinpoint vulnerabilities. It also addresses the challenges in accurately assessing an application's harmful purpose or privacy-invading behavior and evaluates the practical limitations of iOS dynamic analysis tools. The authors provide valuable insights into methods and tools for iOS dynamic analysis and emphasize the need for innovation and improvement. This research is based on empirical studies and provides an in-depth analysis of the challenges related to iOS dynamic analysis and also discussed in [4, 5].

5 iOS Malware Analysis Methodology

After a practical comparison analysis, IDA PRO stands out as my preferred choice among various Reverse Engineering (RE) tools, which include Radare2, Ghidra, LLDB, and Hopper [6–9].

This paper presents a methodology for effective Re-Evaluation (RE) work, focusing on iOS malware. The methodology is divided into three stages: Pre-Analysis Stage, Analysis Stage, and Documentation Stage. The methodology is explained in graphical format for easy understanding, and all relevant details are provided in the department's explanation. This approach ensures a comprehensive analysis of the selected iOS malware (Fig. 3).

5.1 Pre-analysis Stage

We want to get our hands on the malware model's compromised machine. Remember that in order to analyze the malicious payload, unencrypted binaries are needed. Apple has encrypted malware samples that may be downloaded as IPA files, which need decryption. These samples are available on the Apple Store. Instead, we can skip this step if the default dylib is a package.deb file or an application distributed through a commercial installation, in which case the binary file is still unencrypted. To check the model's encryption state, use the "otool" tool with the "−l" option. An encrypted state is indicated by a value of 0, which is the cryptid value of the LC_ENCRYPTION_INFO command. After encrypting the pattern, obtain the unencrypted code by utilizing the "dump-decrypted" utility.

1. CIPHERED IPA FILE BY APPLE
2. DECIPHER THE CODE WITH oTool
3. GET THE UNENCRYPTED CODE

But, in this case, we can skip this stage as we already have the malware sample unencrypted and not ciphered. Therefore, we can directly proceed to the Analysis Stage. We are going to analyze the malware named 'KeyRaider'.

5.2 Analysis Stage

First, we will analyze the strings extracted from the unencrypted CertPlugin.dylib file, and there we have found two links that are entirely external to the iOS world. These links are provided below:

Links are as follows:

1. www.wushidou[.]cn
2. top100.gotoip4[.]com (Fig. 4)

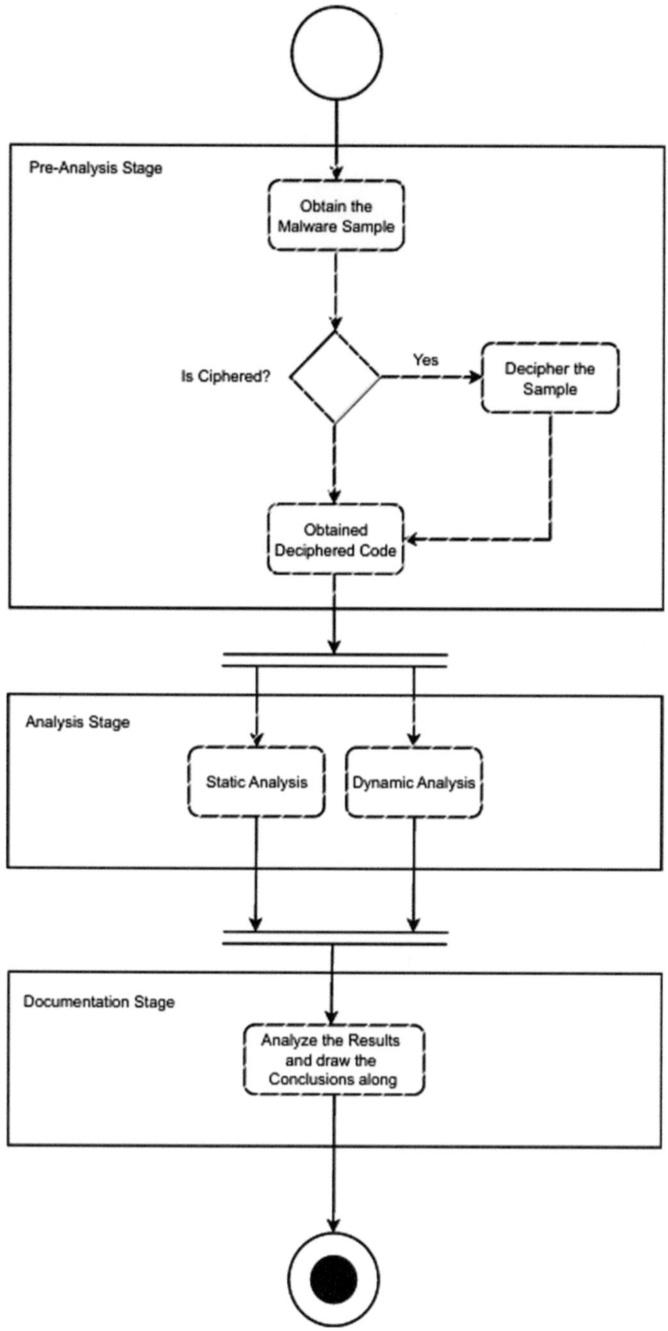

Fig. 3 iOS malware analysis methodology

After performing a WhoIs Lookup on the links, we discovered that both links are registered in the China region, and the registrants have concealed their data with 'REDACTED FOR PRIVACY'. While this is commonly used for privacy purposes, in this case, it appears that they have employed this technique to obscure their identity and avoid easy detection (Refer to Fig. 5).

Here, we can observe that the registered city for the domain is Sichuan, which is located in China. Therefore, these links are associated with China's organization, West263 International Limited (Refer to Fig. 6).

As mentioned in the figure, they have already hidden their data using privacy features to provide minimal information. We can assume that these links might be functioning as C&C Servers, i.e., Command and Control servers, operating on local-hosts. However, it appears that the client has deleted these links, preventing us from connecting to the C&C server.

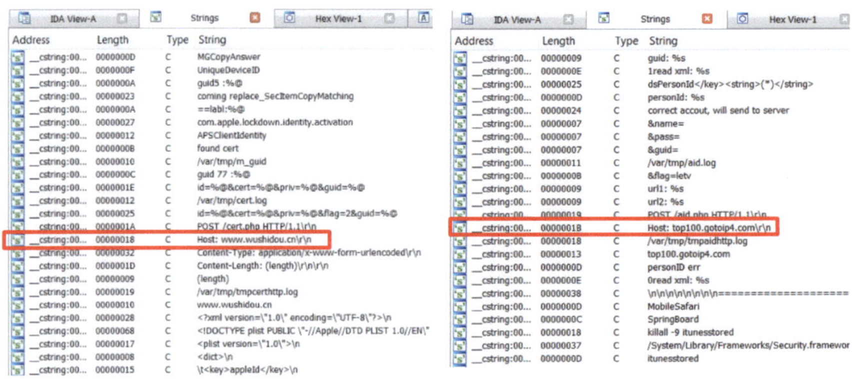

Fig. 4 Suspicious links

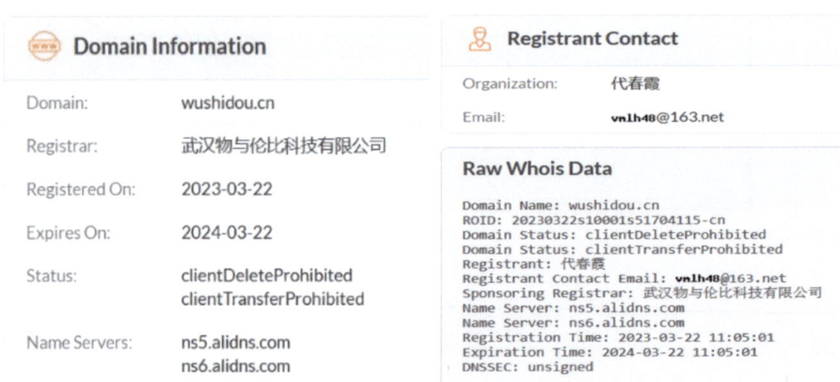

Fig. 5 Suspicious link 1—WhoIsLookup

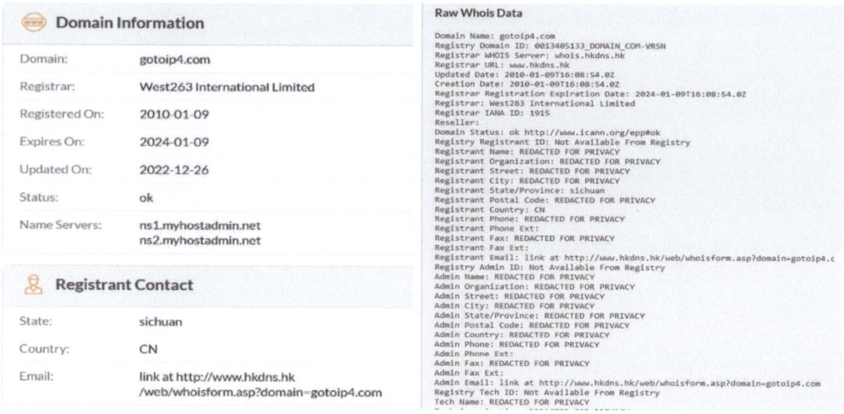

Fig. 6 Suspicious link 2—WhoIsLookup

We have identified traces indicating that this malware attempts to make an App Store purchase by first connecting to iTunes and the Apple official store using the User-Agent as 'AppStore'. Later, it accepts the request and initiates the App Store purchase. Before making the purchase, it also provides details to the App Store and Apple, including relevant information with Encoding Details, Connection Type (Wi-Fi used), Signature Details, and also connects with Game Centre 2.0, maintaining that connection and potentially being persistent. Further in the content, it provides the AppleID, Key, Passwords, etc. (Refer to Figs. 7, 8, 9).

In the further analysis of the file, we have identified some keywords in the Chinese language and observed attempts to connect with other links registered in China (Refer to Figs. 10 and 11).

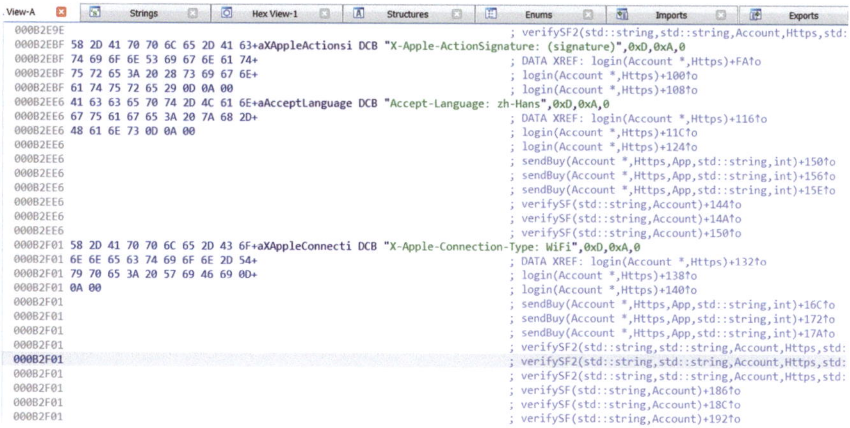

Fig. 7 AppStore purchase 1

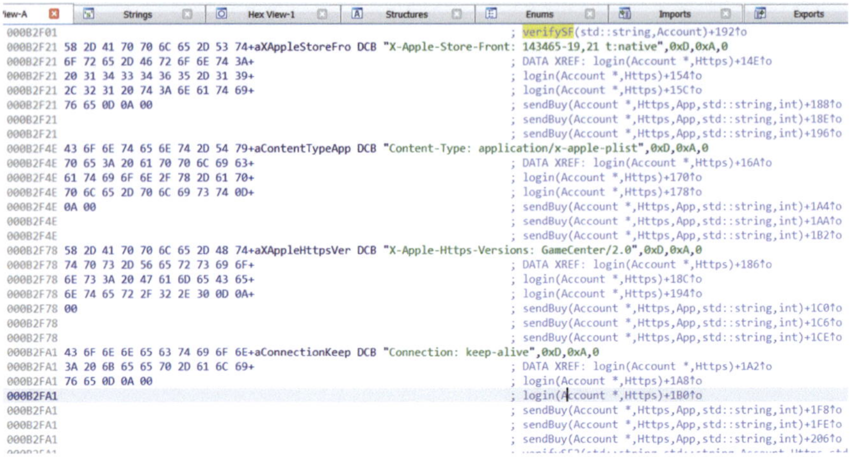

Fig. 8 AppStore purchase 2

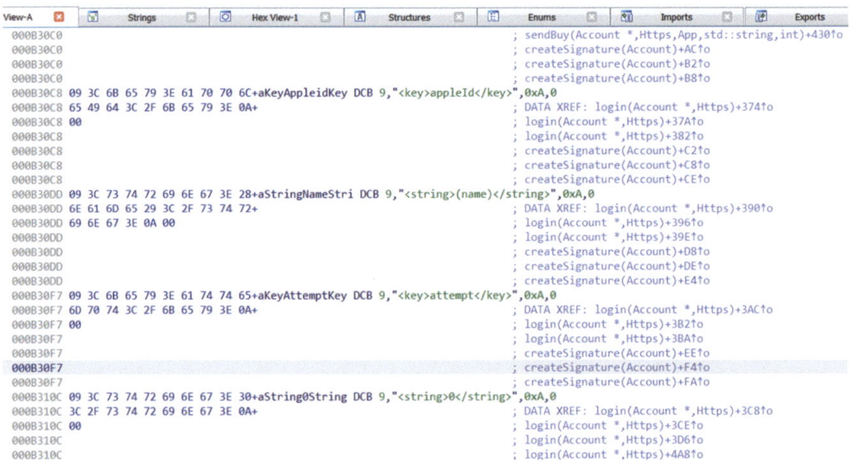

Fig. 9 AppStore purchase 3

Using the mobile substrate framework, the malware hooks itself into functions such as SSLRead and SSLWrite from the process named 'itunesstored.' This process is a daemon that handles both app download and installation, along with purchases and payments.

The SSLWrite function identifies an SSL-encrypted session containing App Store login information to the App Store Server. This function is later hooked by the malware, and it then searches for login sessions using its own patterns to identify the Apple account's username, password, and GUID in the data to be transferred (Refer to Fig. 12).

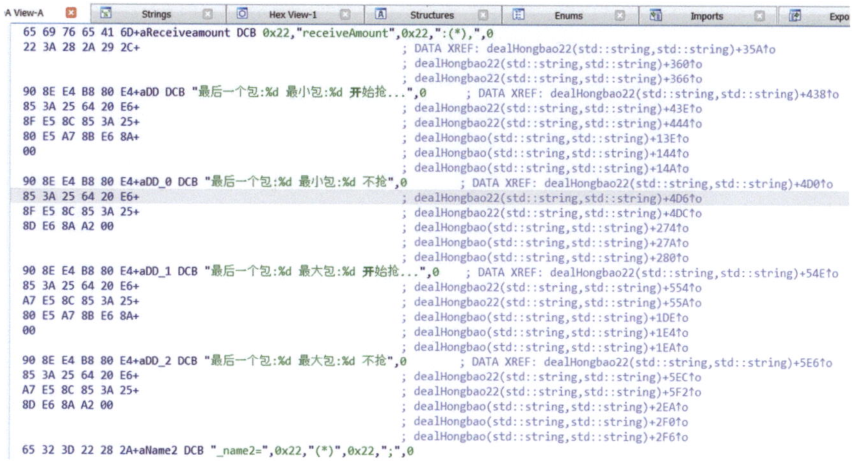

Fig. 10 Suspicious chinese keywords

Fig. 11 Suspicious link

After retrieving the information, the SSLRead function reads the credentials, which are later encrypted with the AES algorithm. The static key for encryption is present in the binary code. Subsequently, the credentials are obtained and sent to its C&C Servers, as discussed earlier (Refer to Fig. 13).

Also, from the analysis of the binary code, it appears that this malware can facilitate forged app purchases from the Apple App Store using the accounts obtained from C&C servers and can emulate the protocols for logins. Unfortunately, dynamic analysis cannot be performed as the C&C servers have been deleted, as per the details retrieved from the WhoIs Lookup. Therefore, we cannot analyze the sample more deeply. However, from the static analysis, we have gathered significant information about the malware and its behavior.

A well-known iOS malware that targeted jailbroken devices was called KeyRaider, impacting users mainly in China. The primary objective of KeyRaider was to obtain services by using stolen Apple account credentials, enabling unlawful in-app purchases. The malware emphasized the dangers of utilizing unlicensed app

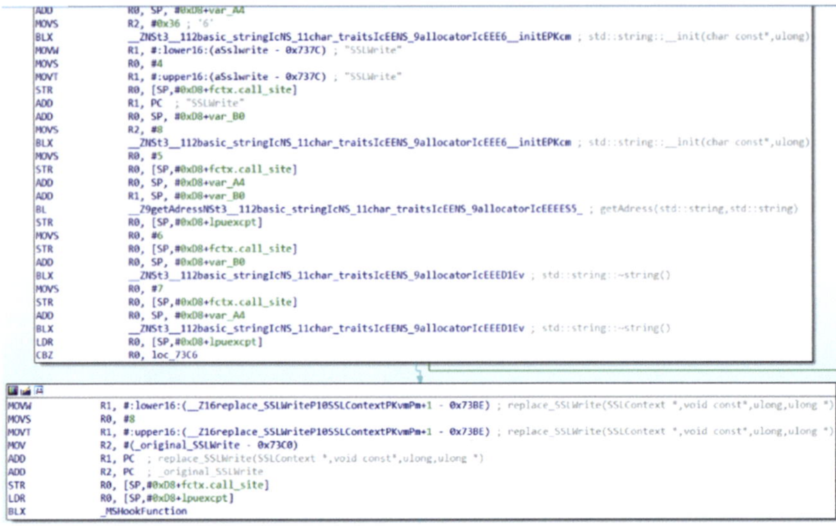

Fig. 12 SSLWrite function

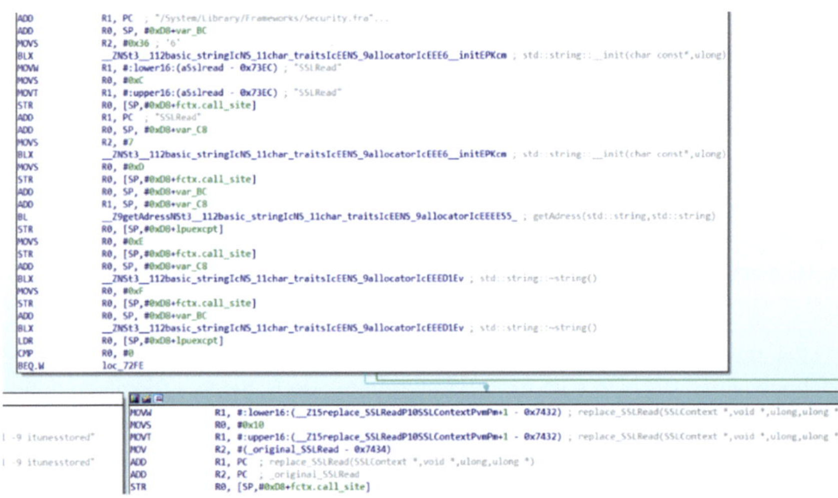

Fig. 13 SSLRead function

repositories and revealed security holes in jailbroken smartphones. It served as a warning about the possible repercussions of jailbreaking iOS devices and installing untrusted apps, compromising iOS security.

Therefore, the malware named KeyRaider, which was earlier identified but not extensively analyzed, has been further examined by the authors, revealing additional insights.

5.3 Documentation Stage

Wiphone Cydia developed the KeyRaider Malware targeting jailbroken iOS devices, infiltrating system processes and capturing sensitive data like account credentials, Apple Push Notification service keys, and purchase details. This malware disabled locking features on over 225,000 Apple accounts, collecting certificates and keys. Exploiting a C&C server vulnerability, it enabled users with specific jailbroken iOS configurations to download App Store apps and make in-app purchases using virtual currency. Now, going back to the main points, we can list the most important topics of the article as follows:

1. **How the sample infects the device?**

Ans: The KeyRaider Malware primarily hooks into the SSLRead and SSLWrite functions in the 'itunesstored' process, intercepting device communication with the Apple App Store. This interception occurs due to the jailbreak of the iPhone, which is considered an infection permitted by the user. The malware also utilizes C&C servers to retrieve login credentials and uses these credentials to log in to the App Store, perform app store purchases, and steal user data, including Apple IDs and passwords.

2. **What Malicious activity is performed?**

Ans: The malware uses the device's iTunes communication to get access to the Mobile Substrate device architecture and obtains Apple account usernames, passwords, and device GUIDs. Furthermore, KeyRaider circulates App Store purchase messages, steals private keys and certificates from Apple Push Notification Service, and disables both local and remote unlocking on iPhones and iPads.

3. **How it can be removed?**

Ans: Firstly, we need to disconnect from the internet, update iOS, change the Apple ID password, remove any suspicious applications, factory reset your iPhone with all settings and erase all contents, install security software, and also enable two-factor authentication. By taking these actions, there are certain chances that we could remove the malware, but it is not 100% guaranteed that it will be completely removed.

6 Conclusion

Practical iOS Malware Analysis provides a thorough examination of various iOS malware, with special attention to the KeyRaider malware. For academics, hobbyists, and cybersecurity experts seeking to enhance their understanding of iOS malware and improve their malware analysis skills, this book is a valuable resource. One of the main focuses of this investigation was KeyRaider, which serves as an excellent case study of iOS malware designed for jailbroken smartphones. The paper dissects KeyRaider's breach of Apple accounts and unauthorized in-app transactions, cautioning against the risks of jailbreaking and third-party app stores. It not only educates on iOS malware but also provides actionable advice for risk mitigation. Equipping readers with essential knowledge, it aids device security, trains cybersecurity experts, and contributes to advancing iOS security measures. Its methodology for KeyRaider analysis is versatile, applicable to various iOS-related malware for effective results.

In summary, Practical iOS Malware Analysis is an invaluable resource for advancing one's knowledge of iOS malware analysis, defense, and detection. In the ongoing effort to safeguard the security and privacy of iOS users in a constantly evolving digital environment, it proves to be an indispensable tool.

References

1. García L, Rodríguez RJ, (2016) A peek under the Hood of iOS malware. s.l., s.n., pp 590–598, Spain
2. Wiki Ti (n.d.) Malware for iOS [Online]. Available at https://www.theiphonewiki.com/wiki/Malware_for_iOS
3. Singh M (2015) Santa Claus malware in Christmas apps targeting android, iOS, PC users [Online]. Available at https://techviral.net/santa-claus-malware-android-ios-pc/
4. Jadhav Bhatt A, Gupta C (2017) Comparison of static and dynamic analyzer tools for iOS applications. Wirel Pers Commun
5. Szydlowski M, Egele M, Krueg C (2012) Challenges for dynamic analysis of iOS applications. s.l., s.n, Austria
6. Alvarez S (n.d.) Radare2 Wiki (Homepage) [Online]. Available at https://en.wikipedia.org/wiki/Radare2
7. Anon. (n.d.) Hex-Rays IDA PRO [Online]. Available at https://hex-rays.com/ida-pro/
8. EURL CA, (n.d.) Hopper homepage [Online]. Available at https://www.hopperapp.com/
9. Team TL (n.d.) LLDB homepage [Online]. Available at https://lldb.llvm.org/

Vulnerability Management and Risk Assessment and its Mitigation in ICS

Nabadeepa Bhowmik and Ujjaval Patel

Abstract Critical infrastructure and industrial automation systems are becoming profitable targets for online predators. Generally, the physical systems that incorporate cyber components, such as programmable logic, micro controllers, sensors, and actuators, field area network controllers, often known as distributed control systems, wide-area networks, etc., are supervised by Supervisory Control and Data Acquisition (SCADA). Following the discovery of Stuxnet in 2009, as well as numerous other incidents of cyberattacks, including one on a chemical plant in Germany and a power distribution system in Ukraine, studies on protecting these systems against cyberattacks, such as plants, have grown to be crucial. But frequently, it is not acceptable to exploit vulnerabilities in the actual operating critical systems evaluation or testing methods for mitigating. We will be concentrating on (i) case studies of the evaluation of the vulnerabilities in industrial components that are frequently used in actual critical systems around the globe. (ii) The security of the exploits consequences; (iii) the mitigating strategies we will be using for defending against such attacks.

Keywords Operational technology (OT) · Cyber security · Critical infrastructure · Industrial control system (ICS) · MODBUS · SCADA · Risk assessment · Risk analysis

1 Introduction

The IEC 27001's initial technical stage is risk assessment [1] standard regarding the implementation of Information Security Management Systems (ISMS). Because of the speed at which state of-the-art attacks evolve, risk assessment needs to be updated often to consider new vulnerabilities or countermeasures. We require tools that can

N. Bhowmik (✉) · U. Patel
National Forensic Sciences University, Gandhinagar, Gujarat, India

U. Patel
e-mail: ujjaval.patel@nfsu.ac.in

B. N. Gohil et al. (eds.), *Information Security, Privacy and Digital Forensics*,
Lecture Notes in Electrical Engineering 1423,
https://doi.org/10.1007/978-981-96-9443-3_25

identify attack scenarios from risk analysis to deploy security controls. Cyberattacks are starting to target ICS. They are frequently referred to as SCADA systems, and they manage industrial processes like transportation, water treatment, and power grid management. Because they are so critical, any misbehavior could put people and the environment in danger. The Stuxnet attack in 2010, in which a worm was able to harm Iranian nuclear centrifuges, was one of the most well-known. This incident made people aware of the tangible effects a computer attack can have on the world [2]. More attacks on these systems have surfaced in the last few years.ICS prioritize ensuring the availability and integrity of their processes over the confidentiality and authentication of data, which contrasts with traditional IT systems. However, their equipment may only last for a few decades, and it can be difficult to update them when vulnerabilities arise. There are many communication protocols that are used by industrial system which are not designed with security in mind and also does not offer any security features. Some of the major complex cyber-physical systems (CPS) that are critical infrastructures (CI), transport, chemical refineries, energy plants, industrial production facilities, gas and oil storage and transport are significant for the country. They are essential to both the health of a country's economy and its expansion. Supervisory Control and Data Acquisition System (SCADA) are employed to enhance the security and efficiency of critical infrastructure. These systems are a type of industrial automation and control system that enables centralized monitoring and controlling of the geographically distributed devices in almost real-time. Many critical infrastructures are using SCADA systems for central monitoring and control of system status in cyber physical systems that include sensors and actuators. Due to IP convergence, SCADA systems have begun exchanging data with business networks more recently [3]. SCADA comprises digital and analog sensors, actuators with Industrial protocols for the transfer of actuator messages from controllers to physical locations, Field data exchange and timing signals, as well as Network Based Data Communication between physical components, controllers, and SCADA stations. Also SCADA systems operate in different layer, have different security requirements than business networks, some of the previous barriers to security breaches have been overcome considering the two networks' current connectivity. In industrial automation, availability, integrity, and confidentiality are typically ranked highest, although at the IT layer, security policies place more emphasis on confidentiality after that integrity and availability. The use of SCADA systems and operational technologies that integrate critical infrastructure with business systems (also known as IP convergence) increases the exposure and connectivity of the infrastructure [4]. This results in additional security threats. Critical Infrastructure has grown to be a desirable target for deliberate attacks and malicious scripts. Furthermore, numerous surveys have revealed that insider threats are to blame for many well-known cyber-attacks. A thorough examination of the 242 cyber security incidents on critical infrastructures that occurred between 1982 and 2014 and resulted in 673 fatalities and 419 injuries was published [5]. Several cases, including the 2016 and 2017 Ukraine blackouts, have been documented since 2014.In this paper, we present a strategy for identifying and creating ICS attack scenarios. Specifically, our goal is to identify situations in which a cyber-attack affects security features. IEC 624431-1 states that security

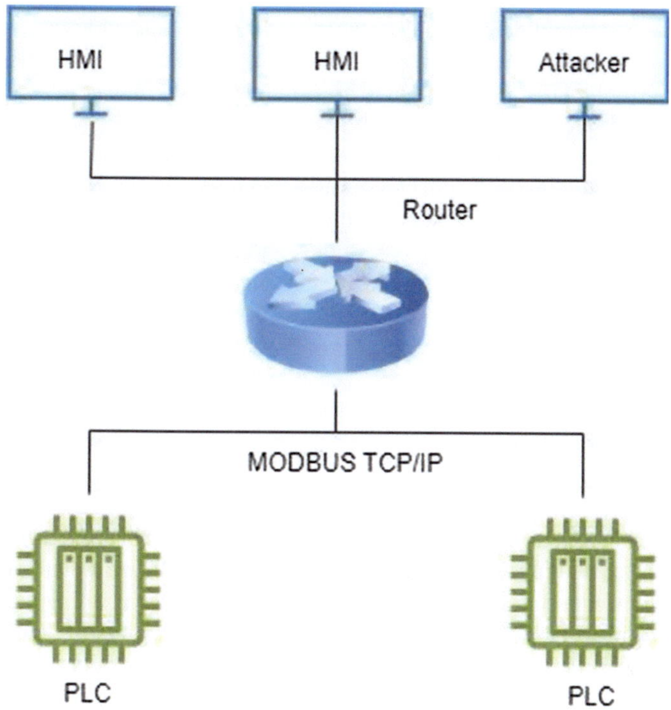

Fig. 1 Basic architecture for testing ICS system vulnerabilities

pertains to the "prevention of illegal or unwanted penetration of, or interference with the proper and intended operation of an industrial automation and control system" and safety refers as "freedom from unacceptable risk" [6].

On Fig. 1, it represents the basic architecture to test the vulnerabilities in ICS systems. Here, in addition to managing the input valve status, regulates the output valve in response to request from other controllers. PLCs that are automated do the controlling, However, the users are capable for overriding control commands by means of a HMI interface. As illustrated in Fig. 1, the HMI oversees presenting all signal values through a console interface to show the current state of the system. It also enables users to transfer control commands interactively, enabling them for forcing the states on the actuators and alter the behavior of the system.

2 Background

The vulnerability assessment and penetration testing, or VAPT, of operational industrial systems may lead to unfavorable circumstances. SCADA integrated production environments must operate constantly, with the exception of planned maintenance.

Any stoppage or slight delay could result in significant financial losses. As such, a platform where users can do penetration tests and vulnerability assessments of the hardware and software they use ought to be available. Furthermore, SCADA systems have numerous interdependent systems and are complex. As a result, conducting penetration testing and vulnerability assessment is quite difficult. To demonstrate the connections that currently exist between cyberattacks and their effects on safety, the main challenge is to be able to model the system according to its physical (safety) and cyber security aspects. Numerous studies attempt to formalize the system, but scaling up is challenging due to the intricacy of the cyber and physical interactions. To identify safety/security risks, two trends can be identified in the related works. The first one suggests using an intersection of modeling techniques to identify safety and security risks in a unified manner. These methods make it possible to address both kinds of risks. On the other hand, integrated approaches seek to identify security threats that affect safety features in order to offer security fixes that safeguard the security of the system [2, 7–9].

In Fig. 2 architecture scenario, the sensors collect data that is sent to PLCs for real-time control regarding the conditions of the plants and the quality of the water. While HMI panels enable direct interaction, the SCADA system offers a visual interface for operators to oversee and manage the plant's operations. For reporting and analysis purposes, the historian server maintains a record of historical data. Cyber threats are thwarted by security measures like firewalls and remote access controls. Operators are guaranteed timely notification of any issues by means of an alarm and notification system.

SENSORS These are positioned all across the water treatment facility and are used to continuously check important factors like temperature, turbidity, pH, flow rate, and water level.

PLC After receiving and processing data from the sensors, the PLC manages the treatment procedures. It communicates with the SCADA for a more thorough overview and with the HMI for operator input.

HMI Process monitoring, parameter setting, and action initiation are all done by operators via the HMI. It gives local control and shows data in real time.

SCADA PLC data is gathered by SCADA, which then presents a consolidated picture of the whole water treatment system. It also permits remote control and observation.

ACTUATORS and VALVES In order to guarantee proper treatment procedures, actuators and valves regulate the flow of water and treatment chemicals in accordance with PLC instructions.

PUMPS and MIXERS As directed by the PLC, pumps and mixers control the flow and blending of water and treatment chemicals.

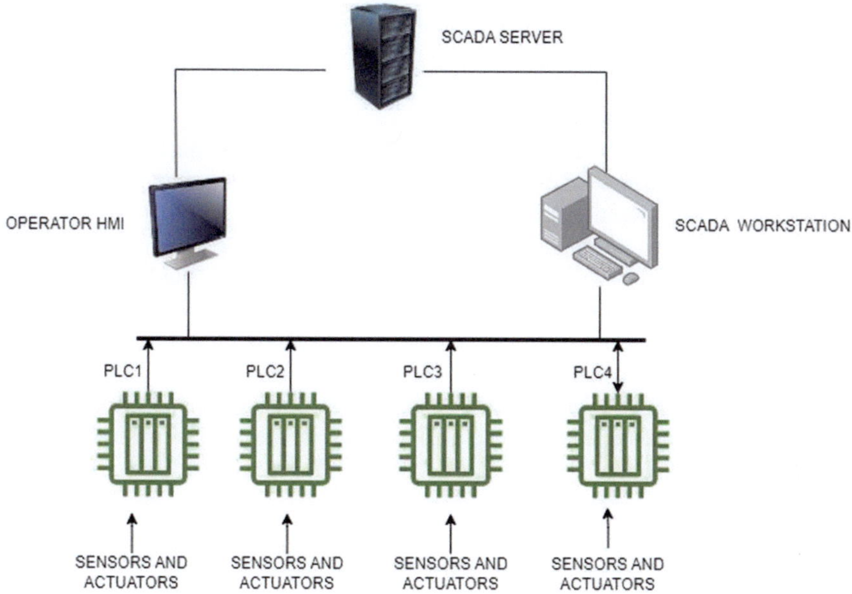

Fig. 2 Basic ICS architecture for water plant

DATA HISTORIAN	A data historian keeps track of and preserves past data for analysis and reporting, which aids in spotting long-term patterns and guiding decision making.
ALARMS and NOTIFICATION	Those, keeps an eye on important parameters and sounds an alarm when something goes out of range, alerting operators so they can take appropriate action.
NETWORK INFRASTRUCTURE	Data interchange between the components is made possible by the network infrastructure, which links them all. Both wired and wireless communication protocols might be used on this network [10].

2.1 *Types of Attacks on Critical Infrastructure*

It has been identified that various attack classes using different VAPT methodology, and some of the following crude classification of attack types are:

A. The common network protocol for transferring computer files to different field devices, like PLCs, is called File Transfer Protocol, or FTP. The majority of the devices implemented them as Java applets that operate on the operators' browsers via the web interface. A Java decompile can be used to disassemble the applets. The decompiled bytecode reveals crucial credentials that are hardcoded, making attacks simple.

B. Denial of service attacks.
C. If control commands are susceptible to MITM, an MITM attack can be used to obtain control over devices by targeting confidentiality and also the integrity of data moving between two entities.
D. Utilizing the devices' plain text communication, the attacker performs unidirectional ARP (Address Resolution Protocol) poisoning to reroute IP traffic.
E. Even though Modbus authentication has been extensively studied, Modbus is still a widely used field protocol in continuous integration and is vulnerable to a number of simple attacks.
F. There are many instances of cross-site request forgery, remote file inclusion, cross-site scripting, and other security flaws in the badly constructed web interfaces intended to configure devices using the http protocol.

3 Vulnerability Assessment and Penetration Testing

Vulnerability Assessment and penetration testing (VAPT) are essential for addressing security flaws in industrial control systems and information technology systems alike. As per the SANS white paper, the focus of a vulnerability assessment is to identify components that are susceptible to cyber-attacks, whereas penetration testing aims to obtain maximum access (Fig. 3).

The design outline makes use of a PLC, router, and computer linked to a SCADA control network in order to gather and display the results. Next, using Kali Linux and Wireshark to examine network data packets, penetration testing is carried out at the access point installed on the network and also during the attack snort rules can be used to monitor the malicious traffic [11].

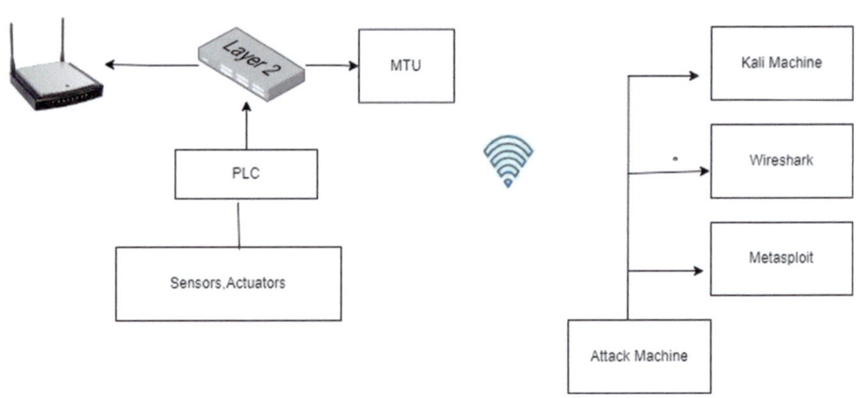

Fig. 3 Attack scenario

3.1 Vulnerabilities in MODBUS-TCP

A. The PLC web interface has an RFI vulnerability that was first discovered in 2015 and hasn't been fixed as of yet. The attacker can perform network scans and other attacks by sending a phishing email that contains a specially crafted link, all thanks to this vulnerability.
B. An attacker can start a denial-of-service attack (DoS) by flooding the server using maliciously constructed Modbus (TCP) packets. This will prevent authorized users from accessing the device. If an attacker overwhelms a server with requests, it will not be able to process requests from legitimate end users. Since all of the addresses in PLC's input and output are disclosed in the Modbus TCP plaintext communication, it is simpler for malware to target particular addresses and compromise the system.
C. An MITM can compromise the PLC because of the plaintext communication and lack of an authentication mechanism in the protocol. Modbus-TCP is used to communicate plant floor data between the PLC and the HMI. Using the HMI, an operator runs the facility. After launching an ARP spoofing attack, the attacker which could be a malicious script replays the packets that are sent from the HMI to the PLC. After an unauthorized device establishes a TCP session, the PLC executes any commands that the attacker sends it.
D. Any malicious script that is operating on a network in accordance with the Modbus (TCP) protocol has the ability to manipulate and damage the control system. The PLC's Modbus (TCP) server accepts connections without asking permission and provides services to the client by carrying out commands.

3.2 Vulnerabilities in SCADA HOST

A. Any process with the equal Integrity level or higher can read the process memory and dump it for credential harvesting because the SCADA client operates as a medium integrity process. According to a host memory analysis, the SCADA application's credentials were stored in the process memory, where any other malicious program could read them. For the duration that the process is active, the password will remain in memory. Additionally, there are links to every URL that has been visited using Internet Explorer, which may reveal confidential.

4 Results

Here Scada Modbus attack has been performed, here by using Nmap scan the open port has identified, and 502 is the port no for the Modbus pal (Fig. 4).

Here by using Metasploit, search Modbus query has been written to get the Modbus matching modules (Fig. 5).

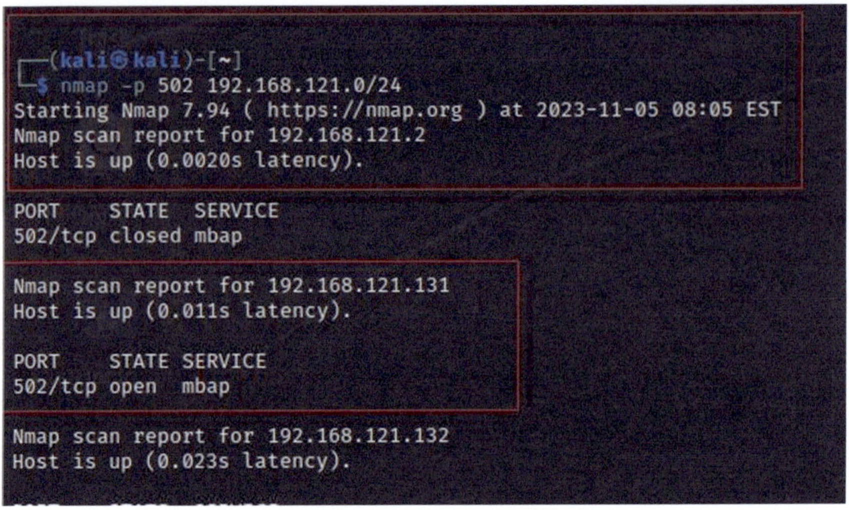

Fig. 4 Nmap scan and open port

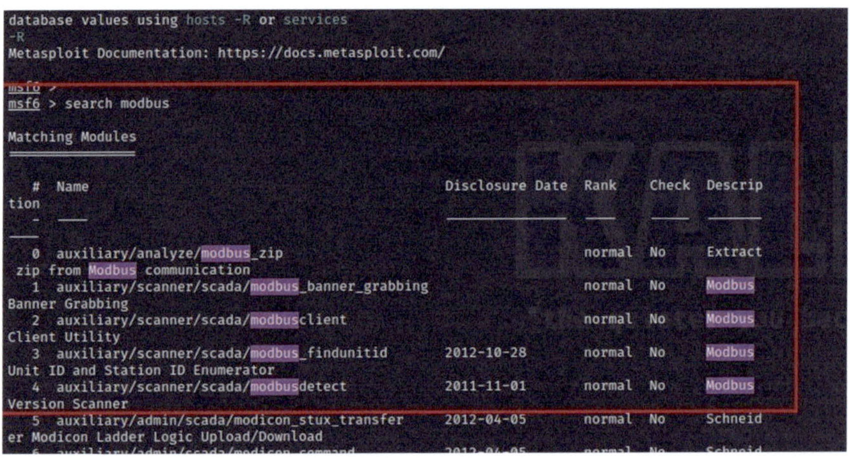

Fig. 5 Metasploit, search query for Modbus

Here, by using *search modbus* it has been identified that Modbus client is there. So, to interact with the module *use auxiliary/scanner/scada/modbusclient* (Figs. 6, 7).

Here by set DATA_ADDRESS the value of the Modbus can be visible and 2 is the address (Figs. 8, 9).

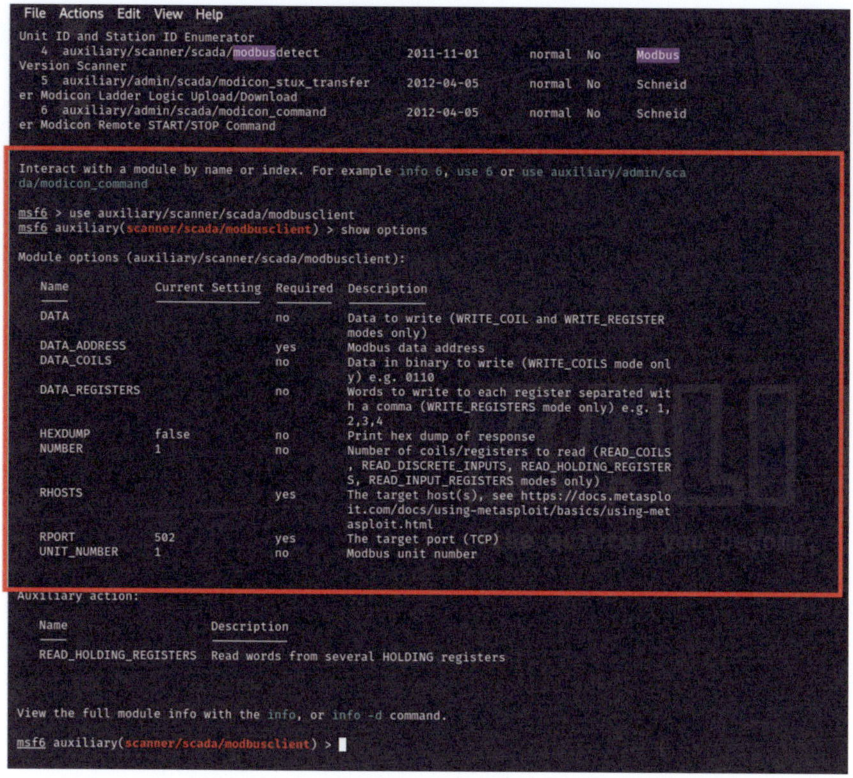

Fig. 6 Module Interaction, for modbusclient

**Here it is visible that the data is 3, Normally Modbus address starts from address 0 but here in Modbus pal we have started the Address from 1, So, if in Modbus Pal the Data address is 3 that means this is data address no 2 (Fig. 10).

By using write command the data can be modified in the Modbus. Here DATA_ADDRESS 2 value has been set to 12590 (Figs. 11, 12).

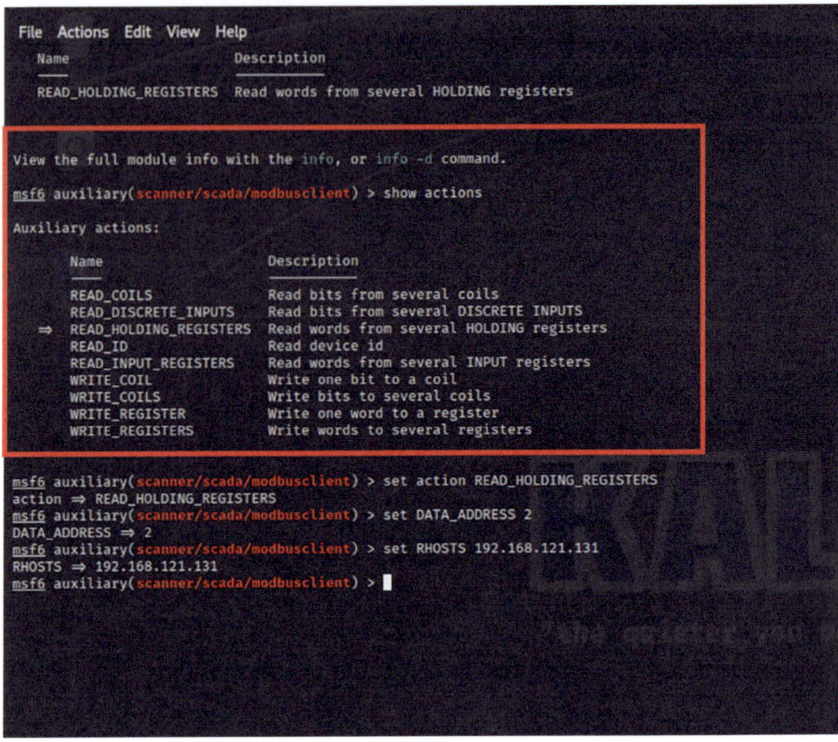

Fig. 7 All auxiliary actions list that *scanner/scada/modbusclient* module can do

5 Countermeasures and Mitigation Technique

Disabling port mirroring on network devices, like Ethernet switches, during installation and commissioning is a good way to reduce the risk of Man-in-the-Middle (MITM) attacks. SCADA systems are secure from interception if network devices do not enable port mirroring. Prompt mode cannot record unicast packet communication between the PLC server and SCADA host. MITM attacks can be avoided by using authentication methods like ECDSA signatures. Authenticity can instill some trust in the reliability of the source. The only thing tamper detection can do is verify whether a message has been changed. One should only permit loading signed DLLs in order to prevent privilege escalation-based exploitation. If successful, an attacker would be unable to load unsigned libraries; however, he or she could still execute malicious code via an API hook or shellcode without having to call Load Library. Additionally, all software that is currently running should have code integrity enforced at the kernel level. This way, even if a process is compromised, malicious code cannot disable code integrity. Combining rate-limiting filters with access control configuration can help reduce DOS. With the right input validation and sanitizing, remote function invocation may be prevented. To prevent CSRF, proper isolation

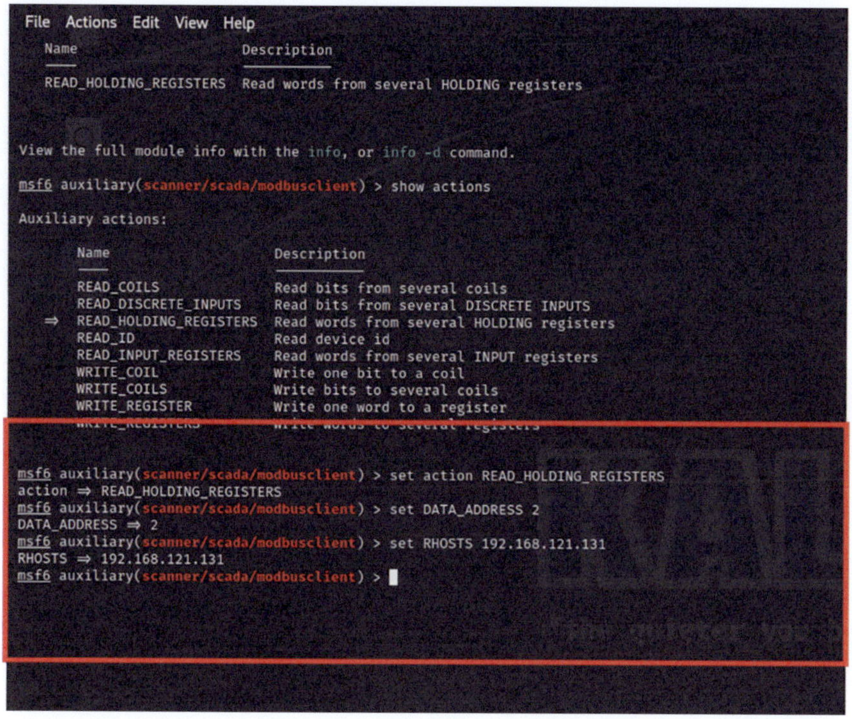

Fig. 8 Read words from Holding Register using *set action READ_HOLDING_REGISTERS*

and header validation in HTML headers can be implemented. Session hijacking can be prevented by using SSL certificates and regenerating the session ID following a successful login. Instead of hard coding of any key or password to access the "first login" mode, it is required to hard code a default username and password and also require the user to create a strong, one-of a-kind password later on. Those test has been used to evaluate these mitigation strategies, and the results have significantly reduced our capacity to exploit the vulnerabilities.

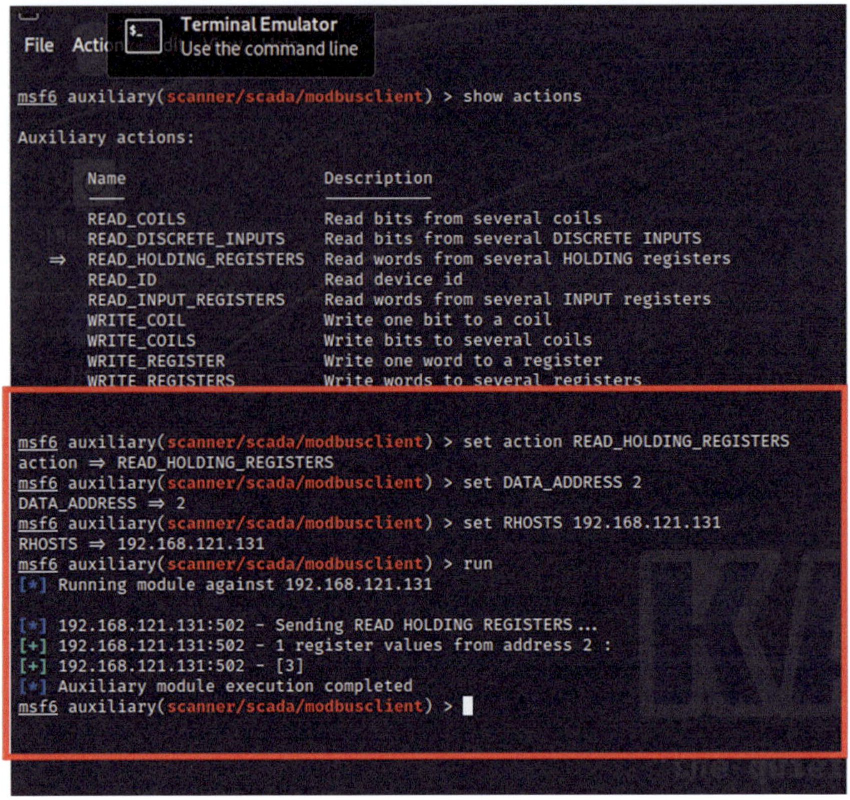

Fig. 9 To go to the target host using *set RHOST* Target host and then run to get the address

Fig. 10 The values for data address of 3 is 3**

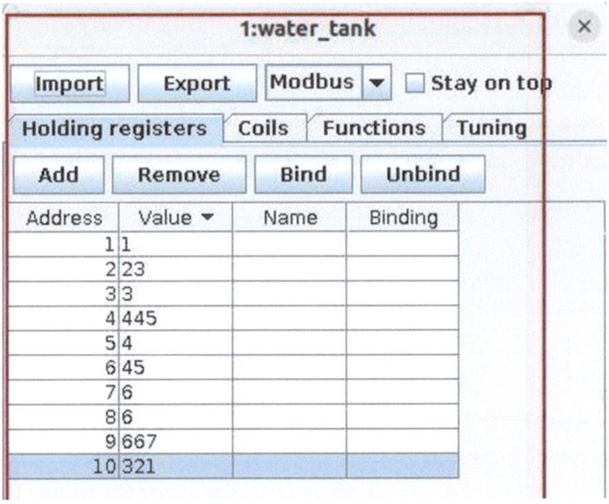

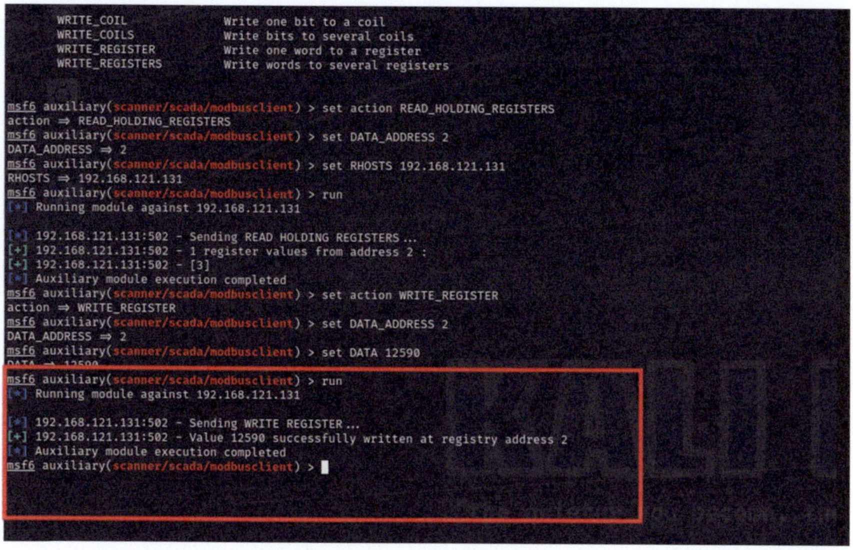

Fig. 11 Using *set action WRITE_REGISTER* the value for Data _Address 2 has been modified

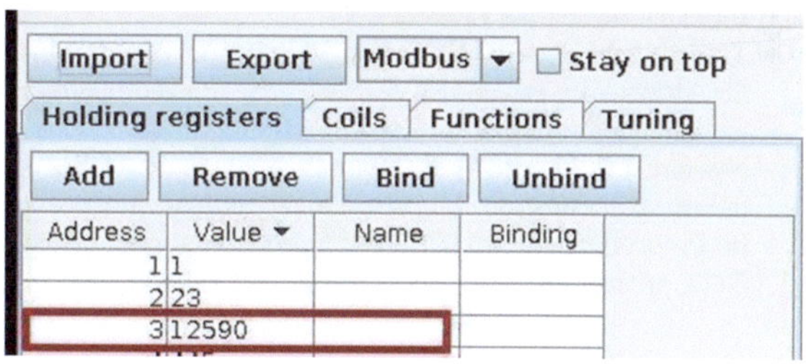

Fig. 12 The value for Data _Address 2 i, e Data _ Address 3 has been modified to 12590**

6 Conclusion

This paper highlights the growing importance of Vulnerabilities in the OT environment and to safeguarding critical infrastructure in the face of evolving cyber threats. Penetration testing on real environment will disclose lot more vulnerabilities which we cannot get from virtual environment. Tools like Metasploit, Wireshark can used for monitor the network traffic, Nmap to scan the open ports, snort rules for monitoring the malicious traffic, here, Modbus vulnerabilities has been shown in the result section other than this more attacks are there which can be vulnerable and also will impact in real ICS industries.

References

1. IEC 27001:2023 (2023) Information security, cybersecurity and privacy protection information security management systems—requirements. International Standard. International Electrotechnical Commission, Geneva, CH
2. Harris B, Hunt R (1999) TCP/IP security threats and attack methods. Comput Commun 22(10):885–897
3. Abbas HA (2014) Future Scada challenges and the promising solution: the agent-based Scada. Int J Crit Infrastruct 10(3–4):307–333
4. Igure VM, Laughter SA, William RD (2006) Security issues in SCADA networks. Comput Secur 25(7):498–506
5. Alcaraz C, Fernandez G, Carvajal F (2012) Security aspects of SCADA and DCS environments. In: Critical infrastructure protection. Springer, pp 120–149
6. IEC 62443-1-1:2010 (2010) Industrial communication networks—network and system security– part 1–1: terminology, concepts and models. International Standard. International Electrotechnical Commission, Geneva, CH
7. Ogie RI (2017) Cyber security incidents on critical infrastructure and industrial networks. In: International conference on computer and automation engineering. ACM, pp 254–258
8. Cárdenas AA, Amin S, Lin Z-S, Huang Y-L, Huang C-Y, Sastry S (2011) Attacks against process control systems: risk assessment, detection, and response. In: Proceedings of the 6th ACM symposium on information, computer and communications security—ASIACCS'11. ACM Press, Hong Kong, China, p 355
9. Huitsing P, Chandia R, Papa M, Shenoi S (2008) Attack taxonomies for the Modbus protocols. Int J Crit Infrastruct Prot 1:37–44
10. Thomas DM, Pandey N, Shukla VK, Singh AV (2021) Attack vectors and susceptibilities of the Modbus in TCP/IP Model. In: 2021 9th international conference on reliability, Infocom technologies and optimization (trends and future directions) (ICRITO), pp 1–2
11. Nyasore ON, Zavarsky P, Swar B, Naiyeju R, Dabra S (2020) Deep packet inspection in industrial automation control system to mitigate attack exploiting modbus/TCP vulnerabilities. In: Proceeding—2020 IEEE 6th international conference on big data security on cloud, May 2020, pp 241–245

Vulnerability Assessment and Penetration Testing (VAPT) of IoT Aided Home Automation System Using Google Home and Sinric Pro Application

Ahmad Adamu Jajere and Ujjaval Patel

Abstract The Internet of Things (IoT) has witnessed rapid proliferation across various domains, offering unparalleled convenience and automation. However, this widespread adoption also introduces significant security vulnerabilities. This research paper aims to address these vulnerabilities through a comprehensive vulnerability assessment and penetration testing (VAPT) approach. By identifying, analyzing, and mitigating security weaknesses in IoT devices, once can contribute to the ongoing efforts to enhance IoT security and protect against cyber threats. In an increasingly connected world, where everyday objects are transformed into intelligent devices, IoT security is paramount. Despite its transformative potential, the IoT landscape is riddled with security challenges, potentially leaving users and organizations exposed to data breaches, unauthorized access, and other malicious activities. Vulnerabilities in IoT devices can have severe consequences, ranging from privacy breaches to operational disruptions. This paper covers how a VAPT was performed using free tools and technologies to achieve the aim of the research. The researchers were able to identify different vulnerabilities which the system is prone to, namely; Denial of Service Attack (DoS), Man-in-the-Middle Attack (MitM), DHCP Starvation Attack, TCP SYN Flood Vulnerability, and Open Port vulnerability. However, all these vulnerabilities identified, proper measures and procedures to securing the system were made for end users and major marketers who employed the use of Sinric Pro Application. The findings and recommendations in this paper serve as a call to action for IoT device manufacturers, security professionals, and end-users to collectively strengthen the security posture of IoT devices. The ultimate goal is to ensure the safe and secure adoption of IoT technology and the protection of sensitive data in a connected world. We hope that this research will inspire further study, collaboration, and the development of robust IoT security measures.

A. A. Jajere · U. Patel
National Forensic Sciences University, Gandhinagar, Gujarat, India

A. A. Jajere (✉)
Yobe State University, Damaturu, Nigeria
e-mail: ahmadjajere1@gmail.com

B. N. Gohil et al. (eds.), *Information Security, Privacy and Digital Forensics*,
Lecture Notes in Electrical Engineering 1423,
https://doi.org/10.1007/978-981-96-9443-3_26

Keywords Cyber threats · Internet of things (IoT) · IoT devices · IoT security · Penetration testing · Security vulnerabilities · Vulnerability assessment

1 Introduction

The proliferation of the Internet of Things (IoT) has transformed the way we interact with our environments, introducing a new era of interconnected devices that promise increased convenience, efficiency, and automation. Everyday objects, from refrigerators to thermostats, vehicles to medical devices, are now equipped with embedded sensors and connectivity, enabling them to collect and exchange data autonomously. This technological evolution has not only revolutionized industries but has also become an integral part of our daily lives [1].

However, the remarkable growth of the IoT ecosystem comes hand in hand with heightened concerns about the security and integrity of these interconnected devices. The vast network of IoT devices, often sharing sensitive and personal information, presents an enticing target for malicious actors seeking to exploit vulnerabilities. Security lapses within IoT devices can have severe consequences, ranging from privacy breaches to physical harm in cases where IoT devices are employed in critical applications such as healthcare or transportation.

The scale and diversity of the IoT ecosystem make it a challenging domain for security enforcement. IoT devices come in various forms, employ different communication protocols, and serve diverse purposes. Traditional security solutions developed for conventional computing environments are often inadequate for addressing the unique challenges posed by the IoT landscape.

The objective of this research is to fortify IoT security through a vulnerability assessment and penetration testing (VAPT) approach. Vulnerability assessments are essential for identifying potential weaknesses and entry points for attackers, while penetration testing validates the effectiveness of security measures and reveals potential vulnerabilities that could be exploited by adversaries. By systematically examining and mitigating security vulnerabilities in IoT devices, we contribute to the ongoing efforts to enhance IoT security, protect user privacy, and ensure the uninterrupted functionality of these devices.

In this paper, we outline the research objectives, research questions, and the scope of our study. We emphasize the critical importance of IoT security and underscore the relevance of vulnerability assessments and penetration testing as vital measures to address IoT security concerns. By conducting a comprehensive VAPT analysis, the main objective of this research is to bridge existing gaps in IoT security research and provide actionable insights into safeguarding the IoT landscape against potential cyber threats.

2 Literature Review

IoT security remains a paramount concern as the IoT ecosystem continues to expand at an unprecedented rate. The literature review presented here delves into the core issues, challenges, and existing research in the field of IoT security, with a focus on vulnerability assessments and penetration testing.

1. ***IoT Security Challenges***: One of the foundational aspects of IoT security is understanding the unique challenges posed by the diverse range of IoT devices. Research by Heiding et al. [2] highlights several key challenges, including resource constraints, heterogeneous device architectures, and the need for secure communication protocols. As IoT deployments span across industrial, healthcare, and smart home environments, these challenges take on different dimensions.
2. ***IoT Penetration Testing***: A significant gap exists in penetration testing specifically tailored for IoT devices. The work by Bella et al. [3] emphasizes the importance of penetration testing in the context of IoT (PETIoT). Their research focuses on the development of testing methodologies and tools that can address the peculiarities of IoT systems. They underline the necessity of penetration testing to unearth vulnerabilities unique to IoT ecosystems.
3. ***Mitigating IoT Threats***: Understanding IoT threats and vulnerabilities is only the first step. Research by Abdalrahman and Varol [4] underscores the importance of proactive defense mechanisms against cyber-attacks on IoT devices. Their work highlights the need for comprehensive security strategies encompassing access control, intrusion detection systems, and secure firmware updates. Such strategies are crucial for mitigating IoT-related threats.
4. ***Automated Security Assessment***: Duan et al. [5] present an approach to automated security assessment for IoT devices. Their research focuses on the use of automated tools to streamline the process of identifying vulnerabilities and weaknesses. Automation is seen as a key element in addressing the rapid expansion of the IoT landscape and the need for efficient security assessments.
5. ***Attack Analysis:*** IoT attack techniques are evolving, and understanding their mechanics is imperative. Thilakrathne et al. [6] conduct an experimental evaluation of cyber-attacks targeting internet-facing IoT devices. Their research provides valuable insights into the anatomy of attacks, their impacts, and potential countermeasures. Such insights serve as foundational knowledge for security experts.
6. ***Security Standards and Regulations***: Shah and Sengupta [7] provide a survey of the classification of cyber-attacks on IoT and Industrial Internet of Things (IIoT) devices. Their work highlights the diversity of attacks on IoT devices and the need for granular classifications to aid in mitigation efforts. This comprehensive view of IoT security threats and tactics underscores the need for adherence to evolving security standards and regulations.

7. ***IoT Firmware Security***: IoT security extends beyond hardware and network vulnerabilities to firmware security. Researchers like Ali et al. [8] focus on the security of IoT firmware, covering aspects like secure update mechanisms, digital signatures, and firmware integrity verification. Their work sheds light on the importance of authenticating and securing firmware updates, which are often the entry point for attacks.

The literature review revealed a notable gap in the field of IoT security, particularly in the context of vulnerability assessments and penetration testing. Existing research provided valuable insights into the challenges and threats faced by IoT devices, but there is a scarcity of studies that systematically examine these issues through VAPT. This research aims to bridge this gap by conducting a VAPT analysis and proposing mitigation measures.

The paper follows a logical progression, beginning with the problem identification, followed by the methodology and tools used. The vulnerabilities identified are discussed, and the results are presented, leading to the conclusion and recommendations for future research and IoT security practices.

3 Architecture of IOT Aided Home Automation System

Figure 1: Sketch Diagram.

This diagram offers a concise overview of the IoT system's architecture, illustrating how devices collect and transmit data, how it is processed and analyzed, and how users can interact with the system while highlighting the critical role of cloud-based infrastructure and security measures.

Figure 2: Network Diagram.

The '電気をつけて' text in the Diagram below is Japanese. Breakdown and translation:

1. Text: 'OK Google, 電気をつけて'
2. Translation: 'OK Google, turn on the light(s)'.

Therefore, this is a common voice command spoken to a Google Home device or the Google Assistant app to control smart lighting. The speaker is asking Google to turn on the lights.

Figure 3: Sinric Pro—Mobile Application.

Figure 4.

Figure 5: Model Diagram.

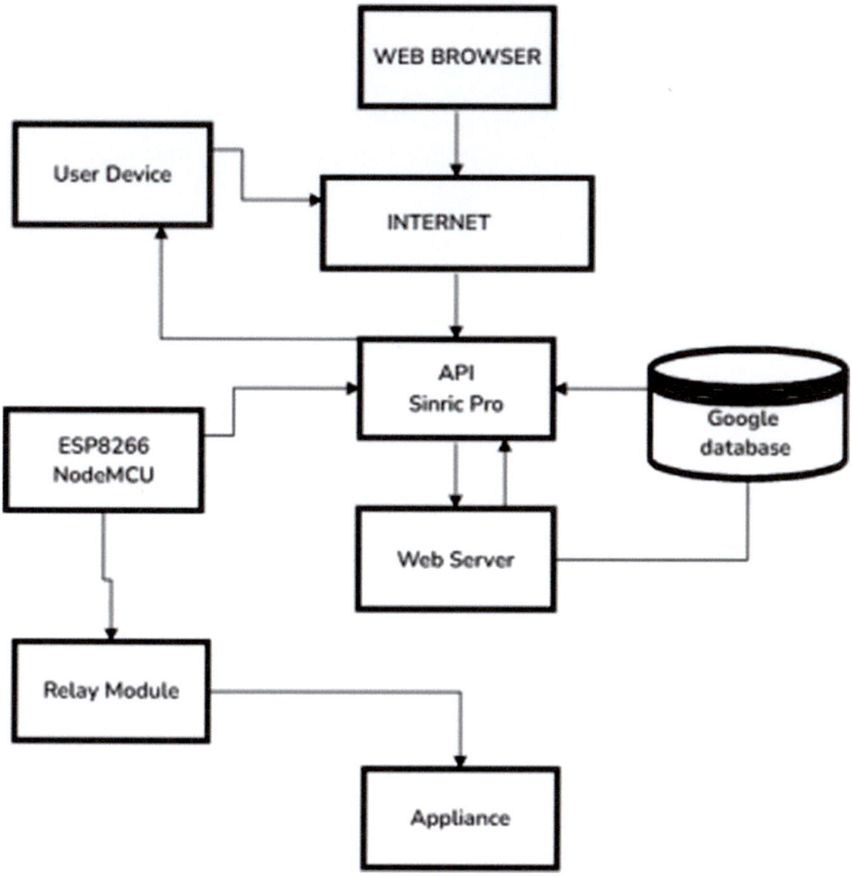

Fig. 1 Sketch diagram of IoT aided home automation system

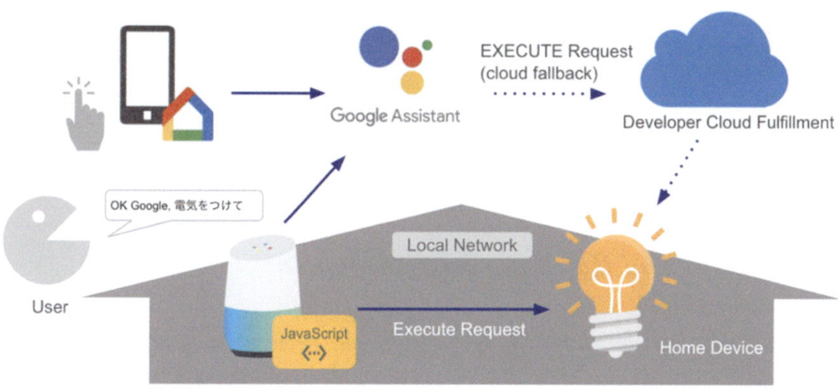

Fig. 2 These diagrams provide a clear and concise way to depict the network's layout, highlighting how data flows and devices interact within the system

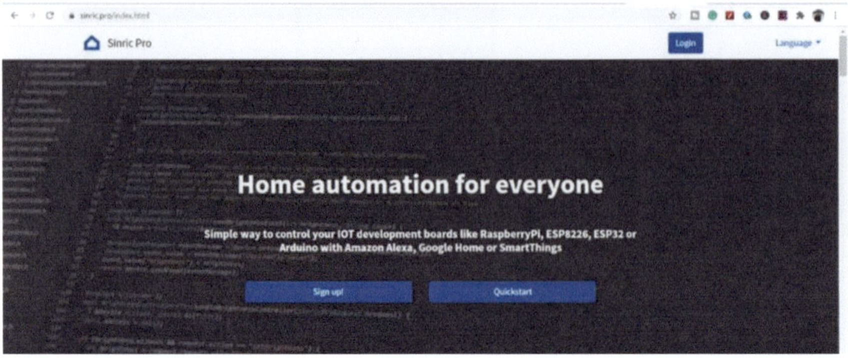

Fig. 3 Sinric pro mobile application landing page

Fig. 4 Google home automation interface

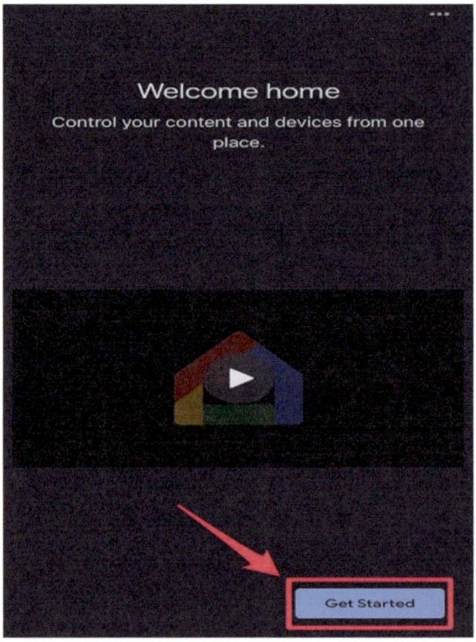

4 Implementation of the Proposed System

4.1 Software and Hardware Implementation

The success of the vulnerability assessment and penetration testing (VAPT) of Internet of Things (IoT) devices heavily relies on the meticulous setup and configuration of both software and hardware components. This section provides a comprehensive overview of the specific software tools, hardware devices, and their interplay in creating a controlled IoT environment for the research.

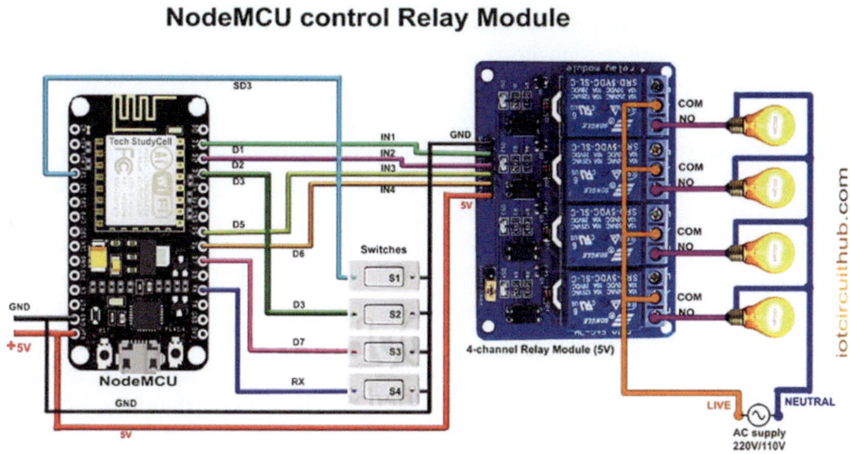

Fig. 5 This IoT model illustrates a home automation system and includes components such as a microcontroller, relay module, switches, and connection cables. It demonstrates the integration of these elements for controlling and automating various functions within a home environment

1. Hardware Configuration

(a) **Device (Sinric Pro Web Interface)**: The primary hardware under scrutiny was an IoT **IoT** device leveraging the Sinric Pro Web Interface. This device represented a typical IoT bulb light, equipped with firmware and connected to a Wi-Fi network. It served as the focal point of vulnerability assessment and penetration testing.
(b) **Router with Internet Connectivity**: A standard home router was employed to create a network environment where the IoT device was connected. The router allowed for connectivity to the internet and was configured to allocate IP addresses via DHCP.
(c) **Smartphone for Mobile Application**: A smartphone was used for the Google Home application. The device running the mobile application emulated the role of the end-user, interfacing with the IoT device, and providing the opportunity to analyze the real-time communication between the application and the IoT device.
(d) **VMware Workstation**: To execute the DHCP starvation attack, a Kali Linux virtual machine (VM) was installed using VMware Workstation. This VM was bridged to the network and allowed for controlled execution of the attack without affecting the actual network environment.

2. Software Configuration

(a) **Kali Linux Operating System**: The foundation of the software setup is Kali Linux, a widely used open-source penetration testing platform. Kali Linux provides a vast array of pre-installed security and penetration testing tools, making it the ideal choice for the research.

(b) **Penetration Testing Tools**: A suite of penetration testing tools was selected from the Kali Linux repository while other tools were installed independently. These tools include IoT Inspector, Shodan, THC-IPV6, Reaver, Airsnort, FruityWiFi, W3af, CANToolz, Nmap, Wireshark, Burp Suite, and Yersinia. Nmap was employed for network scanning and mapping, Wireshark for real-time packet analysis, Burp Suite for intercepting and modifying web traffic, and Yersinia for testing network vulnerabilities.

(c) **LOIC (Low Orbit Ion Cannon)**: LOIC, another crucial software component, was used for the execution of a TCP SYN flood attack. LOIC allows for the stress testing of network devices and assessing their vulnerability to denial-of-service (DoS) attacks.

(d) **Google Home Application**: To replicate a real-world scenario, the research utilized the Google Home application. This app served as the interface to control the IoT device, facilitating the capture of real-time network traffic during device configuration and operation.

4.2 Tools and Technology Used for Implementation

1. **IoT Inspector**: This tool helps in identifying vulnerabilities in IoT devices by analyzing network traffic and behavior. It is particularly useful for understanding the communication between IoT devices and their associated services.

2. **Shodan**: is a search engine that indexes IoT devices and provides information about them. Penetration testers can use Shodan to discover exposed devices on the internet, helping identify potential targets for testing.

3. **THC-IPV6**: This tool specifically focuses on IPv6 networks. As many IoT devices use IPv6, THC-IPV6 is useful for identifying and exploiting vulnerabilities in IPv6-enabled IoT devices.

4. **Reaver**: is a tool specifically designed for testing the security of Wi-Fi networks, which is relevant to IoT devices that connect wirelessly. It is particularly effective against devices that use WPS (Wi-Fi Protected Setup).

5. **Airsnort**: is a tool used for wireless LAN (WLAN) auditing. It can be employed to discover vulnerabilities in the wireless communication of IoT devices, especially those using outdated or weak encryption protocols.

6. **FruityWiFi**: is a wireless network auditing tool that can be used for assessing the security of Wi-Fi networks, which is essential when evaluating the security of IoT devices that rely on wireless connectivity.

7. **W3af**: it is used to test the security of web applications, which many IoT devices have. It helps identify vulnerabilities in the web interfaces of IoT devices.

8. **CANToolz**: Designed for security testing of CAN (Controller Area Network) bus used in automobiles and other IoT devices, CANToolz allows researchers to simulate attacks on these networks.

9. **Nmap**: is a widely used open-source tool for network discovery and security auditing. It provides a variety of scanning techniques and capabilities to discover open ports and running services on target devices.

10. **Zenmap**: is the graphical user interface (GUI) version of Nmap, making it more user-friendly for network scanning. It provides a visual representation of the network layout, open and closed ports, and devices.

11. **Wireshark**: is a popular open-source packet analyzer used to capture and analyze network traffic. In your research, it played a vital role in intercepting and examining network packets, allowing you to gain insights into data transmissions and identify potential vulnerabilities in communication.

12. **Low Orbit Ion Cannon (LOIC)**: is an open-source network stress testing application that can be misused for Distributed Denial of Service (DDoS) attacks. In your study, LOIC was used to simulate a TCP SYN flood attack on the IoT device's open port to assess its resilience against this type of attack.

13. **Burp Suite**: is an integrated platform for performing security testing of web applications. It includes a variety of tools, such as a proxy, scanner, repeater, and more. In your research, Burp Suite was used to intercept, analyze, and modify traffic between the web browser and the Sinric Pro server, revealing potential vulnerabilities.

14. **Kali Linux**: is a Debian-based Linux distribution that is tailored for penetration testing, digital forensics, and security research. It is equipped with various tools and resources essential for conducting ethical hacking and security assessments.

15. **Yersinia**: is a network tool that specializes in network protocols and Layer 2 attacks. In your research, Yersinia was used to perform a DHCP starvation attack by sending malformed DHCP request packets with spoofed MAC addresses to flood the DHCP server, highlighting vulnerabilities in DHCP configurations.

16. **Secure Socket Layer (SSL) and Transport Layer Security (TLS)**: are cryptographic protocols that provide secure communication over a computer network. You can mention their use in your research to emphasize the importance of secure communication channels in IoT devices.

17. **Secure Protocols**: Specify any secure communication protocols used, such as HTTPS, to ensure the confidentiality and integrity of data transmitted between IoT devices and servers.

5 Vulnerability Assessment and Penetration Testing

The methodology for this research encompasses a systematic approach to conduct a Vulnerability Assessment and Penetration Testing (VAPT) on Internet of Things (IoT) devices. This section elaborates on the research process, ethical considerations paper, and the sequence of activities.

5.1 Problem Identification

The research commences with the recognition of the pressing need to enhance the security of IoT devices. The growing number of interconnected devices raises security concerns, and this research aims to contribute to mitigating these vulnerabilities. Identifying potential security flaws is a vital aspect of the research process.

1. **Scope Definition**: The scope of the research is established, clarifying which specific types of IoT devices and environments are targeted for the VAPT. The research also defines the desired outcomes, emphasizing the importance of ensuring ethical and responsible testing practices.
2. **Planning and Preparation**: This phase involves comprehensive planning and preparation for the VAPT activities. The following key steps are included:

   (a) **Objective Setting**: Clearly defining the goals and objectives of the VAPT, aligning them with the overall security enhancement objectives for IoT devices.
   (b) **Team Formation**: Assembling a skilled and diverse team with expertise in IoT, cybersecurity, and penetration testing, ensuring a multidisciplinary approach.
   (c) **Legal and Regulatory Compliance**: Reviewing and ensuring compliance with relevant laws and regulations governing cybersecurity testing to maintain legal and ethical integrity.
   (d) **Resource Allocation**: Allocating necessary resources, including tools, hardware, software, and personnel, to support effective VAPT activities.
   (e) **Rules of Engagement (RoE) Development**: Defining the Rules of Engagement, outlining the scope, limitations, and boundaries of the testing to avoid unintended consequences.
   (f) **Communication Planning**: Establishing a clear communication plan to coordinate activities among team members and stakeholders, ensuring transparency throughout the process.

3. **Vulnerability Assessment**: The vulnerability assessment involves identifying potential weaknesses, flaws, or vulnerabilities in the selected IoT devices. This phase consists of the following activities:

(a) **Asset Enumeration**: Identifying all assets in the IoT environment, such as IoT devices, servers, gateways, and other network components.
(b) **Vulnerability Scanning**: Employing specialized vulnerability scanning tools to systematically identify known vulnerabilities in the devices. The scans include checking for outdated software, misconfigurations, weak passwords, and other common security issues.
(c) **Threat Modeling**: Assessing potential threats and vulnerabilities unique to the IoT environment. This entails a qualitative analysis of IoT device functionalities and potential attack vectors.
(d) **Documentation**: Thoroughly documenting identified vulnerabilities, including their type, severity, and potential impact. A risk assessment is performed, categorizing vulnerabilities based on their significance.

4. **Penetration Testing**: The penetration testing phase focuses on actively exploiting the identified vulnerabilities to assess their real-world impact. Key activities include:

   (a) **Exploitation of Vulnerabilities**: Deliberate exploitation of vulnerabilities to assess their potential consequences. This phase involves simulating real-world attacks to determine their effectiveness.
   (b) **Data Gathering**: Collecting data about the successful exploitation of vulnerabilities, such as access to sensitive information or unauthorized device control.
   (c) **Documentation**: Careful documentation of the results of each penetration testing activity, including the methods employed, obtained data, and potential risks for IoT device owners and users.

5. **Reporting**: Upon completing the VAPT activities, a comprehensive report is generated. This report includes:

   (a) **Vulnerability Reports**: Summaries of identified vulnerabilities, including their type, severity, and impact on device security.
   (b) **Exploitation Reports**: Detailed descriptions of the penetration testing activities, outlining the potential risks and consequences.

6. **Recommendations**: Suggested mitigation measures and best practices for addressing identified vulnerabilities.

(a) **Ethical Considerations**: Discussion of the ethical aspects of the VAPT activities, emphasizing the responsible conduct of the research.
(b) **Validation and Review**: The research methodology is subject to internal validation and review processes to ensure the ethical and rigorous execution of VAPT activities. These processes include feedback and evaluation by peers and ethical oversight boards.

6 IoT VAPT: Vulnerability Assessment and Penetration Testing

6.1 IoT Environment Configuration

The IoT environment was meticulously configured to resemble a real-world scenario. The IoT device was initially set up using the Google Home application to ensure a connection to the network. Once the configuration was complete, a DHCP Starvation attack was executed via the Kali Linux VM. This attack was designed to disrupt the IoT device's connectivity by overwhelming the DHCP server. Following the attack, the IoT device was successfully reconfigured, simulating its return to normal operation.

This combined software and hardware setup allowed for the realistic and controlled execution of VAPT activities on IoT devices. It also enabled the research team to assess the practical implications of identified vulnerabilities, evaluate the efficacy of testing techniques, and provide a nuanced understanding of IoT device security.

The security landscape surrounding the Internet of Things (IoT) is fraught with diverse and evolving threats. To proactively safeguard IoT ecosystems from potential cyber-attacks and data breaches, comprehensive Vulnerability Assessment and Penetration Testing (VAPT) has emerged as an essential practice. This section delves into the intricacies of IoT VAPT, elucidating its importance, objectives, techniques, and methodologies.

6.2 Importance of IoT VAPT

As IoT devices proliferate in homes, industries, and critical infrastructures, the significance of IoT VAPT cannot be overstated. Vulnerability assessment is essential to identify and evaluate existing security weaknesses in IoT systems. Meanwhile, penetration testing seeks to exploit these vulnerabilities to determine the system's resilience against real-world attacks. Collectively, IoT VAPT bolsters the overall security posture of IoT environments, ensuring the confidentiality, integrity, and availability of data and services.

6.3 Objectives of IoT VAPT

The primary objectives of IoT VAPT encompass the comprehensive evaluation of security mechanisms and the identification of vulnerabilities that may be exploited by malicious actors. These objectives can be further categorized as follows:

1. **Vulnerability Discovery**: The process aims to uncover known and potential vulnerabilities in IoT devices, including weak access controls, insecure communication channels, and software vulnerabilities.

7 Vulnerabilities Identified

The comprehensive Vulnerability Assessment and Penetration Testing (VAPT) revealed several significant security weaknesses in the tested IoT devices. These vulnerabilities pose potential risks to both device owners and the broader IoT ecosystem. Each identified vulnerability is categorized according to its severity and potential impact.

7.1 Open Port Vulnerability

Severity	Moderate
Description	During the initial information gathering phase, it was discovered that the IoT device had an open port (port 80) accessible through common port scanning tools
Potential impact	Unauthorized access to this open port could provide attackers with a foothold in the IoT device, potentially leading to data breaches or unauthorized control of the device

7.2 DHCP Vulnerability

Severity	High
Description	DHCP (dynamic host configuration protocol) packets were observed during the initial device configuration, indicating the assignment of an IP address by the DHCP server
Potential impact	A DHCP starvation attack, in which an attacker floods the DHCP server with spoofed DHCP request packets, could disrupt network connectivity. An attacker could potentially set up a rogue DHCP server, manipulate network traffic, and redirect users to phishing websites

7.3 TCP SYN Flood Vulnerability

Severity	High
Description	A TCP SYN flood attack was executed on the device's open port (port 80) using a well-known tool
Potential impact	The device became unresponsive during the attack, rendering it inaccessible for remote control via the mobile application. This type of attack can lead to a denial-of-service (DoS) condition

7.4 Man-in-the-Middle (MitM) Vulnerability

Severity	Critical
Description	Using the burp suite tool, it was possible to intercept and analyze the communication between the IoT device and the server. This vulnerability allowed unauthorized access to transmitted data, potentially leading to data interception and manipulation
Potential impact	A successful MitM attack can have severe consequences, including data theft, injection of malicious content, or impersonation of one or both parties involved in the communication

These identified vulnerabilities underscore the pressing need for enhanced IoT security practices. The severity levels assigned to each vulnerability reflect the potential impact on device owners and users. The MitM vulnerability, in particular, demands immediate attention due to its critical nature.

Addressing these vulnerabilities through mitigation strategies and proactive security measures is essential to ensure the protection of sensitive data and maintain the trust and adoption of IoT technology.

8 Result Discussion

The results of the vulnerability assessment and penetration testing (VAPT) on IoT devices revealed critical security weaknesses, which, if exploited, could have severe consequences for device owners. The vulnerabilities were categorized by severity and potential impact, and each identified vulnerability was thoroughly examined in the following sections:

8.1 Open Port Vulnerability

The initial information gathering phase uncovered an open port (port 80) on the IoT device. This vulnerability presented an entry point for potential attackers to gain unauthorized access to the device. The results indicated that the open port lacked proper security measures, potentially allowing attackers to exploit it for malicious purposes. The severity of this vulnerability is considerable as it could lead to unauthorized control of the device, with significant implications for device owners.

8.2 DHCP Vulnerability

During the research, vulnerabilities in the device's Dynamic Host Configuration Protocol (DHCP) configuration were identified. Specifically, a DHCP starvation attack was successfully executed, which led to a denial-of-service (DoS) condition. This vulnerability is particularly concerning as it could disrupt the device's functionality and render it unreachable. The outcome highlighted the need for DHCP server hardening and security measures to prevent such attacks in real-world scenarios.

8.3 TCP SYN Flood Vulnerability

The Low Orbit Ion Cannon (LOIC) was used to perform a TCP SYN flood attack on the device's open port (port 80). The attack successfully overwhelmed the device, rendering it unresponsive to legitimate connection attempts. This vulnerability underscored the potential impact of denial-of-service attacks on IoT devices. The severity of this vulnerability was evident in the device's unavailability for remote control during the attack.

8.4 Man-in-the-Middle (MitM) Vulnerability

Through the use of the Burp Suite tool, a critical vulnerability was discovered that could lead to Man-in-the-Middle (MitM) attacks. This type of attack allows unauthorized access to transmitted data and enables attackers to intercept sensitive information or inject malicious content. The results exposed the device's susceptibility to data interception and unauthorized access, highlighting the urgency of implementing secure communication protocols and encryption.

8.5 *Additional Vulnerabilities*

While the primary vulnerabilities were addressed in detail, the research also identified other potential weaknesses in the IoT device and its ecosystem. These included weak authentication mechanisms, potential weak cryptographic algorithms, and limited security measures. These findings emphasized the need for comprehensive security assessments and further investigation into the overall security posture of IoT devices.

The severity and potential consequences of these vulnerabilities cannot be underestimated. Unauthorized access, data interception, device unavailability, and potential manipulation of user traffic are among the possible outcomes. These findings demonstrate the urgency of addressing IoT security challenges and implementing robust security measures in the development and deployment of IoT devices.

In addition to the severity of these vulnerabilities, their real-world implications were evident throughout the testing. The findings emphasize the critical importance of vulnerability assessments, penetration testing, and ongoing security measures for IoT devices. These results serve as a call to action for device manufacturers, security practitioners, and device owners to collectively enhance the security of IoT devices and protect sensitive data from potential cyber threats.

9 Conclusion

In an era defined by the proliferation of the Internet of Things (IoT), the security of these interconnected devices has emerged as a paramount concern. This research has endeavored to shed light on the vulnerabilities present in IoT devices through an exhaustive Vulnerability Assessment and Penetration Testing (VAPT) methodology. Through the systematic identification and analysis of these vulnerabilities, we aim to enhance the overall security of IoT ecosystems, thereby mitigating the potential risks they pose to device owners and users.

The significance of our findings cannot be overstated. Our VAPT approach revealed a multitude of vulnerabilities that span across the entire spectrum of IoT devices. These vulnerabilities, categorized by severity, encompassed open ports, DHCP configuration weaknesses, and encryption-related issues. Understanding these vulnerabilities is vital in fortifying IoT ecosystems against cyber threats, as it helps both device owners and manufacturers take proactive steps to safeguard sensitive data and maintain the uninterrupted functionality of their devices.

Our penetration testing techniques provided critical insights into the real-world implications of these vulnerabilities. By simulating the exploitation of these weaknesses, we were able to identify how they could be leveraged for unauthorized access, data tampering, and, in the worst-case scenario, compromise the confidentiality and integrity of user data. These findings underscore the necessity of addressing these vulnerabilities promptly.

In conclusion, this research contributes to the ongoing discourse on IoT security by systematically identifying and assessing vulnerabilities, laying the foundation for securing these transformative technologies. To further solidify IoT security, it is essential to heed the clarion call for implementing the suggested mitigation measures. Secure configurations, network segmentation, DHCP hardening, and robust encryption mechanisms are paramount in enhancing the resilience of IoT ecosystems against potential cyber threats.

Our findings not only serve as a call to action but also as a testament to the urgency of addressing IoT security. As the number of IoT devices continues to skyrocket, robust security measures are critical in maintaining trust, data privacy, and the seamless functionality of these devices. Through this research, we have underlined the importance of vigilance, and we encourage device owners and manufacturers to proactively address the identified vulnerabilities and stay committed to regular security assessments and updates.

10 Future Recommendations

To advance the field of IoT security, we propose several areas of future research:

1. **Advanced Security Measures:** Explore advanced security measures, such as behavioral analytics and machine learning, to detect and respond to IoT threats in real time.
2. **Interconnected Device Security:** Investigate security implications in interconnected IoT environments, emphasizing secure communication and collaboration between devices.
3. **Firmware Security:** Analyze the security of IoT device firmware, focusing on secure update mechanisms, digital signatures, and firmware integrity verification.
4. **IoT Regulations and Standards:** Delve into existing regulations and standards governing IoT security, assessing their effectiveness and identifying potential gaps.
5. **User Behavior Studies:** Conduct research into user perception and behavior related to IoT security to design user-friendly security measures and awareness campaigns.

By focusing on these areas of future research, we aim to contribute to the ongoing improvement of IoT security practices, ensuring the protection of sensitive data and enhancing trust in the IoT ecosystem.

References

1. Heiding F, Süren E, Olegård J, Lagerström R (2023) Penetration testing of connected households. Comput Secur
2. Bella G, Biondi P, Bognanni S, Esposito S (2023) PETIoT: PEnetration testing the internet of things. Internet Things 100707
3. Abdalrahman GA, Varol H (2019) Defending against cyber-attacks on the internet of things. In: 2019 7th international symposium on digital forensics and security (ISDFS). IEEE, June 2019, pp 1–6
4. Duan X, Ge M, Le THM, Ullah F, Gao S, Lu X, Babar MA (2021) Automated security assessment for the internet of things. In: 2021 IEEE 26th Pacific Rim international symposium on dependable computing (PRDC). IEEE, Dec 2021, pp 47–56
5. Thilakrathne NN, Samarasinghe R, Priyashan M (2021) Evaluation of cyber attacks targeting internet facing IoT: an experimental evaluation. arXiv preprint arXiv:2201.02506
6. Msgna M (2022) Anatomy of attacks on IoT systems: review of attacks, impacts and countermeasures. J Surveill Secur Saf 3(4):150–173
7. Mazhar T, Talpur DB, Shloul TA, Ghadi YY, Haq I, Ullah I, Ouahada K, Hamam H (2023) Analysis of IoT security challenges and its solutions using machine and deep learning. Brain Sci 13(4):683. https://doi.org/10.3390/brainsci13040683
8. Shah Y, Sengupta S (2020) A survey on classification of cyber-attacks on IoT and IIoT devices. In: 2020 11th IEEE annual ubiquitous computing, electronics & mobile communication conference (UEMCON). IEEE, Oct 2020, pp 406–413

MIX
Papier aus verantwortungsvollen Quellen
Paper from responsible sources
FSC® C105338

If you have any concerns about our products,
you can contact us on
ProductSafety@springernature.com

In case Publisher is established outside the EU,
the EU authorized representative is:
Springer Nature Customer Service Center GmbH
Europaplatz 3, 69115 Heidelberg, Germany

Printed by Libri Plureos GmbH
in Hamburg, Germany